LAURENCE OLIVIE

JOHN COTTRELL, author and journalist, first
sprang to prominence in 1964 with the publication
of *The World Stood Still,* his best-selling account
of the assassination of President Kennedy. Mr.
Cottrell's subsequent books have been largely
devoted to biography, and particularly to theatrical
biography, his most recent work being *Richard
Burton.*

Acclaim for *LAURENCE OLIVIER*:

'Mr. Cottrell seems to have left no stone unturned
in order to document the work. He weaves his way
through the mass of material neatly and readably.
This is the best book so far on Olivier; indeed it is
an accomplished biography. The story of Olivier's
career is of course absorbing, but Mr. Cottrell sets
it out to full advantage, lucidly and intelligently.
The assessment of Olivier's work at the Old Vic is
especially well done'

The Stage

'Steers a smooth and sensible course . . . a fair
record of the great man's achievement and an
interesting assessment of his work as the first
director of the National'

The Daily Telegraph

Laurence Olivier

John Cottrell

CORONET BOOKS
Hodder and Stoughton

FOR MOTHER AND RENE WITH LOVE

First published in Great Britain 1975 by
Weidenfeld and Nicolson Limited

Coronet Edition 1977

Printed in Great Britain for
Hodder and Stoughton Paperbacks, a
division of Hodder and Stoughton Ltd.,
Mill Road, Dunton Green, Sevenoaks, Kent (Editorial
Office: 47 Bedford Square, London, WC1 3DP)
by Richard Clay (The Chaucer Press), Ltd.,
Bungay, Suffolk

ISBN 0 340 21804 5

SPECIAL ACKNOWLEDGMENT For assistance in the preparation of this biography, my greatest debt of gratitude is due to Mr. Ronald Proyer who, as Research Associate, shared the enormous burden of gathering contributions by way of interview and correspondence. I thank him for his professionalism and his industry, and not least for his unbounded enthusiasm—a great sustaining force.

In turn, the writing of this book would have been impossible without the co-operation of so many friends and acquaintances of Sir Laurence Olivier who contributed personal memories and anecdotes with a unanimous generosity and keen responsiveness that was in itself a demonstration of the extraordinary affection and admiration that the subject commands within his fiercely competitive profession. To all of them, whether their contribution be great or small, my most sincere thanks.

Again, this work would not have been possible without consulting, and often recording, the observations of all leading London and New York film and theatre critics of the past half-century. They are clearly identified in the text and beyond this, quite separately, an immeasurable debt of gratitude is due to Mr. Logan Gourlay for allowing me to quote briefly from *Olivier* (Weidenfeld & Nicolson, London, 1973) and to Mr. Felix Barker, critic of the London *Evening News*, for kind permission to consult his double-biography, *The Oliviers* (Hamish Hamilton, London, 1953), a pioneering work of rare scholarship and authority.

Finally, my personal thanks to Ann Wingar for her diligence as secretary, to Ann Novotny for research in New York, to Elizabeth Harris and Tina Dawson for supplementary secretarial help, and most especially to Mr. John G. Kirk of Prentice-Hall, Inc., whose encouragement and perceptive interest were more valuable and valued than he can ever know.

CONTENTS

1 ★ The Living Legend

Ninety years ago, during a summer holiday in Italy, the singing of an English schoolboy so impressed a famous tenor named Signor Lamberti that the boy was offered the opportunity of being trained for the opera. He returned home flushed with enthusiasm. His Victorian mother froze in disapproval. She handed him a single lira from the residue of his holiday money and said, 'Gerard, if you ever take up that monstrous profession this coin represents all the money you can expect to receive from me.' Ambition faded. The boy, youngest of ten children of a Church of England rector, elected to take holy orders instead.

That Winchester schoolboy was to become the father of Laurence Olivier. Apart from a brief excursion into amateur dramatics at Oxford University, Gerard was never again tempted towards the monstrous profession. He became a clergyman like his father and his grandfather before him. And similarly, if any prediction had been ventured on the day that his son Laurence was born (May 22, 1907), it would have been that he too would one day breathe holy fire from the pulpit. It had been the way of the Oliviers for two centuries. Through six generations the Church had been the predominantly chosen profession of Laurence's male ancestors. He, in turn, had an upbringing strictly designed to prepare him for the ministry. And yet, for all the emphasis on tradition and religious training, Olivier's statement that he was 'born to be an actor' remains definitive, irrefutable. In his own curious way, he *was* predestined to become an actor, just as surely as if he had been born a Booth or a Barrymore. Inherent talent, environment, opportunity—all conspired to forge inexorably a brilliant theatrical destiny.

The magnitude of that destiny is now familiar. Olivier is the pre-eminent theatrical figure of the twentieth century—the first and only lord of his profession, the most distinguished and respected actor of his age. Long before the building of Britain's monumental National Theatre, where his name is perpetuated in the main auditorium, he had achieved celebrity and stature sufficient to rank him forever alongside Garrick and Irving and Kean. In his own lifetime he has secured his place in the pantheon of stage immortals.

But why and how? Why is it that Olivier, the once gauche and ungainly son of an English parson, a boy who never won a prize at school, has emerged with an unrivalled horde of honours and trophies heaped upon him by governments and universities and academies? How has Olivier, who in youth experienced a stuttering start on the London stage and two false starts in Hollywood, who was accused by the distinguished critic James Agate of not just speaking verse badly but of not speaking it at all, emerged exclusively at the summit of a fiercely competitive and over-crowded profession? What precisely makes him stand head and shoulders above all other actors in the world—not a prince among players but the veritable Roscian King?

The first question may be firmly answered: Olivier has won such honour because no other actor has made such a staggering contribution to twentieth-century drama. The theatre has seen him in a hundred parts, classical and modern, lightest comedy and darkest tragedy, including all the great Shakespearean roles, with many more hits than misses and not a few definitive per-formances. The cinema, too, has seen him in such popular classics as *Wuthering Heights* and *Rebecca*, but above all, his name will loom large in motion picture history as the actor–director–producer who adapted Shakespeare to the screen, revealing the brilliance of the Bard to millions who had not previously had access (or perhaps inclination) to the theatre. Add to this Olivier's contribution as a cultural ambassador, as an indefatig-able worker on state and charitable committees, as a servant of the arts who has sacrificed several million dollars declining Hollywood offers in favour of intangible rewards at the Old Vic and the National Theatre, and there can be no wonder that Sir Laurence (as Lord Olivier prefers to be known) has cloaked himself and 'the monstrous profession' in finest ermine.

But is he also the *greatest* actor of our time? Significantly that question is asked about him more than about any other player, and yet it has never been positively answered because there is no recognized yardstick for measuring theatrical greatness. 'You can't say what is best in this business,' he has said. 'It's not like a runner in a race and he does a hundred yards in nine seconds. He is the fastest, so he is the best.' [1] In acting we have only *opinions* of outstanding performances, with no single event to decide the issue. A definitive Hamlet may prove a disastrous Macbeth. No one has ever justified Sir Henry Irving's remark that 'a great actor can do nothing badly'.

If we accept the much-favoured dictum of Victorian critic G. H. Lewes that 'the greatest artist is he who is the greatest in the highest reaches of his art', then only those who have made assault on the loftiest peaks—the truly titanic roles (which Shakespeare most especially provides)—can enter into the reckoning. This narrows the field, but since no actor in reliably recorded history has triumphed in all the great classical roles, it remains difficult to distinguish, without argument, among the giants of the stage.

Yet one undeniable statement can be made on the subject of the greatest English-speaking actor of the twentieth century: If all the relevant information—judgments written and spoken by critics and players—were fed into a computer, Laurence Olivier would take first prize by a mile. No other actor since Irving has generated such electric excitement in the English theatre and maintained a stronger and more lasting magnetic power over playgoers. In the combined realms of theatre and cinema, no other actor rivals Olivier in terms of versatility or the accumulated weight of his memorable achievements.

Curiously, whenever actors are joined in the perennial greatest-of-us-all debate, one name besides Olivier is invariably canvassed with conviction: Marlon Brando. The Brando supporters are matching against Sir Laurence a man with a record of thirty films of widely varying quality and just five Broadway plays, including nothing more 'classical' than Shaw's *Candida*; Brando last appeared on stage in 1947 (at the age of twenty-three) and has never yearned to go back. American actor William Redfield is one who nominates Brando as the greatest actor of our time. In his book *Letters From an Actor* he goes further: 'Ironically enough, Laurence Olivier is less gifted than Marlon Brando. He is even less gifted than Richard Burton, Paul Scofield, Ralph Richardson and John Gielgud. *But he is still the definitive actor of the twentieth century. Why? Because he wanted to be. His achieve-*

ments are due to dedication, scholarship, practice, determination and courage. He is the bravest actor of our time.'[2]

Redfield is absolutely correct in his final answer (the italics are mine). But 'less gifted'? Olivier, who first walked on to a stage at the age of *ten* and played in *Julius Caesar* with such instinctive authority that Ellen Terry noted in her diary, 'The small boy who played Brutus is already a great actor'? Well, yes, if you do not regard determination, courage, unbounded creative energy and acute interpretative intelligence as being gifts of a very special kind. Olivier has displayed these in unrivalled abundance.

Arguments based on opinion of an actor's inborn gifts are highly suspect, and inevitably controversial. Acting is not nine-tenths divine inspiration and one-tenth technique. It is a profession to be worked at and mastered to the best of one's capabilities, and *if* anyone merits the accolade of 'greatest actor' it is surely the actor who masters his craft to the greatest extent and practises it on the worthiest scale—the actor who has developed his art on the broadest canvas, in the finest detail, in the most exciting colours.

Elia Kazan has spoken of Brando as 'the only genius I've ever met in the field of acting'. This is genius of a peculiar and dangerous kind, the wayward genius of a 'mood actor' of dark, unfathomable depths, of an actor possessed of a brooding, stubbornly independent nature that may spur him towards a portrayal of extraordinary elemental power and disturbing intensity or, at other times, make him capable of the most perverse and unprofessional conduct. Olivier, too, with good reason, has been credited with genius, but rejects the distinction. It runs counter to his disciplined, methodical approach to acting—'I don't like the word genius applied to the theatre. I do not think the theatre can cope with genius. I think it too practicable to have to worry with genius.'[3]

It is tempting, for the purposes of biography, to accept Olivier's opinion. 'Genius' has too mysterious a connotation, suggesting some inborn quality that defies rational explanation. Olivier is the theatre's supreme magician, but his dazzling array of conjuring skills is perhaps not beyond analysis, as I shall later endeavour to show. In his case, however, there is an obstacle far more confusing than genius to overcome. There is *the legend*. Attempting to separate the man from the myth is something much more complex. Anthony Quayle once remarked: 'I find it completely impossible to rate actresses or actors. You cannot categorize them like horses in a show. They succeed for different reasons and in different ways, and often their impact depends not so much on what they do as on their "legend" or "image" which renders their audiences peculiarly vulnerable.' No actor has a bigger 'legend' than Olivier, and the biographer is duty-bound to ask: Has the legend grown bigger than the man? How far does it rest on what Thomas Jefferson called 'false facts' and Norman Mailer, *factoids*?

For example, a few years ago John Neville was telling me how he and Richard Burton were rather hurt by notices they received when appearing at the Old Vic as Chorus and Henry V respectively. 'There was one critic in particular who said, "Well, of course, I always remember Laurence Olivier in this role in the late 1930s, and he was magnificent. He had poetry. He had the virility. He was a soldier and he was a king." It was a sort of eulogy, and so Richard and I thought it would be interesting to look up the notices of this particular performance by Olivier. We did, and you know they were not very good at all. In fact, this same critic, who was still writing for the same paper, gave him almost the worst notice of all and said he'd be better off selling cars in Berkeley Street.'

By virtue of the image-inflating publicity that attends him, the truth about any actor is elusive. In Olivier's case it is elusive for additional reasons. First, no other living actor has been and still is being made the subject of so many embroidered, often outrageous, anecdotes by his professional colleagues (even Neville's recollection of the reviews of *Henry V* may unwittingly be a false fact within a *factoid*, since diligent research has failed to uncover that the critic ever referred to Olivier's aptitude as a car salesman). Second, by his mastery of the art of self-effacement, Olivier himself has helped to distort his own history. Just as some of his greatest triumphs are much inflated by his admirers in the retelling, so one finds that some of his so-called disasters have become exaggerated by the actor himself. Furthermore, by the most subtle means at his command, Olivier has calculatingly influenced the shaping of his public image, nurturing it and guarding it with infinite care and, up to a point, admirable discretion.

This actor's chameleon craft, by no means confined to stage and screen characterizations, is so extraordinary that a television critic once hazarded the opinion that Olivier needed to be interviewed in the nude or in outer space—otherwise he immediately took on coloration from his background or mode of dress. Interviewed on stage, in sweat shirt and slacks, he spoke in a voice that had the light, almost ingratiating quality of an old pro. Interviewed in Brighton, he grew more raffish and showbizzy— louder echoes of Archie Rice. Interviewed at the Old Vic, he was dignified and businesslike, every inch the head of a nationalized institution. Interviewed on the American *Dick Cavett Show*, he became the goodwill ambassador for Anglo-American relations, terribly, terribly English, all sweetness and unrelenting humility. Any viewer taking in all these interviews at one sitting might justifiably cry out: And now will the real Laurence Olivier stand up, please?

In his diaries, Cecil Beaton recalls one merry evening in Paris when Olivier outlined the look of his planned film of *Hamlet* through a series of pops, bangs, explosions, farts and other coarse noises. 'It was a most gymnastic performance that we were treated to. Larry's imitations have about them something of the original clown or, at least, the essential entertainer who can be found in some remote music hall or performing in the street outside a pub. This was the real Larry—the mummer, the ale-drinking Thespian—not the rather overwhelmed and shy cipher with the wrinkled forehead that goes out into society.'[4]

But was it the real Olivier? Even Olivier himself has said that he doesn't know what he is *really* like. In 1950 the Canadian-born critic Milton Shulman perceived at least *three* Oliviers: Sir Laurence the actor-manager and theatrical ambassador ('a masterpiece of majestic inflection, studied reserve and unflattering dignity'); Olivier the actor absorbed with almost extravagant energy in the creation of a part; and 'Larry', bon vivant and genial host. 'But,' he added, 'any acquaintance who slaps Sir Laurence Olivier on the back expecting to find "Larry" risks a rather disconcerting experience. Perhaps it is only by compartmentalizing his personality in this fashion that Sir Laurence has managed to accomplish so much in the five years since the war ended.'[5]

Five years later we had zany Salvador Dali coming over to paint Olivier as Richard III, twitching the waxed moustaches that he called his antennae and claiming that they told him to portray his subject with *two* faces. And, of course, in a sense his whiskers were right—just as two centuries earlier Sir Joshua Reynolds was right to paint Garrick standing between the allegorical figures of Comedy and Tragedy, a man torn in opposite directions. There are indeed at least two Oliviers—one the lordly, elder statesman of the theatre, dedicated to upholding the highest traditions of classical acting and recoiling from the garish excesses of showbiz ballyhoo; the other an instinctive comedian who, with pressures removed and no reporters in sight, can abandon the mask of dignity and become the most endearing extrovert. But there is no deep significance, as some would find, in such duality of nature; there may be observed in almost any man some measure of conflict between the public and the private face. The only distinction here is that we are confronted with a consummate master of disguise. 'All the world's a stage . . . and one man in his time plays many parts,' but unlike Shakespeare's man of seven ages, Olivier gives seven scenes to every act, makes his exits and entrances in a bewildering array of parts. He has never taken his ease, never slept through an act or two, never stayed with one character long enough to be nailed by typecasting.

In 1930, when dining with Harold Nicolson, George Bernard Shaw spoke with genuine admiration of the young Larry and called him 'a born actor'. Most actors remain acutely conscious of their own performance in life; to varying degrees they possess the ability to view themselves from a private box and gear their style to suit their situation and audience. Olivier has this capacity developed to a fine art. He has not merely played his part in life; as far as possible he has written his own script, produced, directed and edited.

It has not always been so. In 1930, after a succession of lightweight romantic leads, he complained bitterly of being 'driven by events'. By the end of that decade, however, he had firmly established himself in the driver's seat. He had recognized that talent alone is not enough. It has to be properly harnessed and directed; otherwise—as for example in the case of Richard Burton, once hailed as the natural successor to Olivier—it can drift into shallow waters and founder on the rocks of mediocrity. Olivier set his compass for the highest realms of his art, never allowed himself to be lured off course for long. Yet at the same time, with equal shrewdness, he recognized the immutable truth in the cliché about familiarity breeding contempt and became circumspect of intimate or frivolous publicity. 'There's no glamour about an actor when you get to know him,' he said. The guarding of the legend had begun.

Olivier's extreme wariness towards personal publicity dates from 1939 when the devastating animal appeal of his Heathcliff transformed him overnight into a film star idol, an automatic subject for trifling gossip columnists and the irresistible object of movie-fan hysteria. Twenty years later he explained: 'When I first went on the stage I was looking for fame and réclame. I thought I'd adore the idea of fans, and the feeling of success. But as soon as I got it, I found myself disliking it all intensely . . . I've never stopped feeling a resentment that an actor should have to live in a goldfish bowl, and my public relationship has been awful. But then, actors are such sitting targets, aren't they?' [6]

Inevitably, his publicity-shyness sometimes made him an even bigger 'sitting target'. It happened in 1939 when shunned American interviewers reacted like women scorned. It happened again when he filmed behind closed doors with Marilyn Monroe, and Fleet Street's most acid show business writer accused him of suffering from a surfeit of dignity. In the long term, however, the wisdom of his measured aloofness has been conclusively proven by the results. It has helped to sustain, and indirectly to create, the legend. It was not mere shyness, for example, that prompted him in 1974 to ensure that his Polaroid TV commercial (so successful in the United States) was not for screening in his own country. He is acutely aware of the dangers of over-exposure. Like Irving, he long ago recognized the need for the magician to retain his mystery. And like Irving, he has sensibly taken to heart a code of conduct that was spelled out perceptively by William Hazlitt 150 years ago. It merits repeating:

I conceive that an actor, on account of the very circumstances of his profession, ought to keep himself as much incognito as possible . . . he is the centre of an illusion that he is bound to support . . . by a certain self-respect which should repel idle curiosity, and by a certain deference to the public, in whom he has inspired certain prejudices which he is covenanted not to break. He represents the majesty of successive kings; he takes the responsibility of heroes and lovers on himself; the mantle of genius and nature falls on his shoulders; we 'pile millions' of associations on him, under which he should be 'buried quick' and not perk out an inauspicious face upon us, with a plain-cut coat, to say, 'What fools you all were!—I am not Hamlet the Dane!' ... An actor, after having performed his part well, instead of courting further distinction, should affect obscurity, and 'steal most guilty-like away', conscious of admiration that he can support nowhere but in his proper sphere, and jealous of his own and others' good opinion of him, in proportion as he is a darling in the public eye. He cannot avoid attracting disproportionate attention: why should he wish to fix it on himself in a perfectly flat and insignificant part, viz. his own character? ... An actor, like a king, should only appear on state occasions. He loses popularity by too much publicity; or, according to the proverb, *familiarity breeds contempt*.

Hazlitt's advice still holds good for the great actor, for the one with such towering talent that he may command any stage without recourse to self-publicizing gimmickry. Sir Laurence has followed his counsel subtly and sensibly.

It is also one of the many paradoxical aspects of this extraordinary man's make-up that the actor who today bristles graciously at being regarded as a living monument has also generously furnished the marble. He may, as Kenneth Tynan has observed, put on 'a pose of elaborate humility' when prevailed on to make a speech. Nevertheless, he knows precisely where he stands in relation to the history of twentieth-century drama.

One lunchtime, in the canteen of the National Theatre's old prefabricated headquarters, members of the company were eulogizing over Nicol Williamson's recent Coriolanus. In the background, discreetly silent and looking every inch the senior business executive, was a thick-set, grey-haired gentleman in sober suit and gold-rimmed spectacles. Lord Olivier. He said nothing as they discussed another great actor's performance. The conversation moved on, and later, amid a general exchange of chit-chat, he happened to mention that Olivier cigarettes were about to be withdrawn after eighteen years on the market. Then, with an air of sweetest innocence, he asked, 'Do you think that we will one day be smoking a Williamson?'

More pointedly, the actor-knight once branded in tobacco and dubbed Sir Cork Tip, might have asked, 'Do you think that one day theatregoers will be saying, "Let's go to the Williamson tonight?" ' Olivier and the National Theatre are synonymous now, his legend indestructible.

This book is a study of the actor and his times—neither a gossipy pop-probe nor an intellectual appraisal, but a journey of discovery through a unique show business career. It is an endeavour to recreate the experiences and environmental influences that have contributed to the growth of a colossus, to scrape away accretions of theatrical legend while witnesses still remain and to see this dominoed actor-baron within the context of his art.

2
★
Monstrous Profession

Peter O'Toole, a Yorkshireman by birth and Irish imp by nature, takes fun in puncturing the proud tradition of great English actors by naming theatrical giants from Scotland, Ireland and Wales, and then forestalling protests by adding, 'And of course, Olivier is a Frenchman.' In fact, Olivier has calculated that he is only one thirty-second part French. His ancestral roots trail away in the mists of the early sixteenth century when Oliviers were French Huguenots living in the obscure village of Nay, south of Pau in the Basses-Pyrénées. The name in French means a person who plants, tends, picks or sells olives. A name of trade origin. Like Plowright.

Family legend has it that the Oliviers were set on the move to England in 1685 when Louis XIV revoked the Edict of Nantes that had given partial religious freedom to the French Protestants. The grandfather of David Garrick, the pre-eminent English actor of the eighteenth century, was one who fled across the Channel in that great migration of Huguenots. But in all probability Olivier's direct ancestors left France much earlier, initially emigrating to Holland. At least one, the Reverend Jourdain Olivier, arrived in England as early as 1688, in the office of Chaplain to William of Orange. Through an all-male line, Laurence Olivier is a direct descendant of that king's chaplain.

Amid all the ramifications of the family's lineage, with its preponderance of churchmen, a faint streak of artistry can be traced. There was Laurence's Uncle Herbert with his professional painting, and famous Uncle Sydney, the pioneer Socialist, who had some poems and parodies published. More obliquely, there was old Daniel Josias Olivier, the eighteenth-century diamond merchant who made the first break in the clerical line and reintroduced Gallic blood by marrying a Frenchwoman who was the niece of Jean Baptiste Massé, court painter to Louis XIV.

Before Laurence, however, there had never been an actor in the family, and even if there had been another Olivier of strong acting potential he would not have had the freedom to show himself.

Twelve years before Laurence Olivier was born, Henry Irving became the first actor-knight—indeed, the first actor to receive an honour of any description from the Crown. Soon afterwards, two distinguished actor-managers, Sir Johnston Forbes-Robertson and Sir Herbert Beerbohm Tree, continued the process of cloaking the theatre in a fresh mantle of respectability. But prejudice still abounded. After all, for nearly five centuries, until as late as 1824, actors had been classed under Statute Law as 'Rogues and Vagabonds'. At least there were now powerful precedents for a cleric allowing a son, or even a daughter, to enter the theatrical profession. Matheson Lang, a man of eminent clerical stock, was pursuing a brilliant career on the London stage, and significantly, his cousin Cosmo did not find his progress in the Church handicapped by virtue of the fact that he once dabbled in amateur theatricals and helped to found the Oxford University Dramatic Society. He was soon to be Archbishop of York, later of Canterbury. Then there were the Vanbrughs, Irene and Violet, daughters of Prebendary Barnes of Exeter, both popular actresses; and Sybil and Russell, children of Canon Thorndike, were already established on the stage.

Conceivably, had he been born into this more enlightened age, Laurence's father, the Reverend Gerard Kerr Olivier, might have become the first actor in the family; besides his potential as a singer, he had a commanding delivery and presence and was a natural actor in many ways. Briefly, as a free-thinking undergraduate at Merton College, Oxford, he went astray—lost his faith, accrued heavy debts and joined the dramatic society; but after returning home prematurely, degreeless and disgraced, he began to conform. By way of Durham University he belatedly gained his degree (4th class Classics), and briefly achieved a certain glamour by playing county cricket (for Hampshire). Then, in 1898, he turned to schoolmastering as a career.

This history of questing and sporting youth might in time have endeared Gerard Olivier to his children. But Laurence was told precious little of his father's errant undergraduate days, and now his memories of his father tend to paint a portrait of a stern, commanding, awesome parent, 'a very frightening father-figure, a Victorian father-figure'.[1]

Theirs was a father-son relationship governed by a code of behaviour designed to inspire respect rather than love. Laurence, as the youngest, felt this most, since by the time he was born, Gerard Olivier was in his late thirties. Youthful vigour and romanticism, if not completely spent, were much diminished. Moreover, he had now been reconverted to Christianity. And this time he embraced religion wholeheartedly, with a blazing fervour that left its mark on all his dependents.

Laurence's mother was most immediately affected by his sudden reconversion. As Agnes Crookenden, she had first met Gerard at Boxgrove, a preparatory (junior) school in Guildford, Surrey, where he was an assistant master and she, as the sister of the headmaster's wife, helped out at social functions. She was attractive, vivacious, essentially warmhearted; and ironically she had privately resolved never to marry a clergyman. But this resolution presented no problem when she and Gerard fell in love. They had clearly defined plans. For three years, with more sense than sensibility, they delayed marriage until they had saved enough to go into the education business on their own. Then they took over Tower House, a private residence in the charming old market town of Dorking in Surrey, and developed a thriving little private school. They had a daughter, Sybille; then a son, Richard. Their life seemed predictable and secure.

Then it came—the 'call' that Gerard Olivier felt compelled to answer. In 1903 he became an assistant at the Church of St. John the Evangelist in the near-by village of North Holmwood, and the following year he took up an appointment as curate at the parish church of St. Martin's in the centre of Dorking. Answering the call entailed selling the school, dismissing all the servants except the children's nanny and moving into an infinitely less attractive home in a much less salubrious neighbourhood.

The Olivier's new home was at No. 26 Wathen Road, a street of neat but altogether characterless Victorian villas directly off Dorking's High Street. Here they were displaced 'gentry'. The chimney sweep next door was more prosperous, and his daughter had her own little pony and cart. But little Sybille was never allowed to ask for a ride because she was of a different class. And here, in a plain, semi-detached, three-bedroom house, her second brother was born at five o'clock in the morning on May 22, 1907. Six weeks later he was christened at St. Martin's. They named him Laurence after Laurent Olivier, a sixteenth-century Frenchman, their earliest-known ancestor.

The birthplace of Laurence Olivier still stands today; a drab, outmoded building with nothing to commend it except its convenient position—handy for the High Street shops and the church. No plaque marks the spot, and in any event the house has no memories for Laurence. He was two years old when his father moved the family to a superior residence verging on the Cotmandene common and affording a view of Box Hill.

They named their new home East Dene, and if they had remained settled there Laurence would almost certainly have enjoyed a very normal upbringing. Glorious countryside was all around, affording enormous scope for a boy to lead a vigorous outdoor life. His parents, though far from wealthy, were reasonably secure; and largely through the church—a beehive of social activities—they were becoming rich in friends and much respected members of the community.

Then there was the Dorking Cricket Club for which 'The Rev', as members called him, had played with distinction since the turn of the century. He had topped the batting averages in 1902 when he scored a century against Reigate Hill, and a 40 that helped the town to hold a semi-professional M.C.C. side to an honourable draw. Members and supporters were often heard to express regret that G. K. Olivier, because of his church duties, was not available more often for weekend matches. They had no more attractive batsman excepting Dick Penfold the plumber, who had played for the county second eleven and who, as the club's professional groundsman, had the advantage of being able to 'doctor' wickets to his own satisfaction.

But Laurence never knew the simple pleasures of pastoral and sporting life around Dorking. His path changed direction shortly after his third birthday when the Reverend Olivier was offered a clerical appointment in the slum district of London's Notting Hill. With missionary zeal the curate took up the challenge, again responding to the dictates of his religious conscience rather than to the personal wishes of his family, who had to leave behind friends and exchange a rural demi-paradise for a drab and uninviting asphalt jungle.

Gerard Olivier left Dorking on amicable terms, much liked by his colleagues and by the majority of his congregation. Not so with his next appointment. If his High Church style could occasionally disturb a few parishioners in a sedate country town, it was veritable dynamite in a depressed area like Notting Hill, where his duties as an Anglican curate attached to St. James's Church included taking charge of a tin-roofed mission hut. Here he aroused bitter resentment by practising ritual to the extent of burning incense in his mission church, teaching the local dead-end kids to swing the censer and even walking about the slum area in a habit—cassock and black shovel-hat—that conjured up the image of a Roman Catholic priest.

This time he enjoyed neither the sympathy nor the support of his vicar; after one year he was asked to resign. When he refused on the grounds that he genuinely loved his church and congrega-tion, he found himself dismissed. Back home, in typically stern and dramatic style, he explained to his family what had occurred and why they had to move yet again. 'Imagine!' he thun-dered. 'Sacked. Dismissed. Disgraced. And all for a matter of principle!'[2]

In 1912 the five Oliviers quit their new home at No. 86 Elgin Crescent and began a nomadic life, moving from one town to another as the breadwinner took temporary work where he could, usually acting as *locum tenens* while the regular incumbent was on holiday. Father Olivier, as he was now often called, finally found a permanent position as assistant priest at St. Saviour's in the London borough of Pimlico. The family had a fixed abode again, at No. 22 Lupus Street, near Chelsea Bridge and the Thames Embankment, and they arrived just in time to celebrate Christ-mas in a home of their own. They were to remain there for the next six years.

Laurence, now five years old, had had few opportunities for making friends with other boys. He was learning more and more to contrive his own diversions and, without strong outside influences, the world of his childhood never came to be domi-nated by the popular pursuits of sports and war games. The 'dressing-up game' was the one he knew best—a game inspired by attending so many of his father's services at St. Saviour's. Behind a bedroom door labelled 'Laurence's Shrine', he dressed up in an eiderdown and conducted services of his own before a toy altar, and from that it was but a short step to play-acting on a makeshift stage in the nursery. He was seven years old when his

father helped him to build his own 'stage', comprising a huge
wooden box, old curtains and cocoa tins for footlights. For hours
at a time he would enter the make-believe world of his nursery
'theatre', acting and singing and dancing, and—when his
brother Dickie (two and a half years older) could not be persuaded
to join in—performing all the different parts in his invented
charades. Remarkably, his love of play-acting never faded.

In real life, too, there were semi-theatrical parts to play. At
church services he became one of the 'boat boys' carrying the
incense, and his dream of 'stardom' was to be promoted to
thurifer, swinging the censer extravagantly and commanding
attention as strikingly as the drum major leading a military band.
In 1967, recalling the influence of the splendour of church ritual,
Oliver said: 'My father was an effective preacher, and, as a boy,
sitting in the choir watching him and others in the pulpit, I was
fascinated by the way a sermon was delivered. Those preachers
knew when to drop the voice, when to bellow about the perils of
hell-fire, when to slip in a gag, when suddenly to wax sentimental, when to turn solemn, when to pronounce the blessing. The
quick changes of mood and manner absorbed me, and I have
never forgotten them.'[3]

Laurence's formal education began now at the near-by Francis
Holland Church of England School for Girls (it had one infant
class for boys). It should, in fact, have begun the previous year
when he was due to become a boarder at a school in far-off
Blackheath, but that ordeal had proved too much for a six-year-
old—and for his mother. He wept so profoundly at the separation
that she could not carry it through. Not that the boy cried easily;
at the age of seven he was knocked down by a horse and cart in
the Buckingham Palace Road, and his mother was so impressed
by his dry-eyed fortitude that she bought him his first pair of long
trousers. But he was always emotional about being away from the
mother he adored, and once he started at Francis Holland as a
day-boy a new problem developed—truancy.

One of the teachers was a personal friend of the family and the
new boy exploited this familiarity by going to her with fabricated
stories of why he needed permission to leave school early in the
morning. He invented a 'Miss Finlayson' whom, he said, his
mother wanted him to meet at Ecclestone Bridge for early lunch,
and he was so convincing that the truth came out only when the
teacher finally complained to his mother about his too frequent

cutting of classes. Laurence was punished in the common style of the time—a larruping on the behind with a slipper.

Olivier's tendency to play truant was perhaps symptomatic of rather more than boyish rebellion against discipline or a longing to be back home with his mother. He was never to be what is commonly called 'a good mixer' at school. He had developed in him a curious mixture of extrovert and introvert qualities, both markedly strong. Given an audience, he could be as bright as a new-minted penny, but he also had his long periods of sullenness, and among other boys he could appear to be aloof and downright anti-social. Inevitably this owed something to the influence of a dominant, Victorian-style parent. Recalling their father, Olivier's older sister Sybille has said: 'People were either devoted to him or couldn't take him at all. And talk about a temper—a storming, raging tornado which he'd turn on Larry in a way he never did on our brother Dick and me. Father didn't like Larry, and Larry was terrified of him. Mummy was just everything. She was the most enchanting person. Hair so long she could sit on it. She absolutely made our childhood. Always saw the funny side of everything. She adored Larry. He was hers. He always amused her very much. He was a complete clown. He'd have the whole lunch table shaking with laughter, but he had his sombre side too. He would sit for a long time not saying anything at all. You always felt as though Larry worked everything out in his mind before he spoke. He was always very, very determined. If he was sulking, heaven help all.'[4]

School held no attractions for Laurence until he was nine years old and able to join his brother as a boarding pupil in the small choir school attached to the church of All Saints, Margaret Street, in the heart of London. This unusual school was limited to only fourteen places, and in gaining one of them, through his father's personal connections, Laurence was exceptionally fortunate. His singing voice was sweetly competent, though not of the supreme quality for which the All Saints choir was renowned. In a vintage year of boys coming forward for auditions he might well have been rejected. But he was not. And his entry into that school heralded the most significant step forward in his theatrical development. It exposed him at a highly impressionable age to influences that had an extraordinary effect on his growth as an actor.

All Saints is a High Anglican church—Anglo-Catholic as they

called it then. In 1916, the year that the young Olivier arrived, he heard wags saying of the church: 'It's so high that it's nearly turned.' There was incense everywhere, a profusion of magnificent vestments. And the boys, day in and day out, were exposed to activities that had powerful elements of showmanship: services conducted with pomp and ceremony and professional precision; dramatic and thundering sermons delivered with more than a touch of the theatrical; endless rehearsals for performances by what was generally regarded as the finest church choir in London. The encouragement of self-expression also took more positive forms. Both the vicar, H. F. P. Mackay, and the precentor, Geoffrey Heald, were amateur actors of no mean ability, and they often staged school plays. There were lessons in drama and acting, even rare outings to the professional theatre. In his first Christmas at All Saints, Laurence and his classmates were taken to Drury Lane to see a performance of pantomime (*Babes in the Wood*), and they had the enlivening experience of being escorted backstage to meet such celebrated players as Will Evans and Stanley Lupino.

It is truly astonishing how this smallest of all choir schools so fruitfully sowed the seeds of passion for drama. Of the fourteen boys at All Saints in Olivier's time, three were destined to become successful professional actors. One was named Ralph Taylor, son of actress Mary Forbes. In 1926, as Ralph Forbes, he found fame through the film *Beau Geste* and became a Hollywood star. Another was Lawrence Johnson, the choir soloist, a boy from a family so poor that he was given a free place. After years of hardship as a merchant seaman he eventually changed his name to Laurence Naismith and became a prominent actor in the theatre and in more than fifty films. Today he remembers All Saints with strangely mixed emotions:

It was a terribly tight community, a monastic life really, with just two dormitories for fourteen boys and a day starting like that of a monk—up at 6.45 in the morning to serve in the church, then breakfast followed by choir practice and lessons (plenty of Latin because we often had to sing in Latin) and a walk in the afternoon or out on the playing fields for football or cricket.

I hated the school and I was never happy there. Because I was slack I was beaten more than any other boy. Regularly, like

a gong. And every Saturday we were allowed to go home for
the day and I used to cry every time when I had to go back. Yet
at the same time I loved the whole business of the church, the
services, the festivals, the beautiful music and singing. It was
this wonderful ritual that set Larry and me on the path
towards the professional theatre . . .*

We all used to serve at Mass, and Heald taught us how to
genuflect with perfect grace. Sometimes we had orchestras to
augment the organ, and the midnight mass was especially
enthralling. You actually looked forward to such occasions.
They really were a joy. I have been to Masses in St. Peter's in
Rome and in Florence, but those at All Saints were the more
memorable. They were absolutely impeccable, beautiful,
theatrical. And it was all so deeply moving that it had to rub
off on anyone who was fairly emotional . . .

Larry Olivier? Oh, yes, he was a natural actor all right, even
as a boy. And he had great presence. He was not altogether a
nice boy, or at least so I thought then; a bit of a bully. Yet he
did have this commanding presence, and funnily enough it has
followed me through life in small degrees.

I can remember the first solo I ever sang at All Saints. I was
terribly nervous. But it was very successful and I can remember
some old ladies crying. And I can remember to this day
Larry's actual words as we walked up the stairs to take off our
cassocks. He turned to me and said with an air of quiet
authority: 'Well done. Well done.' It sounded strange from a
boy of fourteen. And yet I have found him much the same in
later years . . . He's always been a rather frightening man.

Olivier was not long at All Saints before he was writing home
for props to enable him to act the part of a policeman in a school
harlequinade. The following year precentor Heald cast him as
First Citizen in the Christmas production of *Julius Caesar*, but
when they began rehearsals the ten-year-old came over far too
strong for that insignificant part and he found himself promoted

* The attraction of ritual was also making a profound and significant
impression on both Ralph Richardson and John Gielgud. Richardson,
aged fourteen, was being trained for the priesthood at this time.
Gielgud went through a religious wave at sixteen when he was 'always
rushing off to the Brompton Oratory to smell the incense and watch
the ceremonial'.

to Brutus. In the reshuffle, Ralph Taylor was switched from Brutus to Cassius. Larry's brother Dickie played Caesar.

As they rehearsed, sometimes during the thunder of World War I air raids, Heald wondered at the way his smallest actor grasped a role demanding so much maturity. The priest had a rare gift for bringing out unsuspected reserves of self-expression in boy players, but even he had never known a pupil to reveal so early a natural flair for verse-speaking and stage movement.

Olivier's amateur stage debut—in a hall seating no more than a hundred—was witnessed by a surprising number of people prominent in the professional theatre. Among them was Ellen Terry, formerly Irving's leading lady, now the most celebrated actress of the day. On hearing that she was in the audience, Laurence innocently asked, 'Who is Ellen Terry?' and met with gusts of derisive laughter. By the evening's end he had won new respect. After the opening performance the Grand Old Lady of the English theatre went backstage and Laurence was introduced to her. 'Oh, don't you love the words!' she exclaimed to the rather overwhelmed boy. Apparently she had genuinely enjoyed the production, for she returned the following night and noted in her diary: 'The small boy who played Brutus is already a great actor.'

Nine months later Heald revived his production of *Julius Caesar*. This time Olivier's performance was seen and admired by Sir Johnston Forbes-Robertson, now retired but still remembered as the greatest Hamlet of the age. Ever after, a supremely proud father would retell the story of how he remarked that perhaps his son had not done too badly, and how the great Forbes-Robertson, with tears in his eyes, replied, 'My dear man, your son *is* Brutus.'

Olivier himself has expressed his doubts about that story; he is inclined to attribute it to an excess of parental pride. What *is* indisputable, however, is that Forbes-Robertson subsequently wrote a letter to Heald in which he observed, 'Brutus delivered his oration to the citizens with a pathetic air of fatalism which was poignantly suggestive—remarkable in one so young.'

Laurence followed that debut next year with the role of Maria in *Twelfth Night*. But he was to make his greatest impact in his final role at All Saints as Katherine in *The Taming of the Shrew*. There were four performances. Again Ellen Terry attended and this time she noted that she had never seen Kate played better by a woman, except Ada Rehan. Also present was another future Dame of the theatre—Sybil Thorndike, then thirty-five, a close friend of the Olivier family and on the threshold of establishing herself as an actress of the first order. Sybil attended with her husband Lewis Casson, and she recalls vividly how the young Olivier was never overshadowed by a Petruchio played by the producer himself, Geoffrey Heald: 'I saw Larry in all those productions at All Saints and most of all I was impressed by his Katherine. His shrew was really wonderful—the best Katherine I ever saw . . . You know, some people are born with technical ability. And Larry was. He didn't have to work hard enough at technical things because he knew it all from the start, instinctively. Now Johnny Gielgud had to work much harder. He wasn't technically equipped as Larry was. Larry was from a little boy.'

Laurence Naismith, who played a minor role in that *Taming of the Shrew*, agrees. 'The evidence was already there—that Larry was born to act. He had the presence. What I remember most about his Katherine was his complete naturalness. I know it was the convention in Shakespeare's day for boys to take the female roles. But Larry was never, in any way, effeminate. He was a very unattractive boy, lean and bony, with very skinny legs. And yet the moment he put on those dresses his image and bearing changed completely. He really became a young girl.'

In March 1920, when Laurence was almost thirteen and away at All Saints, a tragedy occurred that marked the end of what he has since termed 'the paradise of my childhood'. The mother whom he adored died of a brain tumour. She was forty-eight. When Larry saw her for the last time she was lying in bed, paralysed down her left side. She had only two weeks more to live, but he could not know that. He kissed her goodbye as he would any weekend and set off to school.

'I often think, and say, that perhaps I've never got over it,' he said in a B.B.C. television interview some forty-five years later. 'Anyway, my father had to take over, not knowing me very well. I think to him I was rather an unnecessary child. He could look at my sister eating a lot of porridge and my brother eating a lot of porridge with comparative equanimity, but when I was eating a lot of porridge it annoyed him intensely. My sister says I simply got on his nerves, poor man. I don't blame him at all because I was probably very fat and absolutely brainless. However, when my mother died he had to take care of me: my brother was at school and my sister was, I think, already halfway out in the world.'[5]

The death of Agnes Olivier came as a seemingly permanent eclipse of the sun for her children. She was, by all accounts, a woman of infinite patience, fortitude and good humour—as well she needed to be. She was a very clever mimic, and it was she especially who filled the Olivier home with love and the sounds of laughter. Above all, perhaps compensating for her husband's apparent disinterest, she doted on Larry who, though inclined to his dark and sullen moods, often displayed an enormous and mischievous sense of fun to match her own. 'She was an absolute darling,' recalls Dame Sybil. 'Sturdy with a rather gypsy-looking face. And Larry was exactly like her. He and his mother were very close. She understood the boy so well. And I am sure that he got all his humour from her.'

All memories of Mrs. Olivier are of a warm and loving being. Memories of Mr. Olivier are curiously mixed. Popular in his days as a Dorking schoolmaster-cricketer, he emerges as a more dour and dominating figure following his deep involvement in religious duties. One can only speculate that he may have given so much of himself outside the home that he had little left to give when he returned. Yet after the loss of his wife he did give more time to his family, and in May he took them all to the St. James's Theatre to see Sybil Thorndike in *The Mystery of the Yellow Room*—the first time Larry became aware of Sybil as a professional actress. But while Mr. Olivier became closer to his youngest child, the Victorian father-image remained stern and strong, and for several years yet Laurence never suspected how much pride and pleasure his father took in his acting ability.

Since 1918 the Oliviers had been living in a large Queen Anne house in Letchworth, thirty-five miles from London. Mr. Olivier had arrived there at war's end to accept the living of St. Michael's and All Saints. Now, as a widower, he moved the family to a smaller house near the church, and it was from there that Laurence, aged fourteen, set out to face the harrowing experience of being a 'new boy' at an English public school.

Despite the Cassons' remarks about Laurence being a 'natural' for a stage career, the father still had every reason to hope that his boy would eventually make his career in the ministry. The boy's upbringing had been very well designed to prepare him for the Church, and the pattern was being continued now by the father's choice of a public school with a still flourishing ecclesiastical tradition: St. Edward's, Oxford.

'Teddy's' was founded in 1863 by a man with whom Father Olivier could strongly identify: the Reverend Thomas Chamberlain, who, in his early years as a village curate, practised such ritual that he was openly accused of 'popery', stoned in the street and locked out of his own church. Fired by the ideals of the Oxford Movement, Chamberlain saw his school as a nursery for a new breed of clergymen with a stronger, more vigorous sense of purpose. By the 1920s the fees had risen to £125 a year, far beyond the resources of any clergyman without private means but still below the charges of most other English public schools, and within tight financial limits it managed to provide reduced-fee places for many boys from families of the clergy. The demand for such places was excessive, and in securing one for his son, Father Olivier cannot have been handicapped by his acquaintance with the Duke of Newcastle, who, as a patron and churchwarden of All Saints, was well aware of Laurence's talents. In 1911 the Duke had joined the Council of St. Edward's, and that same year members of the Council became trustees and governors of the school.

Laurence went to 'Teddy's' in the fall of 1921, one of seven sons of clergymen in an intake of thirty new boys. Today he is one of the school's most distinguished alumni, remembered in the same breath as Guy ('The Dam Buster') Gibson V.C., Douglas Bader, the legless Battle of Britain air ace, and Kenneth Grahame, author of *The Wind in the Willows*. Yet Olivier never came round to liking public school and, as he would have it, no one at St. Edward's much cared for him. ('I just hated school,' he has said. 'Without wanting to pull out any violins, I think I can say that I was vastly unpopular. I was what my mates would call a show-off. I wanted to show how good I was at games, but I wasn't any good at them at all. And that again gave one this inner *esprit* of wanting, *needing*, to show them.')[6]

A nomadic childhood had not helped to develop a talent for making friends. What he had developed was marked self-sufficiency in making his own escapist entertainments, and that was a valueless ability at public school where you were essentially expected to 'muck in'. His enthusiasms—chapel services, hymn-singing, acting—only helped to isolate him from the mainstream. When placed amid some 300 boys, he emerged as a 'loner', a moody youth whose introspective moments could easily be mistaken for aloofness and conceit.

Sporting prowess was the surest passport to respect and popularity. Olivier had none. Above all, he craved to be a fine cricketer as his father had been, but not a stroke of 'The Rev's' county class batsmanship had been passed on to the son. He never came near to school team selection; not until his final term was he picked to play for his 'house'. How he rejoiced then at seeing his name on the 'house' notice-board: Olivier, L., Number 11. And when he came to bat and took the long walk out to the wicket, he had a vision of achieving lasting glory. Seven runs were needed for victory. He was on stage for the great drama of his sporting life. At the crease he made all the right semi-theatrical gestures—prodding the wicket, surveying the field, crouching in purposeful stance. Dourly, he defended against the first ball. This, he decided, was hardly the stuff of which heroes are made; and so he resolved to be bold. He scored two runs, ran a bye. Then, with only four runs needed for victory, he was clean bowled—by Douglas Bader.

'Games were compulsory in the afternoons at St. Edward's,' Bader recalls. 'And it was the games men that were most admired. I remember Laurence as always being tremendously keen, but never really a player. I myself don't think he was unpopular at all, but he was perhaps introspective, lived within himself, and he had the sort of artistic make-up that might have made him *think* he was unpopular.'

Olivier spent only three years at St. Edward's. And in that time his most notable distinction was achieved outside of the school. It came during the Easter holidays of 1922 when Father Heald was invited by the governors of the Shakespeare Memorial Theatre at Stratford-upon-Avon to stage his production of *The Taming of the Shrew* as part of the Bard's Birthday Festival week. This honour, more than all the praise from visiting stage celebrities, evinced the quality of that original All Saints production, not least the enormous impact the boy Laurence must have had as Kate, and the lasting impression that this Stratford occasion made upon the fourteen-year-old Olivier can scarcely be overstated. He carried the wreath in the ceremonial procession from the theatre to the parish church where Shakespeare has his grave, and there he rejoined the All Saints choir for the memorial service. That same unforgettable day, in rehearsal, he trod the boards of the famous Stratford stage for the first time and met the American actor James Hackett, who was about to play Othello. It was Laurence's first experience of acting in a real theatre, and the calm and instinctive style in which he adapted himself to his awesome surroundings finally convinced Heald that here was a boy born to be a professional actor.

His performance in the special matinée the following day confirmed that judgment. National newspaper critics were present. One, W. A. Darlington of *The Daily Telegraph*, wrote: 'The boy who took the part of Kate made a fine, bold, black-eyed hussy, badly in need of taming, and I cannot remember any actress in the part who looked better.' *The Times* correspondent was similarly impressed: 'If the action halts for a moment, you may be occupied in wonder at the lines so well and clearly spoken, or may ask yourself how it is that boys have so wonderfully learned even to walk like women. You feel that if an apple were thrown to this Katherine she would instinctively try to catch it in her lap.'

After only one performance in a genuine theatre, Laurence was returning to school with favourable national press notices. Again, however, it was not a feat that would impress his fellow pupils at St. Edward's, and hoist him on a par with their gods of the playing fields. 'What, Olivier! Dollying up in dresses and playing a stupid girl during the hols?' He could already hear the cacophony of jibes, and at the start of the summer term he had the good sense to keep button-lipped about an achievement that years later became one of his proudest boasts: that he had actually played in the old Stratford theatre before it was burned down in 1926.

In December 1923, came his one recorded achievement in school life. St. Edward's anniversary celebrations brought boys, alumni and parents together for a long weekend of events that included football matches, a Commemoration dinner, chapel services and a concert. They ended with an 'open stage' production of *A Midsummer Night's Dream*, using the main doors of the school building for most of the entrances and exits. Olivier was already looking for original means of heightening a performance; and as Puck he ensured that he caught the eye by introducing two green lights, worn on his chest and lit by a battery in his pocket. Yet he had no real need of gimmickry. His ability was not to be missed, even by the strictly amateur critics.

A school magazine contributor, simply identified as R. C. M.,* wrote: 'By far the most notable performance was that of Puck. He seemed to put more "go" into it than the others, and succeeded in individualizing his part. To my mind he was a little too robust and jovial for such a quick-footed, light-fingered person, but at any rate he gave a consistent rendering, and showed by his gestures and movements that he has a knowledge of acting and a good mastery of technique.' Another contributor ('A Parent') wrote: 'A word must be said about Olivier's rendering of Puck. It was so distinctly original that it set the audience thinking. Probably more than one went away saying, "That's not at all my idea of Puck." But was it not Shakespeare's idea? That is a very tenable view.' And Douglas Bader now comments: 'After all these years I can clearly remember how frightfully good Laurence was in *A Midsummer Night's Dream*. It seemed to me that he overacted, but with hindsight one could see that he was miles better than anyone else.'

Olivier himself knew he had been good. But he had no illusions about his standing in the school. With telling brevity he recorded in his diary: 'Played Puck very well—much to everybody's disgust.'[7]

That Christmas he went home to a rectory scene of unusual excitement and frenetic activity. Life in the Olivier household was geared to the imminent departure of young Dickie, due to leave in January to begin a career as a tea planter in India. Amid all the emotional fussings and preparations, Laurence had no time to dwell on the significance of the event, but once he had returned from seeing his brother embark at Tilbury he was immediately aware of the new void in his world. The house in Letchworth seemed strangely quiet; and for the first time he went upstairs to a bedroom that was all his own. More than a sense of loneliness disturbed him; he was restless, too, and rather envied the glamour that surrounded his brother in setting off on a great new adventure.

In the evening he had a bath and, as was the family custom, he

---

* R. C. M. was almost certainly Robert Cecil Mortimer, former Bishop of Exeter and now chairman of the Board of Governors of St. Edward's. Remarkably, while accepting the possibility, he does not recall writing the notice.

used his father's bath water to save on the heating. Both father and son were feeling sad at Dickie's departure. Mr. Olivier sat on the bath edge and talked. And then Laurence blurted out his secret thoughts: 'When can I follow Dickie out to India, father, please? In about one or two years? I don't want to go to the university.'

Mr. Olivier's reply came as a total surprise to Laurence. More, it amazed him and puzzled him for years to come—because it revealed that the Victorian-style parent, so often seeming remote and disinterested, had given more thought and feeling to the question of his younger son's future than the boy had ever dreamed possible.

'Don't be a fool,' was the clergyman's crisp and positive reply. 'You are going on the stage.'

Until that moment he had never given a hint that he entertained the professional theatre as a remote possibility for his son. Now, as they talked with an unaccustomed intimacy and easy frankness, it became obvious that this was no snap decision; Mr. Olivier had it all thought out. Next July, he said, the boy would leave St. Edward's and hopefully gain a place at London's Central School of Speech Training and Dramatic Art. And though Laurence still vaguely hankered to join Dickie in India, or perhaps to go into the mercantile marine, he knew secretly and instinctively that his father was absolutely right.

3

The Wayward Drama Student

Shortly after his seventeenth birthday Laurence Olivier faced what seemed to be the most critically important moment of his young life: the hour that would decide once and for all whether or not he might make a professional actor. He had special leave from St. Edward's to attend an audition at a London drama academy. It was not simply a matter of passing the test; he had to come through with sufficient distinction to earn a scholarship worth a year's tuition fees—plus a £50 a year bursary. If he did not merit both honours, so his father said, then they could not afford to send him there, and he could abandon all hope of becoming an actor.

London boasted two actors' teaching establishments of prestige at this time: Herbert Tree's Royal Academy of Dramatic Art in Gower Street, and the Central School of Speech Training and Dramatic Art, more obscurely tucked away in rooms leading off one of the great corridors that encircle the Royal Albert Hall in South Kensington. Olivier's audition was at the latter, and as he approached the imposing building the butterflies in his stomach were gently on the wing. As he made his way up to the Central School he glimpsed the enormous stage and auditorium of the Albert Hall for the first time. The butterflies soared.

Such was his naivety that he actually imagined that he would be required to perform alone on that stage before an audience of hundreds. Instead he found himself directed to a back-room theatre in miniature and asked to say his piece on a tiny stage. Some ten yards in front of him, seated at a table, was his 'audience': a dumpy, fur-caped lady in her late fifties. Olivier launched into 'The Seven Ages of Man' speech, a performance he had rehearsed a hundred times and which he aimed to embellish with his own dramatic gestures. The woman leaned forward on her elbows and scrutinized him across the footlights through an aperture formed with her hands, one palm horizontal above her eyes, the other below.

'Oh, I don't think we need *that*!' she interjected after the boy had made what he thought to be a particularly clever piece of physical improvisation. Olivier went on. He had been forewarned about the informal directness of this lady dressed all in black.

Elsie Fogerty was her name; founder and principal of the Central School, an Irishwoman of rough charm and such formidable personality and determination that George Bernard Shaw once remarked about her, 'She will get her way; there's nobody can stand up to her.' One of her many successful ex-pupils has described her as looking 'like a dignified cross between Queen Victoria and Mr. Punch'.

'Come down, boy, come down,' said the redoubtable Miss Fogerty when Olivier had ended his piece. And when he was down and seated beside her, she began: 'I think you've got a little too strong an idea of the importance of action. It's not really necessary to make fencing movements when you are saying, "Sudden and quick to quarrel." Perhaps just a simple gesture'—and she let her hand fall loosely from her shoulder to her lap as she spoke—'*Sans* everything.' Then, with characteristic bluntness, she went directly to a defect in his physical make-up. She reached out and placed the tip of her forefinger on the base of his hairline and traced a line down to the bridge of his nose. 'You have a weakness here,' she said. 'Remember that.'

Laurence was already privately aware of that 'weakness' (untidy hair well forward, thick eyebrows too close and giving an effect of perpetual frowning); the sharp-eyed Fogie had touched on his most sensitive nerve. Yet she did so in a calm and clinical manner that somehow made it impersonal, and rather than being embarrassed, he was indelibly impressed by her quickness—a point 'brilliantly illuminating, brilliantly observed'. (Soon afterwards he shaved his beetle brows, though for years he was to harbour nagging doubts about his facial image, seeking to cover it up with liberal helpings of putty. Half a century later, he remained uncertain whether his well-known predilection for false noses was not the result of some subconscious hangover from those early years of concern about his face, and he never forgot her observation about too much elaboration in making gestures—a natural tendency that he has always needed to guard against.)

Following that audition, Olivier went into another rehearsed piece: an explanation of how it would be virtually impossible to attend the school without the £50 grant. Miss Fogerty agreed almost at once, and he presumed he had been treated as a special case because his sister had taken a course at the school a few years before. Fogie's decision, however, was probably influenced also by the desperate shortage of male pupils in her academy—only six young men as opposed to more than seventy women, many of whom were there for training in speech and social graces rather than dramatic art to be practised professionally.

Miss Fogerty was a woman of enormous cultural range, prodigious memory and a remarkable vocabulary that she had developed by learning ten new words from the dictionary every night. She was *the* pioneer of what is now known as 'speech therapy', having started in 1914 the first clinic exclusively designed to help people with serious speech defects. Through her Central School, and through pupils she trained to be teachers in other parts of the country, she was responsible more than any other individual for the fine speaking (albeit declining) that was to be heard on the English stage.

Fogie's expertise in the art of voice production and exercise attracted many prominent actors and actresses who came to her for help when faced with vocal difficulties. Among them were Henry Ainley, Elisabeth Bergner, Edith Evans, John Gielgud. She was totally dedicated to the aim of raising speech and drama training to university level and she worked purely for love, profiting nothing materially from her Central School. Only by giving private lessons outside the school did she make a modest living; even then she was hopelessly unpractical about money matters, and Gielgud was one of several 'patients' who complained that she never sent him a bill.

Olivier left St. Edward's to attend Fogerty's in the summer of 1924. In his fierce determination to be totally independent, he took a miserably cheap attic 'bed-sitter' in Paddington and further conserved his money by eating less than was reasonable for a still growing boy. But he failed in his bid to go it alone. It was never possible to live in London solely on his £50 bursary and ultimately he had to accept a £1 a month allowance from his father. Even then it was barely enough—twenty-four shillings a week for food and lodgings and travel expenses. He could have enjoyed greater comfort and regular meals by living at home and travelling thirty-five miles from Letchworth each day, but apart from the tedium of the journey, he preferred to live in London for a strictly personal reason. While at 'Teddy's' he had been shocked by his father's decision to remarry. It was a step fundamentally unacceptable to a boy of strong Anglo-Catholic principles and ideals; it was also inconsistent with the teachings of Father Olivier himself, since he had often and vehemently spoken in favour of celibacy being upheld by the Anglo-Catholic clergy.

His plan to remarry followed a romantic voyage abroad as a member of the Mission of Help to Jamaica, and it coincided with his acceptance of the living of St. Paul's, Brighton. When his intention was revealed, his congregation-to-be refused to accept a married vicar. The issue led to sensational treatment in the Press: SHOULD VICARS WED? was one headline; CUPID V. CONGRE-GATION was another. Through it all Father Olivier stood firm, and so sacrificed a highly attractive living. He was no longer Rector of Letchworth and it was two years before he took up another and final living as Rector of Addington, near Winslow in Buckinghamshire.

Laurence found his stepmother to be a charming and admirable woman, but for a while he could not accept anyone taking the place of his mother and, with a stubbornness worthy of his father, he held out in London and starved himself in the process. He certainly looked undernourished; in his own words, he was 'a shrimp as a child and a weed as a youth . . . a miserably thin creature well into my acting career. My arms hung like wires from my shoulders.'[1]

Between terms at Fogerty's he sought professional stage work to gain extra cash and experience, but work in the theatre was elusive and always low-paying. His first paid engagement came as assistant stage manager and general understudy for a production of *Through the Crack*, by Algernon Blackwood and Violet Pearn, at the obscure little St. Christopher Theatre in Letchworth. He didn't even merit a mention in the programme credits. A few months later, during the Easter holidays, he made his professional acting debut in the same theatre as Lennox in *Macbeth*. The event passed unrecorded.

Out of the paltry proceeds of holiday work, Olivier could afford such rare luxuries as a sixpenny gallery ticket to a West End theatre. Gladys Cooper, every young man's fancy, was his favourite actress and pin-up; Gerald du Maurier was the male

star who shone brightest in his eyes. Recalling that actor many
years later, Olivier remarked: 'Actually Gerald du Maurier,
brilliant actor that he was, had the most disastrous influence on
my generation, because we really thought, looking at him, that it
was easy; and for the first ten years of our lives in the theatre
nobody could hear a word we said. We thought he was being
really natural; of course he was a genius of a technician giving
that appearance, that's all.'[2]

The London theatre of Olivier's student days was not without
its riches. Sybil Thorndike had begun the decade in Grand
Guignol, having her eyes stabbed out with knitting needles in a
lunatic asylum or being crushed with her lover beneath a descending ceiling, but in 1924 she played her definitive Saint Joan,
confirming her position, simultaneously with Edith Evans (in
Tiger Cats), as an actress of the very front rank. It was also the
year that Noel Coward removed his velvet gloves to unveil his
most contentious work, *The Vortex*, a play attacked as decadent
dustbin drama, but one that had a long-term impact on the
theatre of the Twenties as profound as that of *Look Back in Anger*
in the Fifties. Prominent productions the following year were
Lonsdale's *The Last of Mrs. Cheyney*, a popular hit for Gladys
Cooper and du Maurier; *Hay Fever*, dashed off by Coward in
three days of galloping inspiration; and the one new masterpiece,
Juno and the Paycock by one-time Dublin labourer Sean O'Casey.
There was John Barrymore's *Hamlet* at the Haymarket and
belated recognition of Chekhov with the arrival of *The Cherry
Orchard* and then *The Seagull*.

But Shakespeare and Chekhov and O'Casey had no real bearing on the spirit of the times. The West End that Olivier encountered in 1925 was essentially vibrant and glamorous and in
the words of the current catch-phrase, 'Madly gay, darlings!
Madly gay!' Tallulah Bankhead was the 'dahling' of the masses,
Gertrude Lawrence, an irresistible idol. And the popular mood
was best captured in the tuneful hedonism of 'I Want to Be
Happy' that was on everyone's lips from the time that *No, No,
Nanette* opened at the Palace on March 11, 1925, and began its
run of 665 performances. Olivier, befitting a seventeen-year-old
let loose in a world of pulsating freshness and trendy excitement,
was most deeply infected by the romanticism of the age, and
more than ever he was hopelessly infatuated with the show
business life.

He first walked on to a London stage (the Century) on November 30, 1924, five days after *The Vortex* burst the banks of cosy propriety. With bottom billing as 'Lawrence Olivier', he had the minute part of the Suliot Officer in Alice Law's *Byron*. The star and producer was Henry Oscar, one of his teachers at drama school. Ten weeks later, on February 8, 1925, 'Lawrence' made his first London appearance in Shakespeare—two lines as Master Snare and twenty as Thomas of Clarence in L. E. Berman's production of *King Henry IV, Part II*. He passed without critical notice.

If Olivier was 'born to act', it was by no means obvious to everyone at this time. Henry Oscar discerned little talent or potential in the new pupil who came to him so highly commended. He was untidy and defensive and gauche, and the impression stuck with Oscar that the boy would never achieve enough polish and personality to shine as an actor.

In both appearance and manner Olivier was deceptive. Part peasant, part clown in class, he had sufficient flair and resolution to assume a certain princeliness when the curtain rose on a performance that mattered. Then, if little else, he did reveal an indefinable quality, a certain 'style' suggesting hidden power beneath the surface. This faintly showed at the end of his first term when actress Athene Seyler visited the school to judge students for awards. 'Larry was going in for his diploma examination and doing a passage from *The Merchant of Venice*. He was playing Shylock and a bearded Peggy Ashcroft was the clerk in the court. And Larry at the time was covered with hair. His hair grew very, very low on his forehead, and he had frightfully bushy eyebrows and a beard, and I couldn't see his face at all. I should think it was a pretty lame performance, but it was quite obvious to me that here was a young man with a great potentiality, a great gift. I saw this as well in Peggy, merely reading a letter, and so I gave them both diplomas.' (Miss Seyler proved herself to be an extraordinarily perceptive judge of talent. Earlier she had picked out John Gielgud as the outstanding pupil at RADA.)

Olivier and Ashcroft were bracketed for top marks that day. The following term they were the outstanding pupils again. He took the Dawson Milward Cup for the best male student, and she won the girls' prize. Miss Ashcroft's achievement was, of course, much the more significant since she faced far, far greater competition. (Ann Todd was just one of many young talents at the school then.) Laurence, in truth, faced no real contest.

In his one year at the Central School, his basic training covered a remarkably broad range. The curriculum included classes for voice (daily), verse-speaking, prosody and poetics, French, the history of drama, history of costume, deportment, mime, fencing, make-up and stage management. Fencing and make-up attracted him especially and he practised both in his own time. Naturally enough, his approach to acting was all fire and élan; he had, he recalls, a kind of burning ambition to get ahead and show everyone what a magnificent actor he could be; and he longed for great emotional roles. But he had no clear ideas of how he was going to advance his dreams of glory, and despite a year of independence in London he remained a rather ingenuous young man.

For example, although he has since recognized his eternal debt to Elsie Fogerty, he didn't fully appreciate it when attending her school. He still tended to regard his teacher, indeed anyone in that kind of position of authority, as more enemy than friend. This lack of trust showed sadly on the day Fogie offered to give him a letter of recommendation to use as an aid in applying for work prior to leaving school. Ungraciously and unnecessarily, he declined the offer. Asked why, he explained that he had learnt of an agent who had told a fellow student that a letter from the Central School was no recommendation at all. Disconcerted, Miss Fogerty asked for the agent's name so that she might put him straight. Olivier refused to give it. If he had learned anything at public school it was that you didn't 'inform', even on your worst enemy. Fogie was left disappointed. She regretted this kind of invisible barrier between teacher and pupil and later told him: 'If only I were rich enough to pay the students that come to me. It is very strange, but it is true, that when people pay to learn, they never work so well.'[3]

That summer Olivier made his first professional stage appearance since leaving drama school, and he literally fell flat on his face. The occasion was a sketch called *Unfailing Instinct*, put on as a curtain-raiser before a Brighton Hippodrome production of Arnold Ridley's new play *The Ghost Train*. Again and again the eighteen-year-old novice had been warned about the importance of lifting his feet as he came on stage via a door built into the scenery on a wooden base. It made no difference. On the cue for his entrance he stumbled stupidly into the base of the door frame and plunged headfirst into the footlights with sufficient impact to earn his first, brief notice as a pro: 'Mr. Laurence Olivier made a good deal out of a rather small part.'

By accident, and sometimes by feckless design, the young Olivier had a remarkable knack of putting his worst foot forward. He won straight acting roles, and with his natural exuberance, still managed to play the comic. His first chance for regular employment came in October 1925 with an invitation to join the Lena Ashwell Players, a troupe that took culture to the less fashionable London suburbs and performed one-night stands in draughty town halls. The pay was a starvation wage of £2 10s a week, and no travel expenses. Moreover, the troupe was commonly known as 'The Lavatory Players' because they were sometimes required to use lavatories as dressing rooms. Still, it was fractionally better than no work at all. Olivier promptly blew it.

Actor Alan Webb, a contemporary in that troupe, recalls: 'Larry, I remember, shocked my rather prim nature by his fooling about. I was particularly horrified by his loud mirth on stage during a performance of *Julius Caesar*. It was a pretty tatty production and I was playing some old buffer and wearing a particularly ill-fitting sort of cotton wool wig. Well, Larry tweaked my wig on the stage and thought it was terribly funny. He got into trouble for his laughing and I have a distinct recollection of us sitting together on top of an open bus, he in his blue mackintosh, and me saying to him, "Larry, if you don't take your work more seriously you'll never get on." '

While playing Flavius in *Julius Caesar*, Olivier could not get out of his head the idea of projecting anger on the stage by tearing down two wreaths that were pinned to the curtain as a back-cloth. With a little bit of luck, he explained, you might pull down the curtain as well and so expose the naked behinds of the girls busy dressing backstage—'and that was a big laugh'. An even bigger laugh came during a performance at a girls' school at Englefield Green in Surrey. In the first act, Philip Leaver as Marullus was standing on a beer box that served as a rostrum and delivering the 'Knew you not, Pompey' speech. Suddenly the long pants rolled up beneath his toga came adrift. They flopped down and draped over the beer box so that the actor was shackled at the ankles. An experienced trouper might have manoeuvred across to screen the distressed player while he repaired the damage. Not Olivier. He convulsed into hysterical laughter, a fit so uncontrollable that he had to leave the stage.

The next day he was fired.

The wayward actor went hungry for weeks after that. He remained too proud to ask his father for help, and he would have been compelled to seek work outside the theatre if it had not been for the intervention of the Cassons, probably prompted by the vicar of All Saints, who was aware of the boy's difficulties. In December Lewis Casson and his partner Bronson Albery were preparing an extravagant production of Shakespeare's *King Henry VIII*, more pageant than play, and Olivier was offered £3 a week to walk on, understudy if required and serve as one of two assistant managers. It went on two days before Christmas, the programme reading: 'First Serving Man—Laurence Olivier.' He also appeared among an assorted mixture of 'Bishops, Lords, Officers, Guards, Scribes, etc.' When they followed this in March with a revival of Shelley's *The Cenci** for a few matinées, he was kept on as assistant stage manager, also playing the Count's servant, with only a few lines to speak. 'I was a marvellous Assistant Stage Manager,' he recalled, 'stopping people from talking, protecting my saint and heroine. I ought to have stayed an A.S.M. all my life.' In fact, he was so efficient that he aroused his employer's displeasure by shushing Bronson Albery when he was talking in the wings.

In the production of *Henry VIII*, Norman V. Norman played the king, Sybil Thorndike his Queen Katherine and Angela Baddeley was Anne Bullen. Dame Sybil's proud memory of that spectacle at the old Empire Theatre, Leicester Square, is that her train was carried by two future knights: Olivier and a boy called Carol Reed, now famed as a film director. 'They were wonderful boys—quarrelling like fun all the time. And they were both in love with the same girl—Angela Baddeley.' Miss Baddeley, a strikingly beautiful twenty-one-year-old, was then married. But that didn't discourage Olivier from dreaming. He was a seemingly incurable romantic, continually falling in love with young actresses, married or otherwise, and it was all very pure and innocent and quixotic, in keeping with the spirit of the times. This, after all, was the decade that had responded so emotionally

* In this production it was an actor three years Olivier's junior who caught the critics' attention: Jack Hawkins, aged fifteen.

to the exotic romance of *The Garden of Allah* and the young Trappist who breaks his priestly vows for true love; that had accepted the saccharine escapism of *The Blue Lagoon* and made best-sellers of A. S. M.. Hutchinson's *If Winter Comes* and Michael Arlen's *The Green Hat*.

Mad, passionate love was never more in vogue. And as in the song, the young Olivier was forever falling in love with love, and so falling for make-believe and playing the fool. Soon he was to be given the most significant break in his entire career. Yet at once he would become romantically interested in the actress wife of a rival actor and then, as though driven by a death wish, he would put all at risk by clowning on stage in his first leading role.

4

The Repertory Years

On June 3, 1925, King George V created a new knight of the British Theatre. His name was Sir Barry Vincent Jackson and his knighthood 'for services to the stage' represented an extraordinary personal achievement. He had entered into London management only three years before and already his contribution to the national theatre was immeasurable. C. B. Cochran dubbed him 'the Fairy Godmother of the British Drama in the West End', and if Jackson, a chain-smoking, thick-set six-footer scarcely measured up to the part physically, he certainly played it to enormous effect. Quite simply, in the mid-Twenties he was achieving what no one else had dreamed possible: he had founded a little experimental repertory theatre in the cultural wilderness of Birmingham, and by way of it, he was having a profound influence on the theatre as a whole.

Jackson's company (he always called it 'our' company and for years declined to have his name on the playbills) began the process of introducing new plays and players to London with the 1919 production of John Drinkwater's *Abraham Lincoln*. It ran for 400 performances, and that success, more than any before it, demonstrated that the provinces were not entirely wastelands for third-rate touring companies.

Among plays given their first British performance by Jackson's Birmingham Repertory Theatre were *The Farmer's Wife*, *The Barretts of Wimpole Street*, *The Apple Cart*, *Bird in Hand* and *Back to Methuselah*. And today, half a century later, the players who have appeared at the B.R.T. make a remarkable catalogue: a roll that includes Peggy Ashcroft, Felix Aylmer, Alan Badel, Stanley Baker, Leslie Banks, Barry K. Barnes, Brenda Bruce, Sebastian Cabot, Robert Coote, Noel Coward, Roland Culver, Albert Finney, Greer Garson, Cedric Hardwicke, Margaret Leighton, John Neville, Donald Pleasance, Ralph Richardson,

Paul Scofield, Margaretta Scott, James Stewart (later Stewart Granger), Jessica Tandy, Ernest Thesiger and Donald Wolfit. Jackson, as theatre historian J. C. Trewin observed, 'made of his theatre a university of the stage; today its graduates are everywhere'.[1]

Back in the early Twenties, however, Birmingham had little appreciation of what Jackson was doing—which, by his own definition, was 'to serve an art instead of making that art serve a commercial purpose'. His approach was noble, philanthropic and sometimes downright bloody-minded. In 1923, for example, in last-ditch defiance of popular taste, he persevered for two disastrous weeks with a production of Georg Kaiser's *Gas* that played night after night to mini-audiences (forty-seven customers at one count). The play's abject failure left Jackson sour and disenchanted. If the public was not willing to support his theatre, he said, then he was no longer willing to run it. And in January 1924, amid much protest, he closed it down. Seven months later he was to be persuaded to reverse his decision, but for the moment Birmingham's loss was very much London's gain.

With the closing of his steep-raked little playhouse in Station Road (the first building in Britain specifically designed and constructed as a repertory theatre), he concentrated exclusively on London productions: revivals of *The Immortal Hour*; an adventurous staging of Shaw's *Back to Methuselah*, that vast 'metabiological Pentateuch' covering the history of humanity which only the Theatre Guild in New York had attempted before Birmingham ('Are your wife and children provided for?' Shaw asked Jackson); then Eden Phillpott's *The Farmer's Wife*, which London managers in their deplorable insularity had consistently ignored since its first performance in Station Road eight years before. Jackson let London know what they had been missing. *The Farmer's Wife* ran for 1,329 performances.

For his first Shakespearean play in London he chose *Romeo and Juliet*, the 1924 production noteworthy as the first important showpiece for a young man with rare mastery of lyrical effect: John Gielgud. Miss Gwen Ffrangcon-Davies was hailed as the 'ideal Juliet', and the following year she triumphed again as the kitten-queen of Shaw's *Caesar and Cleopatra*. Cedric Hardwicke, using a British Museum bust as his make-up guide, looked every inch the Caesar, and in best repertory tradition he followed his emperor with a butler in Harold Chapin's *The New Morality* and a bowler-hatted First Gravedigger in Jackson's experimental modern-dress *Hamlet*. That so-called 'Hamlet in Plus-fours' prompted plenty of jibes, but it ran from August to November in 1925, an experiment repeated in Vienna and New York and having incalculable influence on future productions.

By now Jackson had been persuaded to reopen his Birmingham theatre (only after four thousand people had guaranteed their support by buying six tickets each at reduced rates) and early in 1926 his 'university of the stage' was welcoming yet another promising new graduate. He was a twenty-three-year-old named Ralph Richardson. Simultaneously, in London the company was preparing a French mystery play, *The Marvellous History of Saint Bernard*, which had already been tried out successfully in Birmingham. Among those who attended the auditions at the Kingsway Theatre was Laurence Olivier, then near penniless and, though not quite starving in a garret, certainly living in somewhat desperate circumstances in a drab bed-sitting room in Maida Vale. Ambitiously he aspired to the leading title role. Instead, he got the microscopic part of 'A Minstrel' and even lost his position as first understudy for the lead, played by Robert Harris. Inexplicably, he found himself relegated to second understudy in favour of another young actor named Denys Blakelock.

If he had reacted with frostiness towards the preferred Blakelock, it would have been understandable. In fact, the reverse happened. Out of their initial meeting at the Kingsway Theatre, a deep and lasting friendship grew—a brotherly relationship so meaningful that nearly a quarter of a century later, when invited to write a foreword to a book by Blakelock, Olivier began: 'Denys Blakelock was the first human being in my life that I could really think of to myself as "my friend". Having lived through my earliest days with a peculiarly desperate wish to be liked unanswered, I embraced this unaccustomed happiness with an innocent young gratitude that I often think must have given Denys, who was a few years my senior, some embarrassment in those early days, though he is kind enough not to say so.'[2]

Blakelock was almost six years older than Olivier. What originally drew them together was their near identical background: both devout Anglo-Catholics, both sons of clergymen, both none too popular at public school, both passionately interested in the theatre. Their paths had crossed just once before, when Blakelock was taken to see the performance of *The Taming of the Shrew* at All Saints, but they had not met at the time. Now, at the Kingsway, Olivier made his own introduction—'I think you know Father Heald'—and thereafter they became the closest of friends, each often being a guest at the other's vicarage home.

In his autobiography, *Round the Next Corner*, Blakelock recalled Olivier's reference to not being liked in his earliest days and explained that he was surprised by it:

At the time it had never occurred to me that Larry was anything else but happy and a boy who was liked by most people who knew him. He was demonstratively affectionate, enthusiastic and interested in everything. He had superabundant vitality, a gift which seems common to all highly creative actors with star quality: that animal magnetism to which they owe their force and their appeal . . .

But to return to the question of his problem of being liked or not liked: looking back I recollect that Olivier could be very blunt in his youthful days, blunt and undiplomatic; and everyone does not care for that. I myself could appreciate it more now than I did then. Once we were sitting in a restaurant called the Cabin in the Strand, I with my hands spread out on the table. Larry looked down at them and said, 'Funny stumpy little hands, aren't they?' He has particularly fine ones himself and I always wanted to be the possessor of beautiful hands.

On another occasion I was driving him out into the country. We were going down the hill from the Heath to Golders Green. I remember the spot, because this conversation had a tremendous importance for me. We were discussing a new play by John van Druten and Larry said, 'I suggested you for the leading part in it but John said, "Denys is a very good actor but *he hasn't got star quality*." ' Those last words went straight to my heart like a stiletto. I think it was my first awareness of that unpalatable truth about myself. Larry was a kind and sympathetic character. He had no malice in him. This was simply said out of a bluntness which belonged to his family. His father was much the same and my over-sensitiveness would often be ruffled by remarks from Mr. Olivier which had no intent to hurt behind them . . .

Larry, too, could be sensitive about his appearance, especially when I first knew him, before he had learned how to dress himself. He was once very cross with his father, who in front of a family gathering, drew attention to his rebel hair. And I was no less irritated with my mother, who after Larry's first visit remarked, 'A nice young man—but very plain.' Thus she dismissed the future Sir Laurence Olivier, and put him to sleep in the boxroom when he came to stay. But she was right. Larry was not good-looking at that time. He had teeth that were set too far apart and eyebrows that grew thickly and without shape across his nose. He had a thatch of unmanageable hair that came far forward in a kind of widow's peak, and his nose was a broad one. He wore very unbecoming suits, much too old-looking for a young man. He told me in later years that they were cast-offs of an uncle, altered to fit him.[3]

The Marvellous History of Saint Bernard opened in London on April 7, 1926. It was highly praised as a production, unanimously so for the acting, and the fact that it ran for no more than two months was solely due to the paralysing effect of the General Strike that brought all Britain to a standstill for twelve mad days in May. Olivier's minstrel part was far too scant to earn him critical notice. The programme did not even get his name right: 'Ollivier.' What mattered, however, was that he had done enough to persuade Jackson to retain him as a member of the company in Birmingham. It was where he wanted to be, unquestionably the best starting point in Britain for any serious young actor seeking a solid foundation on which to build a highly professional career.

Inauspiciously, on his first assignment for Jackson he found himself bound for the obscurity of Clacton on Sea to replace an actor in a Welsh comedy (*The Barber and the Cow* by D. T. Davies), then on tour following its debut in Birmingham. This undistinguished farce had what now impresses as an extraordinarily distinguished cast: Cedric Hardwicke, Ralph Richardson and Olivier, a trio of knights-to-be. Hardwicke, who had joined the company in 1922 after seven years' army service in France, was now an established star of the Birmingham Rep. Richardson, still in his first year with the company, was already recognized as a potential major talent.

In Clacton, Olivier met both actors for the first time. His initial encounter with Richardson was curious, giving neither hint nor hope of the Gordian knot of friendship that would eventually bound the two men together. They took an almost immediate dislike to one another. Olivier judged Richardson unreasonably aloof and superior; Richardson, four years the senior, concluded that Olivier was gauche and immature. Their relationship was not made any easier by Olivier's fanciful notion that he was in love with Richardson's charming young wife, Muriel Hewitt.

A half-century later Richardson still vividly remembers the day on that tour when he offered Olivier a ride in his brand-new 1925 open Morris Cowley. There was no back seat and so the two actors and Muriel Hewitt ('Kit' to her husband and close friends in the theatre) were bunched up in the front. After negotiating a particularly steep hill, Richardson brought the car to a halt. He was gravely concerned because his proud new acquisition was overheating; alarmingly the radiator-thermometer read 'boiling'. Meanwhile his wife and Olivier, talking and laughing with gay abandon, seemed oblivious to his concern. They stayed in the car while its frowning owner got out to inspect the radiator. Finally Olivier left the car, whispered to Richardson that he wanted to ask him something and drew him a few more yards away.

'What the devil is it, Larry?' said Richardson.

And Olivier replied, 'I wanted to ask you, Ralph, if you would mind if I called Muriel, Kit.'[4]

It was as well that the play failed and that the tour was quickly abandoned, leaving Olivier and the Richardsons to go their separate ways. For the moment the former was very much the new boy with the company—a junior rather too impatient to be recognized and too over-sensitive at being ignored. He spent the next six months touring Britain in *The Farmer's Wife*.

Well cast as Richard Coaker, the lovesick young farmer, Olivier clearly made a success of his first regular employment, for when he finally arrived in Birmingham at the end of the year he was invited to stay on as juvenile lead for the second half of the winter season. It was a golden opportunity, and he knew it; the surest gateway to the south since Jackson now had three theatres in London. Yet even now, while fully recognizing his good fortune, he could not resist gagging in a way that put his entire future in jeopardy. His Birmingham debut was in a new one-act comedy by Eden Phillpott, *Something to Talk About*, put on as a curtain-raiser. Olivier—Hitlerish in hair style and moustache—played a monocled aristocrat at a manor house party that is interrupted by the arrival of a burglar. 'Who are you?' the intruder asks. 'We are Conservatives,' was Olivier's haughty reply. But he didn't think this quite funny enough, and on the last night he changed it and said, 'We're Freemasons, froth-blowers and gugnuncs.' [5] He thought that a marked improvement on the script and the audience reaction confirmed him in his opinion. But producer W. G. Fay did not share it. A matter of principle and discipline was at stake, and for once this small and gentle-natured Irishman displayed anger. Olivier has since acknowledged that he was 'a stupid little idiot' and that he might very easily have been fired but for Jackson having mercy on him.

As the so-called juvenile lead, Olivier had the good fortune to be given an enormous range of major parts while still not out of his teens. His roles included the rumbustious Tony Lumpkin in *She Stoops to Conquer*, Chekhov's Uncle Vanya, Jack Borthwick in *The Silver Box* and Parolles in a modern dress *All's Well That Ends Well*, which he portrayed with originality as an amiable and elegant young man in a performance that won favourable comment from Bernard Shaw.

Recalling those early days at Birmingham, Sir Cedric Hard-wicke remembered Olivier as being noisy and lacking in subtlety, 'but I knew instinctively that he'd be a great actor'. Eileen Beldon, who worked many times with him, also noted a certain lack of subtlety. Half a century later she still vividly recalled their dialogue as members of the company were parting at the end of a production. 'He said to me in a very grand manner, "Thank you for a wonderful performance, Miss Beldon. I *do* hope we'll be working together again." And I snapped back, "I *do* hope we don't." '

Actress Jane Welsh also worked with the young Olivier at this time. 'Larry played my uncle, a very wicked and cruel uncle who used to beat me and fly into terrible rages. He was wonderfully inventive all the time and I remember that he said to me at rehearsal one day, "In that scene I think I shall fling myself across the table in my rage." And he did, and it was frightfully effective. It was the sort of thing no one else would think of doing. No producer would say to you, "What about flinging yourself on your face across the table?" I remember, too, that he was rather untidy then. His hair used to stand up on end. But one afternoon he went to see the film of *Beau Geste*, and that evening he came into my dressing room with his hair *à la* Ronald Colman and a little moustache he had painted in. And he said, "I'm going to play Beau Geste when we get to London." That was a real prophecy. He was already showing undoubted signs of his brilliance at this time and was clearly quite outstandingly talented in this rather good theatre company that then included Melville Cooper. I found Larry very lovable, absolutely charming and great fun.'

John Laurie was playing Hamlet at Stratford-upon-Avon in the summer of 1927 and he remembers the young actor visiting him there to seek help, even though they had previously met only briefly at Elsie Fogerty's school:

At Birmingham he was then under H. K. Ayliff, a fine director but a totally unsympathetic one. And I could understand his difficulty because Ayliff had given me a bad time in *The Farmer's Wife* . . . Anyway, this was the man, Ayliff, who had got on young Olivier's nerves and had reduced the boy to a state of nervousness—the worst thing any director can do. When he sought me out at Stratford he was the juvenile lead in John Drinkwater's *Bird in Hand*, and he was very unhappy. The strange thing was that at Birmingham there was no one they could *talk* to.

I was on the roof garden of the Arden Hotel having a drink, when a message was sent up that he would like to see me. I said, 'Send the boy up.' And then this awkward, skinny lad arrived and said very shyly, 'I'm sorry to bother you, Mr. Laurie, but I'm in great difficulty rehearsing this part. In the opening scene Mr. Ayliff wants me to cross over from one side of the stage to the other. But I can't do it.'

'Why can't you do it?' I said.

'Well, there's no reason for it, except that somebody else is coming on and wants my chair.'

'Let's think it out,' I told him. 'Let's find a reason. Is it morning?'

'Yes.'

'All right. Then let's suppose you see the morning newspaper on the seat that you want to reach. And you suddenly think, "I wonder who won last night's football match." And while you are speaking' (it was doubly difficult because he had to move across while speaking) 'don't think of the words, just wonder who won the match. And as you're thinking, reach for the paper, get it, sit down and carry on the conversation and you'll be fine.'

'Marvellous, marvellous,' he said. 'That's it. That's it. Thank you very much, Mr. Laurie.' And he went off back to Birmingham as happy as a puppy with a fat, meaty bone.

The following month Olivier had a far smaller role, as a young American in Elmer Rice's rather weird expressionist drama *The Adding Machine*. The play was far too modernistic for Birmingham tastes. But it was memorable for Olivier. It was the vehicle that transported him back to the London stage.

Cole Porter's not-yet-composed *Anything Goes* would have ideally suited the London stage of 1927–28. It was a time of extraordinary variety, with no discernible fashion beyond its wealth of musical entertainment—the Astaires dancing in *Lady Be Good*, Jack Buchanan and Binnie Hale cavorting through *Sunny*, the lasting melodies of *The Desert Song* and *The Vagabond King*, *The Girl Friend* and *Oh, Kay!* It had its share of memorable plays: *Yellow Sands*, Lonsdale's *On Approval*, Somerset Maugham's *The Letter*, Basil Dean's meticulous production of *The Constant Nymph* with Edna Best as a perfect Tessa and Coward, succeeded by Gielgud, as Lewis Dodd. But only one towering masterpiece appeared, O'Casey's *The Plough and the Stars*. As one critic observed, 'Everything seems to be in a state of flow, or dependent upon whims, caprices and the capacity of individual magnates for making profitable deals.'

Sir Barry Jackson, above all, experimented with a purpose. On January 9, 1928, he launched an experimental season of five plays in London, each to run for one month irrespective of their success or failure. He chose *The Adding Machine* to start the series and transferred almost the entire cast from Birmingham to the Court Theatre. Olivier had a very minor part but he resolved to make the most of it and was especially concerned that his Bowery accent should be flawless. With this aim he gained an introduction to Clare Eames by way of Blakelock, who was then playing her son Robert in a West End production of *The Silver Cord*. The famous American actress not only advised him on the nuances of an East Side New York accent, she volunteered to school him thoroughly, line by line. His determination impressed her most of all. Years later Blakelock recalled: 'Clare Eames said to me at that time, "Larry looks down at me with the eyes of a conqueror." He was just beginning to be conscious of the dynamic power that was in him.'[6]

Miss Eames did more. During one of their meetings he was speaking to her about straight parts and character parts. 'What's the difference?' she said. 'Don't tell me there's such a thing as a straight part. There isn't a part in the world that isn't a character part.'[7] It was a remark that stuck with him ever after and became a maxim in his approach to acting.

In striving for a true Bowery accent Olivier shared a few pointers with Beatrix Lehmann who, as Judy O'Grady, was playing a small graveyard scene with him. But when it came to rehearsals, producer W. G. Fay couldn't comprehend the accent at all. It was authentic but much too foreign to his Irish ear.

'You must stop doing it like that,' he kept saying. 'You had it all right in Birmingham.'

With feigned helplessness, Olivier astutely replied: 'I know how you want it, Mr. Fay. I just don't seem able to do it.'[8] On the opening night he was still using his new accent.

The Adding Machine had a reasonable reception ('I feared the worst, but it turned out quite well,' wrote Arnold Bennett, a critic never easily pleased) but the accents generally came in for harsh criticism—with one notable exception. Olivier was judged to have 'by far and away the best Americanese'. It enabled him to stand out in a minor part and, most importantly, it won him the attention of so influential a writer as dramatist St. John Ervine, who had a regular column in *The Observer*. Ervine concluded his lengthy Sunday review: 'Mr. Laurence Olivier as the young man who accompanies Judy O'Grady into the graveyard gave a very good performance indeed—the best, I think, in the play. He had little to do, but he *acted*.'

Macbeth came next, another modern-dress version with Olivier as Malcolm in a grey flannel suit and felt hat. On the day before the opening fire broke out in the theatre and gutted part of the dress circle. During the first week the scenery fell down, one of a series of minor mishaps. It made no significant difference; the play was so ill-prepared, so ill-suited to modern dress, that it was doomed from the start. Yet it was a profitable experience for Olivier. Again he stood out, a prominence accentuated by the inadequacies of players around him.

'It was my first awareness of Larry as an actor,' recalls Jessica Tandy, who made her debut at the Birmingham Rep that year. 'Not a very inspired production until Larry appeared as Malcolm. The scene in exile with Macduff was electrifying and one left the theatre with an exhilarating feeling of having seen the beginnings of an actor of enormous potential.'

The production for March proved far more popular: a revival of *Back to Methuselah*. Olivier as Martellus had no real opportunity to shine, but his golden chance was now imminent. Jackson was devoting the next month to a more dubious experiment. Tennyson's totally neglected nineteenth-century verse drama *Harold*. Olivier was awarded the title role.

Sir Barry and producer Ayliff jointly share the credit for promoting Olivier into the limelight on the London stage. They judged rightly, and largely on the evidence of his Malcolm, that he had the fire and intensity of speech necessary to conjure up the passionate patriotism of the last Saxon King of England. But would he, they wondered, have sufficient weight of personality to give convincing authority to the role? The whole venture was a gigantic shot in the dark. The play, published in 1876, had never been presented on the regular stage before. Henry Irving had declared it 'quite impossible' for the theatre, and though some cynics said that was sour grapes because it offered no suitable role for him, the remark was not altogether unjustified. Tennyson, by his own admission, was ignorant of 'mechanical details necessary for the modern stage', and the beautiful lyrical qualities that so impressed Jackson were largely lost when transferred from the printed page to the stage.

This was to be Olivier's baptism of fire, his first leading role on the London stage, a challenge all the more demanding since there was no past performance to serve him as a guide. With some pride he has recalled that he learned his 3,000 lines in a single week of studying into the early hours and much brewing of coffee on a small methylated spirit burner. In a sense he profited by being thrown in at the deep end of a somewhat stagnant pool. Tennyson and his tragedy of doom were the principal targets for the critics' barbs; Olivier, as a promising newcomer in an unenviable part, gave them something to be less gloomy about.

With considerable insight, St. John Ervine wrote in *The Observer*: 'Mr. Laurence Olivier, the Harold, varies in his performance, but he is excellent on the whole and has the makings

of a very considerable actor in him. His faults are those of
inexperience rather than of ineffectiveness. The good performance he gave in *Macbeth*, added to the good performance he
gives in *Harold*, makes me believe that when romantic and poetic
drama return to their proper place in the theatre, Mr. Olivier
will be ready to occupy the position of a distinguished romantic
actor.' It marked the arrival of Olivier as a name readily identi-
fiable on the London theatre scene.

Jackson ended his five-play series at The Court with more
Shakespeare in modern dress: *The Taming of the Shrew*. Ayliff
had already staged a successful version at New York's Garrick
Theatre; he knew that the rollicking Elizabethan farce lent itself
far better than *Macbeth* to contemporary settings and allowed all
manner of outrageous novelties such as the introduction of a press
photographer and movie cameraman at the wedding reception,
and the trundling on of an old Ford car, with Petruchio cursing,
'Come on, i' God's name', as he wrestled with the starting handle.
In London the treatment was equally well received, largely
because of the spirited playing of Scott Sunderland and Eileen
Beldon as tamer and tamed, and some wicked scene-stealing
business by Ralph Richardson, who rocked audiences with his
Tranio portrayed as a Cockney chauffeur disguised in morning
coat and silk hat. Olivier, as the Lord in the Christopher Sly
scene, had relatively little to do, but at least his part kept him in
prominent view throughout the performance, and seated in a
box at stage right, he cut a surprisingly dashing figure, immaculate in dinner jacket and with something new added: a trim
'Ronald Colman' moustache.

As he arrived at his twenty-first birthday, the metamorphosis
in Olivier during his seasons at the Birmingham Rep was striking.
Two years before he had been a dark and glowering youth in
ill-fitting suits, still handicapped by the weakness in the face that
Miss Fogerty had noted. Now, as Gwen Ffrangcon-Davies
remembers him, he was 'a ravishing-looking young man'. No one
was more impressed by the change than his closest friend, Denys
Blakelock. He remarked that Olivier had returned to London
looking a completely different person:

He had somehow got his hair to part at last; he had had the
gaps between his teeth filled in, his eyebrows trimmed and
straightened, and he was beautifully and rather gaily dressed.

He had stopped short at his nose, though he has made up for this since by remodelling it with nose clay into one shape after another in almost every part he has played in the last twenty-five years!

All this has something more than a mere personal interest. It is an example of that application and detailed attention to the job, without which no artist can hope to attain to any position of enduring importance, much less make for himself a name that will last beyond his own lifetime.[9]

And the change was not all physical. In character, too, he was smoother, more polished and self-assured. He was still the young man in a hurry, impatient for fame and fortune though without an ambition clearly defined; still the precipitate romantic, eager to fall in love and to marry. But there was greater maturity, more tact in his dealings with people. This had shown during the rehearsals for *Back to Methuselah* when he and Richardson resumed a frosty relationship where they had left off in Clacton more than a year before. For several days they treated one another with the same chilly politeness. Then Olivier finally broke the ice. He invited his young rival to join him for a drink, and over a pint in the pub the first seeds of a great and ever-growing friendship were sown. From then on they were Larry and Ralphy. Each would seek the other's professional advice on many occasions, and only once was their close relationship briefly endangered—on the day that the impetuous Larry reduced Ralphy to a quivering fury by driving his friend's car at breakneck speed over crossroads without slowing down on approach. Richardson said he would never, never forgive him. Olivier replied characteristically: 'It is a well-known thing, Ralphy, that when you get to a point of danger, you get over it as quickly as you can.'

5

Driven by Events

In June 1928, a month after his twenty-first birthday, Olivier was invited by Jackson to replace Patrick Susands in the long-running *Bird in Hand*, taking over his original part of the squire's son who seeks to marry an innkeeper's daughter. His stage sweetheart, first created by Peggy Ashcroft, was now being played by an attractive, dark-haired girl, twenty years of age. For once no husband lurked in the background. Within three weeks of their first meeting Olivier had fallen in love and proposed.

Jill Esmond Moore (as she styled herself then) bore a name of double distinction in the theatre. Her father, who had died in 1922, was H. V. Esmond, actor-manager and playwright; her mother, who would remain active on stage and screen for many years to come, was the celebrated actress-producer Eva Moore. Though six months younger than Olivier, Jill was professionally more experienced (six years on the stage since graduating from RADA) and, as her non-committal reply to his proposal suggests, rather more mature. 'Perhaps,' she told him, 'we should get to know one another better before becoming officially engaged.'

It was the beginning of the most agreeably relaxing period that Olivier had yet known—six months in a familiar and undemanding stage role, not an especially rewarding part, but one that at least afforded him a prominent place in the shop window of the West End theatre. And all the time he was working with the girl he loved. Indeed, for much of the summer he and Jill were able to spend every day together since Mrs. Moore had thoughtfully invited him to escape the drudgery of London bed-sitting room life and stay for some weeks at their country home called Apple Porch near the river at Maidenhead, Berkshire. It made him all the more appreciative of the congenial comforts of family life, all the more eager to marry and make a home of his own. Beyond that he continually hoped for some dramatic bolt-from-the-blue that might lift him out of the common band of so-called juvenile leads and project him towards the Olympian heights of the matinée idol.

One night at the Royalty his hopes of breaking into the 'big time' positively soared. The word went round backstage that Basil Dean was out front. Olivier, ever alert to the long chance, responded as scores of other young actors had done. He went on stage geared up to give a performance too good to be ignored.

Dean was currently the producer that aspiring players most eagerly sought to impress. Originally intended for a career as an analytical chemist, he was a tall, dark and bespectacled man, exceptionally methodical and painstaking, almost excessively intent. He had organized and controlled the Liverpool Repertory Theatre until 1913, the year Barry Jackson was just beginning in Birmingham. He had been managing director of the Theatre Royal, Drury Lane, and then of St. Martin's, and he had given London such memorable productions as *Hassan*, with its musical score by Delius, and *The Constant Nymph*, which he had dramatized with Margaret Kennedy. Opinions of him as a producer were sharply divided. Some held him to be a genius, the greatest exponent of stagecraft; others considered him too extravagant and technical, obsessed with colour and lighting, and tending to 'swamp' the author as he experimented with mechanical devices and introduced extraordinary and elaborate sets. One thing was certain: no one could accuse him of that worst of theatrical sins—dullness.

He now faced a challenge that was daringly ambitious even by his own unrivalled standards: a stage adaptation of P. C. Wren's *Beau Geste*. His immediate problem, as everyone knew, was to find a suitable young man to play Beau. It was his long-drawn-out search that made Ronald Colman moustaches all the rage as actors looked to the 1926 movie for the right touch of suave masculinity. But in Olivier's case it seemed that an abundance of facial hair bestowed no advantage. The story went around that after he had seen Olivier acting like mad in *Bird in Hand*, Dean growled: 'That beetly-browed boy's no good at all.' Dean refutes the story—'just dressing room gossip and obviously untrue'; in reality, he recognized Olivier as one of several possible candidates for the part. Nevertheless Olivier heard the story and feared he had no chance.

Months passed and Dean was still without his perfect Beau. Olivier was summoned for an interview. Falsely informed of the producer's criticisms, he went with eyebrows freshly plucked and hair sleeked back, and he came away full of hope, though no clear promise, that he might get the coveted part. For many weeks more he lived in suspense, and even by December, when he was invited to a trial reading, his part in the play remained unconfirmed. Meanwhile the real million-to-one chance, the break of a lifetime that could have fulfilled his extravagant dreams of overnight stardom, was pushed right under his nose.

In November, while still playing at the Royalty, Olivier was invited by a small-part actor called James Whale to take the lead in an untried war play that he was directing for the prestigious but essentially non-commercial Incorporated Stage Society. The offer left him cold. It involved three weeks of rehearsal for just two performances, one on a Sunday evening, the other a Monday matinée. The pay was a miserable fiver. Moreover, the play, by general consensus, had not the remotest chance of being a success. But Olivier accepted. And he did so for what proved to be entirely the wrong reason. He saw it as a useful opportunity to show off his dramatic muscles in something other than the love-sick juvenile lead of *Bird in Hand*. The merit of the play was irrelevant. Dean would see him in the role of fighting soldier.

The role he accepted was that of Captain Dennis Stanhope, M.C., and the play was R. C. Sherriff's *Journey's End*. In failing to recognize its potential Olivier was in distinguished company. The play, written by an obscure £6-a-week insurance agent, had none of the recognized ingredients for success and had been summarily rejected by London managements and by half a dozen well-known actors. Managers were notoriously prejudiced against war plays. This one, set in a front-line dug-out during World War I, seemed to be without a single redeeming feature—no women, no romance, not even a truly heroic theme.

The snowballing success of *Journey's End* is now a familiar pillar of theatre legend—the play, against the prognostications of every theatre manager in London, became a smash hit overnight and within a matter of months encircled the globe, being performed in twenty-seven different languages, winning rave notices on Broadway, being made into a movie in Hollywood. Above all, the romance of *Journey's End* was heightened in the Twenties by the fact that its author belonged to a Thames rowing club and wrote plays to be performed as amateur fund-raising efforts by other members, their wives and girl friends. Contrary to the publicity handouts, this was not his first attempt at a play but his seventh. No matter. It was his first work to be performed by professionals. Against all probability it was hailed as the greatest of all war plays, a modern masterpiece. And Robert Cedric Sherriff was transformed from struggling insurance agent to Hollywood's highest paid scriptwriter.

All this, however, was beyond imagination on the November morning in 1928 when the author and a handful of actors gathered for the first reading in a drab room over a shop in the Charing Cross Road. They were an odd-looking bunch. Meeting in bare surroundings, dressed in overcoats and mufflers, they might have been anarchists plotting a conspiracy rather than players preparing a West End entertainment. Sherriff told me:

I remember that it was very, very cold. No central heating. Just one small, bleak fire, a long, bare table and some upright chairs. Almost everyone there was a third or fourth choice for his part. Whale had wanted a well-known actor for the leading role, and he had approached Leslie Banks, Robert Loraine and several others without success. Then he said to me, 'Go and see Olivier in *Bird in Hand* and let me know what you think.' I saw him and he was a very good-looking young actor. He had a terrible part in the play, what he called 'providing the love interest', but he had what very few actors had at the time—a strong masculine presence, not at all arty or prissy, and yet not a rough type. I told Whale that I thought he would be fine. But when we met for the first reading he looked slighter and paler than he had seemed to me on the stage, not quite the tough, hard-drinking Company Commander that I had visualized. He was a very shy type, had little to say, and was crouched over the fire trying to keep warm. He looked rather bored and restless, and I got a feeling that he was wishing he hadn't come.

Four of the men present at that meeting were destined to

spend the greater part of their lives in the United States. Maurice Evans was cast as Second Lieutenant Raleigh, the eighteen-year-old virgin soldier who had hero-worshipped Stanhope in their public school days and who finally dies in his arms, his back shot away after only three days in the trenches. Evans would move on to a long and distinguished career as a classical actor on Broadway. George Zucco was there as second-in-command 'Uncle' Osborne, the gentle, grey-haired schoolmaster who read *Alice in Wonderland* before leaving the dug-out to meet certain death. Now he is best remembered as the sepulchral-toned villain of Hollywood horror films. Melville Cooper, playing Trotter, the ranker officer obsessed with the trench food, was to settle in Hollywood, working with Olivier many years later when they filmed *Rebecca* and *Pride and Prejudice*. James Whale, who was directing, would become the master maker of Hollywood horror classics.

Weak as the play might be—and Bernard Shaw was one who had read it and seen no reason to commend it—Olivier at least had the wit to recognize the rare dramatic scope of his role as the young company commander who has been weakened in character by the stress of war and who steels himself with whisky against his haunting fear of being seen as a coward. Casting difficulties left only two weeks for rehearsal. Also Olivier had his performance at the Royalty each evening, with twice weekly matinées. Yet, spurred on by determination to impress Dean, he got deep down inside the character of the sensitive, war-weary Stanhope and later he was to describe it has his 'favourite stage role'.

Journey's End had its first performance at the Apollo Theatre on the evening of Sunday, December 9, 1928. Olivier had borrowed the author's old army tunic, Sam Browne belt and revolver and holster. The whole production, perfectly cast, went off smoothly. Yet the end brought no positive sign of a hit or a miss. The applause at the final curtain was not overwhelming (Sherriff was consoled by his mother with the comment, 'People don't clap when they're crying'), and though Barry Jackson and other London managers commented favourably on the blazing honesty of the play, they held fast to their original opinion that it was never a commercial prospect. But the real test had yet to come—at the Monday matinée when the critics would turn out in force. And this brought astonishing results.

Long-maned Hannen Swaffer, most vitriolic critic of the day, discussed *Journey's End* in the *Daily Express* under the heading: THE GREATEST OF ALL WAR PLAYS. Other notices matched his superlatives. And the supremely influential James Agate took the unprecedented step of devoting his weekly radio talk entirely to one new play which he judged to have extraordinary significance and merit. 'But you will never see this play,' he told listeners. 'I have spoken to several managers, urging them to give you the opportunity of judging it for yourselves, but they are adamant in their belief that war plays have no audience in the theatre.'

Agate was very nearly right. Six weeks went by and all efforts to mount a regular production failed. In the meantime, as far as Olivier was concerned, the playing of Stanhope had fulfilled his original ambition. He had satisfied Dean and was confirmed for the lead in *Beau Geste* at the princely wage of £30 a week.

It was entirely natural that he should seize this opportunity as he had intended from the start. At the same time it made hopes of a new production of *Journey's End* seem all the more remote now that the leading man was no longer available. 'Yet all the rest of the cast stood by the play,' recalled Sherriff. 'They refused other parts in the hope of remaining in it, and they believed in it so much that they tried in vain to form a combine and raise the cash among themselves. But it seemed hopeless.' And then, just as everyone connected with the play was resigned to writing it off as a one-night wonder, all was saved by the intervention of a stage-struck and eccentric intellectual called Maurice Browne. He wore a teddy-bear overcoat, gold earrings and an Old Wykham-ist public school tie, and for years he had trailed around America trying to attract audiences to classical drama presented in small back-street theatres. Browne had never produced a West End play before, but he was totally enraptured with *Journey's End* (he had been a conscientious objector in the war) and he had a millionaire friend who was prepared to back his judgment.

With all the original principal players except Olivier, the new production opened on Monday, January 21, 1929, at the Savoy Theatre, where Dean's long-running *Young Woodley* had just closed. Finding a new Stanhope had presented a major problem, but after some alarming teething troubles a little-known actor called Colin Clive finally came to grips with the character and achieved the kind of sincerity that had been the essential hall-mark of Olivier's performance. There were nineteen curtain calls on that historic first night at the Savoy. Again the critical acclaim was unanimous and the result was a runaway box-office success falling just short of 600 performances. Overnight Colin Clive became a star.

Maurice Evans, who had now played opposite two Stanhopes, thought that Clive was rather better than Olivier. 'I am a little prejudiced because I helped to get him the job after Jeanne de Casalis had persuaded me to see him in some other production, but I thought he was absolutely perfect for Stanhope. Larry was very delicate, a little too romantic looking for the part. With only one exception we really had a perfect cast, even though it was thrown together so hurriedly. Like Larry, I could have left to go into *Beau Geste* as one of the brothers but I turned the part down because I thought the script was quite awful.'

Three men virtually had their lives transformed by *Journey's End*. Before he directed the play James Whale had made no marked progress since his 1919 debut at the Birmingham Rep. He went to Hollywood to direct the film version and never came back; and with such classics of the macabre as the original *Frankenstein* and *The Old Dark House* he firmly established himself as Universal's 'master of horror'. When he updated his style with *The Bride of Frankenstein*, studio chiefs said he had made his monster too human to be frightening, and even Boris Karloff thought it was a mistake to have the monster talking and enjoying a smoke and a laugh. So Whale turned to lighter fare, including the 1936 version of *Show Boat*, before unnerving audiences again with his film of *The Man in the Iron Mask*. He always remained a notable Hollywood enigma, and it rather fitted the life style of the man that his story ended in dramatic and mysterious circumstances, still unexplained. In 1957 he was found drowned in his Hollywood swimming pool.

R. C. Sherriff could have retired on the proceeds from *Journey's End*. Instead he added to his fortune, writing more plays and novels and most impressively making his mark as a screenwriter. Whale invited him to Hollywood to write the screenplay for H. G. Wells' *The Invisible Man*, and over the years he wrote scripts for such outstandingly successful pictures as *The Four Feathers, Goodbye Mr. Chips, Lady Hamilton, This*

Above All, Mrs. Miniver, Odd Man Out, No Highway and *The Dam Busters*.

Most significantly of all, *Journey's End* changed the life of the man who took over the lead from Olivier. Before playing Stanhope, Colin Clive had toiled for £3 10s a week at the Hull Repertory Theatre and played minor roles in the stage musicals *Rose Marie* and *Show Boat*. After Stanhope, he settled in Hollywood and for six years averaged earnings of $75,000 to $100,000 a year. That role was *made* for Clive with his public school-military academy background—a son of an Army colonel, educated at Stonyhurst and Sandhurst. But Clive was never made for the kind of fame and fortune it brought him. He was a sound, useful actor, not a star personality, a soft-spoken, homebird-type who needed the stimulus of several beers to achieve a degree of confidence and sparkle. After his success in *Journey's End* he married actress Jeanne de Casalis, but their respective career paths separated them almost immediately and in Hollywood he had no relatives or close friends. His last film was *History Is Made at Night*, starring Jean Arthur, and he insisted on completing it although he was a sick man. Immediately afterwards he underwent surgery for a pulmonary ailment. He never recovered; he died in hospital in June 1937. He was thirty-seven years old.

How drastically might the course of Olivier's career have been changed if he had remained as Stanhope and experienced instant stardom? Actor John Laurie believes it could have been disastrous for him. 'If Larry had remained as Stanhope he might have shared the fate of the man who succeeded him. Colin Clive never could shake the damn part off. Larry instead went on to do other parts; he was learning his job. While *Journey's End* went on and on, here and in America, Olivier the actor emerged.'

At the time, Olivier supposed that he had made an extremely costly mistake in viewing *Journey's End* merely as a steppingstone to a far greater prize. Yet it was an error of judgment that any young actor might have made at the same point in his career. After all, why should he have seen, where men of infinitely greater experience were blind? He was wrong again in assuming that the lead in *Beau Geste* would be an immensely rewarding role; he failed to see that the best-seller, so successfully filmed with Colman as Beau and Noah Beery as the sadistic sergeant, could never effectively be adapted to the narrow confines of the stage. But again, who was he to have doubts about an opportunity that glittered like pure gold—a Basil Dean production, the spotlight of His Majesty's Theatre in the Haymarket, a cast of 120 including Marie Lohr and Madeleine Carroll?

Beau Geste was nothing if not spectacular, and probably no one but Dean would have dared so much with special effects in trying to recreate a full-scale military battle on stage. There was much firing of rifles, even a Maxim gun blazing away with blanks that brought showers of splinters up from the boards. Nor did Dean duck the problem of Beau's promised Viking's funeral. Olivier was to be laid out on a bed by his brother John (Jack Hawkins) and draped in a flag, with the sadistic sergeant (Edmund Willard) dumped at his feet. Then 'petrol' was to be poured over the bodies and the appearance of a funeral pyre given by smoke from offstage and electrical effects for simulated flames. Realism was obviously essential; so rehearsals included close-order drill for three quarters of an hour each day under a Regimental Sergeant Major, and much hand-to-hand fighting practised so fiercely that Hawkins was knocked out by a studded Army boot.

The play opened on January 30, one week after *Journey's End* began so auspiciously at the Savoy, and for sheer effort it deserved a fair mark. Dean recalls it having a 'rapturous' reception, mainly from the cheaper seats, but on the evidence of the reviews it was a disastrous production: absurdly overlong, badly constructed, chaotically staged—a fact emphasized when the relief fireman, alarmed by the billowing smoke and electrical flames, rang down the safety curtain of iron and asbestos much too soon. By the time it was raised and the cast prepared to take their bows, the bulk of the audience had left.

Some critics judged that Olivier had done as well as could reasonably be expected. But Agate, who had so greatly admired his Stanhope, was dissatisfied. Olivier, he thought, had rightly made Beau an ass—'but not a commanding ass'. He awarded the chief acting honours to eighteen-year-old Hawkins, 'a young actor with a future'.

An ice-cold February and an influenza epidemic contributed to a failure that cost its three backers some £24,000. The play remained at His Majesty's for four weeks, just long enough for

Dean to mount his next spectacular production, *The Circle of Chalk*, and Olivier's gloom over the reviews of *Beau Geste* was promptly dispelled by the news that he would again be the leading man, this time playing a Chinese prince called Po who falls in love with a teahouse girl sold into slavery. The role offered him plenty of scope to experiment with his tricks of make-up. His leading lady was a popular star of the silent screen, Chinese-Californian Anna May Wong, daughter of a Los Angeles laundryman. But the result was the same; another over-elaborate production that failed. Indeed, the first night was a nightmare. Miss Wong, physically perfect for her role, shattered the oriental illusion with her broad American accent. Olivier, recovering from laryngitis, sang a solo number with a voice cracking into an embarrassing falsetto. The scenery turntable became jammed. And when two coolies slipped on the black lacquered stage, portly Bruce Winston was sent flying out of his rickshaw and across the footlights into the percussion instruments.

It now seemed to Olivier that every opportunity turned to fool's gold-dust as soon as he grasped it. Yet it was never through any real failure on his part. His personal notices varied from excellent to mediocre, those of the plays from lukewarm to petrifying sub-zero. A month at His Majesty's; now only one month at the New Theatre. The next brief stop was the Lyric, playing Richard Parish in *Paris Bound*, a domestic comedy with Herbert Marshall and Edna Best. Then, after three successive failures, he moved on to the Garrick to play John Hardy in *The Stranger Within*, with Olga Lindo as his leading lady. For once he was in a play praised by the critics, and he and Roland Culver were judged to be excellent. It made no difference. The public, inexplicably, stayed away and the play soon folded.

As plans to film *Journey's End* were announced, Olivier gloomily reflected that he had missed his chance now that Colin Clive was accepted as the definitive Stanhope. Yet he was not totally dismayed. The past five months had brought him some positive benefits: a boosted income enabling him to improve his lodgings and his wardrobe, and the satisfaction of his name, boldly displayed in the West End, steadily becoming more familiar to theatregoers and managers. And his run of ill-luck seemed about to change. In July he was offered the part of Hugh

Bromilow in the New York production of *Murder on the Second Floor*, a play already established as a success in London. Olivier grabbed at the opportunity, which involved his first visit to America. He had long dreamed of playing on Broadway, and there was special incentive for doing so now. Jill Esmond was already over there, playing in the long-running *Bird in Hand*.

In New York, where the newcomer finds life suddenly accelerated and strangely exhilarating, it was obvious that their romance would now either blossom or fade. It flourished. They decided to marry as soon as they were returned to England. Unhappily, Olivier had to leave New York long before his fiancée. Frank Vosper's *Murder on the Second Floor* had a chilly reception from the audience at the Eltinge Theatre and survived only five weeks—a rather surprising flop since the notices were not especially bad and another British thriller, *Rope*, was currently a runaway success on Broadway.

Olivier wanted to remain in New York, but American Equity limited foreign actors to one stage role in six months. So, with Miss Esmond committed indefinitely to *Bird in Hand*, he reluctantly returned to London and 'rested' for several months until, in December, he joined a strong cast (O. B. Clarence, Athene Seyler, Nicholas Hannen and Frank Lawton) in Tom Walls' production of *The Last Enemy*. As the nerve-shattered pilot Jerry Warrender, he now had his most interesting and worthwhile role in a year of disappointments, and his performance encouraged the view that here was an actor of rare potential. Ivor Brown wrote in *The Observer*: 'As the airman Mr. Laurence Olivier gives a rendering of the first lustre, as vivid in its nervous brutality as in its later gentleness. This actor, who be it remembered, after some fine work with Sir Barry Jackson's team was first in the part of Stanhope in *Journey's End*, has during the past year given a series of consistently brilliant performances in consistently ill-fated plays. May this one break the unlucky series. At any rate, his time will come.' But *The Last Enemy*, too gloomy for Christmas-time fare, failed like all the rest. And Olivier's fortunes changed only for the worse.

The New Year marked the beginning of his leanest spell in the theatre, eight months that yielded only one day's work on the stage, an unpaid Sunday night appearance at the Arts Theatre, playing opposite Elissa Landi and Cathleen Nesbitt in John van

Druten's *After All*. True, he also gained his first experience in the new-fangled talking pictures, but the two films in which he appeared were insignificant and involved only a few weeks' work. One was *The Temporary Widow*, an Anglo-German production starring Lilian Harvey, the English dancer who had become a film idol in Germany. The other, more primitive picture was *Too Many Crooks*, directed by George King and involving Dorothy Boyd, Bromley Davenport, Mina Burnett, Arthur Stratton and Ellen Pollock. This totally inconsequential 'quickie' was one of many churned out with indecent haste to satisfy the British Quota Act, which demanded a certain proportion of British-made productions be shown at home besides the myriad imports from Hollywood. It was such a trivial work that Ellen Pollock, also making her screen debut, does not even remember Olivier's being in the same picture.

In April 1930 Jill Esmond at last returned from New York and in contrast she immediately found work, taking over Kay Hammond's part in the long-running play *Nine Till Six*. She commanded far more publicity than Olivier at this point in her career, and when they announced their plans to marry in July she became a focus of very special attention from the Press. This was because the bride-to-be had recently expounded highly controversial views on marriage. Her views, given a full-page spread in a national newspaper, make very familiar reading in today's climate of Women's Lib. In the Thirties they were sensational.

Under the headline WHAT I THINK OF MARRIAGE, she argued, reasonably, that wives were now partners, not playthings; intellectual equals, not domestic comforts:

> Victorian girls must have looked forward to marriage as a partial escape from a domestic cage. Today, marriage is in some ways more like an entrance into a cage. For whereas marriage is bound to mean more ties and responsibilities, the freedom of unmarried women is now greater than it has ever been since the days of the Romans.
>
> Many of our elders are fond of talking about the 'rights' and 'duties' of husbands and wives, as though marriage were a business contract with obligations set forth in black and white. If ever the man I married behaved decently towards me, or I

towards him, only because it was laid down in an unwritten marriage contract, I should feel it was high time we parted. Not that I expect married life to be one long romantic dream. It is impossible that the first careless rapture should last forever, and luckily too, for nobody could endure such a mental condition for long. Sooner or later, but inevitably, one settles down on an even keel. There is a mutual readjustment. And if one could look forward to that readjustment and see it clearly and dispassionately under conditions of the present day, then the first problem of modern marriage is as good as solved.[1]

Now that her own marriage was imminent, Miss Esmond was asked whether she still maintained the intentions she expressed when she wrote, 'I should certainly have secrets and friends unknown to a husband of mine, and I should sometimes have a holiday from him as well as from work.' She answered that she still held those views. Also, as a matter of principle, she saw no reason why a wife should not support her husband. 'She might, for instance, be a better wage-earner, while he might want to take up some sort of work not likely to bring in any money for some time.'

In the summer of 1930 she was certainly a better wage-earner than Olivier. But it mattered to her not at all. She explained years later: 'When we were courting I was, I suppose, a bigger name than he was. But I was always, *always*, conscious that his potential was enormous. I always knew he was the much more important person . . .'[2]

For Olivier, however, it was not so easy to accept the idea of starting married life with the wife as the principal breadwinner. It was largely a matter of masculine pride. At the same time professional pride tended to pull him in the opposite direction: After experiencing star billing in the West End and making himself known as a leading man, he was averse to going back to minor parts unless they were of very special merit. When at last he was offered work (a supporting role in a new London production) he stubbornly declined it.

The offer came from Noel Coward, who invited him to his Chelsea home to look over the script of *Private Lives* and the part of the boorish husband, Victor Prynne. The play, written in four days while Coward was recovering from influenza in

Shanghai, was essentially a flashy vehicle for the author and
Gertrude Lawrence. Olivier did not relish the idea of a back-seat
ride behind those two irresistible dazzlers. He demurred.
Coward, realistic and incisive, quickly made him think again. He
knew all about Olivier's appalling string of failures. 'Look, young
man,' he said, 'you'd better be in a success for a change.' And
he threw in another compelling reason why Olivier should
accept. The pay was £50 a week. It was an offer that no out-of-
work actor on the verge of matrimony could responsibly refuse.

On July 25, 1930, shortly before stepping into *Private Lives*,
Olivier married Jill Esmond Moore at All Saints, Marylebone. It
was a high-society affair; a *Tatler* scene far removed from his
early years in that neighbourhood when the Oliviers were so
poor that Laurence had to use his father's bath water to save on
heating, and luxury was a chicken so finely carved that it could
serve the entire family for three separate meals. Now it was
champagne and caviare. They were married in the presence of a
vast array of friends, including Jack Hawkins, Margaret Webster,
Alison Leggatt, Richard Goolden, Ralph Richardson, Nora
Swinburne and Frank Lawton. Wedding gifts included a Persian
necklace of black pearls and brilliants from theatre-loving
Princess Marie Louise, a granddaughter of Queen Victoria, and a
necklace of aquamarines from Lady Gilbert, widow of Sir
William Gilbert, the bride's godfather. And Lady Fripp, widow
of an eminent surgeon, lent the newly-weds her country house as
a base from which to make motoring tours on the honeymoon.

Ostensibly, Olivier was a very fortunate young man indeed.
Six years before he had been living in a drab bed-sitter, hungry,
out of work and not a little frightened of the future. Now, at
twenty-three, he had a beautiful and famous bride, social
prominence, a legion of fascinating friends and the immediate
promise of working at a higher salary than he had ever enjoyed
before. Yet he remained restless, growingly dissatisfied with the
way his career was shaping. However attractive the money, he
could not easily reconcile himself to playing so trifling a role as
the dull, deserted Victor of *Private Lives*. More than that, he
feared for his image. He wanted desperately to be seen as the
strong, romantic hero, never as a dreary and priggish husband.

Private Lives began its pre-London warm-up in August, and
according to Coward the whole tour was 'swathed in luxury' as

they travelled the country by car. 'The touring days of the past belonged to another world. Assurance of success seemed to be emblazoned on the play from the first; we had few qualms, played to capacity business and enjoyed ourselves thoroughly. We felt, I think rightly, that there was a shine on us.'[3]

But there wasn't much shine on Olivier. His restlessness and melancholy were reflected in a curious interview, conducted by a Manchester *Evening Chronicle* reporter identified simply as 'S.P.' She wrote:

What struck me most was that nothing seems to surprise him. The whole world holds no surprises for this most virile youth—he is nothing more than a youth. He knows everything and has thought about everything. But, sad to relate, he is unusually pessimistic—almost cynical.

'Only fools are happy,' he told me. Of course, he said that in an unguarded moment when he had forgotten to ply me with his terribly pointed questions.

'I suppose,' he went on, 'it is because they don't really know what they want in life, and so every little pleasure that comes along they regard as a paradise of happiness. I somehow can't get that way. I always examine things so very closely that immediate pleasures are dwarfed by my insistence on ultimate benefits.

'I want events to go my way, and I don't want to be driven by events.' That is just how this young man talks, and yet I can find no reason whatever for his gloomy outlook. He has had a career which would make other young men green with envy.

I told him this . . . And yet he would not be consoled. 'All this may sound very well,' he said, 'but I have with very few exceptions always had parts that I have not liked. They have not always been difficult parts but I have not been too fond of the characters I have had to portray.

'I hate the part I am playing now.' He said this with emphasis. He stopped suddenly, however, and proceeded to explain. 'I don't mean that I hate playing the part of Prynne, but I think it is a most hateful character.

'Audiences, you know, find it very difficult to dissociate the actor from the part he is playing, but I do hope Manchester is different. I dearly wish they wouldn't think I am actually what I appear on the stage.'

Despite all Lawrence [sic] Olivier told me about his misfortunes, I refuse to believe he is the unluckiest man on the stage . . . the time is not far distant when he will find the part he is searching for, and then become a really brilliant luminary in the theatrical firmament.[4]

In *Private Lives* Olivier at least saw the theatre at its most luxurious and glamorous, and for the first time he knew the comfort of being associated with a truly regal smash hit. The opening was *the* event of the year in the West End—a first night for the new Phoenix Theatre as well as for the play, a glittering, aristocratic occasion when hordes of the social elite turned out in their tiaras and tuxedos and paid exorbitant prices to savour a cocktail that was frothy with upper-class refinement and wit and expertly mixed to their champagne tastes. But, as they had anticipated, Olivier and Adrianne Allen, the female second lead, received short measure in the copious and glowing reviews. Coward himself noted their misfortune and later wrote: 'Adrianne played "Sibyl" with a subtle tiresomeness and a perfect sense of character, more character actually than the part really had. Larry managed, with determination and much personal charm, to invest the wooden "Victor" with enough reality to make him plausible. I frequently felt conscience-stricken over them both, playing so gallantly on such palpably second-strings.'[5]

While appearing nightly as Victor, with matinées on Thursdays and Saturdays, Olivier also played another cold-fish character by day: the male lead in the film *Potiphar's Wife*, adapted from the stage comedy by Edgar Middleton and now described as a 'sex drama'. It told the story of an aristocratic married lady (Nora Swinburne) who becomes bored with her prosaic husband and starts an affair with her handsome chauffeur, tempting him into misconduct, then charging him with assault when he displays indifference to her advances. As the unemotional chauffeur, Olivier won moderate praise. But remarkably some critics condemned the picture on the grounds that the theme was immoral and in very bad taste; and in Britain in the Thirties, unlike today, fuddy-duddy disapproval did not assure box-office success.

Meanwhile the Elyot–Amanda duet was so effectively seducing audiences at the Phoenix that *Private Lives* could have packed

the theatre for at least six months, probably far longer. But
Coward made it a firm rule never to remain in one production for
more than six months divided between London and New York.
So, after three months the hit was taken off and transferred to
Broadway—a decision attacked at the time as being totally
unreasonable and an author's invitation to future disaster. For
Olivier the bloom of Manchester now seemed far away, and if he
was still being 'driven by events' they were at least going very
much his way. He was returning to Broadway, this time in a
thundering success hailed as 'unique theatrical magic'.

And he was going back with his wife. Jill Esmond, blonde-
wigged, was taking over the role of the tiresome Sibyl Chase since
Adrianne Allen was pregnant and could not make the trip. It was
an ironic ending to what had seemed to be his most unrewarding
year in the theatre. So often he had been disappointed after
accepting attractive roles in plays that failed. Now, when he took
on a role he rather despised, it had a profound and lasting
influence on his career. *Private Lives* was his passport to New
York at a time when the talking-picture boom had sent Hollywood talent scouts scouring Broadway for actors who could
speak effectively.

Also, as he has explained, he benefited enormously from the
experience of working with Coward for six months:

I think Noel probably was the first man who took hold of me
and made me think. He made me use my silly little brain. He
taxed me with his sharpness and shrewdness and his brilliance.
He used to point out when I was talking nonsense, which
nobody else had ever done before. He gave me a sense of
balance of right and wrong.

He would make me read: I never read anything at all. I
remember he said: 'Right, my boy, *Wuthering Heights*, *Of
Human Bondage* and *The Old Wives' Tale* by Arnold Bennett.
That'll do, those are the three best. Read them.' I did. I also
read *The Forsyte Saga*. I began to read a bit of Dickens . . .
Noel was a tremendous influence. He made me a little bit more
sensible than I had been up till then, I think.[6]

Coward also succeeded with Olivier where all others had failed
by curing him at last of that disruptive tendency to clown

uncontrollably on stage. 'Larry was a terrible giggler on stage and I had to stop him. It was one thing to have an actor's joke, but it's not very fair on the audience. If I did anything in the part that was at all·funny, Larry would be in fits of laughter instead of being cross, so I said, "From now on I'm going to try to make you laugh, and every time you do so, I'll kill you." He got so angry with himself for falling for it, and I ruined several of his performances, but it was worth it.'[7]

6

Adrift in Hollywood

In the summer of 1932 Olivier flew down to Mexico for a fishing vacation and promptly found himself arrested at Ensenada airport and bundled off to the local jail. He explained that he was an Englishman on his way to join American friends for a two-weeks' holiday. It was useless. The *policia* apparently spoke only Spanish and judging by their gesticulations he gathered that something was wrong with his passport. At the jailhouse an official imposed a thousand pesos fine—far more than the innocent abroad had brought with him. Without payment there could be no release. Olivier was frantic. He argued heatedly, demanded to be put in touch with the British Consul in Mexico City. And then, half an hour after the arrest, his fishing pals arrived. Within minutes he was set free.

The friends were actors Douglas Fairbanks, Jr., and Robert Montgomery and soon after his release, Olivier cottoned on. Their suppressed grins told that he had been the victim of yet another of their outrageous practical jokes. The Mexican police had been in on the caper from the start, and really spoke and understood English very well.

He should have guessed it sooner. After more than a year in Hollywood he had learned to expect most anything from those two irrepressible jokers. The same team had once paid an ex-prizefighter five dollars to invade his dressing room and threaten to beat him up for having taken off with his non-existent wife. Coward might have cured him of his high jinks on the stage, but he had since discovered that a generous sense of humour was an invaluable aid to survival in the film colony and especially in the swinging Fairbanks set.

Laurence Olivier and Jill Esmond went to Hollywood for the first time in the spring of 1931, when the silents, with the notable exception of Chaplin's *City Lights* and his much later *Modern*

Times, were on the verge of obsolescence. More than eighty per cent of the theatres in the United States were equipped for sound. It was three and a half years since Jolson had sung from the screen in *The Jazz Singer*, one year since Garbo in *Anna Christie* had spoken her first immortal line: 'Gimme a visky with chincher aile on the saide—and don't be stingy, baby.' The hams and the mumblers and the heroes with high-pitched voices were on the scrap heap, and the movies were suddenly wide open to actors who could actually talk.

So many silent stars—Clara Bow, John Gilbert, Corinne Griffith, William Haines, Colleen Moore, Norma Talmadge, Billie Dove, Vilma Banky—could never sustain their popularity once they opened their mouths to speak. And under the new order an English accent became a positive advantage. Aristocratic, monocled George Arliss gave voice to Disraeli (1929) and won the Best Actor Academy Award. Other British actors who transferred easily from silents to talkies included Clive Brook, Ronald Colman, C. Aubrey Smith, Herbert Marshall, Nigel Bruce, Basil Rathbone and, much to some people's surprise, a clergyman's son with the face of a concrete mixer and fists that had gone six rounds with world heavyweight boxing champion Jack Johnson. With a gravel-gargling voice to match his looks, the lovable ruffian Victor McLaglen became another Oscar-winner of the early talking pictures. And the Thirties saw hordes of new British actors and actresses heading west to reap the gold dust of the talkies—Charles Laughton, Leslie Howard, Evelyn Laye, Claude Rains, Ray Milland, Ida Lupino, Diana Wynyard, Cary Grant, Elissa Landi, Reginald Owen, Freddie Bartholomew, Valerie Hobson, Cedric Hardwicke, Reginald Gardiner. Some stayed only briefly. Others never left.

The Cinderella days when talent scouts might find a Lana Turner sipping soda at a drugstore fountain hadn't quite arrived. Broadway was the obvious and most rewarding hunting ground for genuine talking actors, and the Oliviers, with the right combination of looks, talent and elocution, were automatically tested for a number of studios while they were in New York with *Private Lives*. MGM had the longest look at them, since that studio filmed the stage production, but this scrutiny served only as a guide for the movie version they were making with Norma Shearer and Robert Montgomery. On February 25, 1931, a young executive named David O. Selznick cabled Paramount chief B. P. Schulberg: PLEASE WIRE INSTRUCTIONS CONCERNING LAURENCE OLIVIER AND JILL ESMOND. OPINION HERE DIVIDED, WITH MAJORITY BELIEVING ESMOND MORE DESIRABLE FOR STOCK THAN OLIVIER. HOWEVER, FELIX YOUNG [Production executive] AND MYSELF ARE ONLY TWO THAT HAVE SEEN OLIVIER APART FROM TEST AND WE BOTH CONSIDER HIM EXCELLENT POSSIBILITY. MY OWN FEELING IS THAT, IN SPITE OF THEIR UNQUESTIONED MERIT, THEIR SALARY IS WAY OUT OF LINE FOR BEGINNERS, ESPECIALLY AS WE HAVE NO PARTS IN SIGHT FOR EITHER. WOULD RECOMMEND HAVING NEW YORK TRY TO USE THEM . . .[1] But Paramount didn't sign them either. Instead the Oliviers secured $700-a-week contracts with RKO. At the time, Jill Esmond was judged the more valuable property, and this opinion was strengthened a few days later with the release of her first British film, Alfred Hitchcock's *The Skin Game*. Some critics thought she gave the best performance in the picture and it was noted that, from some camera angles, she looked remarkably like Norma Shearer.

Radio Pictures was then situated on Gower Street, next door to Paramount and not far from the United Artists, Columbia and Metropolitan production centres. There, for the first time, the Oliviers saw a film studio that was a city in miniature—ten huge sets giving space for production for six feature films, and sound trucks at the ready for location work; a studio with a twenty-strong private police force, its own fire brigade, hospital and huge restaurant. The company had just completed the Oscar-winning *Cimarron*, its biggest spectacle, with over 2,000 extras used for scenes of the pioneer days in the Oklahoma oil fields. Among its busier stars were Joel McCrea, Mary Astor and Helen Twelvetrees. Miss Esmond was put to work almost immediately, on loan to Paramount to play Ruth Chatterton's daughter in an appalling picture called *Once a Lady*.

As a Hollywood new boy, Olivier spotted plenty of familiar faces around the swimming pools of Beverly Hills and Bel Air and Malibu. With *Journey's End* completed, James Whale had stayed on to work on the dialogue of *Hell's Angels* for Howard Hughes. Now he was making his first horror classic, *Franken-stein*, catapulting Englishman William Pratt (renamed Boris Karloff) to international fame; and later, when Karloff declined the faceless part, Whale would do the same for another Englishman (Claude Rains) in making *The Invisible Man*. Colin Clive was also working at Universal Studios, picked by Whale to play

Dr. Frankenstein because he appeared suitably neurotic and high strung. He was approaching his $2,000 a week heyday when he would be Katharine Hepburn's leading man in *Christopher Strong* and appear in a film based on the life of his ancestor, *Clive of India*.

Hollywood even had one of Olivier's thirteen choir-mates from those far-off days at All Saints. Ralph Forbes (Cassius to his schoolboy Brutus) had arrived in 1925, scoring a hit in his first American movie *Beau Geste* and acquiring some irrelevant celebrity because of his supposed physical resemblance to the Prince of Wales. His wife, Ruth Chatterton, was now recognized by *Movie Fan* readers as 'The finest actress on the screen', but their eight-year partnership was nearing an end. (At their 1932 divorce one of the divergencies was said to be that Miss Chatterton sometimes wore pyjamas at the dinner table after a hard day at the studios, while Mr. Forbes, the traditional Englishman, favoured formal dress even when they dined alone.)

Among Olivier's closest friends in Hollywood was British stage actor Anthony Bushell, who had moved west from Broadway to appear in the films *Disraeli* and *Journey's End*, and who was a founding member (with C. Aubrey Smith, Ronald Colman, Boris Karloff, P. G. Wodehouse and Murray Kinnell) of the film colony's first cricket club. Olivier also renewed his acquaintance with Raymond Massey, who arrived out there in 1931 after a British film debut as Sherlock Holmes and a Broadway first appearance as Hamlet. But his most valuable ally on the west coast was an American—Douglas Fairbanks, Jr.—who, after seven years in the movie business had finally established himself as a major star through his work in *Little Caesar* and *Dawn Patrol*. Defying paternal opposition that bordered on the pathological, he had entered his celebrated father's profession at the age of thirteen, back in 1923 when Fairbanks, Sr., was undisputed king in Hollywood, with Mary Pickford, his second wife, as queen, and 'Pickfair' as the palace where they held court to visiting royalty, nobility, politicians, artists and sundry sports stars. His first film had been a flop, but at sixteen he had made his mark in *Stella Dallas* with Ronald Colman, and two years later he had scored a hit in his stage debut in *Young Woodley* at Los Angeles Majestic Theatre. In the distinguished audience on that first night at the Majestic was a fast-rising young actress, lithe, vital and saucer-eyed, publicized as the star whose geometry most closely resembled that of the Venus de Milo. Her name was Joan Crawford. They married in June 1929, made one movie (*Our Modern Maidens*) together and soon afterwards, as separate work and conflicting interests kept them more and more apart, they became victims of the matrimonial hazards so familiar in Hollywood.

By the time Olivier arrived on the scene, the Fairbanks–Crawford marriage was beginning to founder. Olivier, too, was not without minor marital troubles, and he and Fairbanks released their tensions with late-night sprees at a Russian club in Los Angeles where they swilled vodka, sang to the sentimental strains of the balalaika and became very much involved with White Russian members who were quixotically plotting the counter-revolution.

RKO's fond hope in signing Olivier was that they had the makings of another English star in the mould of Ronald Colman, who had bridged the silent-talkie gap so impressively as Bulldog Drummond and who was now recognized as the pre-eminent actor in the media. Olivier had the Colman moustache and good looks, and like Colman he helped to project the Anglo-Saxon image by gravitating for a while towards the Hollywood Cricket Club, led by former English captain C. Aubrey Smith. But in acting style he was obviously different—more aggressive and intense and lacking Colman's peculiarly gentle and unassuming manner. So the studios tried a different tack; they switched to presenting him as the dashing Englishman who was really an all-American guy at heart. For publicity pictures they togged him out in baseball gear!

Olivier's first Hollywood picture was *Friends and Lovers*, a Northern Indian Army romance about a woman used by her husband to blackmail susceptible men. The temptress was Lili Damita, a gorgeous French firecracker who, between a two-dollar marriage in Yuma and a divorce worth a fortune to her in alimony, was destined to endure six tempestuous years as the wife of Hollywood's great sexual rover, Errol Flynn. Erich von Stroheim and Adolphe Menjou were others involved in this insignificant sixty-six-minute programme picture that traded on big names with moderate box-office success. Victor Schertzinger directed.

Olivier recalled the shooting of his first Hollywood film as a comic-tragic experience. 'Von Stroheim was preoccupied with a bit of business throughout the rehearsals. To appear ultra-sinister, he was to wear a black patch over one eye and a monocle over the other. But which ornament for which eye? He kept reversing black patch and monocle for Schertzinger's approval. He was a hard worker, but off the set he seemed to be distracted, worried, lost. Years later when I saw him in *Sunset Boulevard*, it occurred to me that he was very much like that in real life, even in 1931, the fallen giant of the silent era, dazed by his fall.' [2]

In *Friends and Lovers* Olivier played blackmail victim Lieutenant Nichols. One critic described his performance as 'too precious'. Most ignored it altogether. Yet RKO was sufficiently impressed to keep him on the payroll at a time when savage economies were being made at all the studios.

Soon both Oliviers became bored with the months of inactivity between pictures. As Jill Esmond later explained: 'The studio didn't seem to understand when we complained. We were receiving our weekly cheques. What had we to grumble about? That was their attitude.' Both were ambitious; both were irritated by idleness and the lack of worthwhile roles. J. B. Priestley, after a visit to Hollywood in the Thirties, well expressed their uneasiness when he wrote: 'Its trade, which is in dreams at so many dollars per thousand feet, is managed by businessmen pretending to be artists and by artists pretending to be businessmen. In this queer atmosphere, nobody stays as he was; the artist begins to lose his art and the businessman becomes temperamental and overbalanced.' [3]

Olivier, however, put a rather high premium on his art. He was now a vigorous twenty-four, brimful of ambition but so often finding that he was preparing for films that never materialized. In 1931 he made only one picture of any merit and that was while on loan to Fox. It was called *The Yellow Passport*, co-starring Elissa Landi and Lionel Barrymore, with Boris Karloff and Mischa Auer in trivial supporting roles. The dialogue was a trifle verbose, but stylish direction by Raoul Walsh lent some credence to the melodramatic story of a Jewish girl being hounded in St. Petersburg by the sinister Baron Andrey (Barrymore), head of the Czarist secret police. Olivier persuasively played Julian Rolph, the young British journalist who befriends her. In the original play the girl finally kills the debauched and licentious baron with a hat pin. In the film they wisely let her shoot him. Less intelligently, however, it introduced a fully equipped airfield for the final escape sequence; this in pre-war Russia!

The following year was even more frustrating for Olivier—just one new picture: *Westward Passage* (1932), a story of love turned to disillusionment, with Ann Harding, Zasu Pitts, Juliette Compton and Bonita Granville, then nine years old. By now he had become desperately disillusioned with the movie colony, and his frustration finally came to a head when he returned from his Mexican fishing holiday and discovered, after completing retakes on *Westward Passage*, that more months of inacivity lay ahead.

It was a familiar enough situation in the Hollywood of the early Thirties; the chill winds of the Depression were now biting hard into the movie industry that had borrowed extravagantly to expand in the transition to the talkies. All the film studios worked in fear of bankruptcy and their economies were necessarily drastic, alarming and utterly confusing. Movie projects were liable to be abandoned as soon as they were begun; actors were commonly forced to accept half-cuts in salary if they wished to stay on.

Olivier's studio had weathered the storm better than some, thanks in no small part to the arrival in mid-1931 of David O. Selznick, the twenty-nine-year-old whiz-kid formerly with Paramount. One of Selznick's shrewdest moves at RKO was to encourage the making of *King Kong*. He also showed fine judgment in building up an impressive stable of new stars, though he nearly missed out with an unknown actress who arrived from New York in 1932. She was an angular girl in her mid-twenties. She dressed casually in slacks and sandals, wore no perceptible make-up and spoke with an upper-crust Connecticut twang. Selznick exclaimed, 'My God, that's the worst scarecrow I ever saw. If we need someone to play the Witch of Endor, she'd be the one.' Director George Cukor, whom he had brought over from Paramount, thought otherwise. The girl's New York screen test (a scene from Philip Barry's *Holiday*) was mediocre; yet he detected some indefinable quality, something arresting about the way she placed a glass on the floor during the scene. Her name was Katharine Hepburn, and Cukor recommended her for the lead in Selznick's hottest new film property, *A Bill of Divorcement*.

Clemence Dane's controversial play proposing insanity as grounds for divorce was a 'natural' for screen treatment, and the plum role of Sydney Fairfield became a coveted prize as soon as it was known that John Barrymore would play her deranged father, with Billie Burke as the mother. Norma Shearer hoped to be released from MGM to play it. RKO's contract star Irene Dunne was an obvious possibility. Eighteen-year-old ex-child-star Anita Louise made a promising test. But Selznick came up with a more original idea. He offered the part to Jill Esmond.

Miss Esmond, previously wasted on insignificant film roles, leaped at the chance. Olivier, in contrast, remained grimly unimpressed. First, and with some reason, he suspected a late switch in casting. Why, if Selznick was so enthusiastic about Jill's playing the part, was he asking her to take a severe cut in salary and at the same time signing up a newcomer called Hepburn who had held out successfully for the extraordinary starting salary of $1,500 a week? Second, he himself was itching to get out of Hollywood.

Even Selznick, who strove to make his own name synonymous with quality in the movies, had once said: 'If you are primarily concerned with something that is usually called personal artistic integrity, you don't belong in the business of making commercial pictures. You should get yourself a paintbrush or a typewriter.' By that yardstick Olivier had no business in Hollywood. He wanted something artistically worthwhile and he saw more hope of getting this in Britain, where he had the chance of starring opposite Gloria Swanson in *Perfect Understanding*.

The Oliviers now faced the first major clash of interests in their respective careers. Finally he concluded that he must return to England and that Jill would have to decide for herself whether to remain on for a chance of stardom. There could be no question of compromise in respect to his Hollywood career. He firmly believed that he was quitting the place for good and that after working with Swanson he would concentrate on the stage. His conviction about never coming back was a key factor in influencing Miss Esmond. Greatly disappointed, she decided to give up the part. They sailed for home in July. Two months later *A Bill of Divorcement* was released. It was a smash. And just as the stage production had made Katharine Cornell a star, so the film rocketed Katharine Hepburn to international fame.

Meanwhile, Olivier's return to British films had proved rather pointless. *The Perfect Understanding* was a complete disaster, far inferior to anything he had done in Hollywood, and a project especially unfortunate for Miss Swanson. The film, dealing with the fallacy of a married couple trying to live independent lives, was her first British-made talkie. It dismally failed to launch the hoped-for comeback of the supreme movie queen of the Twenties, and it persuaded her to abandon producing.

Olivier now resolved to return to the London stage, and he came back in April 1933 in Keith Winter's *The Rats of Norway*, one of those dramas about the emotional involvements of the staff at an English boys' school, a breed of play spawned by John Van Druten's *Young Woodley* six years before. His role as an idealistic young schoolmaster corrupted by his elders was not a leading one, but he accepted it unhesitatingly because it had strong dramatic possibilities and also because it meant working with his old friend Raymond Massey and the actress he had adored since schooldays, Gladys Cooper. Cecil Parker complemented an admirable cast. The result was a positive hit, and although *The Observer* critic advised Olivier to beware of dropping his voice at the end of sentences ('I found him frequently verging on inaudibility') the general reaction to his playing of the young preparatory schoolmaster Stevan Beringer was overwhelmingly favourable, and not for the first time the 'sincerity' of his performance was stressed.

The Rats of Norway provides an early example of how Olivier could make a striking impression in an essentially quiet role, without any strong physical or vocal effects. He impressed especially with his moving delivery of a little poem, and although the part was too modest to win him great critical attention, it is surprising how vividly it is now remembered by other players who saw it. Harold Hobson, veteran critic of the *Sunday Times*, has since included it among the seven occasions in his life in the theatre when he felt on the strength of a single experience that he was in the presence of greatness. 'The feeling was,' he said, '*coup de foudre*, a thunderclap.'

With a long run assured, the Oliviers took over the lease of a house once owned by the artist Whistler, in Chelsea's fashionable Cheyne Walk. They anticipated a settled life in London. Then, just as they were about to move in from their rented apartment, Olivier began to receive a series of fresh overtures from Hollywood. He immediately dismissed the first offer: a one-year contract for $40,000, involving forty weeks' work for MGM. But a second approach, two days later, dangled a bait that no ambitious young actor could sensibly ignore. His agent in Los Angeles cabled that he was wanted in two weeks—*to star opposite Garbo!*

Here, on the face of it, was the opportunity of a lifetime. Being the male lead opposite Garbo was in itself a guarantee of international fame. Yet he responded with characteristic caution. Ever alert to the devious and erratic ways of the Hollywood film planners, he demanded an assurance of being given first-class return transportation and an appropriate salary (not less than $1,500 a week) to commence from the time of his arrival. Metro agreed. They further promised that, if for some unforeseeable reason, the Garbo picture was never made, he would be offered the lead in another major movie. Still Olivier haggled. Cables flew back and forth. His conditions were met. He had exhausted all reasonable arguments against returning to Hollywood.

With delays over negotiations and arrangements for his release from *The Rats of Norway* (Louis Hayward took over his part) more than a month went by before he was ready to leave for Los Angeles. Even then, incredibly, he still did not know what kind of part he had to play. In the end it was from a London film correspondent that he learned that he was to be a Spanish envoy to the court of Sweden in the seventeenth century, and that Garbo, as Queen Christina, would fall in love with him during an incognito journey when she was masquerading as a man.

Olivier sailed for America in mid-July, accompanied by Jill Esmond since she had both stage and screen work in the offing. The publicity attending him now was extraordinary—front-page news stories, photographs and interviews in all the national press. 'This is the big part that Larry Olivier has deserved for so long,' wrote the London *Evening Standard* film correspondent. 'To every part he has brought a great ability, personal charm and good looks. His screen likeness to Ronald Colman has frequently been noticed.' He was amused but not deceived by the sudden attention. All the same, the future looked undeniably bright, especially when he arrived at the studios to find production in a rare state of readiness. His wardrobe, based on cabled measurements, was already prepared; only two weeks of rehearsals, he was told, and then they would begin shooting.

Apparently many actors had been considered for his role of Don Antonio, among them Ricardo Cortez, Fredric March, Nils Asther and Franchot Tone. They had all been rejected.

Garbo, as he was given to understand, had personally approved him after seeing his work as a young lover in *Westward Passage*. The producer was Walter Wanger; the director, Armenian-born Rouben Mamoulian.

One thing, however, did strike Olivier as being curious: the announcement that they would begin shooting with the most crucial scene of the entire picture, the bedroom scene at a country inn where Don Antonio meets the disguised Queen for the first time and arouses such overwhelming passion in her breast that she is later prepared to sacrifice the Swedish throne for her one true love. This choice was especially awkward for Olivier. It involved playing a highly sensitive love scene with an actress who was virtually a stranger, for in the short time available before the first rehearsal he found it impossible to establish any kind of rapport with Garbo. Her icy, aristocratic façade, as everyone took pains to tell him, was really a shield for a star who by nature was desperately shy. So he made allowances for this, turned on his quiet English charm when they were introduced on the set, and in private conversation did his utmost to make her feel at ease. All to no effect.

Disconcertingly, Garbo's lack of warmth remained evident when they came to rehearse their historic love scene. Olivier later recalled: 'The stage was set for our most important scene when as Don Antonio, I meet Garbo in her boudoir at the inn and there discover the warm, tender woman beneath the boyish masquerade. And this is the part of my story I shall always look back upon with a mixture of amazement and disappointment. The director explained that I was to come forward, grasp Garbo's slender body tenderly, look into her eyes and, in the gesture, awaken passion within her, that passion for which she is later to give up the Swedish throne. I went into my role giving it everything that I had, but at the touch of my hand Garbo became frigid. I could feel the sudden tautness of her, her eyes as stony and expressionless as if she were marble.'[4]

Those first rehearsals were an embarrassing nothingness. The combination of Garbo and Olivier produced as much exciting chemistry on the screen as the mating of Ma and Pa Kettle. Soon afterwards MGM issued a sensational press release: Olivier was out—replaced by John Gilbert.

Even Hollywood, so accustomed to sudden shocks and sensations, was rocked by the news. John Gilbert as the new Don

Antonio? Surely not! Not *the* John Gilbert, the fallen idol of the silent screen whose image as 'The Great Lover' had been so cruelly shattered when he opened his mouth in *His Glorious Night* and said, 'I love you' in a disillusioning pipsqueak voice? Not Gilbert the prince of has-beens who used to propose regularly to Garbo and once actually got so far as an elopement until, on that dramatic drive to Mexico, she gave him the slip and bolted herself in a hotel ladies' room?

At the time, Gilbert's return was popularly interpreted as an act of charity on Garbo's part, repaying a debt to the man who had helped her make a success of her first international movie, *Flesh and the Devil*. This explanation was altogether easier on Olivier's wounded pride. It meant that he had not necessarily failed. Garbo had turned to Gilbert when he most desperately needed her friendship, and no actor in Olivier's position could be expected to compete in that kind of strictly personal situation. But if this were true, why did she wait until the first rehearsals before pulling Gilbert back from the edge of oblivion? Her contract gave her the privilege of approving her leading man; she could have vetoed all other candidates.

Garbo, as in all things, has remained silent about the affair except to say that she was very unhappy with the way Olivier was treated; and with her silence the story of Olivier's dismissal has become badly distorted. Numerous books record that, after the first emotionless test, Garbo went to Louis B. Mayer and asked for a new leading man; that Mayer stalled and the movie goddess responded in the traditional prima donna fashion, by sending word that she was sick when shooting was about to begin. In this way, so the story goes, Mayer got the message, and Garbo got the leading man she really wanted. The inference has been that Garbo was incapable of registering emotion with Olivier.

But there is one other, much simpler explanation of this unfortunate affair: that Olivier was simply inadequate or unsuited to the role. This is in fact confirmed by Rouben Mamoulian. He recalls:

In preparing *Queen Christina* I had all the parts cast to my satisfaction but had difficulty in finding the right Don Antonio. There was a young actor who, I thought, might fit the part in looks and in the quality of his personality—that was young Olivier. Whenever I feel confident of my hunch and/or judgment in casting I do make a test of the person in question. However, in this case two elements were of equal importance: (1) Does the actor fit the part? (2) Can he hold his ground in experience and authority opposite Garbo? Miss Garbo, was, naturally, past the stage of making tests, but the only way I could arrive at a final judgment was through a test of Olivier with Garbo and not with some substitute. Miss Garbo agreed, so I made a very comprehensive test. The result re Olivier was negative. Although he had qualities that suited the part, he didn't have enough maturity, skill and acting weight to balance Garbo's. In short, he was too young and inexperienced for Don Antonio. Thus, finally, John Gilbert got the part.

Generously, Olivier has come to accept this explanation. 'I just didn't measure up,' he recalled in 1972. 'She was an absolute master of her trade. She had an enormous image to the public. And me, I was just grovelling like a puppet, but that was not the way to play her great lover. It became apparent to me really, and I wasn't really surprised when I was fired. She had to fire me because there was nothing else to do. I simply wasn't up to her—a horrible experience.' [5]

He now had the option of an alternative role, and Walter Wanger suggested the idea of his testing for *Romeo and Juliet* opposite Norma Shearer. Olivier dismissed it with the comment that he didn't think Shakespeare was suitable for the screen! (Three years later Leslie Howard got the part.) With Jill Esmond he fled Hollywood as soon as could be arranged. They took a vacation in Honolulu and after a few days there he received a cable offering him a new 1,500-dollar-a-week contract with MGM. He did not bother to reply.

Queen Christina had its New York premiere on December 26, 1933, opening at the Astor Theatre to great critical acclaim and becoming best remembered for its final, fading shot of Garbo leaving Sweden after the death of her lover, and standing statuesque like a figurehead in the prow of her ship as she gazed out to the setting sun. It mattered not that her hair billowed back against the prevailing wind. Everyone praised Garbo. Gilbert was mostly ignored. His career continued to decline and four years later he died. The official cause was a heart attack; but he had literally drunk himself to death. He was thirty-nine.

How fundamentally might the course of Olivier's career have been changed if he had starred opposite Garbo as originally planned? Very probably the prominence alone, irrespective of his performance, would have established him as an international movie star. Very possibly Hollywood would then have made him an irresistible offer and, once under the usual seven-year contract, he would have found his development as a stage actor seriously restricted. As a non-starter, however, he gained nothing in screen status from his much-publicized casting opposite Garbo. He was still a man of the theatre first and of the cinema second. When the British film annual 'Stars of the Screen' appeared in 1934, it contained a section 'devoted to biographies of stars who were, or will be, leaders on the screen'. Only one Olivier was listed: Jill Esmond.

7

★

Bolts of Lightning

When the wounded Olivier quit the Hollywood jungle in 1933 he was at least spared the discomfort of returning directly to London and facing searching questions about his fate as Garbo's rejected screen lover. Fortuitously, that ordeal was postponed since both he and Jill Esmond had been engaged for a Broadway production of Mordaunt Shairp's *The Green Bay Tree*. New York, however, did not provide quite the pleasant interlude that he hoped for, even though he was appearing in an enormously successful play and working again with his wife and with English actor James Dale, whom he had met seven years before in the *Saint Bernard* production. A dark shadow was cast over the entire proceedings by the formidable figure of Jed Harris, the Vienna-born American producer and impresario and by far the toughest, most acid-tongued task-master that Olivier had yet encountered. Harris was an outstanding theatre talent whose life story might have been entitled, 'How to Make Enemies and Influence People'.

In the summer of 1933 Harris planned two Broadway productions: *The Green Bay Tree*, a notorious and contentious drama of homosexual life, and *The Lake* by Dorothy Massingham and Murray MacDonald, already a British stage hit. In the former he thought it would be clever to have such masculine types as Olivier and Dale cavorting on stage as a couple of classy queers. The latter was planned as a spectacular stage return for Kate Hepburn following her triumph in Hollywood. Knowing how Broadway could be cruelly uncharitable towards a bright young film star assuming a leading stage role, Harris suggested that it would be a shrewd move if Miss Hepburn made a more modest entrance on Broadway, first taking a supporting role in *The Green Bay Tree* before opening in *The Lake*. But the actress suspected his motives. It looked very much as though he was trying to prop up his first play with a sure-fire box-office name. So she declined and Jill Esmond got the part.

Whatever his motives, Harris's advice proved sound enough. *The Green Bay Tree* opened in October, a smash hit. The first night of *The Lake* (December 26) was one of the historic catastrophes of the theatre. Miss Hepburn had won an Academy Award for *Morning Glory*; her film fame brought a record advance sale of $40,000. Now she plunged out of her depth, and it was during the first intermission, in the lobby of the Martin Beck Theatre, that Dorothy Parker uttered her classic remark: 'She ran the gamut of emotions from A to B.' Although *The Lake* continued to do good business, it was taken off on February 10, 1934, after its sadly miscast star had paid Harris to release her from their verbal agreement.

Before leaving Broadway, Miss Hepburn visited the Cort Theatre to see Olivier's much-praised work in *The Green Bay Tree*. 'I can remember vividly his extraordinary emotional performance. I said to him, "My God, Larry, you are brilliant."

' "Yes," he said. "I hate Jed so, I have to get rid of all drive to kill him." '

James Dale felt much the same way. 'What Katharine Hepburn says about Jed Harris is quite correct. Only I don't think *he* hated anybody really. He was just frightfully in love with himself. He thought himself wonderful and we cordially disliked him, all and sundry. And he depressed Olivier beyond words. But then Jed Harris would have depressed anybody . . . we had four weeks of this man, rehearsing every day, and it was one of the most unhappy experiences for both of us.'

However much Harris bullied and badgered, however tyrannical his approach, there was no denying his ultimate effectiveness. Olivier, as the tormented crypto-queer Julian Dulcimer, earned notices of a higher calibre than he had ever known before. Brooks Atkinson of the *New York Times* gave it a rave review (as did others): 'In the two chief parts, James Dale and Laurence Olivier play like bolts of lightning . . . Olivier's Julian is an extraordinary study in the decomposition of a character. His ability to carry a character through from casual beginnings to a defeated conclusion, catching all the shades of meaning as he goes, is acting of the highest quality.'

Florence Fisher Parry (for the *Pittsburgh Press*) wrote:

I cannot remember ever having been more impressed with a young man's *immersion* in a role. Julian does more than spring to life—we feel that he has grown upon us over the period of a lifetime. His entrances seem not to be made from the wings of a stage—but from an adjacent room where he has been conducting his life as vividly as upon the visible stage. And in the horrifying scene where he is beaten into slavish submission by his benefactor's abnormal attraction for him, his acting becomes not *acting*, but an exhibition of emotional collapse so painful to witness that the eyes of the audience are torn away; the spectacle of his ignominy actually becomes too terrible to bear.

James Dale, however, has reservations about Olivier's performance:

He was inclined to speak with his mouth shut and was very fidgety onstage. He was restless and active, which made it difficult for the others, who never knew what he was going to do. It had an unsettling effect on me, but I liked him so much that I just put up with it. I had a long dinner scene with him, the best part of a whole act, a dinner *à deux*. And it was the most terrible experience because he would never do the same thing. Night after night, I never knew what he was going to do—I got the impression he didn't know himself. But the audience liked it very much indeed. It came over to them perfectly.

Of course, Larry is a man of action. When he thinks of a thing, he jumps up and rushes away and does it before he stops and considers it. That is his temperament. The character in *The Green Bay Tree* was a limp, wet, lackadaisical, rather effeminate lad—the very last thing that Larry Olivier was, is, or ever will be. I understood that he didn't like himself in the part.

Actually Olivier detested it. He had scored a resounding personal success and yet he counted the days until he and Jill would be free to head for home. The end came in March 1934, by which time he had been invited by Noel Coward to play in his new London production of S. N. Behrman's *Biography*. It seemed a good bet for his return to the West End stage after a year's absence. The play was a long-running hit on Broadway. In London it would have the same leading lady, Ina Claire, making her first stage appearance in England since *The Belle of Bond Street* twenty years before.

This was Coward's first venture into management, backing his own plays with his New York stockbroker friend, Jack Wilson, and it proved a disaster. Yet Olivier was successful in his role of Richard Kurt, the intolerant and ill-mannered American editor who persuades a celebrity painter to 'tell all' in her autobiography. He works, wrote Ivor Brown (*The Observer*) 'as well as any man could to hold our interest in this boor; he feels his way into the very heart of roughness and it is not his fault if, at the close, we are tired of the fellow and his raucous self-righteous ranting at the world'.

Back on the London roundabout of mostly short-lived plays, Olivier next went into Gordon Daviot's *Queen of Scots*, a play specially written for Gwen Ffrangcon-Davies. Ralph Richardson had been playing Bothwell in rehearsals and finding himself uncomfortably out of character in a flashy romantic role that involved strong love scenes, and so eight days before the opening date he asked if he could be released from the part. At this point Olivier boldly came to the rescue and in the circumstances, with no time to develop a profound interpretation, he did remarkably well. He played in a swashbuckling style, 'more Hollywood than Holyrood', but generally his notices were good. His Bothwell, said Agate of *The Sunday Times*, was 'an excellently conceived and executed portrait, except that I think he is a little too light, especially in the voice which has the tennis club, will-you-serve-first-partner-or-shall-I ring about it'.

Olivier now received another invitation to be an emergency replacement, this time a much less flattering one. Coward wanted him for the dashingly eccentric Tony Cavendish in his production of the Edna Ferber–George S. Kaufman play, *Theatre Royal*, but just for three weeks while they were out of town. Once they reached the West End, it was explained, the part would be taken over by Brian Aherne, who had been unavoidably detained in Hollywood by overtime shooting on the MGM movie *What Every Woman Knows*. Ostensibly, it was a lousy deal. But after reading the play he decided that his role was so exceptionally attractive that it was worth taking a gamble. Hollywood schedules, as he well knew, were maddeningly erratic; perhaps, just possibly, Aherne might be delayed even longer. And there was another, even remoter possibility: might he not play the part so supremely well that Aherne would be nervous about trying to take over from him?

The play, known in America as *The Royal Family*, had been renamed for British presentation to avoid ambiguity, since the 'royals' it satirized belonged to Broadway not Buckingham Palace—namely the Barrymore family. Tony Cavendish was an obvious and outrageous take-off of John Barrymore. Olivier, who had met Barrymore in Hollywood, recognized it as a magnificent opportunity for justifiably extravagant acting combined with plenty of daring, scene-stealing athleticism—in every way a near perfect part for himself. By the time Aherne arrived on the scene, the play had opened in Glasgow. The cast (it included Marie Tempest, Madge Titheradge, Mary Merrall and George Zucco) had rehearsed together for a month before opening and they gave Aherne a rather frigid reception. Miss Tempest, now nearly eighty, was especially haughty, and the new leading man from Hollywood became even more ill at ease after watching Olivier's performance with a certain awe. 'It was a wonderful performance and I was deeply impressed, and terrified to watch him jump from the upper landing over the bannisters and down on to the stairs below. Could I possibly do it? I thought not! Several sleepless nights later, the problem was unexpectedly resolved for me. Miss Tempest refused to rehearse all over again and at the same moment Katharine Cornell, with whom I was to appear in six productions, telephoned from New York begging me to return to be with her in *Romeo and Juliet*. Noel released me and I left at once, thankful that I wouldn't have to risk the jump.'

Everyone profited. Coward recouped his losses on *Biography*. Aherne, as Mercutio, joined a remarkable cast that included Basil Rathbone (Romeo), Cornell (Juliet), Edith Evans (the Nurse), Orson Welles (Tybalt) and a then little-known actor called Tyrone Power. As for Olivier, his impact on the West End was tremendous, both physically and artistically. His Tony Cavendish represented a major personal triumph, a performance hailed as the best thing he had yet done and bringing forth the highest praise for his typhonic entrances and exits, his Fairbanks-like gusto and swordplay, his extraordinary bravura.

After playing Cavendish for two months at the Lyric Theatre, Olivier misjudged his prodigious, eight-foot leap over the balcony and broke an ankle on landing. His understudy, Valentine Dyall, quit a game of bridge to take over the remainder of the performance, and his friend Robert Douglas played out the run. Olivier saw in the New Year on crutches. Yet he never regretted having introduced his paratrooper-style fall. Just as success as a New Yorker in *The Adding Machine* had made him fanatically painstaking in grasping accents, so success in *Theatre Royal* encouraged his indulgence in highly physical action on stage. (In one performance he played a fencing sequence so furiously that his sword went flying across the stage and struck Dame Marie Tempest on the breasts.) It was not all for theatrical effect. It was partly a compulsion that grew out of youthful consciousness of his weak physique. He had always worked hard to compensate for early frailty. Now physical fitness became vitally important to him in work, and even in the movies he was to insist on executing his own stunts wherever practicable.

Recalling this early reputation for athleticism, he has explained: 'I was, of course, absolutely swept overboard by Douglas Fairbanks and John Barrymore in films, and indeed, John Barrymore playing Hamlet at the Haymarket was tremendously athletic. I admired that greatly, all of us did. In fact a lot of the silent film stars were very full of muscle and torso. I remember Milton Sills, Ramon Navarro in *Ben Hur*—they all had to show very manly biceps and chest. It was part of their glamour. One thought of oneself, idiotically skinny as I was, as a sort of Tarzan. It appealed to the girls, it gave one a tremendous special kind of glamour. In films, of course, it was all physical glamour. It had to be—Rudolf Valentino, Fairbanks—it was physical prowess, the brilliant use of the sword, the wonderful way of leaping over ridiculous heights, which probably they never used to do at all.'[1]

By a curious coincidence Olivier was crippled in *Theatre Royal* at a time when he had already bought the rights in a Keith Winter play that was built around a character confined to a wheelchair. *The Ringmaster* concerned the semi-paralysed proprietor of a Torbay guest house who, by force of personality and by continually cracking the whip of his sardonic comment, contrives to dominate the lives of everyone around him. When the play opened in London in March 1935 Olivier had clearly profited from his months as an invalid; he simulated painful movements with extraordinary realism and in the final scene, where the deserted cripple breaks from his chair to scream and writhe on the floor, he went into agonizing contortions that had the audience cheering at the end.

The volume of that first-night applause suggested another stage triumph. Strangely the reverse was the case. *The Ringmaster* had an impressive cast: Dame May Whitty, Colin Keith-Johnston, Nigel Patrick, Jill Esmond, Cathleen Nesbitt, Dorothy Hyson. The producer was Raymond Massey. The few who attended, adored it. But the word never spread and after the eighth performance, with a modest audience applauding strongly enough for six curtain calls, the play had to be taken off. The trouble was that the critics did not care for it. Agate praised the players and then damned the play. Ivor Brown felt the treatment was wrong. And not for the first time he complained of Olivier's delivery. 'I wished he would not clip his speech and throw away the last words of a sentence; it was a continual strain to hear him.'

It was the shortest run Olivier had so far known in London. And his next play, *Golden Arrow*, survived only one week longer, doubly disappointing because it was his first experience as an actor-manager, the first play to have 'Laurence Olivier Presents' atop the playbills. Originally he went into it as both leading man and director, resuming his association with producer Maurice Browne, who had bought the rights in this comedy by novelist Sylbia Thompson and Victor Cunard. But the two men held irreconcilable views in the rehearsal stage. Olivier, less pessimistic about the way the play was shaping, sought and obtained full responsibility for the production. Browne, in being severely critical and pulling out, showed sound judgment, just as he had done in backing *Journey's End* to the hilt.

Golden Arrow, though often sharp on wit, was far too slow-moving in the early scenes. However, it did have one very attractive saving grace. For the role of an American girl, Olivier and Browne had wanted Carol Goodner, a New York actress then working regularly on the London stage. When they failed to get her they agreed to take a chance on a twenty-year-old red-

head from County Down who had studied at London University
to become a teacher. She had a Bachelor of Arts degree but very
limited acting experience: two seasons as a £4-a-week toiler
with the Birmingham Rep and one in Regent's Park Open Air
Theatre. Her assets were an uncommonly sure American accent,
strikingly good looks and a beguiling Irish charm.

James Agate (*Sunday Times*) noted that the girl was obviously
inexperienced and wrote: 'Throughout the evening Mr. Olivier
had not one single word to say that was worth speaking or
hearing, and undoubtedly his best utterance was when at the
end, in his capacity as impresario, he invited us to welcome a
young actress "in whom there are undeniable and obvious po-
tentialities". The ears nearly fell off my head at hearing the title
of transcendent greatness specifically declaimed for a newcomer!'

Future events proved Olivier right. The girl whom he eulo-
gized was Greer (formerly Enid) Garson, and following this
break she became a successful West End ingénue. Three years
later she was signed to a Hollywood contract by Louis B. Mayer
who, in a single excursion to Europe, also brought back a Vien-
nese film actress called Hedwig Keisler. Miss Keisler became
Hedy Lamarr. Miss Garson became a star with her first picture,
Goodbye Mr. Chips.

Denys Blakelock, who had a secondary role in *Golden Arrow*,
later wrote:

> I wish there were something more positively interesting to
> record about that first Olivier production. But the play,
> though witty and entertaining, was very lightweight and did
> not give him much chance to stretch his imaginative powers.
> His own performance was immaculate as ever. So were his
> clothes. Olivier was then at his most smart and sophisticated—
> quite a different personality from what we know today . . .
> He had travelled far already since the days when Clare Eames
> had said, 'Larry looks down at me with the eyes of a con-
> queror.' The conqueror had arrived. The building of his
> Empire was about to begin.[2]

★

8

The Shakespearean Revival

Olivier had spoken of a certain intuitive sense of destiny in his youth, of a vague knowing that he would attain the heights, and yet up to this point in the mid-Thirties there had been no hint that his greatness might be achieved as a classical actor. He had been schooled in the classical tradition, but in nearly seven years since graduating from the Birmingham Rep he had consistently played contemporary roles with the one brief exception of Bothwell in *Queen of Scots*. Largely by necessity, he had moved with the tide of popular taste, and that taste in post-war England was overwhelmingly in favour of innovation, experiment and freshness.

In the early Twenties it required a peculiarly dedicated and non-materialistic actor to seek to establish his reputation in doublet and hose. And then there came the talkies, a creeping menace that inevitably accelerated the drive for novelty. In such a progressive climate even the stark realism of Sean O'Casey won popular acclaim, and in 1929 when Dublin's Abbey Theatre rejected his tragi-comedy *The Silver Tassie*, the play still found a stage in London, enabling Charles Laughton to make his harrowing appearance as Harry Heegan, the Irish football hero returned from Flanders, paralysed from the waist down.

Shakespeare, of course, was not completely ignored. In its drab setting across from Waterloo Station, a one-time flea pit and gin palace now known as the Old Vic flourished under Lilian Baylis; and with new leading man, John Gielgud, it came to a certain popularity in 1930 when West End theatregoers crossed the Thames to see a Hamlet that was acclaimed by Agate as 'the high water mark of English Shakespearean acting of our time'. All the same, this Old Vic production, the first to be transferred to the West End, did not survive long in the commercial glare of Shaftesbury Avenue, and though the Bard was often and brilliantly served elsewhere, generally he needed to be cloaked in experimental modern dress to appeal to the unconverted who demanded something at least different if not new.

The decade in which Olivier had won his spurs in the theatre was the decade when the great sin was to be seen as 'theatrical', when the 'ham' was positively out and so-called naturalism was in, when managers actually looked askance at actors with pretty verse-speaking voices and when, at auditions for contemporary plays, it could be a distinct disadvantage to have a reputation in the classical theatre. The stage was left open to a host of presentable personalities who were judged to have the ability to 'act naturally', to somehow be themselves on the stage. This became the day of the non-actor, the time when so many young men took Gerald du Maurier as their model and failed to appreciate the skilled technique behind his facile façade. But fashions were beginning to change in the early Thirties, and once they had changed, the non-actors were doomed.

In these circumstances, Olivier was exceptionally fortunate. He never carried the handicap weight of the classical player. He had appeared in modern dress from the beginning; the mind's eye never automatically placed him in costumed drama. Yet, by both temperament and training, he was essentially 'classical', and now, as the tide turned and a new generation was beginning to discover what great classical talents abounded, he could enjoy the best of both worlds. In the mid-Thirties the modern and traditional theatre remained equally within his compass.

Many things were possible for Olivier in 1935. He still resisted Hollywood offers, but now he could enjoy film star riches without sacrificing his more valued work on the English stage. In April he was signed to a long-term film contract by Alexander Korda, who three years earlier had sealed the success of his London Film Productions with the making of *The Private Life of Henry VIII* and was now building up a great movie empire with vast new studios at Denham in Buckinghamshire. Olivier's name was added to a fast-growing stable of stars that included Laughton, Chevalier, Massey, Richardson, Merle Oberon and Leslie Banks. Life was most agreeable for him now. Both he and Jill Esmond never wanted for stage work. And in their new Cheyne Walk home, with its magnificent sixty-foot-long studio rising to the second floor, they had a house ideally suited for entertaining their theatrical friends: Coward and Gertrude

Lawrence, the Richardsons, the Bushells, Robert Newton, George Relph and Mercia Swinburne, among others. They hob-nobbed with such giants of the day as Shaw and Barrie and generally shone as two bright stars amid a social scene of rare brilliance.

It was just one month after gaining the financial security of a Korda contract that Olivier ventured into theatre management with the misdirected *Golden Arrow*. Two weeks after that play failed he was at Denham, using the cinema to pay for his labours of love in the theatre. His first film for Korda was *Moscow Nights*, with Penelope Dudley Ward, Athene Seyler and that grand old man of the French cinema, Harry Bauer. *The Observer* critic wrote: 'The surprise of the picture is Laurence Olivier, who plays the young officer with as much wit and feeling as if the tomfool fellow were really a possible character. Such pleasure as I got from *Moscow Nights* was largely due to Mr. Olivier's recurrent appearances on the screen.' Though intelligently directed by Anthony Asquith and a marked improvement on a French version of only eight months before, it was an undistinguished movie.

Meanwhile, in the theatre something extraordinary had been happening. A Shakespearean play had been presented on the West End stage and it had been a smash hit. This was Gielgud's own production of *Hamlet* with himself as the Prince, Jessica Tandy (Ophelia), Frank Vosper (Claudius), Laura Cowie (Gertrude), Jack Hawkins (Horatio), George Howe (Polonius), Glen Byam Shaw (Laertes) and a frail nonentity named Alec Guinness (Osric), who, after ten days of rehearsals, had been told: 'It's no good. Go away for a week and get someone to teach you how to act.'

When this *Hamlet* had opened at the New Theatre in November 1934, Olivier was performing his Fairbanks–Barrymore acrobatics in *Theatre Royal*. Shakespeare was still alleged to be an unpopular dramatist in the West End and Gielgud's production was being openly greeted as a test case. Had the climate changed? Was there a future for the classics in the commercial theatre? The critics' reaction was not encouraging; it was 'Everest half-scaled' . . . a Hamlet 'too purely the intellectual' . . . 'Ophelia miscast.' But they were only the judges. The paying public formed the jury and their verdict was a resounding 'yes' for the Bard. When the production closed on March 30, 1935, it had run for 155 performances, a total then surpassed only by Henry Irving's (200) sixty years before. Theatre historian J. C. Trewin has called that *Hamlet*, 'the key Shakespearean revival of its period'. It was this revival that so positively spurred Olivier's ambition to return to the classical theatre

His chance came in the autumn of 1935. Bronson Albery and Gielgud were planning a revival of *Romeo and Juliet* with Edith Evans and Peggy Ashcroft again as Nurse and Juliet respectively. This time, however, it was proposed that Gielgud should share the roles of Romeo and Mercutio with another actor, and Robert Donat was their choice. Donat was the new 'golden boy' of the British cinema following his triumph in Alfred Hitchcock's *The Thirty-Nine Steps*. He had already refused $100,000 clear of income tax to play Romeo to Norma Shearer's Juliet in a Hollywood movie, and now he declined Gielgud's offer because, by chance, he was planning his own stage production of *Romeo and Juliet*. Seeking a second choice, Albery and Gielgud remembered their emergency replacement for Bothwell in *Queen of Scots*. They invited Olivier to play the two roles.

Only three weeks were available for rehearsals of *Romeo and Juliet*, since Gielgud was then committed to filming by day in Hitchcock's *The Secret Agent*. Probably this was to their un-realized advantage. Had they been given any longer, it is entirely conceivable that the marked differences between Gielgud and Olivier over the playing of Romeo could have assumed proportions resulting in deadlock. As it was, the rehearsals never lacked for argument arising out of the conflict between Olivier's realism and what he calls Gielgud's 'irrepressible sense of beauty'. This clash surprised no one. Gielgud was already firmly established as the supreme master of lyrical effect, the euphonic quality; instinctively, he sought to safeguard the beauty of the poetry, the correctness of the rhythm. Olivier, in contrast, had trodden a rougher path from his classical nursery, and after so many years in the 'modern' theatre, he sought equally instinctively to breathe reality and true-to-life honesty into every part he played. His first concern was not for the poetry but that his Romeo should come across as a genuine, living character: a tousled sixteen-year-old boy, hesitant and impetuous, and recognizably gripped in the exquisite agony of adolescent love. Too often, it seemed to him, Romeo was presented as an unbelievably sweet and smooth-talking romantic.

As the curtain went up at the New on October 17, 1935, the stage was perfectly set for the kind of dramatic duelling that had been a popular sport in the English theatre of a century before: a joust between flamboyant egotists, each jealously guarding his reputation and seeking to eclipse the other. Such rivalry was never the original intention, but once recognized, it was an undeniable box-office asset.

Predictably, the first round went to Gielgud. Olivier was roundly blasted by the critics for butchering the poetry, and their barbs penetrated more deeply than any before, simply because he cared about this performance, his first major test in Shakespeare, more than anything he had previously done. The following night he was so despondent that he offered to relinquish the part. Albery dismissed the idea. He did not share Olivier's gloom and events bore him out. *Romeo and Juliet* ran at the New for 186 performances, a record for the play first produced 338 years before.

Over the years a great deal of emphasis has been given to the devastating criticism of Olivier's Romeo. He himself has said that he was shattered by it. Certainly, by extracting sentences from all the reviews ('his blank verse is the blankest I have ever heard' . . . 'plays Romeo as though he were riding a motor-bike . . .') one can build up a picture of overwhelming condemnation. But, examined fully, the notices were not nearly so bad as we have been led to believe. In some notable cases, the savage criticism of his poetic delivery was curiously balanced by extravagant praise of other aspects of his performance. Agate, for example, has been much quoted for his comment in a radio broadcast: 'If Romeo were just a lovesick gumph, occasionally falling into a deeper trance in which he speaks unaccountable poetry, then Olivier is your Romeo. But if it is a question of playing Shakespeare's analytical and critical lover, then Gielgud's the man.' Examine, however, what the same critic had to say in his *Sunday Times* review and one finds him, after some characteristic splashing of acid, describing Olivier thus:

Mr. Olivier's Romeo suffered enormously from the fact that the spoken poetry of the part eluded him . . . Apart from the speaking there was poetry and to spare. This Romeo looked every inch a lover, and a lover fey and foredoomed. The actor's facial expression was varied and mobile, his bearing noble, his play of arm imaginative, and his smaller gestures were infinitely touching. Note, for example, how lovingly he fingered first the props of Juliet's balcony and at the last her bier. For once in a way the tide of this young man's passion was presented at the flood, and his grief was agonizingly done. 'Is it e'en so? Then I defy you, stars!' is a line which has defied many actors. Mr. Olivier's way with this was to say it tonelessly, and it is a very moving way. Taking the performance by and large, I have no hesitation in saying that this is the most moving Romeo I have seen.

First-night performances can be notoriously misleading and certainly Olivier grew in stature in the ensuing weeks as Romeo. Innumerable members of the profession sent him letters of praise, including director Tyrone Guthrie, who congratulated him on a performance of 'terrific vitality—speed and intelligence and gusto and muscularity'. And when St. John Ervine went to the play—at the prompting of Fabia Drake, who had acted with Olivier at All Saints—he came away enthralled and devoted his weekly column in *The Observer* to what he judged the best Romeo he had ever seen.

Even Gielgud, with strong reservations about the verse-speaking, has since praised that Romeo, strikingly Italianate and romantic. 'I remember Ralph [Richardson] coming to see it and saying, "He just stands against the balcony with such an extraordinary pose that this animal magnetism and vitality and passion come right over." And I was very busy enunciating all the poetry very beautifully but I was very cold aesthetically compared with him. And I was struck then, as we all have been since, by his extraordinary power and originality, and the way he dashes with a part, and really wrings its neck without self-consciousness or worrying whether he's attractive or good or bad, or what. He's a great performer without caring, you feel, what is said. He doesn't act with the sort of caution and fear that some of the rest of us have.'[1]

A generous tribute, but posterity should perhaps allow for Gielgud's acutely modest nature and his instinctive tendency to lean over backwards in always seeing the best rather than the worst in most everyone. It might be fairly balanced by requoting Sir Alec Guinness: 'I was only the Apothecary and twenty-one years old, so not much of a judge. But I remember feeling jealous for Gielgud who, at that time, had no romantic rival in the English theatre. Larry Olivier was undoubtedly glamorous but he seemed a bit cheap—striving after theatrical effect and so on—and making nonsense of the verse. Yet his personal success was undoubted and he made himself look remarkably beautiful as Romeo.'[2]

Also John Laurie provides a rather devastating postscript on Olivier's verse delivery.

When he was playing in *Romeo and Juliet* he sent for me one day and asked, 'What is this thing called *blank verse?*' And I said, 'Well, Larry, it's five beats to the line.' And he said, 'Is that all?' 'No,' I said, 'it isn't all. There's a lot more to it than that, because the five beats are hardly ever there. You have to make all kinds of allowances, as in syncopation. There are a thousand subtleties.' I tried to explain it to him, but it was impossible to make a man speak blank verse who hadn't much idea of it in one quick lesson between shows at the New Theatre. Now, however, he speaks blank verse well, and combines it with a totally realistic approach.

After six weeks of Romeo, Olivier faced the challenge of Mercutio—a natural part for him and one he was determined to exploit to the full. Ralph Richardson happened to be playing the same role on tour in America with Katharine Cornell and Maurice Evans, and at Olivier's request he wrote to him briefly about the lessons he had learned and the little bits of theatrical business he had introduced. Most especially he stressed the importance of not hurrying the Queen Mab speech. Olivier has never forgotten that letter and even now, almost forty years later, can quote its concluding paragraphs word for word: 'You should try to produce a different key every time you come on—and wear your clothes in a different way. I have a tremendous circular scarlet cloak of fine red flannelette; this I can do a great many things with. I hope that you are not bored with all this my dear boy—but one thing more—the difficulty is to keep sober enough in the one hour twenty-five minutes wait you have before the end to take your call without falling into the orchestra pit. This takes years of skill and cannot be overestimated, as much of the effect of the poetic "Mab" speech may be lost by such an incident.'

Olivier profited from his friend's experience and, working in a few frivolous gestures of his own, he presented a Mercutio of swaggering extravagance and sardonic wit that was as far removed from his adolescent Romeo as one could imagine. It effectively drew attention to his extraordinary versatility, though in rehearsal it was a loud performance that again instilled his director with dark forebodings. Altogether this was an appallingly worrying and testing time for Gielgud. He was directing. He was preparing his own Romeo with parting affection since he recognized that, being thirty-one, he would surely never play it again. He also had to contend with working by day on the Hitchcock film with Madeleine Carroll, Robert Young and Peter Lorre—an experience he found both disturbing and uncomfortable. (Hitchcock unnerved him. Lorre was liable to disappear from the set to take a morphine fix and when present to indulge in all manner of scene-stealing tricks. There were maddening time-wasting delays and a train-crash sequence that required Gielgud to spend several days prostrate beneath iron girders and rubble.) Still, he was the complete professional and he coped, and though he was far from satisfied with his own Romeo, the audience reaction was one of overwhelming approval and the recast production proved an enormous success. The traditionalists hailed a hero speaking poetry purely and lyrically and if Mercutio did not caress the verse so sweetly it mattered much less. Olivier's characterization—a dashing cavalier who partly lifted the Nurse's voluminous skirt with his sword's point as he chirped, 'A sail, a sail, a sail!' and who duelled so fiercely with Tybalt (Harry Andrews) that they literally drew blood from each other—was irresistible, always arresting.

After seven years out of Shakespeare, Olivier was now having a triple taste of Shakespearean roles. Late in November, while still playing Mercutio, he landed what was recklessly hailed as 'the most coveted prize in screen-acting in the country today': the role of Orlando opposite Elisabeth Bergner's Rosalind in the film of *As You Like It*. He remained highly sceptical about Shakespeare's suitability for screen treatment, and he still regarded himself as a stage actor at heart and the cinema as being artistically unattractive. Yet it required a fanatical conviction for anyone to refuse this particular offer: a then colossal salary of

£600 a week. Also, he said, he welcomed the chance of playing in any medium with Miss Bergner.

'I have always wanted to play Shakespeare decently. Not with genius—God forbid—just decently and intelligently. I had hoped to do it with Romeo—no, good heavens, not a screen Romeo, but in the theatre. Perhaps I did. I don't know. Anyhow, I don't believe I could have been nearly as rotten, or half as good, as the critics made out. In the meantime I hope I can do something with Orlando—something reasonably intelligent. No one can play with Bergner without learning something from her.'

As You Like It, committing him to filming for thirteen weeks by day while playing Mercutio on stage every evening, kept Olivier busier than ever before. At the start, he was encouraged by assurances from Paul Czinner, the producer, director and husband of Miss Bergner, that Shakespeare would not be mutilated. Sir James Barrie, no less, had made a screen treatment involving only a few discreet cuts. But many more changes emerged in its making. In order for the story to be appreciated, every word had to be followed; and yet to exploit the advantage of the screen, more action and movement had to be introduced. Marrying these two needs was where attempts to film Shakespeare had consistently failed. *As You Like It* was no exception.

Characteristically Olivier trained with two professional all-in wrestlers to prepare for his wrestling match as Orlando, but no amount of realism and dramatic action could veil the fact that the play was awkwardly ill-suited to the screen. After only a few days of shooting he recognized his mistake in accepting the part. As for the incentive of working with Bergner, that quickly evaporated since they scarcely ever met. She usually chose to start work in the afternoon, the time when Olivier, on the set since shortly after dawn, was eager to get away and rest briefly before playing Mercutio. Czinner, unperturbed, was quite content to shoot close-ups of Orlando's reaction to words spoken by a Rosalind who wasn't there.

At the New in the evenings Gielgud listened with interest and scepticism to Olivier's daily experiences on the film set. The previous year Gielgud had been appalled by the butchering of verse in Max Reinhart's lavish production of *A Midsummer Night's Dream*, now best remembered for its extraordinary cast—James Cagney, Mickey Rooney, Joe E. Brown, Victor Jory, Dick Powell, Olivia de Havilland and Anita Louise. He clung firmly to the opinion that Shakespeare could not satis-factorily be presented on the screen, a view strengthened by the failure of so many earlier attempts, including the 1929 Fair-banks–Pickford version of *The Taming of the Shrew* that had the unforgettable credit line: 'additional dialogue by Sam Taylor'. His attitude was not to be changed by the Shearer–Olivier *As You Like It*, nor the following year by a dreadful *Romeo and Juliet*, with Leslie Howard and Norma Shearer, which Gielgud endured for ten minutes before fleeing from the cinema.

As You Like It received extremely mixed notices. So did Olivier. Nevertheless, the making of this picture was a valuable experience for him. He learned much from Czinner's work about the pitfalls to be avoided in filming Shakespeare, and he came away with his own theories of how such a film might be im-proved.

And yet, like Gielgud, who was to turn down Hollywood offers to film *Hamlet*, he still could not shake off the opinion that Shakespeare on celluloid was really something better left un-tried.

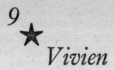

9

Shortly before Christmas of 1934, when Olivier was revelling in his newly won matinée idol status as the dashingly eccentric Tony Cavendish of *Theatre Royal*, his performance was watched intently by a dark-haired, elfin-faced beauty, just twenty-one years old. She had a kittenish quality and looked—and indeed felt—much too young to be the mother of a one-year-old daughter.

Apparently she was impressed by rather more than Olivier's acting and athleticism. For she turned to a girl friend sitting beside her and said in an extraordinary matter-of-fact tone, 'That's the man I am going to marry.'

'Don't be ridiculous,' her friend said. 'You're both married already.'

The girl smiled, a hint of devilment in her wide-set, blue-green eyes. 'It doesn't matter. I'll still marry him one day.'

At this time the sum total of Vivian Hartley's professional achievement was the delivery of just one line ('If you are not made headmistress, I shan't come back next term') in a Gainsborough movie called *Things Are Looking Up*, starring Cicely Courtneidge and unusual for the brief appearance on film of tennis champion Suzanne Lenglen. Vivian had looked very convincing as a schoolgirl in gymslip and broad-brimmed straw hat. She had wrung the maximum possible emotion from her single line. But that was several months ago. Professionally she had done nothing before or since.

Yet, within six months of seeing Olivier in *Theatre Royal*, this unknown untried actress would be a West End star.

She had been born in India, soon after sundown on November 5, 1913, in a bungalow on a hillside overlooking Darjeeling, within sight of the snow-capped peaks of the Himalayas. Her mother was an Irish Catholic, married two years to Ernest Hartley, a prosperous, Calcutta-based exchange broker who was also an enthusiastic amateur actor, reputedly of outstanding ability. Vivian had been encouraged to play in children's concerts from the age of three and a half, and she revealed a passion for acting as a seven-year-old school boarder at the Convent of the Sacred Heart at Roehampton, South London. Her first part in a school play was as Fairy Mustardseed in *A Midsummer Night's Dream*. She then told another girl that she was positively decided on becoming an actress when she grew up. The other girl, two years older, had failed to keep her part in the play. She professed a higher ambition. 'I want to fly when I leave school. I'd like to be a pilot.' Her name was Maureen O'Sullivan. Ten years later she was spotted by a talent scout and taken to Hollywood, where, without dramatic training, she won international stardom as Tarzan's Jane.

At thirteen, Vivian left Roehampton to join her parents on the Grand Tour of Europe. Mr. Hartley had made his fortune while still relatively young and fully intended to profit from his early retirement. For years they travelled to the fashionable tourist centres—Biarritz, Paris, Dinard, Cannes, San Remo, Salzburg, Zurich, Kitzbühel—and after an unusually varied education Vivian emerged from a finishing school in the Bavarian Alps as a highly cultured and sophisticated young lady: eighteen years old, equipped with all the social graces, well versed in the arts in general, fluent in German and so perfect in French that she would later be able to dub her own movies.

In the spring of 1932 stage-struck Vivian was enrolled at the Royal Academy of Dramatic Art. It was where she wanted to be and, judging by the promise she revealed, where she rightly belonged. But after two terms she disappointed the principal, Sir Kenneth Barnes, with the news that she was leaving to get married. Her fiancé was a young barrister named Leigh Holman and she had met him one year before, at Christmas, at the South Devon Hunt Ball held on Torquay Pier.

For any woman content to play a wifely role (something Vivian by her very nature could never be) it was casting of an eminently attractive kind. After honeymooning in Kitzbühel, they set up home in a small but stylish London apartment. Vivian had everything she needed and more: a housekeeper, numerous friends, a full social life, a special allowance from her

husband of £200 a year for clothes and accessories. Yet it would
never be enough. The excitement and pace of those years gone
by, continually introducing her to new places and faces, had
prepared her for everything but leisurely living and domestic
routine. She was young and high-spirited and imaginative and
with an artistic flair that cried out for some outlet for expression. The immediate solution was simple. She returned to
RADA. But within a few months she was pregnant; she could
complete only one more term at drama school.

The baby, expected on or about Vivian's twentieth birthday,
arrived one month premature, on October 12, 1933. 'Had a
baby—a girl' was all that the young mother noted in her diary.
To a friend visiting her in the nursing home she confided that it
had been 'a messy business' and one she wouldn't want to go
through again. The girl, named Suzanne, was to be her only
child. The Hartleys now moved into a charming Queen Anne
house in Little Stanhope Street near Shepherd's Market in
Mayfair. Vivian adored it and rejoiced in the fact that Lynn
Fontanne had once lived there. Again she seemingly had everything—a nurse now in addition to the maid, and plenty to occupy
her as she planned interior designs and shopped around for
antiques. Indeed, for nine months she was completely content
with her nest-building role. But it could not last. She was
essentially a young woman who thrived on excitement, adventure and challenge.

The first marital crisis came in August 1934. The Holmans
were on a yachting holiday in the Baltic when Vivian received a
cable saying that she *might* be wanted for a film starting on the
12th, only a few days away. The part, she knew, would be no
more than a walk-on, but at least it was the beginning that she
hungered for. On the other hand, it scarcely justified ruining a
holiday planned so carefully and elaborately, and at no mean
expense. Leigh Holman found it extraordinary that she should
contemplate even for a moment the idea of abandoning their
holiday, not yet half complete, for the sake of the vague possibility of crowd work on a film at a paltry guinea a day. He had no
intention of returning home when the yachting tour was going
so well. And that decided it for Vivian. Partly out of stubborn
pride, partly with a feeling that this was the moment of truth in
her often-declared ambition to become a professional actress,
she quit the yacht in Copenhagen. Leigh sailed on without her.

Her decision seemed all the more like an idiotic impulse when her husband arrived home at the end of the month and she had to confess that her premature return had been for nothing. Shooting on the film had been delayed by bad weather. In fact, while he was sailing on round the Baltic, she had spent the rest of their holiday staying in Sussex with their friend Clare Sheridan. But Vivian's embarrassment and feeling of guilt only served to harden her determination. In September she worked as an extra in crowd scenes in *Things are Looking Up*, and because she made such an attractive schoolgirl she was brought to the forefront of the action and given one line to speak. That line automatically raised her wage from one guinea to thirty shillings a day and qualified her to be chauffeured home every night.

Still, no one else took her ambition seriously. She was seemingly just one more of the many young socialites and ex-debutantes who amused themselves by flirting on the fringes of show business. Then, shortly before seeing Olivier in *Theatre Royal*, her career was suddenly accelerated by a young theatrical agent named John Gliddon. He was an ex-actor and journalist and and he had been telling actress Beryl Samson that he wanted to introduce something of the Hollywood star-building system to Britain, that he was eager to find unknown girls of exceptional personality and beauty who might be groomed for the stage or screen. The actress recommended Vivian to him. They met one day in September in Gliddon's Regent Street office. She wore a large picture hat and a light summer frock, and he was enchanted by her on sight. On the bus journey home, she told Mrs. Samson that he had liked her but thought her maiden name too unappealing. They discussed alternatives—among them Gliddon's horrendous suggestion of April Morn—and before the journey was over they had agreed that she should use her husband's first name as a surname. She would be Vivian Leigh.*

Gliddon worked hard for his hoped-for percentage. For weeks he gave his protégée the full promotion treatment, introducing her to useful connections, escorting her to all the smart places and celebrity functions where a budding young actress might be seen to advantage. With her arresting and photogenic beauty

* Although Miss Leigh gave this account of how she acquired her stage name, Gliddon has credited Ivor Novello with first suggesting 'Vivien Leigh'.

it was inevitable that she would get work in the so-called 'quota-quickie' movies. She started as leading lady in *The Village Squire*, made at Elstree in one week and earning her five guineas a day. A month later she appeared in another dreadful 'quickie', *Gentlemen's Agreement*. It was moderately useful experience. But could she really act?

The real test came when David Horne, her leading man in the 'quickies', recommended her for the role of his young, flirtatious wife in the play *The Green Sash* being presented at the Q Theatre, South London. She had insufficient time to rehearse and she was dissatisfied with her own performance, but her playing of this lengthy, emotional role did establish her potential as a dramatic actress, and at Ealing Studios she was now cast as the heroine in a feature film, *Look Up and Laugh*, starring Gracie Fields and directed by Basil Dean. Like Olivier in *Beau Geste* five years before, she soon discovered how effectively Dean could play the sharp-tongued martinet. She had a brief love scene with John Loder and was exceptionally nervous. Dean, by his own admission, made insufficient allowance for her nervousness, and without cheerful encouragement from Gracie, her morale would have been shattered.

Vivian, however, had one reason to be grateful to Dean. He decided not to take up the option on her contract. If he had done so, she could have been condemned to appearing in mediocre Ealing comedies for the next five years. Instead, she was free to soar far higher.

Miss Leigh's meteoric advance is now part of theatrical legend—a Cinderella story familiar enough in the myth-making realms of Hollywood but almost without equal in the history of the London stage. Once in a generation an undiscovered girl with an exceptional singing voice may leap to overnight stardom in a musical, but it is quite another matter for an unknown straight actress, devoid of stage experience in lesser parts, to achieve instant fame in a play. Miss Leigh did the impossible. After one night in what was only the second stage role of her professional career, she emerged as the 'golden girl' of the English theatre, massively publicized, sought after by both British and Hollywood film studios.

Of course, luck played its part. It just happened that theatrical manager Sydney Carroll was casting a new West End play called *The Mask of Virtue* at a time when not one of the actresses approached—Peggy Ashcroft, Anna Neagle, Jane Baxter, Diana Churchill—was available for the important role of Henriette Duquesnoy, a French street girl masquerading as a sweet young virgin. Largely because she *looked* perfect for the part, Carroll took a chance on Vivian.

'I didn't know a thing,' she later recalled. 'And every day during the three-week rehearsal they nearly fired me because I was so awful. I remember someone saying at the Ivy Restaurant, "She'll have to go—she is terrible." I was lucky enough to wear a lovely pink dress, a lovely black dress and a wonderful night-dress for the part. But I didn't know what to do . . . Someone in the play had the line to say to me, "I shall make many demands on you," and I said, "Not more than the gentlemen, I'm sure," and it brought the house down and I never knew why. I was that much of an ass. I suppose, though, I must have had some sort of timing to get the laugh.'[1]

Miss Leigh had timing and much more. She made that first night—May 15, 1935, at the Ambassadors—a night all her own with a performance that was totally captivating. Her voice was perhaps too soft, but something magical and extraordinary came across the footlights, more than just beauty and charm and grace, that something extra that has always defied precise definition. Star quality.

Carroll had recognized it already, for he advised Alexander Korda to attend that first night. And he did something more; he suggested that she change the spelling of her first name to the more feminine Vivien. In this way Vivien Leigh, actress and star, were born as one. She went into *The Mask of Virtue* as a £10 a week 'newcomer'. The next morning she was the most publicized young actress in Britain. Hollywood wanted her. But Korda won with his bid—a five-year contract, requiring her to make only two films a year and allowing her six months' freedom in every twelve to appear on stage. The London evening papers reported it as a £50,000 contract and (thanks to the publicity-conscious Carroll) her age was generally given as nineteen.

During the run of *The Mask of Virtue* Vivien and Larry met for the first time. John Buckmaster, Gladys Cooper's son, took her to dinner at the Savoy. He observed Olivier with his wife at a near-by table, and after pointing them out he remarked, 'What an odd little thing Larry looks without his moustache.' Vivien found his comment strangely irritating. 'I was very indignant and I said rather pompously that he didn't look funny at all. Then Larry came over as we were leaving and he invited me to join a party at the weekend. I said that he presumably meant the two of us—my husband as well—and so we went and we played football, and I remember Larry roaring around one minute and then unaccountably falling fast asleep under the piano the next.'²

It was not an especially romantic beginning. The introductions had been made very casually when they were in the Savoy Grill Room, waiting for taxis to be called. The weekend party, held at a house leased by the Oliviers at Burchett's Green, near Maidenhead, gave them no opportunity to become well acquainted. But the mutual attraction was there, and sooner or later, professionally or socially, their paths were sure to cross since they were both Korda contract stars and shared so many friends in the theatre.

Olivier and Miss Leigh almost met again in January 1936. He was then playing Romeo at the New. Vivien, now finished with *The Mask of Virtue* and awaiting Korda's call, went to that theatre to audition for Gielgud and Byam Shaw, who were preparing to direct a production of *Richard II* on behalf of the Oxford University Dramatic Society. While Olivier was in his dressing room, unaware of her presence, she was on stage reading and winning the small part of the Queen. Four months later, in a different theatre, they saw one another across the footlights. Ivor Novello had taken Vivien to the Lyric to see a matinée performance of J. B. Priestley's new play *Bees on the Boat-deck*, which was being presented by a new partnership comprising Olivier, Richardson and the author. Olivier had no difficulty in spotting her up in a box. The theatre was almost deserted.

This play's failure was a severe disappointment to Olivier. In rehearsals he had thrown himself into his part with familiar zest, promptly injuring his fingers in sliding down a rope on to the 'boat-deck'. But the play failed to draw the public and the critical reaction was curiously mixed. Indeed, one might have thought that leading critics Agate and Brown had seen entirely different first nights. Ivor Brown thought it wonderfully entertaining: 'I have not seen Laurence Olivier better than in the raillery and the comic invention of Second Officer.' Agate judged it a dreadful play, poorly played: 'Mr. Olivier is even less happy, for his second officer is no second officer at all, but a young gentleman from behind the counter of a bank or stores.' It was time for Olivier to recoup his losses by making his second film for Korda.

In May, a few days after seeing *Bees on the Boat-deck*, Vivien had met Larry for lunch, their first time alone together. Now, in August, Korda brought them together for three and a half months, cast as the young lovers in *Fire Over England*, a spectacular romantic drama of Queen Elizabeth and the Spanish Armada and built around two fictitious characters, Cynthia, the Queen's lady-in-waiting, and Michael Ingoldsby, a dashing young naval officer who escapes from the Spanish after seeing his father burned at the stake.

At Denham Studios they initially met in the corridor outside the self-service canteen. She remarked how pleased she was that they were working together. He grinned. 'We shall probably end up fighting,' he said. 'People always get sick of each other when making a film.'

A few weeks later Olivier was celebrating the birth of a son. When he first knew that Jill Esmond was expecting a baby he had told her, 'He will be a son and his name will be Tarquin.'* And Simon Tarquin he was now christened. Olivier had wanted a boy. It so happened, however, that the starting of a family coincided with the first occasion that he and Vivien were working together. The weeks of filming ran into months and all the time they became increasingly aware of a rare and undeniable affinity between them—one that grew rather than faded with familiarity. Their love scenes were played with a noted naturalness, and off the set it became obvious to everyone around them that they were twin souls, suddenly and inexorably and fatefully drawn together. Lunch was traditionally a communal affair at Denham, the cast assembling around large tables. But the co-stars began to separate from the crowd and sit alone, totally immersed in each other's company; also in the long rest periods between shots they spent more and more time together.

Then, as now, it was the familiar hazard so peculiar to show business marriages. Years later Miss Leigh explained to Paul Tabori, Korda's biographer: 'It was during the making of *Fire Over England* that Larry and I met—and fell in love. Alex

---

* The name Tarquin appears in *Macbeth* which Olivier was studying at this time.

was like a father to us—we went to him with every little problem we had. We usually left convinced that he had solved it—or that we'd got our way, even when we hadn't. Well, one day we went to him and said, "Alex, we must tell you our great secret— we're in love and we're going to get married." He smiled and said: "Don't be silly—everybody knows that. I've known it for weeks and weeks." '³

In building his movie empire Korda had been signing up talent faster than he could hope to make use of it, but in the great majority of cases he eventually profited by his investments and now, more than a year after putting Olivier and Miss Leigh under contract, he was ready to promote them into international stars. *Fire Over England* was the first screen opportunity he had given Vivien. Olivier had already made *Moscow Nights* for Korda, but it was not a spectacular vehicle and he was still far less prominent in films than two other British actors working for Korda at Denham at this time. Charles Laughton, son of a Scarborough hotel owner, a one-time kitchen-hand at Claridges, intended for a career in catering, was Korda's most consistently successful star, now following his bawling, unfeeling Captain Bligh with his quietly sensitive Rembrandt. Then there was Robert Donat, making a delayed start in *Knight Without Armour* with Marlene Dietrich after asthmatic trouble had confined him to a nursing home. He was still plagued with asthma, needing to suck cocaine lozenges to stave off coughing fits, and if his illness proved obdurate it was planned that Olivier should take over his role. But Donat kept going and soon became the highest paid film star in Britain.

Olivier had been much less fortunate in his screen opportunities. He remained sceptical about the movie-making business in general, and at Denham he was disappointed to see that *Fire Over England,* scripted by Clemence Dane, bore no resemblance to A. E. W. Mason's best-seller on which it was supposedly based. Only the title and the name of its heroine remained the same. Yet he recognized that it had more potential than most of his previous movies: a distinguished producer in the German Erich Pommer and a highly professional cast that included Flora Robson, Leslie Banks, Raymond Massey, Robert Newton, Lyn Harding and veteran Morton Selten. Playing the Spanish Ambassador was Henry Oscar, the drama teacher who had perceived no spark of brilliance in Olivier as a pupil.

When filming began, American director William K. Howard
was amazed to find that both Miss Robson and Oscar were word
perfect after the first rehearsal. So they went direct into shooting,
completing in one and a half days a sequence scheduled to take at
least a week. But the film still took an inordinate amount of time
to complete, largely because it involved so much action and so
many elaborate sets for the court sessions at Westminster and
the burning of the Armada. Olivier had the most athletic part,
and as usual he insisted on doing his own stunts, even when he
had to leap on board a galleon (built in a field at Denham),
throw a firebrand along the petrol-soaked deck and then dive
head-first overboard (into a concealed net) as the ship burst into
flames. After each 'take' the fire was extinguished by hoses.
But on one occasion they failed, the water only extending the
flames as it ran along the deck with the burning petrol on top.
In his haste to escape burning, Olivier slipped as he leaped on the
bulwarks and crashed heavily into the net. Pommer feared that
he might have broken his neck and afterwards ordered that he
should have a stand-in.

Olivier protested. In his support Miss Robson argued, 'He
would feel a fraud to be praised for a scene he did not do himself.'

'All film acting is a fraud,' replied the producer.[4]

Fire Over England was a huge success in Britain. Lionel
Collier, the *Picturegoer* critic, enthused: 'This picture stands
head and shoulders above any historical drama yet made in this
country and it has had few rivals from other countries . . . As the
young lovers Vivien Leigh and Laurence Olivier are exceedingly
good. Their love scenes have a naturalness and tenderness that
is particularly attractive.' Generally Olivier's notices were excellent, though it should be stressed that the film was first and
foremost Miss Robson's special triumph. She dominated as a
Virgin Queen that even won the historians' approval.

On the Continent, too, the film was well received, winning a
French gold medal award and, rather curiously, the fanatical
approval of one Adolf Hitler. A copy of the picture was seized in
Prague when the Germans invaded Czechoslovakia and several
prominent Englishmen who visited Hitler before the war came
back with the news that the Fuehrer was running *Fire Over
England* again and again and praising it lavishly.[5]

In the United States it did not have the same impact, its highest honour being a *Life* nomination as 'movie of the week'. In the hope that it might repeat the success of *The Private Life of Henry VIII*, it was the first British film production to be given a full-scale Hollywood send-off, including a preview at Grauman's Chinese Theatre; this amused American critics no end since 'the great British movie' had Hungarian backers, a German producer, an American director, a Chinese director of photography, a Russian art director, another Russian collaborating on the screenplay and a Frenchman designing the costumes. Its box-office appeal in America was limited by its lack of marquee names, the best-known member of the cast being Massey, who had only a powerful cameo part as Philip of Spain. Moreover, American audiences were not prepared to see Olivier, in what was otherwise an Errol Flynnish role, weeping hysterically over the ashes of his father at the foot of the stake. This scene was 'razzed' every time it came on the screen in the United States and was finally cut out altogether.

Nevertheless, both Olivier and Miss Leigh had reason to be well pleased with *Fire Over England*. Vivien—like such Korda newcomers as Merle Oberon and Binnie Barnes—made an immediate and favourable impression in Hollywood, and the film advanced Olivier's screen reputation more than any of his ten pictures that had gone before. Remarkably, however, while they were destined to form the most famous stage partnership of their time, they would be disappointed at having only two more opportunities of filming together.

10

★

Fame at the Old Vic

'Vacant—the position of screen's classic romantic actor No. 1'

The announcement appeared in the British press following the arrival in England of Hollywood director Edward H. Griffith in the fall of 1936. He had provoked debate by telling reporters: 'There has been no real successor to John Barrymore as the screen's leading classic romantic actor. Now the place is there to be claimed.' And who did he think was the likeliest claimant? Fredric March was one possibility, he said. Leslie Howard another. 'But my own tip is Laurence Olivier. He had a bad break in Hollywood but his return ticket is ready whenever he wants it. They think a lot of him in the United States . . . That boy's got the most to catch up, but he looks to me the safest bet of the three.'

Olivier was now twenty-nine years old, at a point in his career where three courses seemed open to him. He might consolidate his reputation as a leading man on the West End stage, earning in excess of £100 a week. He could concentrate more profitably on his film career, perhaps achieving the kind of superstar status that Griffith judged within his reach. Or, as appeared most probable, he could continue to combine the roles of matinée idol and Korda contract star. What seemed absurdly improbable was that this young man, at such an opportune juncture, would elect to face the severest challenge of his career for the lowest financial return. Yet such was Olivier's fateful choice. For a mere pittance of £20 a week for fourteen months he turned his back on the bright lights of Shaftesbury Avenue and crossed the Thames to appear at Lilian Baylis's Old Vic off the grey and dingy Waterloo Road. It was the most daring gamble of his life, and one that had the most profound influence on his professional image.

★

The Old Vic, a solitary playhouse on London's unfashionable south side, was so named because it was the survival of the Old Victoria Theatre (originally the Royal Coburg), notorious in the early nineteenth century as the haunt of prostitutes, pickpockets and gin-soaks, and the roughest clientele in town. It was on passing the Victoria's doors—jostled by 'a herd of ragged boys, vomiting forth slang, filth and blasphemy'—that Charles Kingsley was inspired to write in *Alton Locke* his protest against 'these licensed pits of darkness, traps of temptation, profligacy and ruin'. Half a century later, in 1880, licence ended abruptly as the theatre's lease was taken over by Miss Emma Cons, a dedicated social worker and passionate servant of God and Temperance. She aimed to advance the good fight against bars and brothels by offering low-cost 'purified entertainment' fit for all the family, and so a squalid flea pit became the respectable Royal Victorian Coffee Music Hall, with a clean bill of fare that included wholesome vaudeville acts, extracts from opera, concerts, Sunday afternoon religious talks and 'penny lectures' by public-spirited men of distinction. Its principles were high, its commercial aspect inevitably bleak. And then, at the turn of the century, the extraordinary Lilian Baylis arrived to take over the management from her elderly aunt.

By the time Olivier came to the Old Vic, Miss Baylis was a legendary character in London—the dynamic missionary of the arts who had successfully brought culture to the masses as the initiator (in 1914) of the Old Vic Shakespeare Company, and more recently as the founder of Sadler's Wells, with its opera and ballet. Critic Ivor Brown described her as an 'odd little Empressario, with her fire of faith, her queer face, her spluttering speeches, and her vanities of cap and gown'. More than that, she had a 'style' unique in the realm of theatrical management. She prayed daily for guidance, taking problems both professional and personal to God; she addressed the highest and the lowest in a homely, down-to-earth manner ('Hurry home, dear, you've got to give the King his tea,' she told Queen Mary after a matinée); she cooked meals on a gas-ring in the prompt corner (the smell of frying kippers or sausages regularly engulfed the stalls on matinée days); she watched performances from her own box in which she had a kitchen table hidden behind a red curtain so that she could carry on her paper work; she stressed to job applicants the importance of rectitude in her company ('Are you pure, dear boy? I'm not narrow-minded but I won't have anything going on in the wings'); she resisted anything new that cost money—from electric lighting to a higher wage scale for actors; and she argued that critics should pay their own way ('Why should we give the bounders free seats and then let them say scurrilous things about us?'). Above all, she was renowned for her thrift: rigid in her economy, ruthless in her bargaining, endlessly begging and bullying to obtain more money wherever she could. She wanted nothing for herself and everything for her theatre. She wanted to raise artistic standards but one thing she would never raise was admission prices. The Old Vic was nothing if not 'The People's Theatre'—all the people's. At the same time, standards had risen so high that it no longer drew its audiences predominantly from the slum quarters.

Olivier knew all the popular stories about the God-fearing Miss Baylis, stories illustrating her wrath, her simplicity, her dedication and her eccentricity; and he was not disappointed on meeting her for the first time. In her office of purposeful disorder he confronted a grey-haired woman of sixty-two, stout, bespectacled, with a slight squint in one eye and a mouth partly paralysed on one side. Her accent, commonly mistaken for cockney, was, as he discovered, really South African; before joining her aunt, Miss Baylis had been teaching music and dancing in Johannesburg. Nor was she quite the 'old dragon' that some stories might have led him to suppose. She came to treat him with the loving firmness of a Victorian mother-figure, and later, when he was playing a full-length Hamlet twice on matinée days, she actually tucked him up in an old eiderdown to ensure that her star player was resting warm between performances. On matters of temperance and money, however, he found that nothing had been exaggerated. Once, rather foolishly, he enthusiastically explained to her a splendid way to raise more money—by opening a theatre bar. She looked aghast. 'My dear boy, don't you realize that if it hadn't been for drunken men beating their wives, we'd never have got this place.'

Basically, two groups of actors indulged in 'financial slumming' down the Waterloo Road. There were the ambitious young professionals with nothing to lose and all to gain in experience: innumerable names of the future such as Alec Guinness, James Mason, Glynis Johns and Anthony Quayle, the latest and most notable recruit in this category being Michael Redgrave, a schoolmaster only two years before and now stepping direct into the Old Vic's top salary bracket. The second group comprised actors and actresses firmly established as skilled and dedicated classical players—old stalwarts in supporting roles and a handful of towering talents such as Gielgud, Edith Evans and Sybil Thorndike. Olivier belonged to neither group.

He was, of course, something of a star in his own right, but in the modern tradition, and lacking a reputation so gilt-edged that it could not be debased by a season of failure at the 'Vic'. He might profit immeasurably in experience and prestige; he also had a very great deal to lose. It was proposed that he should tackle a variety of great Shakespearean roles, commencing with *Hamlet* performed in its four-and-a-quarter-hour entirety. But could he do it? Would he suffer by comparison with so many formidable talents around him? Understandably, after all the savage criticism of his verse-speaking, he was full of nagging doubts. Yet a masochistic streak in his nature, compounded of ambition, stubbornness and pride, demanded that he should at least try.

Charles Laughton had displayed equal, if not greater, courage in going direct from Hollywood to the Old Vic in 1933—possibly greater because he had never played in a major Shakespearean production before and was less well-equipped with his husky, sibilant voice to handle the verse. But there was a difference. The opening of Laughton's nine-month season had coincided with the unveiling of his monumental, Oscar-winning performance in *The Private Life of Henry VIII*. That one movie was the rock on which Korda's empire was built, arguably the most significant single event in the development of the British film industry. And from that moment on, whatever his fate at the Old Vic, Laughton was always assured of star status and security in the movies. Olivier did not have such a spectacular screen triumph behind him. His greatness as an actor was more opinion than established fact. He was going to the Old Vic as a theatrical thoroughbred screaming with potential that had yet to be fulfilled in a classic event.

It was in the early days of filming *Fire Over England*, during a weekend at his mother-in-law's country home, that Olivier was approached by producer Tyrone Guthrie with the idea of joining the Old Vic. He consulted all his close friends, and the clincher came when he put through a transatlantic telephone call (a rare

extravagance in those days) to seek the advice of Richardson in
New York. The reply was: 'Very good idea, dear boy'—nothing
more. Beyond this, Olivier has since stated that he would never
have gone to the Old Vic if Gielgud had not done so first and
made that ill-sited theatre so fashionable. Indeed, he said that
but for Gielgud he might never have become a classical actor at
all, choosing instead to devote himself to plays by modern
writers.

In October the Oliviers left for a three-week holiday in
Capri. He took with him a copy of *Hamlet* plus books of analysis
and criticism of the play. Past comments on his verse-speaking
had made him sharply aware of the need to strive for much more
than a conventional, finely spoken portrayal. He could never
compete on strictly lyrical terms with the pure rendering of an
Ainley or a Gielgud. He needed something different, a way to
play his own strengths, and he knew full well that it is imperative for the actor to bring something of himself to his particular
role if he is to achieve convincing power.

Guthrie, keen to have an unconventional interpretation, had
called Olivier's attention to one book in particular, *Essays in
Applied Psycho-Analysis* by Dr. Ernest Jones, President of the
International Psycho-Analytical Association. This work, published in Vienna in 1923, presented a Freudian approach to
examining Hamlet's make-up and was most notably concerned
with the author's theory that Hamlet's delay in avenging his
father's murder most foul could be attributed to an Oedipus complex, i.e., the prince hesitated to kill Claudius because he was
confused about his real motives, whether he was motivated by
hatred arising from love of his father or by jealousy and self-
interest arising from an unnatural love for his mother. Olivier
found the notion totally appealing, infinitely more persuasive
than the obvious presumption that Hamlet delayed for want of
proof of his uncle's guilt. It provided an attractive guide-line for
his overall approach to the part. Conveniently, too, for an actor
of his pronounced athletic leanings, it did not preclude a playing
of the traditionally gloomy Dane as a man of action. Within
reasonable limits, he could still indulge his penchant for acrobatics and swordplay. Shackled by subconscious self-guilt, it
was only in the killing of Claudius that this prince lacked decisiveness.

During the holiday prior to his first Hamlet, Olivier and Jill

Esmond were joined for two days in Capri by Vivien Leigh and Oswald Frewen, a forty-nine-year-old Royal Navy Commander and, as the son of Clara Jerome and Moreton ('Mortal Ruin') Frewen, a first cousin of Sir Winston Churchill. Frewen and his sister Clara Sheridan had been close friends of Leigh Holman since long before his marriage, and he was now escorting Vivien while her husband was tied to business commitments in London. Together they had toured Sicily, then they stopped over in Capri to make up a spirited foursome with the Oliviers. It was a lively reunion enjoyed by all, but the abrupt parting only served to make Vivien and Larry more painfully conscious of how much they hated to go separate ways. Back in London, however, they would often meet. And she was to see his Hamlet no fewer than fourteen times.

January 5, 1937, marked the most terrifying first night of Olivier's career. It was not simply the ordeal of playing for the first time the most testing role he had yet known. It was the ordeal, because of limited rehearsal time, of playing *Hamlet* in its entirety without ever having a complete run-through of the part. That was handicap enough for any actor. And Olivier faced another. He needed to overcome the prejudice and positive hostility of some of the theatre's older supporters who objected to his selection as leading man for the new season. They saw him as something of a carpetbagger, a stage and screen 'pop' star picking plums deserved by long-serving and more obviously dedicated classical actors.

With so much weighed against him, his first of all nights at the Old Vic must be counted as an astonishing success. A few years earlier, youthful eagerness to make an impression would surely have stampeded him into the trap of playing loud and strong too soon. But he was rich in theatrical cunning now. He opened in a low key, bringing the audience to him rather than blustering out to grab them from the start. And the soft-pitched beginning was wholly effective. It disarmed and intrigued, and it spared the house any jarring ice-cold shock as he gradually unfolded a dark and urgent and virile Hamlet far removed from Gielgud's intellectual prince of elegance, sadness and sensitivity; a Hamlet with a cat-like agility of body as well of mind, who would accompany 'Why, let the striken deer go weep' with a prodigious leap from the raised throne into the mimic stage below and then down to the footlights. Inevitably, his performance could not satisfy the die-hard traditionalists. The interpretation was 'too dashing', the verse-speaking not sufficiently melodious; and the notion of an Oedipus complex went unrealized by the vast majority. But for all the fault-finding, this Old Vic audience had the wit to recognize an actor of rare courage, originality and virtuosity. The blazing sincerity of his performance was the winning factor and the prolonged applause at the final curtain told of his hard-won acceptance by the members of this 'private club'.

How high does Olivier's 1936 Hamlet rate? The dreaded, often self-contradicting Agate responded to the big occasion with a masterpiece of confusion—some 2,225 words, to be precise, and culminating with the prize remark: 'Lots could be said about Mr. Tyrone Guthrie's highly imaginative production, but not, I think, at the fag-end of an article.' Agate, quite simply, said everything and said nothing. Ingredient by ingredient, he picked at the *pièce de résistance* of the Old Vic season but conveyed scant appreciation of its entertainment value as a whole. He it was who made the oft-quoted statement: 'Mr. Olivier does not speak poetry badly. He does not speak it at all.' But in the same review he praised the 'remarkable cogency' of the soliloquies. Again, as often recalled, Agate complained of a Hamlet 'entirely without melancholy' and acidly described it as 'the best performance of Hotspur that the present generation has seen'. Not so readily recalled is that he also judged that this Hamlet excelled all others of recent years in 'its pulsating vitality and excitement'.

It is true that most critics shared Agate's disapproval of Olivier's handling of the verse. But some of the notices were staggeringly good. The London *Daily Express* said that with this one performance Olivier had leaped to star class as a dramatic actor. W. A. Darlington of the *Daily Telegraph* said that, verse-speaking apart, he did not see how the performance could have been bettered.

Amid all the conflicting opinions of Olivier's first Hamlet, it is perhaps interesting to note what his fellow actors and his director thought of the performance. Alec Guinness, who understudied him, was 'outraged at the gymnastic leaps and falls required by his example. I never liked the performance or Guthrie's production', he said, 'but it was huge box-office. Looking back at it with wiser hindsight I realize it was necessary for Olivier to do what he did—and it laid the foundations for his becoming a truly great actor.'[1]

Michael Redgrave (Laertes): 'The truth is that I thought he was a bad Hamlet—too assertive and too resolute. He lacked the self-doubting subtleties the part demands. Every actor, even one as gifted and versatile as Olivier, is limited in his range of parts by his own temperament and character. The very boldness of Larry's personality, his natural drive and his pragmatism make him unsuitable to play an introspective, wavering character like Hamlet.'[2]

And Guthrie: 'Offstage he was not notably handsome or striking, but with make-up he could achieve a flashing Italianate, rather saturnine, but fascinating appearance. The voice already had a marvellous ringing baritone brilliance at the top; he spoke with a beautiful and aristocratic accent, with keen intelligence and a strong sense of rhythm. He moved with cat-like agility. He had, if anything, too strong an instinct for the sort of theatrical effect which is striking and memorable. From the first moment of the first rehearsal it was evident that here was no ordinary actor—not everyone's cup of tea, no strong personality can be that; not necessarily well cast for Hamlet, but inevitably destined for the very top of the tree.'[3]

In box-office terms, this *Hamlet* was a smash hit. Night after night it packed the Old Vic in spite of its seven o'clock start, and it benefitted from the prolonged publicity given to its star. Olivier stayed in the news through the injuries he received in his quest for realism in the duel scene. During one rehearsal he had been cut slightly by Redgrave's rapier. In a matinée performance he was cut over the right eye, and a few days later he was caught bending to avoid a lunge and was struck over the head. Blood from the scalp wound ran down his face on to his tunic, yet he played out the remaining fifteen minutes and afterwards made light of it all.

For the Old Vic's production, in February, Olivier suggested *Twelfth Night* with himself as Sir Toby Belch. He saw it as an opportunity to demonstrate his versatility as an actor and his inventiveness with make-up. In both purposes he succeeded. This was the first role that gave him full scope for elaborate disguise. On came a beaky nose of putty, pouches under the eyes, an untidy walrus moustache; and when this corpulent, grotesque figure first swayed on stage, hiccoughed twice and fell down, the gallery gasped with surprise. He was, *The Times* said, 'now and then recognizable only by a gleam of teeth'.

At his suggestion, Jill Esmond joined the company to play Olivia, her first stage appearance since the birth of their son. Revue-star-impressionist Ivy St. Helier was Maria, her first Shakespearean part after a quarter of a century of taking off other people. And Jessica Tandy gave up the security of a West End success to appear. 'It was my first experience of playing with Larry,' she recalls. 'He had all the physical attributes of a romantic juvenile; yet there he was having the time of his life as Toby Belch. A hilarious, robust, inventive performance. I played Viola *and* Sebastian—God help me!—and the duel scene with Aguecheek (Alec Guinness), Toby Belch and Sebastian was a romp for audience and actors alike. My greatest difficulty was keeping a straight face when Larry insisted on poking Sebastian in the chest to see what kind of man this Sebastian was.'

It was, in fact, too much of a romp. Some critics thought it overplayed and complained that Olivier's outrageous acrobatics —'a super-abundance of comical crawling, stumbling and staggering'—unbalanced the production The playing became less disciplined as weeks passed and the impression was given of an Olivier–Guinness duel for laughs. The latter has since denied this, stressing that Olivier was always in charge of the stage and helped him enormously with advice. Guthrie, however, judged that Guinness was the more amusing in 'a baddish, immature production of mine'.

Twelfth Night gave Olivier the light relief needed after the strain of a full-length Hamlet that, on matinée days, involved almost nine hours on stage within a ten-hour period. Now, in the spring of 1937, with the Coronation of King George VI being imminent, something more serious and stirringly patriotic was required, and *Henry V* was the obvious choice. Olivier intensely disliked the character of the soldier king and his glorification of war. So did Guthrie, and rebelliously they toyed with the idea of a version designed to hold the play's blatant jingoism to ridicule. Olivier's distaste for *Henry V* showed through in his performance. Critics noted a certain monotony of speech and coldness of mien. He made the king a calculating, fairly magnetic figure, but he rushed some of the long speeches, exercised emotional restraint where none was needed, and in his underplaying could not give himself wholeheartedly to the kind of full-blooded, stirring patriotic roar—'God for Harry, England and Saint George!'—that later had such impact in his film version.

By all accounts he vastly improved in the ensuing weeks, partly through the encouragement of Richardson, who had earlier played the role. Richardson told him that, however much he disliked the character, the supreme majesty of the poetry was all that really mattered. 'You might say he was a cold bath king. You might say he was a scoutmaster. Yes, if you wanted to. But, of course, you must remember that he is the exultation of scoutmasters. Shakespeare does that to everybody. Without Shakespeare, Macbeth would be rather a common murderer, instead of which he's a great poet.' Shedding his cynicism Olivier found that the sheer, irresistible power of the poetry began to work its magic upon him, and once uninhibited by the facile heroics, he enthralled audiences with a truly regal English lion. Laughton visited him in his dressing room after one performance and said how profoundly he had been moved. 'Do you know why you're so good in this part?' he asked.

'No,' said Olivier. 'Please tell me.'

And Laughton, in grand Churchillian manner replied, 'You are England, that's all.'

Jessica Tandy played Katherine and was no less moved by the grandeur of his lion-king. 'I hardly ever missed going to the wings to watch Larry's soliloquy before the battle, *Upon the King!* How marvellously and powerfully he played it! Hardly speaking above a whisper but with what ease and depth! The audience held their breath. Fortunately we have his performance preserved in his own production of the film—but I shall never forget the "live" performance.'

Guthrie, too, was impressed. He judged this *Henry V* to be his best production to date. It broke all box-office records with its run of eight weeks instead of the usual four, and after the final curtain Miss Baylis came on stage to address the audience, whom she always called 'My people'. They anticipated some words of gratitude for their enthusiastic support, but they should have known better. Instead, she reprimanded them severely for having let their company down by not coming to see *The Witch of Edmonton*, which had flopped early in the season.

At the end of this season the Old Vic company was honoured

by an invitation to inaugurate an annual festival performance of *Hamlet* at Elsinore's Kronborg Castle in Denmark. Lilian Baylis and her producer were intrigued by the idea of presenting the tragedy where Shakespeare had set it, but besides the sheer mechanics of playing in an open courtyard they faced serious casting problems. Both Redgrave (Laertes) and Cherry Cottrell (Ophelia) were no longer available; more awkwardly, Olivier was due to begin filming *The First and the Last* with Vivien Leigh at Denham. The main obstacle was eventually cleared, thanks to Korda's agreement to interrupt shooting of the Olivier picture at the appropriate time. And a worthy replacement for Redgrave was found in Anthony Quayle. There was also a new king (John Abbott for Francis L. Sullivan) and a new Horatio (Leo Genn for Robert Newton). But who would play Ophelia? The answer was surprising. Miss Baylis invited a young actress of enchanting presence but precious little experience with Shakespeare: Vivien Leigh.

A certain mystery has been allowed to surround Miss Leigh's invitation to join the Old Vic. Olivier denied that it was at his suggestion—but then he certainly had no wish for her to imagine that she had been chosen as Ophelia because of anything more than her own talents. The *Hamlet* in Elsinore was the brainchild of Robert Jorgensen, a London-based Danish journalist and publicity man. He suggested it to his country's Tourist Board. Coincidentally, Jorgensen was also the publicist for *The Mark of Virtue*, Miss Leigh's vehicle to overnight stardom. Did he perhaps suggest her for the Old Vic production? No. His understanding was that Olivier had asked for her.

However it came about, the arrangement suited Olivier and Miss Leigh very well indeed. It meant that during their first three weeks of filming together he could help her prepare her Ophelia. He rehearsed her each day in the car they shared to and from Denham Studios. He was at hand to encourage her through the early rehearsals when Guthrie was critical of her stage mannerisms and of a small voice that he feared would be inaudible in an outdoor arena.

The Old Vic company left for Denmark in late May, and at the Renaissance-style castle of Kronborg, site of the fortress of Elsinore, the stage was set in a great stone-flagged courtyard for the first performance there by an English company since 1585. The 2,000 courtyard seats could have been sold many times over. Royalty, diplomats, and hordes of pressmen were attending. The visit received massive publicity and such co-operation that the hundred officer cadets quartered in the castle were put at Guthrie's disposal to use as extras as he willed. In just one respect the organizers had slipped up. They had neglected to close the castle to visitors. So the company found it best to conduct their week of rehearsals from midnight until six each morning. By day they could then enjoy boating and swimming after getting in a bare ration of sleep. Unfortunately, however, the nights were almost always wet. Scenes were played out in raincoats and beneath unbrellas, and steadily the weather worsened.

When John Abbott, as Claudius, came out into the cobbled courtyard bearing a brolly, he brought new feeling to his line: 'Is there not rain enough in the sweet heavens?' And on the eve of the opening the 'stage' was so fiercely lashed by wind and rain that a complete run-through was impossible. The tempest mounted, and by six o'clock on opening day all hope of an out-door performance had been washed away. Guthrie, Miss Baylis and Olivier held an emergency conference. Cancellation was unthinkable since a trainload of V.I.P.s had already left Copenhagen. They would have to switch the production to the ball-room of the Marienlyst Hotel, about one kilometre away.

At first it seemed a profitless gesture. The hotel had only a tiny cabaret stage; the seating was hopelessly inadequate, back-stage facilities non-existent. Yet everyone worked frantically to make a show possible, and no one thrived more on the challenge than Olivier. He responded with a sense of urgency bordering on relish, conducted a hurried rehearsal, improvised exists and entrances. The 'stage' was created by ringing off the dance floor with three-quarter circles of 870 basket chairs in a style that anticipated the term 'theatre-in-the-round'. It would have worked better if they had been able to make entrances by a double door at the head of a flight of steps, but permission for this was refused—because a pair of blue-tits were nesting in the architrave!

The whole operation was a miracle of improvisation and its success astonishing. While stage movements were sometimes badly confused, this problem was entirely excusable. Only the acting really mattered, and the sympathetic audience judged that to be of the highest quality. Ivor Brown of *The Times* rated it 'as good a performance of *Hamlet* as I have ever seen'. George Bishop of *The Daily Telegraph* described it as one of the most exciting evenings he could remember. 'In an odd sort of way this improvisation suited Laurence Olivier. The simplicity of the setting, the almost charade-like character of the performance, the strain and tension of the quick preparations, the uncertainty of what was going to happen next, the knowledge that he was the first English actor to play Hamlet in Denmark, the distinguished and expectant audience . . . all these things put this wiry and virile young actor on his mettle. There was electricity in the air and next morning he, Vivien Leigh and the rest of the company basked in the plaudits of the Danish press.'[4]

It was a triumph for everyone, including Miss Leigh, whose Ophelia had all the vocal power necessary in such a crowded and intimate 'theatre'. And the company repeated their triumph the following evening when clear skies allowed them to play in the castle courtyard as originally planned. At the time a greater success was barely imaginable. Yet two years later, on a calm evening in July 1939, Gielgud was to make his Elsinore bow with a production hailed by the Copenhagen press as 'The World's Best Hamlet'.

The visit to Elsinore coincided with Olivier's thirtieth birthday. It also brought him to a crisis point where he had to make the most difficult decision of his private life. Everyone in the Old Vic company was aware that he and Miss Leigh were ecstatically in love. And it was in Denmark—just one year after their first meeting—that they finally agreed that they could no longer live apart. What made it exceptionally painful for all concerned was the fact that neither of them was really unhappily married. Both had, and continued always to have, the utmost regard and respect for their partners. But in Vivien's case she and Leigh Holman were light years apart in temperament and belonged to two completely different worlds. She was a late-night creature, loving to socialize into the early hours; he worked by day and, by nature, could never fit easily into a social scene crowded with theatrical types who called each other 'darling', threw out four-letter words like confetti, and talked incessantly of show business or of themselves. Once Vivien became a star and found that she loved to live as a star, it was difficult to see how her marriage could possibly survive.

Following the triumph in Elsinore she and Olivier began to

live together. They were also working together and immediately returned to Denham Studios to complete the filming of *The First and the Last* in which they were again cast as lovers. The film plot concerned the brother of an eminent barrister who accidentally kills the husband of his mistress. When an innocent man is accused and remanded in custody for twenty-one days, the guilty one chooses to spend three weeks of high living with his girl friend before surrendering himself to the law. On their final day together, the lovers take a steamer trip to Southend and the murderer wrestles with his conscience and the temptation to keep his freedom. Much to Dean's chagrin, Korda insisted that this climactic sequence should be completed in a single day.

The pleasure steamer *Golden Eagle* was hired for the river trip from Tower Bridge down the Thames to Southend, and the outing was memorable for one curious incident that illustrates the extraordinary ambition and vision of Miss Leigh at this time. It has been recalled as follows by a first-hand witness, film critic C. A. Lejeune:

'From the moment we cast off it rained inexorably. There was nothing for anyone to do but wait for the weather to clear, watch the grey docks sliding by, read the newspapers, play gin rummy and talk. The talk inevitably came round to the film that MGM was planning to make of *Gone With the Wind*. No casting had yet been announced, but there were hot tips that Paulette Goddard, Bette Davis, Barbara Stanwyck, Miriam Hopkins and other celebrated stars were certainties for the Scarlett O'Hara role. Somebody turned to Olivier and said, "Larry, you'd be marvellous as Rhett Butler." He laughed it off, but the suggestion was not too preposterous; by this time he had an international reputation as an actor. Somebody else ventured that she saw Rhett Butler as Robert Taylor. Others saw him as Gary Cooper, Errol Flynn and Cary Grant. Discussion of the casting went on in a desultory fashion, until the new girl, Vivien Leigh, brought it to a sudden stop. She drew herself up on the rain-swept deck, all five-feet-nothing of her, pulled a coat snug round her shoulders and stunned us with the sybilline utterance: "Larry won't play Rhett Butler, but I shall play Scarlett O'Hara. Wait and see." ' [5]

For all her affected confidence, Miss Leigh seemed to be cherishing an impossible dream. In the summer of 1937 she was still relatively unknown in America. By the most generous reckoning her chances of becoming the screen Scarlett might have been rated a hundred to one against. And anyone catching a sneak preview of Miss Leigh's latest film with Olivier might have been forgiven for concluding that she had absolutely no chance at all. *The First and the Last*, scripted by Basil Dean and Graham Greene, disappointed all concerned. Korda thought it so bad that he had it shelved indefinitely. Not until its two stars had become international celebrities was it judged a commercial proposition. Then one year after its trade showing, it was released by Columbia under the new title of *Twenty-One Days*. To Dean's surprise it received some excellent notices in America which he felt were entirely undeserved. Olivier and Miss Leigh saw it for the first time in a New York cinema during the war. They walked out before it was half over.

On completion of *Twenty-One Days* the co-stars began their new life together with a holiday in Venice. Then they returned to separate film work in London. She was loaned to MGM for *A Yank at Oxford*, co-starring Robert Taylor and Maureen O'Sullivan, who had been her contemporary at the Roehampton Convent. He started on *The Divorce of Lady X*, an expanded remake of an early London Films production, *Counsel's Opinion*. In this, he played a smart young divorce lawyer who, quite innocently, finds himself in compromising circumstances when a young woman invades his hotel bedroom. The next day he is visited by a good-natured, dunderhead peer (Ralph Richardson) who wants a divorce on the grounds that his wife (Binnie Barnes) has been seen in another man's hotel room. Wrongly the lawyer presumes that he himself is the alleged co-respondent.

It is an indication of the stuffiness of the age that this film was later attacked in a book (*The Film Answers Back* by E. W. and M. M. Robson) for its 'major psychological mistakes' and generally low moral attitude. In reality, it was a very light, highly polished comedy of errors, never intended to be taken seriously, and it was acclaimed by those critics who judged it purely on entertainment values. Its major visual attraction was the first screen appearance in colour of Merle Oberon. Formerly a dance hostess called Queenie O'Brien, then an actress under her real name of Estelle Thompson, Miss Oberon had been discovered and raised to stardom by Korda, whom she was destined to marry in 1939. *The Divorce of Lady X* was her second film since a near-fatal car crash that had been the pretext for abandoning the ill-fated epic, *I, Claudius*. She combined well with Olivier. Some critics thought it was his best screen performance to date. But it was Richardson, as the amiable Lord Mere, who shone brightest of all. He virtually stole every scene in which he appeared.

Olivier now returned to the Old Vic for his second series of great Shakespearean roles, beginning with *Macbeth*. In this, for the first time, he rehearsed under the direction of Michel Saint-Denis, the French producer who had led the *Compagnie des Quinze* with great distinction and had since settled in London, founding a drama school through which Stanislavsky's ideas on naturalistic acting were beginning to filter into the English theatre. Gielgud, Guthrie, Olivier, Byam Shaw, George Devine and many others were to be influenced by Saint-Denis. It was after taking his French class to see the *Compagnie des Quinze* in London that Redgrave had resolved to abandon schoolmastering for professional acting.

Olivier, who had reacted against the ham acting of the Twenties and strived so strongly for realism, found in Saint-Denis a director in whom he had complete faith. During rehearsals of *Macbeth* his fundamental approach to playing Shakespeare was put into words by the Frenchman when he told him: 'It must be absolutely true, and you must find the truth *through* the verse, and you must not discard the verse and pretend it's prose, and you mustn't be carried away by the verse into utter unreality. Therefore, you must find the truth *through* the verse.' The production, however, never lived up to the high hopes that Olivier had for it in the early days of rehearsal.

Macbeth, of course, has a reputation as Shakespeare's most haunted and ill-starred play. Over the centuries productions have been interrupted by political riot and arson, even by attempted murder. Scores of minor mishaps have fed the legend of a jinx: Donald Wolfit almost breaking his neck in rehearsal, Diana Wynyard spraining her ankle in the sleepwalking scene, a Stratford opening being postponed when producer Peter Hall came down with shingles. However irrational or exaggerated this theatrical superstition may be, Olivier's first appearance in the title role was certainly accompanied by an extraordinary number of misfortunes. Saint-Denis was involved in a taxi accident before the opening. Lilian Baylis grieved when a dog that she loved was run over and killed. Olivier developed a severe cold, and rehearsals were so bedevilled with interruptions that the opening had to be postponed for four days—an action unprecedented at the Old Vic. Olivier's chill, given as the official reason for the postponement, served to cover up a multitude of production problems. Quite simply, the play was not ready in time.

Andrew Cruickshank, who played Banquo, recalls that things went so alarmingly wrong that Guthrie, then directing Gielgud in *School for Scandal* at the Queen's Theatre had to be summoned to the Vic. 'The night before the opening we were at dress rehearsal and Motley had designed a very difficult set. Everything seemed to go wrong, and by midnight we had only got through the first scene.'

Real tragedy was to follow. Miss Baylis suffered a heart attack, and on the day before the rescheduled opening it was announced at rehearsal that she had died. She was sixty-three and had been battling ill health for more than three years. Her last expressed wish was that her illness should not be allowed to interfere with *Macbeth*'s opening as planned.

On every Old Vic first night for thirty years Lilian Baylis had conspicuously occupied her private box—a dumpy, matronly figure usually wearing a sable cape lined with bright mauve over a black taffeta coat with painted enamel buttons. Now her chair was empty, and before the curtain went up Lord Lytton, chairman of the Governing Body, paid a tribute to this 'masterful woman of genius'.

Not until he had completed his performance was Olivier given a note that she had left for him several days before. On a visiting card she had written: 'Welcome return to dear Laurence Olivier. May you be as happy in *Macbeth* as in *Hamlet* last season.'

Olivier was not happy in *Macbeth*. He has referred to the production as an 'utter disaster' for everyone concerned, including himself. But he exaggerates. Its fixed one-month run made a profit for the Old Vic and the play was so well received that it was transferred to the New Theatre. True, Saint-Denis's elaborately stylized treatment came in for some hostile criticism, but generally the reviews were thunderingly good. 'Mr. Laurence Olivier is a magnificent Macbeth,' wrote the *Daily Express* critic. 'He plays the part at full stature; every line rings out, trumpet-tongued with a regal and resonant splendour; every point is grasped and flourished with a spaciousness that recalls the great actors of the past.' 'He has only to walk on stage to set it alight,' wrote Lionel Hale. And *The Times* said, 'His attack upon the part itself, his nervous intensity, his dignity of movement and swiftness of thought, above all his tracing of the process of deterioration in a man not naturally evil gave to his performance a rare consistency and power.' Even Agate had a good word for it, though he suggested that the actor—who had 'registered another step in a career of considerable achievement and increasing promise'—would play Macbeth twice as well when he was twice as old.

The *Macbeth* jinx manifested itself one more time during the run. Ellis Irving was playing Macduff when he had his hand so badly injured in the sword fight with Olivier that he had to be replaced. Roger Livesey took over and found his duelling opponent no less ferocious.* 'Larry used to put up a tremendously vigorous fight, and on one occasion I broke his sword. The broken bit, made of steel, whizzed out into the audience, and we stopped fighting and waited to hear a cry from someone impaled on it. The audience also waited for something dramatic. But nothing happened and so we resumed. At the end of the matinée a dear old lady appeared with the piece of sword. She asked Larry to autograph it for her and then she proudly took it away.'

As past experience showed clearly, a sell-out Shakespearean production at the Old Vic will not necessarily enjoy the same success when transferred to the West End. But the lesson was now ignored in moving *Macbeth* to the New, and to the great disappointment of Olivier, who saw it as his big opportunity for winning new fame, it failed to break the pattern. Each night he was growling, 'So fair and foul a day I have not seen . . .' and Bronson Albery would come into the dressing room and say, 'It'll get better. It can't do anything else.' But it didn't get better. It survived the transplant for only three weeks and its losses wiped out the profit made in the previous month.

Fortunately, the Old Vic had come out with a winner in the meantime: a spectacular Christmas show of *A Midsummer Night's Dream*, set in Victorian period, with dazzling decor by Oliver Messel, a flying ballet of fairies under the direction of

---

* There is a popular story (alas, apocryphal) that a stagehand was posted in the wings every night with instructions to hiss during Olivier's last scene, 'Hey, Larry! You've got to *lose* this fight.'

Ninette de Valois, and incidental music by Mendelssohn. Ralph
Richardson made a hilarious Bottom. Alexander Knox had just
five lines as Tom Snout, the tinker. Robert Helpmann, as
Oberon, had his first important speaking part on the stage.
Titania was played by Vivien Leigh.

This production was, incidentally, the first Shakespearean play
ever attended by the child princesses, Elizabeth and Margaret.
For the eleven-year-old future Queen of England it might also
have been her last. As Guthrie recalled the occasion: 'The heiress
to the throne nearly lost her life by falling from the box; so interested was she to see how the fairies flew that she hung out by
the heels. On the same afternoon, Helpmann and Miss Leigh
were brought round at the interval to the Royal Box, to be
presented. In the process of making their bow and curtsy the
elaborate wire head-dresses of the Fairy King and Queen became
inextricably twisted together. The pair remained head down,
literally with locked horns, until wrenched apart by the Queen
and the two delighted children.' [6]

A Midsummer Night's Dream had been more pantomime than
play, a glamorous spectacle owing more to the visual effects of
Messel than the poetry of Shakespeare. However, in February
1938 Guthrie believed that he was following it with a production worthy of the highest traditions of the Old Vic: *Othello*,
with Ralph Richardson as the Moor and Olivier his Iago. The
cast had great strength in depth, all the ingredients were thought
to be present for the making of an outstanding theatrical event.
Yet the outcome was a dismal failure—bluntly, because Guthrie
and Olivier were too clever by half. As with *Hamlet*, they
revelled in the game of psycho-analysing fictional characters and
now their theorizing centred on the Iago–Othello relationship.
Again they turned to Dr. Jones, Freud's biographer, for guidance.
Again the Welsh professor had a notion that was instantly
appealing. Iago's hatred for Othello was not the straightforward
envy and jealousy that it seemed, but a reaction that stemmed
from his subconscious homosexual love for his master, a love
he could not comprehend. In theory it explained a great deal in
the play; in practice it was a concept fraught with problems,
particularly because Richardson would never go along with
an interpretation with such perverse undertones. Guthrie has
since expressed the view that a good, plain-speaking row might

have cleared the air, but instead everyone behaved with gentle-manly restraint. Larry and Ralphy begged to differ, the latter arguing that the magnificent rhetoric of the play was what really mattered, the former quietly going his own subtle way and accepting the idea of Iago's repressed homosexual desire as the key to 'get inside' the character.

At one rehearsal, in an effort to get the message across, this twisted Iago gave open expression to his perverted passion. He threw his arms around Othello's neck and kissed him full on the lips. And Othello responded by patting him sympathetically on the back of the head, rather as one might go about humouring a harmless lunatic, and saying, more in sorrow than in anger, 'Dear fellow; dear, dear boy.' Richardson was not conceding one wink or fleeting smile in favour of this fanciful approach, and the production resulted in a major disappointment for two actors who had looked forward so eagerly to working together on the stage again. It was, in Guthrie's own words, 'a ghastly, boring hash'. Richardson's Othello never caught fire. He was an actor with a rare facility for making poetry out of prose but was never so at ease with pure poetry, and in the great roles this disposition showed. As for Olivier's Iago, the critics liked it not at all; it was 'too cheery', 'too puckish', and, as with his Prince of Denmark, the novel psychology behind his interpretation escaped them entirely. After the excitement of his Hamlet and the rich promise of his Macbeth, he was judged to have taken a back-ward step.

There now followed an extraordinary departure for the Old Vic—the experiment of interrupting a season of Shakespeare with a play both new and having a contemporary setting. This was James Bridie's *The King of Nowhere*, a curious comedy about an actor who has been mentally ill and, though officially cured, escapes on impulse from a nursing home before formal discharge. A rich and repressed spinster helps him to become leader of a new political party and a neo-Fascist campaign to save Britain and reform the world. Finally he is taken back to the asylum—a king of nowhere. Both Marda Vanne (the spinster) and Olivier proved outstanding in this production; the critics, however, concentrated far more on the play than the playing, and the public, so engrossed at the time with the Munich crisis, showed no interest in it. Quickly, the Old Vic reverted to safer, traditional fare: *Coriolanus*.

In this enormously demanding role Olivier scored the greatest
critical success of his pre-war Old Vic period, and he did so
partly through the influence of Lewis Casson, the man who had
come to his rescue when he was an out-of-work actor thirteen
years before. As producer, Casson wrung some concessions to
traditional Shakespearean playing from the actor dedicated to the
modern and realistic approach. Sybil Thorndike, a magnificent
Volumnia in her husband's production, recalled: 'I think Lewis
did make Larry get rid of some of his little tricks on stage and be
more orthodox. Not that he was very tricky as Coriolanus. But
if there were tricks, Lewis hated them. He liked straightforward
honest-to-God playing. He and Larry got on terribly well. Of
course they fought—naturally, because they were both so violent.
But they only argued like fun because Lewis loved a good argument. On one occasion Lewis said, "You've got to do this speech
all in one breath." And Larry said, "I bet *you* couldn't." So Lewis
did it in one breath and said, "Now you do the same." And, of
course, Larry could do it. After all, they used to have contests
in breathing and Larry had a longer breath than anybody else.
He could do the general Confession, "Almighty and Most Merci-
ful Father", from the morning prayer twice through in one
breath. Lewis could only do it one and a half times. I was so
ashamed when he broke off and was beaten.'

Olivier himself did not rate Coriolanus as his best performance
at the Old Vic. He liked his death scene fall, yet another piece
of mad acrobatics, somersaulting down the staircase and rolling
over three times to end within a foot of the footlights. But
flattering though it was, he could not honestly agree with the
praise of critics who hailed his performance as truly great. 'I'd
been on the stage now thirteen years,' he recalled. 'I think,
honestly, the critics thought it was about time they were kind
to me.'[7]

In fact, the critics were not unanimously kind. The London
Daily Herald headline was MAGNETIC OLIVIER GABBLES. But all
the critics who mattered were entirely on his side. Ivor Brown
observed how he had grown immeasurably greater since joining
the Old Vic: 'His voice has gained in volume, in reach and passion. It has notes of exquisite appeal, delicate finesse and such
attack as makes the syllables shimmer like a sword's blade.'
Alan Dent judged that his faults were in abeyance and that he

was 'of a stature to come within the line of the great tradition'. J. C. Trewin called his Coriolanus 'a pillar of fire on a plinth of marble'.

And Agate? Well, he did complain of Olivier's 'clowning' and his 'excessive make-up', but he also acknowledged his gain in pathos and in vocal depth and resonance and proclaimed him 'the nearest thing we have today to the heroic tradition. The only thing to be settled is whether he is going to have the genius which includes a feeling for poetry.' More significantly, one critic wrote: 'There is now no doubt in my mind that the only sign of a great actor in the making in England today is Laurence Olivier.'

It was Agate again, writing under one of his pseudonymns!

Thus, shortly before his thirty-first birthday, Olivier had finally passed with full honours the examination of critics both traditional and modern in outlook. By the end of that Old Vic season, on May 21, 1938, his importance as a classical actor was generally recognized; for the first time he found himself being regularly mobbed by fans waiting outside the stage door. It was what he had always wanted. And yet, just as he was coming to this peak of personal glory, he disappeared from the English theatre. Six eventful years would pass before this freshly acknowledged prince of players was seen on the London stage again.

11

Heathcliff and Scarlett

Towards the end of June 1938, Olivier and Miss Leigh left London in the latter's old Ford V8 on a 1,000-mile drive to the South of France. In this last full summer before World War II they were beginning their most idyllic holiday together. He had completed his labours at the Old Vic. She had just finished her ninth film, *St. Martin's Lane*, with Charles Laughton and Rex Harrison. Now they aimed to put all professional cares aside for a month of sunsoaking idleness. In reality, however, they were both too successful to escape their careers entirely for any appreciable time. Only a week or two later a cable found them at a small hotel in the coastal village of Agay, east of St. Raphael. It read: ARE YOU INTERESTED GOLDWYN IDEA FOR SEPTEMBER FIRST FOR VIVIEN YOURSELF AND OBERON IN WUTHERING HEIGHTS STOP ANSWER AS SOON AS POSSIBLE STOP. As added bait, a script by Ben Hecht and Charles MacArthur arrived soon afterwards.

Hecht himself had suggested Olivier for the role of Heathcliff. Director William Wyler had agreed that he was the best choice. But Olivier, having no desire to work in Hollywood again, declined the offer. He did intimate that he might be tempted if there was also a suitable part for Vivien. But there wasn't. Merle Oberon had the female lead and he was strongly opposed, as a matter of policy, to Vivien's returning to supporting roles.

Back in London he was approached again, this time by the director. Wyler recalls: 'We met several times at Larry's house where he and Vivien Leigh lived together. I presented what I considered a "plum" part for any actor, particularly one relatively unknown in America at the time. But Mr. Olivier was less than enthusiastic, though he agreed that it was a good script. I assumed his reluctance was due to a previous unpleasant experience in Hollywood, until he took me one night to see a film in which Vivien appeared. This, I thought, was a subtle suggestion that I might use her in the film as well. She was excellent in what I saw. Fortunately, there was Isabella, a secondary role, not yet cast, and later played by Geraldine Fitzgerald, which I immediately offered her—and which she immediately rejected. "I will play Cathy or nothing," she said. I tried hard to persuade her. Since she was still unknown in America, I assured her that she could never get a better part than Isabella in her first American film. So much for my prophecy!'

Olivier now returned to British film work at Denham. Korda had seen a newspaper story about an aircraft that went up and apparently never came down, and he had asked screenwriter Brock Williams to use it as the basis for a film plot. The result was *Q Planes*, a fast-moving adventure film about spies who made new bombers mysteriously disappear on their test flights. Ralph Richardson played Major Hammond, the eccentric Secret Service man called in to investigate; Olivier as a dashing young test pilot (Tony McVane) and Valerie Hobson as Hammond's sister provided the love interest. The story was technically far-fetched but it had a deft, slightly frivolous treatment, and the film, so very topical when released in 1939, was no less popular when reissued five years later. Olivier, however, made no significant impression in a rather colourless role, and not for the first time he was in a movie in which Richardson, creating a delightfully scatterbrained character, never missed a trick in a grand slam bid for the acting honours.

During the making of *Q Planes*, and following an unsuccessful test with Robert Newton as Heathcliff, Olivier was again approached by Wyler for *Wuthering Heights*. Again he declined. But now Vivien Leigh's attitude was changing. She realized that he was particularly attracted by this role and that he was rejecting it solely because he did not want them to be kept apart. She also recognized that such an attitude, with never a compromise, could seriously restrict their careers. So ultimately Olivier agreed. As before, when faced with a difficult decision, he made a final check with Richardson. 'Bit of fame! Good!' was Ralphy's simple comment. And that settled it.

Olivier's third period in Hollywood, though infinitely more productive, proved as daunting as ever. He left London on November 5, Miss Leigh's twenty-fifth birthday, with his hopes falsely raised by news that Miss Oberon might be leaving *Wuthering Heights* and that Vivien was a possible replacement. On arrival he found that there was no longer any question of a casting switch. It unsettled him from the beginning and set his mood for working on a picture that was to be plagued with troubles almost from start to finish.

Wuthering Heights was a major production somewhat misguidedly envisaged by Sam Goldwyn as being primarily a vehicle for Merle Oberon. It had a predominantly British cast, including David Niven, Flora Robson, Hugh Williams, Donald Crisp, Leo G. Carroll, Miles Mander and screen newcomer Cecil Kellaway, and the Yorkshire moors were painstakingly recreated some fifty miles out of Hollywood, deep in the Conejo Hills where Joel McCrea had his ranch.

Some 500 acres of rolling hills had been stripped of native flora and replaced with some 14,000 tumbleweeds sprinkled with a purple sawdust to resemble heather. A thousand genuine heather plants, raised in hothouses, had been planted for the close-ups. Unfortunately, this effect was rather marred when Miss Oberon sprained her ankle while running through the heather in the climactic love scene. Shooting had to be postponed four days. By that time the California sun had raised the newly planted heather to the height of full-grown wheat—far higher than on any Yorkshire moor. In addition, filming was disturbed by Olivier's contracting athlete's foot and Miss Oberon's suffering with such a severe cold that she needed to wear a diving-type wet-suit beneath her silk dress for scenes in the 'rain'.

These were less serious troubles. Olivier's real misery in filming *Wuthering Heights* arose from his uneasy relationships with his leading lady, the producer and the director. There had been no difficulty when he co-starred with Miss Oberon in *The Divorce of Lady X*. Now, however, the atmosphere became strained, and it showed particularly when they came to play love scenes. In one scene they had to deliver their lines while face to face, only inches apart. Olivier, required to convey great passion, spoke one line slightly gushingly.

'Please don't spit at me!' said Miss Oberon.

They tried the scene again. Unintentionally he spluttered a second time.

'You spat again,' said the star.

Olivier reacted with such a torrent of abuse that the exchange ended in both stars stalking off the set. Wyler allowed them time to cool off, then called them back to try it again. This time it was a dry run. And remarkably, while still feeling mutual hostility, they succeeded in playing the tender love scene to Wyler's complete satisfaction.[1] In fact, they were to have only one scene together that was unconvincing. When Olivier was required to slap her face in a moment of uncontrolled rage he dared not play for realism but gave his co-star an absurdly gentle pat on both cheeks.

The role of Heathcliff—'rough as a saw-edge, and hard as whinstone'—is an exceptionally difficult one. It demands great power and passion in the playing; and yet with a shade too much *forte* in the villainy the result can be disastrously melodramatic. When Douglas Fairbanks, Jr. (a most improbable choice) tested for the part, he overacted so grotesquely that the reel became a collector's item, shown again and again at Hollywood parties and never failing to send audiences into fits of convulsive laughter. Olivier had never before had a film part of such extraordinary emotional range; in struggling to master the part of a man, both human and inhuman, he looked for all the help he could get. But it seemed to him that help was all too rarely forthcoming, that the criticism he received was mainly destructive, and that however hard he might try, someone would find fault.

For example, plenty of Hollywood's pampered leading men would have refused to work with the irritation of athlete's foot. Not Olivier. He could not resist the opportunity to make a great performance of the crippled actor heroically reporting for work on crutches, a touch of gallantry that he thought could not fail to make a big impression. But it achieved nothing of the kind. Since his foot looked like a miniature American football, he spent a day finishing close-ups on a revolving stool. Then producer Sam Goldwyn appeared on the set and started talking to Wyler. Olivier made a show of limping past him, expecting the producer to put a sympathetic hand on his shoulder and say, 'Willie, you must send this poor chap home. He's obviously in terrible pain.'

Sure enough, Goldwyn did put a hand on his shoulder. Then he turned to Wyler and said, 'Willie, look at thees actor's face. He's the ogliest actor in pictures. He's dirty. Hee's acting ees stagey. He's hammy and he's awful. If he goes on playing the way he is I'll close up the picture. Otherwise he will ruin me!'

All that concerned him was the actor's make-up, which he judged to be disastrous. Ever striving for realism, Olivier had taken pains to look suitably grubby for his initial scenes as a stable boy. But his make-up, a shade too light for the stage, was much too much for the magnifying lens of the camera—a fact he accepted only after seeing the early rushes. His performance, like his make-up, also needed toning down, to be more subtle and less theatrical. The truth of the matter was that, with fifteen movies behind him, he still had to learn respect for the medium and to appreciate fully that film acting was a craft peculiar to itself, often requiring techniques very different from those on the stage where everything by necessity is slightly exaggerated. Only now, and somewhat painfully, was the lesson to be hammered home.

A few days later he finished the scene where Heathcliff puts his hand through the window (made of sugar). His hand was made up with blood and gashes, and he was standing outside the kitchen door waiting for Flora Robson (Ellen) to open it for him. At that point Goldwyn reappeared. By now Olivier was visibly sulking, and rather than lose his co-operation completely the egocentric producer made a rare conciliatory gesture. 'How are you?' he said. 'It's very bad, isn't it? I know it must be very painful—athletical feet!' It was an uneasy truce.

Trouble with his leading lady, trouble with the producer, but worst of all was his initial falling-out with his director. Olivier had never encountered a director quite like Wyler before. Jed Harris might be downright cruel and bloody-minded. Basil Dean might play the martinet. But at least they made positive demands. Wyler was something else—a supremely demanding taskmaster, endlessly striving for perfection, but without explaining exactly how it might be achieved.

Olivier's misery was shared by David Niven, who had initially endured several weeks' suspension rather than appear in *Wuthering Heights*. He hated the cry-baby role of the dull and effeminate and virtuous Edgar Linton, and after his experience in *Dodsworth*, he hated the idea of working with Wyler a second time. In the end he accepted the part only on Wyler's personal assurance that he was 'no longer a sonofabitch'. But it turned out very differently. Niven recalls that Wyler again put him through absolute hell. 'No one was spared by Willie. The girls were reduced to tears on several occasions and even Olivier was brought up all standing.

'The most talented and most reasonable of performers—after being told twenty or thirty times to play some long scene once again, without any specific instructions as to how to alter it—he finally confronted Wyler.

' "Willie, look—I've done it thirty times—I've done it differently thirty times—just *tell* me, that's all. *What do you want me to do?*"

'Wyler considered this for a long moment—

' "Just . . . just be *better*"!' [2]

No wonder Olivier became exasperated. Yet, like the long-suffering Niven, he finally came round to recognizing Wyler's brilliance, and five years later was to pay him the highest tribute by inviting him to direct his film of *Henry V*.

Wuthering Heights was destined to transform Olivier into an international film star. An immediate benefit followed when David O. Selznick came to casting his picture of Daphne du Maurier's best-selling novel, *Rebecca*. William Powell was eager to play the male lead, but he would cost $100,000 more than Olivier. In a cable dated June 15, 1939, to Lowell V. Calvert, his general manager, Selznick wrote: POWELL IS MUCH MORE RIGHT AS TO AGE, WHEREAS OLIVIER IS BETTER PERHAPS FOR THE MOODY SCENES, ALSO HIS ENGLISH, AND PERHAPS HE HAS THE MORE OBVIOUS EDGE ROMANTICALLY. THE DECISION SHOULD PROBABLY REST NOT AT ALL UPON WHICH IS BETTER FOR THE ROLE, SINCE COLMAN IS THE ONLY PERFECT MAN AND WE CANNOT GET HIM AND THEREFORE WE ARE POSSIBLY EQUALLY WELL OFF WITH EITHER OF THESE SECOND CHOICES FROM STANDPOINT OF ACCURATE CASTING. THE DECISION INSTEAD SHOULD BE BASED SOLELY ON WHETHER WILLIAM POWELL IS LIKELY TO ADD HUNDREDS OF THOUSANDS OF DOLLARS TO THE GROSS.[3]

After *Wuthering Heights*, Olivier was in a position to compete on a box-office attraction basis. The real importance of the picture, however, was not so much that it established him as a front-rank movie star, but more that it fundamentally changed his attitude towards film making. Years later he explained his debt to Wyler: 'Looking back at it, I was snobbish about films. Then I had the good luck—but what hell it seemed at the time— to be directed in a film by William Wyler, *Wuthering Heights*. He was a brute. He was tough. I'd do my damndest in a really exacting and complicated scene. "That's lousy," he'd say, "we'll do it again." At first we fought. Then when we had hit each other till we were senseless, we became friends. Gradually I came to see that film was a different medium, and that if one treated it as such, and tried to learn it, humbly, and with an open mind, one could work in it. I saw that it could use the best that was going. It was for me a new medium, a new vernacular. It was Wyler who gave me the simple thought—if you do it right, you can do anything. And if he hadn't said that, I think I wouldn't have done *Henry V* five years later.'[4]

Miss Oberon, too, now remembers *Wuthering Heights* with a pride that has vanquished any bitterness felt at the time. She writes: 'It is really interesting to look back and realize we were witnessing a great actor adapting his art from Stage to Screen, even though we all suffered a bit from the growing pains. I was essentially a screen actress, and though only twenty-two at the time, was treated like an old shoe. But the results of Larry's performance are now notable in the prouder annals of the history of motion pictures. The film itself (in spite of the old shoe) is honoured by being in the archives of the Library of Congress of the United States government.'

Olivier never dreamed during the making of *Wuthering Heights* that he was about to take the most significant leap forward in his film career. He corresponded almost daily with Vivien Leigh and his letters were heavy with gloom and heartache. She was then in London, awaiting rehearsals for a revival of *A Midsummer Night's Dream*. Within a week of their parting they had both deeply regretted their agreement to a three-month separation for the sake of their careers, and now, after three weeks of receiving his accounts of cumulative despair, Vivien could bear it no longer. On a sudden impulse she booked a ticket on the *Queen Mary* and a flight from New York to Los Angeles. With Old Vic rehearsals imminent, she could have only five days in Hollywood. She still judged it well worth the effort and expense.

In her romantic day-dreams she imagined Merle Oberon withdrawing from the picture just as she arrived in time to step into the breach. But she knew this was no longer a real possibility. And she had an even wilder fantasy—that somehow she might still be chosen as Scarlett O'Hara, the role she had hungered for these past eighteen months. On the voyage she re-read *Gone With the Wind* for the umpteenth time. It seemed a masochistic exercise.

Almost two and a half years had now elapsed since the independent producer David O. Selznick had hesitatingly paid $50,000 for the screen rights of *Gone With the Wind*, a record sum for a first novel and a gamble immediately justified as the book became a runaway best-seller. Yet not a single frame of the picture had been shot; still, after two years of ballyhoo, the great nation-wide Search for Scarlett had not produced a leading lady. The current gag was that Selznick was waiting for Shirley Temple to grow up and play the part. For a long time he encouraged the belief that an unknown would be cast as Scarlett; literally hundreds of new faces were tested, among them a New York model named Edythe Marriner (later Susan Hayward). But no one really believed that now. The role was far too demanding to be entrusted to a novice. An established star would surely be chosen and rumours centred on at least a dozen actresses far more eminent than Vivien Leigh.

Joan Crawford was the first 'possible' mentioned by Selznick, even before he had secured the screen rights. Then he suggested Miriam Hopkins or Tallulah Bankhead. Norma Shearer, the first publicly named candidate, was not interested and said, 'Scarlett is going to be a thankless and difficult role. The part I'd like to play is Rhett Butler.' Katharine Hepburn *was* interested, only to be told by an ungallant Selznick, 'I can't imagine Rhett Butler chasing you for ten years.' Other actresses considered included Joan Fontaine (who rejected the part of Melanie and suggested her sister Olivia de Havilland), Margaret Sullavan, Paulette Goddard, Bette Davis, Jean Arthur, Claudette Colbert, Carole Lombard, Ann Sheridan, Joan Bennett, Frances Dee (Mrs. Joel McCrea) and—believe it or not—Lucille Ball. The lovable 'Lucy' was so overcome by nervous excitement that she went down on her knees at the audition and forgot to get up until three scenes later.

Of all these stars, none coveted the role more passionately than Bette Davis. She regarded herself as the perfect Scarlett, as natural a choice as was Clark Gable for Rhett Butler. She felt that the role should have been hers by divine right and that her failure to get it was final proof of the insanity of Hollywood. Ironically, in the early days of casting, when Errol Flynn was a possible Rhett Butler, Warner Brothers offered a package, pro-

viding both Flynn and Miss Davis on loan. But she was understandably horrified at the idea. ('When I was sitting on the throne
of England, in *The Private Lives of Elizabeth and Essex*, I used
to close my eyes as Errol Flynn advanced towards me delivering
his awful colloquial dialogue and I'd pray, "Please, God, may I
open my eyes and find he has turned into Laurence Olivier." ')
So she rejected the deal. After the casting of Gable there was to
be no second chance for Miss Davis—only a huge consolation
prize in the shape of another wilful Southern belle called Julie
Marsden. It enabled her to win her second Oscar in William
Wyler's *Jezebel*.

On the evidence of later performances—most notably as the
fiery, ungovernable redhead of *Reap the Wild Wind* (1942)—one
can now see that Paulette Goddard might have been a 'natural' as
Scarlett. The story is told that she was passed over because
Selznick, fearing scandal, requested and failed to get evidence
that she was really the third Mrs. Charles Chaplin (they were
secretly married in 1936). But if so, it was only a temporary
setback. Miss Goddard remained a spirited front-runner until
the very last hurdle.

According to the studio publicity department, 1,400 young
women were interviewed in the Search for Scarlett. In all this,
as Selznick's monumental memos reveal, Miss Leigh had not
been overlooked. As early as February 3, 1937, he memoed:
I HAVE NO ENTHUSIASM FOR VIVIEN LEIGH. MAYBE I WILL HAVE,
BUT AS YET HAVE NEVER EVEN SEEN PHOTOGRAPH OF HER. WILL BE
SEEING 'FIRE OVER ENGLAND' SHORTLY, AT WHICH TIME WILL OF
COURSE SEE LEIGH.[5]

Such was the background to Vivien's flying visit to Hollywood
in 1938. She did not seriously believe that she could overcome
such competition, and on arrival her pessimism was reinforced
by Olivier's friends. They advised her that an English girl
could not be cast as Scarlett because the South would never accept it. Secondly, too much capital was at stake, and too little
time available, to gamble on a comparative newcomer in the
key role. And yet, much less obviously, there were two vital
circumstances that conspired in Vivien's favour. First, her
arrival was most opportunely timed—when the vast confusion
of candidates had at last been whittled down to only three
(Paulette Goddard, Joan Bennett and Jean Arthur), and time for
a decision was running out because Gable was contracted to start

filming no later than February 1939. Second, Vivien had an invaluable contact in Olivier's agent, Myron Selznick, brother of David and one of the most powerful agents in Hollywood.

When Olivier received Vivien's cable that she was *en route* for Hollywood, he acted on his own initiative and asked Myron whether it would be possible for her to test for the role of Scarlett. The filming of *Gone With the Wind* was due to begin only a few days later. On a forty-acre back lot of the old Pathé studios at Culver City dozens of abandoned sets, including part of the jungle for *King Kong*, had been demolished and reconstructed as a replica of 1864 Atlanta, and on the night of December 10, the faked city—$25,000 worth of timber soaked in kerosene—was due to go up in flames for the filming of General Sherman's ruthless act of destruction. That night, while Myron entertained Olivier and Miss Leigh at a dinner party, David Selznick, friends and studio executives were gathered on a platform specially erected to give them a grandstand view of the Burning of Atlanta. David did not want his brother to miss the spectacle, and when Myron failed to appear he delayed the midnight holocaust for one hour. Then, with twelve fire companies from Los Angeles standing by, he could wait no longer. He signalled for his 'city' to be set ablaze. Myron, a little high on drink, arrived with his guests too late.

'Where the hell have you been?' growled David.

Myron just grinned.

And then he steered Vivien Leigh forward. 'Dave,' he said, 'I want you to meet Scarlett O'Hara.'

It was said lightheartedly, but the introduction could not have been better stage-managed if Myron had been calculatingly cold sober. The setting was dramatic—a night sky glowing orange from the flames. Vivien, her eyes dancing with excitement, her hair swept back by the breeze, looked refreshingly radiant. Olivier, more than anyone, was alive to the brilliance of the situation. 'Just look at Vivien tonight,' he had remarked to Myron as they approached the platform. 'If David doesn't fall for that I'll be very surprised.'

David Selznick had never seen Miss Leigh before—at least not beyond screenings of *Fire Over England* and *A Yank at Oxford*, which had left him favourably impressed. If she had immediate impact on him now he did not register the fact. Later, however, when they met for drinks in his office, he referred her to George Cukor, and in the early hours of the morning, without any attempt at a Southern accent, she read a scene for the director.

The following day, December 12, Selznick memoed his wife in New York:

> . . . Saturday night I was greatly exhilarated by the Fire Sequence . . . Myron rolled in just exactly too late, arriving about a minute and a half after the last building had fallen and burned and after the shots were completed. With him were Larry Olivier and Vivien Leigh. Shhhhh: she's the Scarlett dark horse, and looks damned good. (Not for anybody's ears but your own: it's narrowed down to Paulette, Jean Arthur, Joan Bennett and Vivien Leigh.) . . .[6]

After the filmed test with Leslie Howard, Vivien commented wryly, 'There were so many girls being tested and popping in and out of the costume that it was quite warm from the previous occupant when I came to put it on.' Again she had not attempted a Southern accent (though she assured Cukor that she could quickly acquire one) and she remained pessimistic about her chances of getting the part. But in the evening, relaxing at the Beverly Hills Hotel, Olivier continued to encourage her.

Besides her nationality and her lack of Hollywood star status, there was one other factor that might handicap Vivien in her bid to play Scarlett. She had left her husband and daughter and was living with a man who had left his wife and son. Hollywood already had enough troubles trying to placate the puritanical elements in America. The power of these forces was still in evidence as late as 1964 when Richard Burton and Elizabeth Taylor were pilloried as they ran the gauntlet to the altar. But the romance of Olivier and Miss Leigh was rather different. They lived together in England at a time when the private lives of celebrities were not subjected to such a flashbulb-popping glare of publicity. And in America they were not quite yet prominent enough to have acquired real notoriety. There was, then, at least a chance that their relationship might not influence Selznick's decision.

The immediate problem that Vivien discussed with Olivier was her scheduled engagement at the Old Vic. Her five days in Hollywood had expired; rehearsals of *A Midsummer Night's Dream* were about to begin. They agreed that she could not abandon her bid to play Scarlett, so she cabled Guthrie for extended leave and followed up with a letter tactfully explaining her dilemma. Guthrie was understanding and he found a replacement in Vivien's friend from drama school days, Dorothy Hyson, who made her Old Vic debut as Titania.

Four consecutive days were allotted for the decisive Scarlett tests, one complete day for each candidate. Vivien's turn came last, on Wednesday, December 21. On looks alone, she was a strong contender. Her one visual fault—blue eyes whereas Scarlett's were pale green—had been eliminated by a yellow spotlight that changed the colour image. Now all depended on her acting range. 'The girl I select must be possessed of the devil and charged with electricity,' said Cukor; and here she did well, giving Scarlett the right measure of petulance and arrogance, playing down her sentimental qualities.

For the next three days Vivien lived in suspense, with never a hint to suggest whether she had passed or failed. In the evenings she and Olivier fitfully attempted to work out their future plans. But in this tense atmosphere, serious planning was out of the question.

The fourth day was Christmas Day, and George Cukor had invited them to his Beverly Hills home for a lavish party. Vivien, by now resigned to disappointment, regarded it as her last social fling before returning home. The majority of the cast for *Gone With the Wind* was there. Vivien and Larry arrived late. Soon afterwards Cukor took Vivien to one side and, as they stood drinking in the garden, he casually mentioned that they had at last made their choice for Scarlett O'Hara. Miss Leigh, trying to appear equally casual and not register disappointment, waited for him to elaborate.

'Well,' he said quietly. 'I guess we're stuck with you.'

The contract was signed on Friday the thirteenth of January, 1939, with the studio's cameras turning and the Press looking on. For added impact the long-delayed announcement of the casting of Olivia de Havilland (Melanie) and Leslie Howard (Ashley) was made simultaneously. Such secrecy had been observed that the signing came as news even to Olivier. As Vivien later explained, 'I didn't want to tell Larry right away because a seven-year contract went with the part and we didn't want to be separated.'

Olivier reacted by storming into the producer's office and

telling him that he and Vivien planned to get married and that he definitely did not want her committed to an agreement that might involve long separations. According to Selznick's biographer, Bob Thomas, the following dialogue was exchanged:

'Larry, do you remember when I was head of RKO and I wanted to star Jill Esmond in *A Bill of Divorcement*?'

'Yes.'

'And you insisted that your wife give up the part and go back to England with you?'

'Yes.'

'Larry, don't be a shit twice.'[7]

However strongly Olivier objected to that seven-year commitment, he recognized the necessity to seize a great opportunity. He later wrote to Miss Leigh's mother: 'It is difficult to make a decision to work apart, but I believe we were wise to make it, and that it will bid more for our ultimate happiness together to choose to work (even if we don't like it very much) at the expense of our temporary personal happiness.'[8]

Vivien began filming on January 26, playing the opening scene, in which Scarlett, aged sixteen, is flirting with the Tarleton twins on the porch at stately Tara and petulantly complaining, 'Everyone is talking of war, war, war.' She revelled in her work for just three weeks, during which time she found Cukor to be a supremely sensitive and sympathetic director, good-humoured, gently persuasive, able to free her of nervous tension and inspire the self-confidence that she badly needed. And then, to her horror, Cukor was fired. The scenes he had filmed with Scarlett were excellent, but Selznick, intent on achieving the biggest as well as the best, felt that insufficient attention was being given to the vast panorama of the picture. Both Miss Leigh and Miss de Havilland argued passionately in favour of Cukor, but neither their reasoning nor their tears could move Selznick to reconsider. Victor Fleming, responsible for such contrasting classics as *Captains Courageous* and *The Wizard of Oz*, took over. Gable, who had been directed by Fleming in *Red Dust* and most recently *Test Pilot*, totally approved the change. Leslie Howard remained disinterestedly neutral. He did not like his goody-goody role of Ashley Wilkes and his only concern was that filming should be completed as quickly as possible so that he could get on to *Intermezzo* with Ingrid Bergman (her first Hollywood film and, tragically, his last).

On March 13 Vivien wrote to her husband in London that Cukor had been her last hope of ever enjoying the picture and that now she was praying to see the end of it. She felt lost without her favourite director, and her sense of isolation was accentuated because Olivier was no longer in Hollywood to raise her spirits after a sixteen-hour daily stint at the studios. With *Wuthering Heights* completed, he had just left on a pre-Broadway tour in S. N. Behrman's play *No Time for Comedy*.

Several factors persuaded Olivier to leave Hollywood at this time. He wanted to act with Katharine Cornell; he was eager to return to the stage, and he liked his light triangle-comedy role as the tempestuous young playwright Gaylord Eastbrook. Most especially he judged it important to his career to re-establish himself in New York. His success in this last respect, however, was even greater than he might have wished. The release of *Wuthering Heights* and his brilliantly successful Broadway opening came almost simultaneously and combined to bring him to a new peak of popular appeal that he found at first flattering, then uncomfortable and finally intolerable.

New York theatre critics were unanimous in their praise of *No Time for Comedy*. And the film critics let loose a broadside of superlatives in salute of *Wuthering Heights*. Frank Nugent (*New York Times*) wrote: 'Mr. Olivier's Heathcliff is one of those once-in-a-lifetime things, a case of a player physically and emotionally ordained for a role . . . he is Heathcliff, heaven-sent to Brontë and to Goldwyn.' In Britain, *Wuthering Heights* was not entirely well received. Lionel Collier, the often generous critic of *Picturegoer* magazine, said that in spite of the technical brilliance the film left him strangely unmoved—'mainly, I think, because the artists concerned consciously "acted" rather than "lived" their parts'. But this was strictly a minority view. Mostly the notices varied from good to outstanding, and Olivier's impact was the most sensational of all. Before the film's screening in Britain it was listed in the main trade publication as having David Niven as the principal star. Once shown, Olivier became an international film star every inch the equal of Niven.

The film impressed many of the highbrow critics and at the same time lent itself to mass marketing gimmicks. It was billed as 'The Strangest Love Story Ever Told', and throughout America the public became familiar with the beetle-browed features of Olivier who, dark and sinister, glowered from a million posters bearing the red-lettered legend: THE MARK OF HELL WAS IN HIS EYES. The immediate response to so much personal publicity caught the conservative Olivier off balance. He found himself being mobbed everywhere in the style of a latter-day pop star—fans massing outside the stage door of the Ethel Barrymore Theatre, pursuing him to his hotel, perching on the running board of his car, tearing at his clothing for souvenirs. Finally, after one particularly nasty mauling by the fans, he decided it was time to call a halt: he announced he would no longer sign any autographs in the streets. Inevitably the Press followed up the story and he furnished them with the rather indelicate quote: 'As for autograph-hunters themselves, they want to see you, they want to touch you, but they are not nice about it. In fact, they're dreadfully rude.'

However honest this remark might have been, it was somewhat undiplomatic, coming as it did from an actor profiting by work in a foreign country. It made him an easy and automatic target for the popular press, and predictably they took him severely to task, portraying him as a rather conceited and ungrateful young upstart. In June, when it came to reviewing the film *Q Planes*, released in America as *Clouds Over Europe*, the *New York World-Telegram* commented: 'A strange man is Laurence Olivier. He handles such difficult roles as the male leads in the movie *Wuthering Heights* and the current Katharine Cornell play *No Time for Comedy*, but at the mere suggestion of being interviewed by a girl reporter last week he folded and fled like a horse thief. Seems perfectly at home here, talking about coffee and stuff with lovely Valerie Hobson . . .'

Ironically, five days later the *World-Telegram* did carry a girl reporter's interview with Olivier. And this story particularly distressed him because it said that he found acting opposite Miss Cornell very dull. It appeared under the headline, LIFE AND LAURENCE OLIVIER ARE VERY DULL—BUT DEFINITELY, and began:

Life is very dull for Laurence Olivier. Being a matinée idol is very dull. Having a couple of dozen adoring women waiting in the alley of the Ethel Barrymore Theatre is very dull. Giving interviews is ditto, and playing opposite Katharine Cornell in the hit *No Time for Comedy* is also very dull. In fact, he is going stale in the role, so he is leaving the cast in the beginning of July . . . 'Really, playing the same thing day after day is very trying,' he said. 'I feel I am definitely going stale in this play. I find myself doing things automatically instead of thinking things out. I find—a few seconds after I have done something—that I have done it like an automaton, without thought. And these girls with autographs. Really it is quite embarrassing. I suppose it is part of being an actor. But it gets embarrassing.' . . . 'Really I'm just a dull fellow,' Mr. Olivier repeated. 'Really I am. I don't ever know what to say to you reporter fellows. I suppose it's because I don't have a viewpoint about anything. One should have viewpoints about things, I suppose, but I just don't. I just sit here and realize I am becoming more and more boring, and then I try to say something dangerous just to be interesting. Or else you take one little thing I've said and pull it way out to make headlines . . .'[9]

It was tame, inconsequential stuff on present-day standards, trivial journalism that no intelligent reader could take seriously. But it touched a sensitive nerve and Olivier over-reacted, withdrawing tortoise-like into his austere English shell and refusing to come out. If he could not give interviews without being misquoted or misrepresented, then it was better not to give interviews at all—a defensive action that only made the Press more virulent in their personal criticism. Eventually, of course, the subject became tired copy and was dropped altogether. But the experience left a permanent scar on him, and his deep-rooted distrust of the Press can be traced back to this point.

Olivier's professional stock had never stood higher than in that spring of 1939. Yet it was not a happy time for him. Early in the tour of *No Time for Comedy* he had been saddened by the news that his father had died following a stroke. The Reverend Gerard Kerr Olivier was in his seventieth year when he died, and he was buried in the village churchyard of his last parish at Addington in Buckinghamshire. For the past fifteen years he had followed his son's career with immense pride, taking no small satisfaction from the knowledge that some of the theatrical talent was inherited. Recalling him, Olivier remarked, 'I can remember him in later life, smirking a little and putting his thumbs into his waistcoat arm-hole, and saying, mock self-deprecatingly, "Your father wasn't a bad actor." '[10]

In New York *No Time for Comedy* was assured of a long run. but this brought him no cheer since it only prolonged the separation from Miss Leigh. Once he tried weekend commuting to California, making a sixteen-hour flight after his Saturday night performance and flying back late on Sunday. On such a trip he sent a postcard to Ralph Richardson, who received it at Denham Studios while preparing for his sun-blinded scene in *The Four Feathers*. Olivier sounded light-hearted and he invited his great friend to come out and enjoy the sunshine and absurd luxury of Hollywood. But once back in New York his high spirits faded and, because any flight delay might cause him to miss a Monday night curtain, the theatre management had to ban all further coast-to-coast trips. Meanwhile Vivien continued to write home about how much she loathed working in Hollywood. And without Olivier she came to rely more and more upon Cukor for professional guidance. Each Sunday she would go over to his house to discuss the next scenes for filming, and soon she discovered that Olivia de Havilland was secretly doing the very same thing. In this way, though taken off the movie, Cukor was virtually still directing Scarlett and Melanie.

Until she became accustomed to his more direct and forceful manner, Vivien had many clashes with Fleming. And then there was always the great mother-hen figure of Selznick hovering in the background and pestering her with all kinds of details. In the early stages he was continually fussing over Vivien's accent, her visual image, and especially what he termed the 'breastwork situation'. He requested a series of 'experiments' with her figure, most importantly her bosom, and he memoed: 'Tell him [Fleming] that if she doesn't look at least as good as Alice Faye in this particular department I'll consider that his whole life has been wasted.'[11]

Eager to finish filming without delay, Vivien drove herself at a fearful pace, usually working fifteen or sixteen hours a day, six days a week. Both she and Gable were struggling with the most demanding roles of their careers and the emotional strain showed. They came to the emotion-charged scene where Scarlett rejects her husband. 'I can't do it!' Vivien cried. 'I just can't. The woman is a terrible bitch.'

'While we're at it,' Gable chipped in, 'I might as well tell you,

Vic, that I can't do that "don't give a damn" scene.'*

Glaring at Gable, Fleming turned on Vivien. 'Miss Leigh,' he snarled, 'you can insert this script up your royal British ass!' Then he threw the script at her feet and stormed off the set. For two days he failed to reappear. On the third day, Selznick, Gable and Miss Leigh arrived at his home bearing a cage of love-birds. Mollified, he returned to the picture.

Even this rugged director, who had flown in World War I, hunted tigers in India and raced motor cars, was cracking up under the strain of shooting the world's longest and costliest movie. Soon afterwards he had a nervous breakdown and a third director, Sam Wood, who had just completed *Goodbye Mr. Chips*, took charge of *Gone With the Wind*. After a month in a nursing home, Fleming returned and he and Wood shared the last few weeks of direction.

Late in June the filming was virtually complete, except that Selznick insisted that they go back to the beginning and re-shoot the opening barbecue scene at Tara. This meant that Scarlett needed to reappear as a virginal sixteen, but Vivien, after six months of severe nervous and physical strain, was beyond artificial rejuvenation. She looked pale and emaciated and, after seeing the rushes, Selznick realized that it was hopeless and told her to take a vacation first.

Joyfully she rushed off to join Olivier in New York and a few days later he was released from the Broadway play, being replaced by Francis Lederer. He, too, had a long leave before going to work for Selznick, on the film of Daphne du Maurier's *Rebecca*. So they sailed together on the *Isle de France* for a brief visit to England and a holiday on the Riviera. Neither was named on the passenger list and when they disembarked at Plymouth on July 28 reporters were told that it was 'just a coincidence that the two stars were on the same liner'. Such discretion was, quite simply, in keeping with the style of the age. No prominent figure in Britain, unless hell-bent on self-destruction, went out of his way to flaunt conventions publicly. At the same time, within their own circle, Olivier and Miss Leigh never attempted

* Rhett Butler's final line was: 'Frankly, my dear, I don't give a damn.' It qualified as profanity under the rigid censorship regulations of the time and so it was changed to: 'Frankly, my dear, I don't care.' But this lost all the impact and so Selznick reverted to the original at the expense of a $5,000 fine payable to the Producers' Association.

to make any secret of their relationship. They were hopelessly in love. All their friends knew it, the most casual acquaintances could see it. And for a considerable time now they had both been busily engaged in seeking divorces so that they might marry without delay.

Back home they found the country in a more advanced state of preparedness for war—air raid shelters mushrooming in the parks, sandbags piled high outside public buildings, queues for pig-snout gas masks. And on August 9 London was plunged into darkness for the first trial 'black-out'. Yet, in mid-August, as Selznick's two British stars, accompanied by Vivien's mother, sailed from Southampton to America, the international situation seemed to them to be less menacing than it had been after the 1938 Munich crisis. This was the majority view. In an opinion poll conducted on August 31, 1939, only one Briton in five said that he or she expected war—far fewer than in the poll of eighteen months before. On arrival in Hollywood, they now found that Selznick had changed his mind about reshooting the Tara scene for *Gone With the Wind*. After five months of production and an expenditure of a fraction under $4 million, the longest film in cinema history was complete. And within only a few days Vivien's first scene line as Scarlett O'Hara was to be given a terrifying topicality: 'Everyone is talking about war, war, war.'

12 ★ Triumph and Disaster

'Enjoy your day while you may. All this is coming to an end . . .'

Larry Olivier was playing the role of Jeremiah, with a row-boat as his improbable stage; and if his speech was unusually blurred it was strictly the fault of too much champagne in the Californian mid-day sun. 'You're all washed up,' he went on, 'finished . . . done for . . .' Then he sat down in his dinghy and pulled within hailing distance of another luxury yacht and roared out his prophecy of Armageddon all over again.

The place was Catalina Harbour, twenty-two miles south of Los Angeles, and Olivier was a weekend guest aboard the yacht of Douglas Fairbanks, Jr., and his new Virginia-born wife Mary Lee. Over the ship's radio a few hours earlier, he had heard the metallic voice of Neville Chamberlain querulously delivering his fateful broadcast: 'I have to tell you . . . that this country is at war with Germany.'

Other Britons at Santa Catalina Island on that historic Sunday of September 3, 1939, were Vivien Leigh and her mother, and actors David Niven, Ronald Colman, Nigel Bruce and Robert Coote. Vivien had wept at the news of war and finally Fairbanks had dispelled their holiday gloom by breaking open a crate of champagne and proposing a toast to victory. They drank many toasts. Niven went overboard on water-skis—still wearing his dinner jacket. And now Olivier was taking perverse pleasure in touring the harbour to tell the white-capped yacht set of the black days ahead.

Not everyone was amused. An official complaint was lodged with the yacht club secretary, and one hour later a bemused Ronald Colman, on board his schooner *Dragoon*, received notice that he was expected to apologize for drunken and insulting behaviour. Olivier did not correct the mistaken identification, and Fairbanks, seeing wisdom in retreat, had his yacht put out to sea for the rest of the Labour Day weekend.

As with the Friday of John Kennedy's assassination, everyone old enough to do so can recall precisely where he was and what he was doing on that first Sunday of September when the world erupted into war. Some, like Olivier's old drama teacher Elsie Fogerty, were in church praying for peace. Others, in their hundreds of thousands, were sunning themselves on beaches or sheltering from sudden thunderstorms. Alexander Korda heard the news on the radio in his London office, together with his family, close friends and associates. His wife, Merle Oberon, broke into tears. John Justin, his newest star-in-the-making, immediately decided to join the Air Force Reserve, and then tried in vain to get himself called up without completing *The Thief of Baghdad*. His co-star Conrad Veidt, Berlin born and educated, announced that he would remain in British pictures. But *The Thief* had to be completed in America and he stayed there, often playing Nazis and giving more of his salary to British War Relief than most British stars in Hollywood.

On September 4 Korda's magnificent new spectacular, *The Four Feathers*, was due for release. But that day all cinemas in England closed down and the film was shelved, its release long delayed. Meanwhile, Ralph Richardson, one of its stars, had reported for duty as a temporary Sub-Lieutenant in the R.N.V.R.

On September 5, the misnamed Labour Day over, Charles Laughton reported back early to the Hollywood studios where he needed five and a half hours each morning to be transformed into the grotesque gargoyle called Quasimodo in *The Hunchback of Notre Dame*. He didn't get along with his director and now the tension between them was markedly worse. The director, who had a curious habit of always working in white gloves, was a real Hun—William Dieterle. Laughton, as a soldier, had been badly gassed in the trenches just before the World War I Armistice. In the same movie, playing the villainous Frollo, was Sir Cedric Hardwicke. He had been the last British officer to leave France after World War I. Now, eager to resume his Army commission as captain, he hastened off to see the British Consul. To his immense disappointment he was told that his British Army Reserve status had been cancelled. He was too old at forty-six.

In the twelve months before World War II, 264 feature films had been shown in British cinemas. Of these only 50 were made at home. Hollywood contributed 172. It was then very much the capital of the movie world and consequently a large number of British stars were working there in September 1939. Like Hardwicke and Laughton, the majority found themselves too old or unfit for an active role in a real-life drama. Other World War I veterans included Colman, who had served in France with the London Scottish Regiment before being invalided out with a fractured ankle; Herbert Marshall, who had been severely wounded and had his right leg amputated while serving with the B.E.F.; Basil Rathbone, who had won the Military Cross as an officer in the Liverpool Scottish Regiment; Leslie Howard, invalided home from the Western Front suffering from shell shock (as therapeutic treatment his mother had suggested he take up acting). But whatever their age or fitness, most members of the British colony in Hollywood immediately contacted their consul in Los Angeles to ask what they could or should do to help. For all of them the official advice was the same: 'Do nothing for the moment but stay put and await further instructions.' Some British actors who were beyond military age argued that if they could not get into uniform, they might at least go home to share the common danger. Lord Lothian, the British Ambassador in Washington, answered: 'You are here in America on legitimate business. Yet what would Germany give to have such a corner as you actors have in the making of American pictures for the world market? And if Englishmen are to be portrayed in those pictures, how much better that real Englishmen act the parts rather than have them appear on the screen as portrayed by America actors with monocles and spats?'[1]

For Niven, son of a soldier killed in World War I, the future seemed clear. As a former Regular Army officer in the Highland Light Infantry, he belonged in the fight as soon as possible. He was thirty years old and Lord Lothian had advised him to stay in Hollywood and represent his country on the screen. But Niven wouldn't listen. He became the first British star to leave Hollywood for home. Fairbanks gave him a farewell 'stag' party attended by a host of compatriots including Olivier, Colman, Cary Grant, Nigel Bruce, George Sanders, Brian Aherne, Roland Young, Basil Rathbone, Herbert Marshall, Reginald Gardiner and Robert Coote. Within a few weeks he was back in uniform, in the Rifle Brigade.

Olivier rather envied his prompt and positive action. But

unlike Niven, who had finished shooting *Raffles* on September 1,
he was committed to film work that was just beginning. Moreover, at the age of thirty-two and without service experience, it
was extremely unlikely that he could get into uniform at once.
On the first day of war all fit men between eighteen and forty-
one became liable for military service. But registration of men
in age groups advanced at a snail's pace. It began on October 21,
1939, with those aged twenty to twenty-three. By May 1940 it
would still not extend beyond men aged twenty-seven.

Although Olivier was now impatient to complete his next film,
Rebecca, the sense of urgency soon abated for him, just as it did
for so many British citizens at home. For this period, up to
May 10, 1940, was variously known as the 'phoney war', 'the
Bore War' and the 'funny war', or, as the Germans called it,
'*Sitzkrieg*'. By Christmas, 1939, Britain had over 1,128,000 men
in the Army and they had not fought a single battle. Because of
black-out regulations the number of fatalities in road accidents
had immediately doubled, but not until December 9, when Cor-
poral T. W. Priday was shot dead on patrol, did the British Ex-
peditionary Force in France lose a single man. In these circumstances it was not so difficult for Olivier to resign himself to
working on in Hollywood. Again and again he was advised that
he could serve no useful purpose by stampeding home long
before his call-up was due. So he remained, and during the
'phoney war' he made two of his most memorable films—
Rebecca and *Pride and Prejudice*.

On December 15 Olivier took a break from *Rebecca* to escort
Vivien to the Atlanta premiere of *Gone With the Wind*. Selznick
had decreed that it should be the most extravagantly impressive
film opening of all time. And it was. A state-wide holiday was
proclaimed by the governor of Georgia, and a three-day festival
by the mayor of Atlanta. The Grand Theatre, scene of the
premiere, was refaced with white pillars to resemble the stately
Tara, and a grand costume ball was arranged with everyone
required to wear appropriate 1864 dress. Olivier flew from
Hollywood in a specially chartered plane, along with Vivien,
Olivia de Havilland, Claudette Colbert and other celebrities.
Gable followed independently with Carole Lombard and MGM
publicity chiefs. He had declined to join the V.I.P. plane out of
sympathy for Fleming, who had refused to attend the premiere
after coming across a press release that stated: 'There were three

directors on *Gone With the Wind*, all supervised by David O. Selznick.'

The Atlanta premiere was followed by another one, almost as spectacular, in New York. Throughout these glittering events Vivien remained the central attraction. Though often at her side, Olivier was officially attending independently, as one more Selznick star being kept in the limelight. And for the moment he was very much in the supporting role. *Wuthering Heights* had made him an international movie personality, but Vivien, now twenty-six, was being elevated to superstar. Two months later Olivier was to accompany her to the Cocoanut Grove of the Ambassador Hotel in Los Angeles for the twelfth annual awards ceremony of the Academy of Motion Picture Arts and Sciences and see her collect the Best Actress Oscar—one of a record total of eight won by *Gone With the Wind*.

Miss Leigh was too intelligent to be deceived by so much adulation and ballyhoo. She recognized that one colossal triumph in a role ideally suited to her talents did not suddenly transform her into a highly accomplished actress. At the same time, her unchanging professional attitude to Olivier was extraordinary in the circumstances—and it reflected well on them both. For now, when she was the far bigger movie star, she still bowed to his superior experience, still recognized him as being an infinitely greater talent.

Vivien's great disappointment at this time—and one shared by Olivier—was that she had not been chosen to co-star with him in *Rebecca*. With the notable exception of Florence Bates as the domineering Mrs. Van Hopper, the cast was by necessity all British and Irish. It included Judith Anderson, George Sanders, Nigel Bruce, Reginald Denny, C. Aubrey Smith, Melville Cooper, Leo G. Carroll, Lumsden Hare and—in her first Hollywood film—Gladys Cooper, who visited Los Angeles 'just for three weeks' and loved the California sunshine so much that she never left.

Olivier was working with old friends, and under a British director; with Vivien there, the illusion of being back home could have been complete. But persistently as he tried, he could not bring this about. Selznick felt she was far too spirited a personality ever to be right for the submissive second Mrs. Maxim de Winter—a view shared by playwright Robert Sherwood, who was working on the script, and by director Alfred Hitchcock.

Excluding Scarlett, the female lead in *Rebecca* was then the most sought-after role in Hollywood. For a long time Selznick favoured Joan Fontaine, but influential colleagues pooh-poohed the idea. She was too wooden, they said, and insufficiently talented. Her sister Olivia de Havilland was a popular choice, but contractual difficulties proved too formidable. Anita Louise and Loretta Young were suggested and quickly ruled out. Finally three candidates remained: Margaret Sullavan, Joan Fontaine and Anne Baxter. Miss Sullavan was eliminated because it was impossible to imagine her being dominated and unnerved by the darkly sinister Mrs. Danvers. Miss Baxter gave the most touching performance in her test and was desperately unlucky not to win the part (Selznick pointed out that she was ten times more difficult to photograph than Fontaine and that it was harder to understand Max de Winter marrying her). So it was back to Fontaine.

Joan Fontaine, at this point, was about to marry Brian Aherne and abandon her career. In four years as a film actress she had made no real progress, being confined mostly to indifferent 'B' pictures and briefly and unsuccessfully being groomed to succeed Ginger Rogers as Fred Astaire's partner. It was entirely fortuitous that she ever became a candidate for *Rebecca*. Sitting next to Selznick at a dinner party at Charles Chaplin's house, she had modestly argued in favour of Margaret Sullavan for the lead in *Rebecca*, and it was then that he first surmised that she herself might be perfect as the sweet, shy and timid heroine. In September 1939 she abandoned her honeymoon to take the part.

Miss Fontaine faced a stern test in this, the first significant role of her career. Her acting ability was being stretched to the full, and life on the set was not made any easier by Olivier's painfully obvious disappointment at not having Miss Leigh for his screen bride. Several members of the cast sympathized with him, and Manderley became a house divided. This schism showed when not everyone joined in a surprise party organized on the set to mark Miss Fontaine's twenty-second birthday. Reportedly, a flustered Reginald Denny admitted to her in private that he had tried to enlist Olivier, Judith Anderson and Gladys Cooper for the celebration, 'but they said they couldn't be bothered'.[2]

A certain personal tension on the set was not altogether unhealthy for a film in which Olivier had to project a moody superiority over his young and nervous and inexperienced bride. Beyond this, Miss Fontaine was fortunate in having a quietly sympathetic director with the skill and patience and understanding to bring out the best in her. This was Hitchcock's first Hollywood film, following immediately upon his screen version of another Daphne du Maurier novel (*Jamaica Inn*), and he worked in a highly individual and economical style that puzzled the profligate producer of *Gone With the Wind*. Selznick had soaked up his father's philosophy: 'Live expensively! Throw it around. Give it away! Always remember to live beyond your means. It gives a man confidence.'

Selznick originally wanted no expense spared in creating a full-scale Manderley, but he was finally persuaded that a huge miniature on the scale of one inch to one foot would serve equally well. And when it was time for Manderley to be ravaged by fire, he thought it would be a clever touch to have the smoke billowing up to form a spectacular 'R' in the sky. But as Hitchcock proved, a simpler idea was far more effective: a close-up of a pillow with the monogram 'R' being consumed by flames in Rebecca's bedroom.

Hitchcock refused to have Selznick on the set of *Rebecca*, but the producer still saw the film as being their joint creation and continually bombarded him with memoed suggestions and complaints. Those written about 'Larry' indicate that despite the lessons learned under Wyler's direction, Olivier had still not eliminated his more obvious faults in acting for the cinema. In particular his old tendency to gabble became more noticeable as he slowed his reactions on camera.

On October 13, 1939, the producer wrote to his director:

'Dear Hitch:
Larry's silent action and reactions become slower as his dialogue becomes faster, each day. His pauses and spacing on the scene with the girl in which she tells him about the ball are the most ungodly slow and deliberate reactions I have ever seen. It is played as though he were deciding whether or not to run for President instead of whether or not to give a ball. I realize that he is not anxious to give the ball, and the reasons therefor, but even if the decision were a much more important one, for screen purposes the timing is impossible. For this reason I think you had better plan on picking up close-ups,

as you discussed . . . And for God's sake speed up Larry not
merely in these close-ups, but in the rest of the picture on his
reactions, which are apparently the way he plays on the stage,
where it could be satisfactory. But while you are at it, you will
have to keep your ears open to make sure that we know what
the hell he's talking about, because he still has the tendency
to speed up his words and to read them in such a way that an
American audience can't understand them . . .'[3]

Ten days later Selznick wrote to Hitchcock: 'I have been
meaning to speak to you for some time about Larry's habit of
throwing away lines too much—for instance as he did in the
dining room with his line in which he contradicts Frank's suggestion that he was ill at the time. I know that this is the modern
style of acting, but it's also a modern style of losing points! He's
been better lately, but I'd appreciate it if you would be on your
guard about it in the remaining sequences.'[4]

Nevertheless, the finished version was a triumph for Hitchcock
and its two stars; Olivier's performance, brooding and sinister
in a curiously individual style, won considerable critical acclaim.
The film became a smash hit abroad. It was not such a huge
financial success in America on its first release—largely because
it was not pushed hard by United Artists, who were annoyed
by having missed out on the *Gone With the Wind* bonanza.
(Customarily they released Selznick's films, but when it came to
his most valuable property, he had gone to MGM. He wanted
Gable, and MGM's price had been Gable and half of the estimated production costs of $2·5 million, in exchange for the
releasing rights of *Gone With the Wind*—and half of the profits.)
But once *Rebecca* had won the 1940 Best Picture Academy
Award (the only Hitchcock movie to do so), it soon received the
wide distribution it deserved and went to the head of the year's
top ten films in the Motion Picture Herald Poll. Olivier and
Fontaine were both nominated for Oscars but lost out to James
Stewart (*The Philadelphia Story*) and Ginger Rogers (*Kitty
Foyle*). Seemingly as a consolation, Miss Fontaine was awarded
the Best Actress Oscar the following year for her performance as
another uneasy wife (Cary Grant's) in Hitchcock's *Suspicion*.
And she won it in direct competition with her sister, nominated
for *Hold Back the Dawn*.
During the making of *Rebecca*, Olivier and Miss Leigh had

high hopes of being able to work together next time. Following a winning formula, MGM planned to film another Victorian classic, *Pride and Prejudice*, to be scripted by Aldous Huxley and Jane Murfin. The role of the haughty Darcy, long ago turned down by Gable, seemed a 'natural' for Olivier, and director George Cukor thought Vivien would make an admirable Elizabeth Bennet. The studio bosses had other plans. They saw Vivien as Myra, the sweet and tragic dancer of *Waterloo Bridge*, who turns prostitute when wrongly informed that her one true love has been killed in the war. This topical 'weepie', based on the Robert Sherwood play, opened with an English colonel recalling on the first night of World War II his heart-rending experience as a captain in World War I. If Vivien could not play in *Pride and Prejudice* as Miss Bennet, then Olivier might easily join her as the colonel and captain in flashback. They had two throws of the dice, as it were.

And ironically both chances came to nought. Vivien preferred *Pride and Prejudice* and urged Cukor to lobby on behalf of Joan Crawford for the lead in *Waterloo Bridge*. But again her Scarlett image was too strong. She was regarded as too high-spirited for the gentle and well-bred Miss Bennet, but not too pert and vivacious to play a professional ballet dancer. Robert Taylor was favoured for the role of the captain, and to add to the irony, the part of Miss Bennet, originally intended for Norma Shearer, went to an actress whom Olivier had promoted years before: Greer Garson.

The outcome, however, was entirely in their interests. Miss Leigh gave her most touching screen performance to date as the doomed dancer. Olivier, as Darcy, was admirably cast for the third time in succession. In fact, *Pride and Prejudice* was well cast throughout. Mary Boland played Mrs. Bennet; Edna May Oliver made one of her last screen appearances as Lady Catherine de Bourgh. The predictable choice for Mr. Bennet was Edmund Gwenn, who had previously made films with both Jill Esmond (*The Skin Game*) and Miss Leigh (*A Yank at Oxford*).

It mattered little now that Olivier and Miss Leigh were engaged on separate movies. Both were working at the MGM studios, and in all their spare moments on the set they were secretly preparing for a joint venture. Between scenes of *Pride and Prejudice*, he was to be seen scribbling private notes; in her lunch break when making *Waterloo Bridge* she was closeted in her dressing room for coaching in verse-speaking from Dame May Whitty. And soon their secret was out: they were preparing for Olivier's own stage production of *Romeo and Juliet*, an ambition that had remained with him, undiminished by his experience with Gielgud four years before. Anticipating that it could be his last great flourish in the American theatre before going off to war, he was determined to achieve something extra-ordinary, and to this end he and Vivien (prematurely, Hollywood was now calling them 'the Oliviers') sank their entire savings of about $60,000 into the project. A similar amount was put up by Warner Brothers, who were hoping eventually to star Olivier in another film of the life of Disraeli. And Selznick, as a personal favour and much against his better judgment, agreed to release Vivien at a time when he was anxious to protect her gold-plated Scarlett image and continue her story in a sequel to *Gone With the Wind*.

The two stars were more than business partners in this venture; they now planned to marry in six months' time, just as soon as their respective divorces became final. On January 29, 1940, in an undefended suit, Jill Esmond had been granted a decree *nisi*; and on February 19 Leigh Holman, now a Sub-Lieutenant in the R.N.V.R., had also brought a successful action. While both Olivier and Miss Leigh lost custody of their children, they were assured of being able to see them whenever it was practicable, and the marital breaks were made with a minimum of rancour. Throughout the long drawn-out period of separation, Miss Esmond and Mr. Holman had done their best to secure recon-ciliations. They emerged from their private ordeals with great dignity, and they maintained such understanding and generosity of spirit that they would always remain on the friendliest of terms with their ex-partners.

Olivier and Vivien were not free to marry until August. Until then they expected to be fully occupied with *Romeo and Juliet*. No expense was to be spared on the production. He wanted the best costumes and scenery and he had Motley design an in-genious and elaborate set built on a revolving stage, allowing quick changes for twenty-one scenes. Olivier persuaded Dame May Whitty to play the Nurse. Alexander Knox, whom he had met at the Old Vic, was recruited for Friar Laurence, Edmund O'Brien came direct from *The Hunchback of Notre Dame* to play Mercutio, and Cornel Wilde, not yet a movie star, was

Tybalt. For months in advance Olivier and Miss Leigh talked
and thought of little else. He was not only directing and acting,
but making the production all his own, even to the extent of
composing entrance music. Meanwhile Vivien recognized the
limitations in her technique, particularly in doing justice to the
long lyrical passages of the love scenes, and no actress could
have worked more conscientiously and single-mindedly to
overcome them. She believed totally in her partner. As much for
his sake as her own, she desperately wanted to succeed.

In view of all the thought, industry, expertise and money that
went into this production of *Romeo and Juliet*, its abysmal failure
remains one of the more perplexing and curious disasters in
theatrical history. It opened in San Francisco, preceded by
massive publicity that fairly measured the excitement generated
on the West Coast by the appearance of two Hollywood stars
so appropriately cast as the best-known lovers in English literature. The week in San Francisco was a sell-out. They had their
teething pains, of course. On the first night Olivier made a solo
entrance with the lines:

> *Can I go forward when my heart is here?*
> *Turn back, dull earth, and find thy centre out.*

Then, as a Romeo of sixteen in spirit but not in body, he
attempted to vault over the wall of Capulet's orchard. He never
made it. Instead he found the centre of the wall and was left
suspended there, unable to save a scene strangled at birth.

Nevertheless the critics gave it a fair mark. Romeo, again a
hesitant, awkward youth as in the Gielgud production, now
spoke to greater lyrical effect; and while Miss Leigh was never
more nervous than on the first night, this only served to make
her all the more convincing as a fourteen-year-old virgin in love.
Greatly encouraged, they moved to Chicago. One critic there
called the play 'Jumpeo and Juliet', another likened Romeo to a
'bumptious football half-back'. But Olivier was not disconcerted
by such frivolous comments; after all, wildly enthusiastic
audiences were filling the 4,000-seater Chicago Auditorium.

In New York, as in Chicago, they received advance publicity of
blatant vulgarity. 'See real lovers make love in public' was the
most tasteless slogan that preceded them. News reports told of
enormous advance bookings and predicted one of Broadway's

most dazzling first nights. It was no time for a fainthearted entrance. Olivier booked an expensive hotel apartment, ordered crates of drink for the parties they would be expected to give. Many friends were in town to see them. From England came scores of 'good luck' cables.

And then, after months of painstaking preparation and keen anticipation of the feast to come, their great coronation cake collapsed in ruins at the first cutting. The so-called Butchers of Broadway swung their cleavers as one, and even Olivier, with the experience of a hundred first nights behind him, was left dazed and bewildered by the overwhelming and unanimous condemnation 'The worst Romeo ever' . . . 'Laurence Olivier talked as if he were brushing his teeth' . . . 'plodding and uninspired' . . . 'Explosive and incomprehensible'. The reviews never wavered in their contempt.

Next day Olivier telephoned the 51st Street Theatre for news of the public's reaction to the appalling notices.

'They're queueing up right round the theatre,' said the box-office manager.

'Queueing?' said Olivier, unable to believe his ears.

'Yes, queueing. They're queueing to ask for their money back. What should I tell them?'

Angrily Olivier snapped, 'Oh, give them their money if that's how they feel.'

Two weeks passed before he cancelled his instruction to refund money on advance bookings. By then it was too late. His proud gesture had already ensured that he and Vivien would lose their entire savings.

They moved out of their hotel apartment and into the house at Sneden's Landing on the Hudson that Katharine Cornell had offered them for weekends. And they sent back the crates of drinks put by for entertaining friends. Then, entirely contrary to their mood, they felt obliged to keep a promise to attend a Radio City ball being organized by Noel Coward in aid of war relief. Their host greeted them with a line they would never forget: 'My darlings, how brave of you to come.'

Why was this *Romeo and Juliet* such a total disaster? Various alibis have been offered, including the suggestion that New York critics were prejudiced against the idea of two Hollywood stars attempting to storm Broadway amidst a blaze of ballyhoo, but no amount of rationalization can really whitewash such a complete failure. Publicity no less vulgar and public demonstrations far more sensational did not prevent Richard Burton's winning critical acclaim on Broadway as a Hamlet who had only just made an 'honest woman' of Miss Elizabeth Taylor. On the weight of all the critical evidence it must be concluded that Olivier failed through misjudgments of his own. He was totally in love with the play as well as with his Juliet, and in the high summer of their romance he seems to have been blinded to major flaws in his production. On film, an approach with so much passion for detail and spectacle might well have succeeded; on stage, his dual role of leading man and director gave him less opportunity to stand back and view dispassionately the production as a whole. It was an intensely painful, but perhaps needed, lesson.

13 ★

Admiral Nelson and the Acting Sub-Lieutenant

As *Romeo and Juliet* limped through its last week on Broadway, Olivier's theatrical disaster was dwarfed to insignificance by world events of rather more catastrophic proportions. In London, American Ambassador Joseph Kennedy was saying that England was defeated and degenerate, and Churchill was preparing to growl his bulldog defiance: 'We shall fight on the beaches, we shall fight on the landing grounds, we shall fight in the fields, we shall fight in the hills, we shall never surrender.'

It was June 1940. The 'phoney war' had ended the month before. Belgium and the Netherlands had fallen; France was all but lost. Each day brought more despairing news and, with the invasion of Britain seemingly imminent, Olivier presumed that every able-bodied Englishman would be needed for the fight for survival. On May 30 he announced that he and Miss Leigh were leaving for England on the first ship available after the closing of *Romeo and Juliet* on June 8. He explained that they had written to the Ministry of Information offering their services; they had just received a cable of acceptance.

Olivier's announcement was premature. At this point the Embassy in Washington instructed him, along with all other British citizens over thirty-one, to remain in the United States until further notice. There followed a cable from Lord Norwich (then Mr. Duff Cooper, Minister of Information, and a personal friend of Olivier) advising him somewhat cryptically to stay put until it was decided how best they could use his services to help the war effort. Finally, to complete his frustration, he received a discouraging reply from Richardson about the chances of joining him in the Fleet Air Arm. His friend saw no immediate hope of his being accepted for the service. The age limit for unqualified pilots was twenty-eight, though older men might be accepted

according to their flying experience. Olivier was thirty-three.
Impatiently, he went on with his flying lessons. And then,
indirectly, he learned the kind of 'service' that Duff Cooper had
in mind for him. Alexander Korda arrived in New York and
explained that he planned to work from Hollywood on films
with a strong propaganda angle. Would Olivier be prepared to
work with him?

The fact that Korda had left England just at a time when the
war was heating up was widely criticized. But those who abused
him misunderstood his motives and failed to appreciate the value
of having him in Hollywood. There he could make semi-
propaganda movies assured of far wider distribution. He could be
a useful contact with Hungarian exiles abroad; also he had sufficient influence and powers of persuasion to gain the support of
many American stars for strongly pro-British films. His value
was properly recognized when he was put on the Black List by
the Nazis and on the Honours List (for a knighthood) by Britain
in 1942. Then, after risking twenty-eight transatlantic trips,
many of them rough journeys in bombers, he returned to England permanently.

In 1940, however, Korda's value was by no means obvious,
and when he approached Olivier and Miss Leigh in New York,
they told him that they had no enthusiasm for remaining in
America. A few weeks later he contacted them again, this time by
telephone from Los Angeles. He explained that he had found the
perfect screen subject for them, one widely appealing and at the
same time stirringly patriotic: the story of Nelson and Emma
Hamilton. Vivien was doubtful about the subject; Olivier kept
talking about going home. But Korda, the supreme diplomat,
persisted. They would film it at maximum speed, in roughly six
weeks. And, he stressed, with all their savings gone, it would be a
golden opportunity—perhaps their last—to earn enough money
to see them through the uncertain time ahead and to cover the
expense of having their respective children evacuated to America
for the duration of the war. That persuaded them.

There was just one drawback in Korda's scheme. Filming
could not begin until September. R. C. Sherriff, having tried in
vain to rejoin his World War I infantry regiment, had just landed
in America to work on the script. So far not a single word was
written. With two months to spare, Olivier and Miss Leigh
decided to take a final holiday. From mid-July until early

August they stayed with Alexander Woollcott at his island home
on Lake Bomoseen, Vermont, and then were guests of Katharine
Cornell at Martha's Vineyard, four miles off the coast of Massa-
chusetts. A few weeks still remained before they began filming
and Olivier used this time in Hollywood to make a concentrated
bid for his pilot's licence.

Each day he took lessons at Clover Field and later at the
Metropolitan Airfield. Each day Miss Leigh and Korda prayed
for his safety and steeled themselves for the worst—with some
cause. He was not a born flier and in his quixotic determination
he smashed up three training planes. Yet, after months of being
bullied and badgered by a red-necked, military-style instructor,
he completed the 200 flying hours necessary to qualify. Off stage,
it represented the proudest achievement of his life.

There is an old saying about matadors that goes: 'To fight a
bull when you are not afraid is nothing. And to not fight a bull
when you are afraid is nothing. But to fight a bull when you are
afraid—that is something.' Olivier fought when he was afraid.
Ralph Richardson had introduced him to flying a few years
earlier, taking him up for spins at his London Aero Club and
encouraging him to have a few lessons. But Olivier never felt at
ease in the air, and now he only continued flying because he
wanted so passionately to qualify for some truly active role in the
war. Ironically, his private air training happened to coincide with
a great wave of defamatory attacks on British citizens who had
moved to America to avoid the war or who were still out there
almost a year after hostilities began. The British film colony in
Hollywood bore the brunt of these attacks launched in England.
'*Gone With the Wind Up*' was the scurrilous label attached to
them. A few certainly deserved it. Many others, including
Olivier, were unfairly caught in the indiscriminate fire.

Much-loved Gracie Fields, in particular, was harshly treated.
In the fall of 1939 she had been boosting the morale of British
troops by singing to the B.E.F. in France, most popularly 'Wish
Me Luck As You Wave Me Goodbye'. But in 1940, when Italy
entered the war, her husband Monty (Mario Bianchi) Banks was
declared an alien, though he had lived in America since the age of
ten, and nobody wished Gracie luck as she joined him in the
United States. British newspapers accused her of deserting her
country and taking all her money with her. Overnight she
slumped from national darling to *persona non grata*. She gave

concerts in Canada and the United States, donating all the proceeds to the British war effort (she put her earnings at £1·5 million), toured the world entertaining Commonwealth troops, returned to Britain to sing in munitions factories. But it took a long time to overcome that initial hostile publicity.

The 'Gone With the Wind Up' smear reached its crisis point on August 25, when the *Sunday Dispatch* published a 1,500-word attack by producer Michael Balcon on British stage and screen workers who remained in America. He wrote:

Suppose a hundred of the finest aviation engineers were to walk out to America—to work, let us say, for American manufacturers not exporting planes to this country; what would you call them? Deserters? Yes. And you would be justified. So I consider that I am justified in giving this title to the scores of producers, directors, writers, artists and technicians who have migrated to Hollywood and New York since Munich. Deserters. Just that . . .

In this country the public is asked to make every possible sacrifice. These isolationists are being allowed to accumulate fortunes without sharing in any way the hardships their fellow Britons endure gladly for our cause. Are they the real war profiteers? I think they are. And this is to be a war without profiteers . . . Can this situation of those who remain at home be reconciled with the claim that all Britons over 31 in Hollywood were urged to stay there by our own Consul? It cannot. I find it hard to believe that any such suggestion was ever made.

Suppose these people had stayed at home and had helped us make films expressing the British view and interpreting our ideals for the film audiences of other countries. Well, they could have done three things: (1) They could have helped to build up an industry. (2) They could have helped organizations like ENSA—as many of the greatest stars have been doing ever since the war began. (3) They could have done what real troupers like Robert Donat and Michael Redgrave have done—gone round the country touring great plays for nominal salaries, keeping the tradition of the theatre going, keeping the people happy, putting the British viewpoint to the world. That is the one thing we want them for—not to fight, but to make propaganda.

They could have done what fine fellows like Ralph Richardson and young Pen Tennyson have done—contributed to the industry which trained them and entered the service as well. For people like these the show goes on. For the isolationists the curtain should be rung down.

If Mr. Balcon's explosive 'Deserters!' article had expressed only one man's viewpoint, its impact might have been momentary. But it was augmented by other commanding voices and sent shock waves full across the Atlantic. J. B. Priestley wrote that he agreed with much of what Mr. Balcon said so vigorously. George Formby commented: 'He is only saying what all we chaps in the business feel . . . I am glad someone has had the guts to speak out on the subject. We've got a good word in Lancashire to describe the people who have run away—and it's a bit stronger than "deserters"!'

Finally there came the support of influential Sir Seymour Hicks, Controller of ENSA, who was then busy at Drury Lane rehearsing six separate shows for the troops:

Mr. Balcon has not gone far enough. I would deny these so-called Englishmen the right ever to set foot in this country again. I am thinking of starting a 'Roll of Dishonour' for film and theatrical runaways . . . Actors like Edmund Gwenn, Sir Cedric Hardwicke, Nigel Bruce and John Loder fought gallantly for England in the last war. I would never think of asking them to return. It's the other younger men I'm thinking about.

Meanwhile the German consul in Los Angeles was exploiting the situation to the full. Britons who had met him at Hollywood receptions knew him to be a charming gentleman, but it was his duty to try to prevent pro-British films from being made and now his staff distributed hundreds of copies of a British newspaper story headlined: COME HOME, YOU SHIRKERS. A radio broadcast from England further helped him in the propaganda war and aroused such alarm in Washington that Lord Lothian cabled Lord Halifax (Foreign Secretary) on August 31, 1940:

I think the short-wave broadcast to the U.S. on Thursday night by J. B. Priestley supporting accusations against British actors here made in *Sunday Dispatch* on August 25 was very undesirable, and will do our cause no good. Nearly two months ago, after consultation with the War Office, I issued a public statement to the effect that all British actors of military age, that is, up to thirty-one, should go home, and that older actors should remain at work until new regulations about military age were issued. I understand that this ruling has been, to all intents and purposes, obeyed. It is therefore quite unfair to condemn older actors, who are simply obeying this ruling, as 'deserters'. Moreover, the maintenance of a powerful nucleus of older British actors is of great importance to our own interests, partly because they are continually championing the British cause in a very volatile community which would otherwise be left to the mercies of German propaganda, and because the production of films with a strong British tone is one of the best and subtlest forms of British propaganda. The only effect of broadcasts like this is quite unjustifiably to discredit British patriotism and British-produced films; neither do Americans like having British dirty linen washed for their benefit in public.

At the same time the British Consul in Los Angeles called a meeting of British actors to explain how important it was to silence such damaging publicity. There was no purpose, he explained, in an immediate stampede home; the great immediate need in Britain was for more equipment rather than more man-power. But it would be constructive if each actor put an offer of his service in writing and held himself ready to be called when-ever needed. Also they should do their best to contribute to British war charities and be available for personal appearances. Cedric Hardwicke and Cary Grant were deputed to fly to Washington for a meeting with the Ambassador. There, Lord Lothian gave them a copy of his cable to Lord Halifax. He was satisfied with the letters volunteering service, but proposed further that the British film colony should form an advisory committee to liaise with the consul in Los Angeles. This com-mittee, which met once a week under the chairmanship of a retired British Army colonel, comprised Hardwicke, Ronald Colman, Basil Rathbone, Herbert Marshall and Brian Aherne.

Aherne has recalled: 'We reviewed, and as far as possible, controlled the wartime activities of our British Colony; a couple of them, who shall be nameless, were worth nothing, but the rest behaved extremely well and more than justified Lord Lothian's faith in them. One name I must mention is that of Basil Rathbone, President of the British War Relief Association (West Coast Division) who travelled endlessly and worked tirelessly all over the West and deserved a large share of credit for the enormous sums of money and gifts of comforts and supplies that were collected by this Division. Had he been in England, he would surely have received a knighthood.'[1]

For the moment, Olivier was not directly involved in these developments. He was preoccupied with events of far more personal and lasting significance in his life. On August 28 he and Miss Leigh received news that their decrees had been made absolute and that they were at last free to marry. For three years they had waited for this day, and they were not prepared to delay their wedding one more day than was necessary. They planned to marry after the minimum three days' notice required by California law and as quietly as possible. Olivier sought the advice of Ronald Colman, who had managed his wedding to Benita Hume so discreetly. Colman explained that the Press was almost certain to be tipped off if they registered in the Los Angeles area. He suggested that they drive the hundred miles to Santa Barbara and register there. They could have the ceremony at a cottage on his San Ysidro ranch, then slip away on his schooner *Dragoon* for the honeymoon. They gratefully accepted.

Vivien could still not resist holding a pre-wedding party for friends, but they kept their secret so well that only the Colmans were aware of what they were actually celebrating. As added security, Benita ordered the wedding ring, pretending that it was an additional one for herself. Remarkably, they even kept their secret from Garson Kanin, who was sharing their rented Beverly Hills property. On the evening of Friday, August 30, Kanin was at Katharine Hepburn's house having an important after-dinner discussion about a possible new film. Their business meeting was going well when Olivier telephoned. Could Kanin come back to the house immediately? Yes, it was urgent. No, he could not say what he wanted on the phone. And no, it could not possibly wait. Kanin hurried back, intensely annoyed that a story conference with such an important star might have been jeopardized by his abrupt departure, and fully prepared to make a scene. On arrival he found Olivier and Miss Leigh wreathed in smiles and looking as though they fully expected him to share in some enormous private joke. But he was in no mood to play their guess-what game and so they told him: they were leaving for Santa Barbara immediately to get married. And they wanted him to be best man.

'Rather a good part,' said Olivier.

'Great,' said Kanin. 'Thank you very much. I'm honoured. And who's my partner? You know, maid of honour. Dame May Whitty?'[2]

Vivien looked alarmed. A maid of honour had never occurred to them. But Kanin had a solution—and one that would partly salvage his own disrupted evening. They would call on Kate Hepburn *en route* and ask her to join them.

Miss Hepburn had already retired for the night and was asleep when they called, but she sportingly agreed to join them on the night ride to Santa Barbara. It was a bizarre affair. They made a wrong turn that put them way behind schedule and caused the bride and bridegroom to start bickering and make spirited exchanges about whether they ought to get married after all. Meanwhile, at the Colman ranch the justice of the peace was being plied with drinks to persuade him to await their arrival. When they did at last arrive, one and a half hours late, the official was only half sober. But their delay proved fortuitous, since they now discovered that the statutory three days' notice for a wedding was not completed until midnight. The moonlit ceremony was therefore performed at one minute past the witching hour, outside on a rose-covered terrace with Kanin and Hepburn the only witnesses. The Colmans went ahead to prepare the honeymoon yacht.

Kanin has recalled the occasion as 'a forerunner of the Theatre of the Absurd'. He was busy sneezing with hay fever. The justice of the peace called the bridegroom 'Oliver' and the bride 'Lay'; and he omitted to ask Vivien for her vow and forgot to ask the best man for the ring. Finally, after pronouncing them man and wife, the pixilated judge let out the improbable cry, 'Bingo!'[3]

As part of the elaborate plan Kanin and Hepburn now dropped the newly-weds at a secret rendezvous where they were picked up by the Colmans' chauffeur and driven to the *Dragoon* in San Pedro harbour. Their hosts greeted them at three in the morning. Then, after the smallest of wedding receptions— wedding cake and champagne for four—they weighed anchor and headed out to sea, bound for Catalina Island once more. Operation Quiet Wedding had been a hundred per cent success.

It was September again off Santa Catalina, the first anniversary of World War II, precisely one year since the time Olivier and Miss Leigh had been sailing back to Los Angeles to work on separate films. Now, after a three-day honeymoon, they were sailing back to work together as Nelson and his mistress, as co-stars and partners on a professional and social scale that was destined to make them known the world over as 'The Oliviers', the royals of show business. The weeks ahead, working on *Lady Hamilton*, were the happiest they ever experienced on a film. For weeks they had been pouring over books on Nelson and Emma, and Olivier was especially fascinated by the character he had to play. Also they enjoyed working under Korda, who was directing the picture himself and who was an inexhaustible source of humour with his engaging fractured English and his own brand of Goldwynisms, such as 'Print both three'. At one time, however, it seemed that this picture might never be completed. They were beyond the halfway stage when Korda suddenly realized that in his all-out haste he had overlooked one vital formality: he had not checked the script with the U.S. censor. Sherriff was sent along to see Joseph Breen, head of the Hays Office, and the verdict was shattering.

Breen cheerfully told him: 'You can't possibly make this picture. It's not just a matter of changing a scene. The whole story is unacceptable. Here's a man living in sin with another man's wife. But his own wife is still alive and her husband's alive, and she has a baby by him and still neither of them shows the slightest remorse or even consciousness of doing wrong. Impossible!'

'But we've practically finished the picture!' Sherriff protested. 'They've spent a million dollars on it!'

'That's just too bad,' said Breen. 'If you'd shown me the script before you started I could have put you wise and saved them all the money . . . The big trouble is that in your script you condone the offence. You glorify it, make it exciting and romantic; and you let 'em get away with it.'

Korda was horrified. They had already shot the Battle of Trafalgar, spent far too much money to abandon the project now. But in the end Sherriff and his co-author Walter Reisch came up with a solution. Knowing that Nelson's father was a country parson, they hit on the idea of writing in an additional scene in which they had the gout-stricken old man, in his wheelchair, berating his son for immoral behaviour. 'What you are doing is wrong. It is an evil thing that all right-minded people will condemn. It will do you great harm, and I beg you to see no more of this woman.' Nelson looks suitably contrite. 'I know. You are right in all you say. I realize it is a wicked, inexcusable thing to do and I am ashamed at my weakness in surrendering to it.' This one invented exchange, totally without basis in history, satisfied the censor and saved the picture.

Lady Hamilton must rate as the most surprising success of Olivier's screen career. It was a low-budget movie, completed incredibly in six weeks, with only models serving as ships for the great naval engagements and the scriptwriters providing additional dialogue on a day-to-day basis. Yet the result was a blatantly jingoistic piece that became a box-office hit in many countries, not least in Russia. With its obvious parallel to current events (Britain's 'finest hour' as she stood alone for long periods of the Napoleonic Wars) it fitted perfectly into the mood of the time and significantly it had the distinction of becoming Churchill's favourite film. He had it shown on board the *Prince of Wales* in August 1941, on his way to the Atlantic Conference with President Roosevelt. He kept a copy at his Chartwell home and showed it whenever important guests came to stay.

It was one of Korda's most effective pieces of propaganda. In 1941, when the Senate Foreign Relations Committee held hearings to examine the problem of foreign agents in the United States, the film was exhibit 'A' in the case brought by Senators Nye and Vandenberg, who accused Korda Productions of being an espionage and propaganda centre for Britain and so operating in violation of a law that demanded the registration of all foreign agents. The movie's damning scene was said to be the one set in the Admiralty boardroom where Olivier as Nelson makes an impassioned speech against dictators and declares that you cannot make peace with them. 'You have to destroy them—wipe them out.' He referred to Napoleon, but the allusion to Hitler was inescapable. Korda was asked to furnish proof of the historical accuracy of this scene. There wasn't any.

Korda and his fellow Hungarian producer Stephen Pallos were subsequently summoned to appear in front of the Committee.

Korda's biographer Paul Tabori recalls: 'Though Alex was in the middle of a film, the Senators insisted that he should drop everything and come to Washington. The date of the hearing was set for December 12, 1941. On the 7th, as we know, something happened that made such investigations rather silly and pointless. The Japanese planes dived over Pearl Harbor and America was at war.'[4]

In mid-September 1940 there occurred one of the greatest tragedies of the war at sea, an action described on both sides of the Atlantic as fiendish and outrageous. On Friday the 13th, the 11,000-ton Ellerman liner *City of Benares* defied superstition and sailed from Britain for Canada with 100 child evacuees on board. Four days out, 600 miles from land, she was torpedoed while riding a tempestuous sea in gale-force winds—an attack that defied a firm and accepted law of the sea war that liners should never be sunk in conditions offering very remote chance of survival. The death roll was 258; of the children only 13 were saved.

The Oliviers had an eye-witness account of this tragedy from author and playwright Arthur Wimperis, who had sailed on the liner for a meeting with Korda in Los Angeles. It filled them with horror, and a very profound appreciation of their personal good fortune. Only two months earlier their own children had safely made that perilous Atlantic crossing. Vivien's daughter Suzanne, now almost seven years old, made the voyage with her grandmother Mrs. Hartley. His son Tarquin, just four years old, was on the same boat, travelling with his mother. The Oliviers flew to Toronto to meet them, combining the trip with personal appearances in cinemas to support Canada's drive for war funds.

By late December all the loose ends in the complex life of the Oliviers were neatly tied. They could rest assured that their children were safe for the remainder of the war. They had no more stage or screen commitments. And he had won his civilian 'wings'. At last they could satisfy what Vivien described as their 'overwhelming longing' to return home. A week before Christmas they invited a few friends for farewell drinks. Their ship, the *Excambion*, sailed from New York for Portugal on December 28. At the quayside Olivier told reporters: 'I won't be back until the war's over.'

Although Sunday the 29th was the night of the second Great

Fire of London, when the city suffered its severest blitz of the war, the Battle of the Atlantic had not yet reached its height. All the same, it was a menacing time for the crossing, with the monthly average tonnage lost standing at almost 300,000, and the Oliviers were prepared for the worst, especially when they discovered that their American ship had three senior officers, including the captain, who were German. Vivien spoke German fluently and she overheard snatches of conversation that strengthened her suspicion that they were really in the hands of Nazi agents. Soon the slightest wink or nod was taking on dark significance and their voyage was played out in a cloak-and-dagger atmosphere suitable for a spy melodrama starring Conrad Veidt and Erich Von Stroheim. Yet it passed without any genuinely dramatic incident, and once they had landed safely in Lisbon, the Oliviers concluded that they had been far too imaginative. Later, however, they knew differently; they heard that several crew members had been arrested on espionage charges.

The Battle of Britain had made it impossible to continue the regular London–Lisbon civil air service that had been operated during the 'phoney war' by the Dutch wing of B.O.A.C. But since December 17 that wing had resumed flights to Lisbon and back by operating from Whitchurch Airfield, near Bristol, with four Royal Dutch DC-3 aircraft that had the range to bypass the main theatre of the war in the air and fly south-southeast towards the Spanish peninsula. After three days in Lisbon the Oliviers secured seats on one of the seven-hour flights to Bristol. All possible security measures were taken on this service—planes blacked out in the air, departure times kept secret even from the passengers —but in reality such precautions were worthless. Lisbon was the espionage capital of the world. At Sintra Airport there was the singular situation of Lufthansa and B.O.A.C. having offices directly across a passage from one another. Allied and enemy pilots passed each other in the wide corridor. German mechanics at the airport could easily telephone the Intelligence Department at their Embassy as soon as they saw a plane being made ready for take-off to England. Thus, at the time of the Oliviers' departure, the element of risk seemed considerable.

The Lisbon–Bristol line had then been operating for less than a month without incident; it was far too soon to assess the risk factor. In time, however, it was to become evident that the danger was minimal. German fighters made no effort to intercept the Dakotas, and it was concluded that German Military Intelligence regarded it as against their own interests to put these flights out of action. For both sides this was an attractive means of delivering spies; it was also useful for the passing of information and the carrying of prisoner-of-war mail, neutral diplomats and diplomatic bags. In its first year the Lisbon line would carry 1,500 passengers without interception; in the second year, some 4,000. Not until June 1943 was there a fatal incident. Then a cluster of Junkers 88 tailed the Bristol-bound Dakota called *Ibis* and shot her down in flames into the Bay of Biscay. There were no survivors. The thirteen passengers included Leslie Howard and a young Englishwoman who was the first wife of actor Raymond Burr.

For the Oliviers the introduction to wartime Britain was an unforgettably dramatic experience after two years of luxurious living in California and New York. In sharp contrast to Lisbon, no bright lights shone out of the darkness to pinpoint the vast, sprawling city of Bristol with its half-million inhabitants. They landed at a bleak and isolated airstrip overshadowed by the awkward flying hazard of Dundry Hill and were then driven to a hotel that had all its windows shattered by bomb blast. Along their route they saw scenes of massive destruction, much of it the recent result of the city's devastating air raid on the night of Sunday, November 24. In their hotel it was so bitterly cold that they went to bed fully dressed—an especially practical step, as it happened, since they were very soon disturbed by the banshee wail of the sirens so familiar to everyone else. Outside, bombs were falling, ack-ack barking, searchlights crisscrossing the sky— a Wagnerian *son et lumière*. They felt cold and exhausted, and yet strangely exhilarated. Most of all they felt profoundly happy. They were where they really belonged.

Olivier was the third prominent British actor to return from Hollywood, following David Niven and Richard Greene, now both in the Army, and he came back fully expecting that his flying experience would give him an advantage in applying for active service. At thirty-three he had no hope of qualifying as a fighter pilot, but there seemed a fair chance that he could gain some kind of flying role in the Fleet Air Arm (Richardson, after all, was a pilot in the service at thirty-seven), and so he applied for entry as soon as he and Vivien resettled in their bomb-damaged London home. Then, at the first medical, he was shocked to learn that they proposed to reject him on the evidence of a slight nerve defect in one ear, damage caused a year before when flying through a blinding storm in America. It was a trivial fault, and by privately getting a specialist to back him up he managed to have the verdict reversed and to win acceptance for non-operational flying. In the meantime he and Vivien joined a group of professional actors who were presenting concerts at aerodromes and helping to launch the R.A.F. Benevolent Fund.

While awaiting call-up, Olivier also made a 'guest' appearance as Johnnie the Trapper in an all-star propaganda film called *49th Parallel*. The film, jointly produced and directed by Michael Powell and Emeric Pressburger, concerned the adventures of a stranded German U-boat crew, on the run in Canada and trying to reach the safety of neutral America. Its stars included Leslie Howard, Anton Walbrook and Raymond Massey, and they all agreed to a half-cut in salary. Elisabeth Bergner was said to have waived her salary altogether, but as it happened she quit the film after only a few days' work on location in Canada. She was never happy with her role as a member of a Hutterite community in Alberta and had an unfortunate experience when she came face to face with genuine members of that religious sect. They were fundamentalists who regarded any make-up, jewellery or personal adornment as being sinful, even to the extent of never having buttons on their clothes. But when Miss Bergner arrived on the 'lot' in a Hutterite settlement, she was wearing—apart from a suitably modest gingham frock—full make-up, bright red lipstick, false eyelashes and polish on her nails! The Hutterite ladies were outraged, and one of them was so offended that she ran forward and soundly boxed the film star's ears. Miss Bergner remained in the picture, but only as a bonneted figure seen in two or three long shots. Her role, somewhat changed, was taken over by a child actress who gave an irresistible performance and immediately made a name for herself: Glynis Johns.

Above all, this film was a personal triumph for Eric Portman, until then a stage actor without a screen reputation. After seeing a rough-cut of the picture, Leslie Howard insisted that Portman should be given star billing—a view fully endorsed by the critics who raved over his compelling performance.

For once Olivier missed the physical rigours of shooting on location, completing his contribution in ten days in the comparative luxury of Denham studios. In a part occupying only ten minutes of screen time he had an opportunity to show off his range and virtuosity to rare effect, starting at a loud and rollicking pace as the hunt-weary trapper singing joyfully in his bathtub, moving subtly into a softer key and then closing with the pathos of his slow death from gun wounds. Coached by a genuine trapper (Tony Onraet), who was in England with the Canadian troops, Olivier captured perfectly the accent and gusty mien of a French-Canadian frontiersman. After seeing the rushes, Vivien declared with some justification that it was 'the best thing he's done in films'.

One morning in mid-April 1941 Olivier received in the mail an envelope containing a tiny sprig of white heather and two four-leafed clovers glued to a piece of paper. It was from Elsie Fogerty. Somehow his old drama teacher, with her great mother-hen instinct, had managed to discover the precise day that he was leaving to begin his service in the Navy and was wishing him luck. That same morning he and Vivien shut up Durham Cottage and drove to Lee-on-Solent where Acting Sub-Lieutenant (A) Olivier, R.N.V.R., began his training on British aircraft. Ralph Richardson was already there to welcome them and they rented a furnished house at Warsash overlooking Southampton Water, a few miles northwest of the seaplane base. When the war began, John Casson, eldest son of Lewis Casson and Sybil Thorndike, had also looked forward to the day when he might welcome Olivier to Lee-on-Solent and serve over him as squadron commander. Casson had been a pilot officer in the Fleet Air Arm since 1926. But he failed to realize his ambition of having both Olivier and Richardson under his command. In 1940, while leading a dive-bombing attack on the German battleship *Scharnhorst*, he had been shot down in a Norwegian fjord and was now languishing in a German prisoner-of-war camp.

Olivier was stationed with Richardson for only three weeks of basic training. Then he was on the move again, being posted to Worthy Down, near Winchester. There, again, he had an actor friend to show him the ropes: Lieutenant R. Douglas-Finlayson, otherwise Robert Douglas, the man who had replaced him in *Theatre Royal* after he broke his ankle in a reckless leap over the bannisters. Like Richardson, Douglas had learned to fly before the war and had joined the Fleet Air Arm as soon as it began. He recalls: 'It was my job to help Larry become accustomed to the "routine". He seemed so desperately keen to "go into battle" instead of doing the dreary job we were stuck with, namely, training observers, gunners, etc. in antiquated old Swordfish or whatever else could stagger into the sky. But he had barely got started when he was involved in a hideous incident.'

The incident occurred on Olivier's first day at Worthy Down. Douglas was away from the station for much of the day, but in the evening he returned and on arrival in the Ward Room he casually asked the Commanding Officer if Lieutenant Olivier had settled in all right.

The C.O. said nothing. He just glared and then pointed out of the window at a wrecked plane and two other aircraft that had been damaged when Olivier was taxiing on the runway for the first time.

'Good heavens, sir!' Douglas exclaimed. 'Not *three*!'

From the beginning of his service days Olivier found his acting reputation to be a handicap in trying to win recognition as a serious pilot-officer. Some forty officers, mostly regulars, were seated at the Ward Room long-table on the first day that he joined Douglas there for tea. Immediately two old Commanders began to discuss the new arrival in voices clearly audible to the rest and in a style worthy of a scene played by C. Aubrey Smith and Nigel Bruce.

'New fellah over there,' said the first Commander. 'Know who he is?'

'Yes,' said the second Commander. 'Another actor fellah— name's Olivier.'

'Oh! Heard the fellah played Nelson in a Hollywood film not so long ago.'

'Quite so.'

'Ridiculous!' the second Commander snorted. 'Chap doesn't look a damn bit like Nelson.'

Olivier smiled. But his amusement at such recognition soon passed. He could never escape his film star image altogether, and rather as in his public school days, he soon found himself confronted with an indefinable and invisible barrier that seemed to deny him acceptance as 'just one of the boys'. He desperately wanted recognition as a Fleet Air Arm officer in his own right, as a pilot who also happened to be an actor, but he seemed doomed to remain 'that actor fellow' who also played at being a pilot.

For the time being Vivien Leigh the movie star was resigned to playing the obscure role of just another young service wife, following her husband from station to station. When the Theatre Guild invited her to New York to be Cleopatra to Cedric Hardwicke's Caesar, she declined. 'My place is here beside Larry,' she wrote. But she could never tolerate indefinitely such a humdrum and inactive life, and Olivier, recognizing her increasing restlessness, encouraged her to find a play suitable for her return to the London stage. They were anxious that her comeback be in a role well within her range, and in the end it was Olivier who shrewdly suggested Jennifer Dubedat in Shaw's *The Doctor's Dilemma*. Hugh Beaumont, managing director of H. M. Tennent Ltd., agreed to put on a revival—one with lush settings and elegant Edwardian costumes designed to give audiences a happy escape from the drabness and austerity of wartime Britain.

On August 7, 1941, Olivier accompanied Vivien to London and they saw *Lady Hamilton* at the Odeon. Four days later she began rehearsals. The play was to tour the provinces for six months before opening in the West End, six months during which they could see one another only on weekends, and then usually for only a few hours after long and tedious train journeys. Once the play had opened at the Haymarket in March 1942, they were able to live together at their bungalow near Worthy Down, but it meant rising every morning at 6.30 A.M., he to ride his motor-cycle to the air station, she to take the train to London. Few people, if any, recognized the world-famous Scarlett O'Hara as she huddled each day in the corner of some drab railway compartment, an unassuming figure, usually in plain raincoat and head scarf, and always reading a book by Dickens. On one such journey she heard two men from the Worthy Down air station discussing her husband's prowess as a pilot, particularly in formation flying. 'He's a duck out of water,' said one. And Vivien knew that the man was right in a way. Training air gunners and running a camp for teenage members of the Air Training Corps fell far short of the kind of active role Olivier saw for himself in the war, and it depressed him greatly when he thought how many of his actor friends were risking their lives in action. In addition, he was being increasingly called upon for 'entertainment duties'. They always assured him that it was vital morale-boosting work, but it gave him no real satisfaction, and sometimes it seemed a downright waste of time.

In February 1942, for example, he found himself committed to organizing a concert party on behalf of Fleet Air Arm. His own contribution comprised singing a sea-shanty and appearing in an arrangement of excerpts from *Henry V*. All went well until the show was given a special performance at the Garrison Theatre, Aldershot. It could not have been more ill-timed. By chance it coincided with what was far from the 'finest hour' in the history of the Fleet Air Arm.

On February 12, Hitler had ordered that the battleships *Scharnhorst* and *Gneisenau* leave their hide-out at Brest. In a cunning and daring operation they slipped through the British defences, steamed up the Channel with a powerful escort and reached the safety of Heligoland. The Navy and R.A.F. were caught by surprise and some forty aircraft were lost in a vain bid to sink the German ships—a humiliating blow that badly damaged British morale and aroused fresh fears of invasion. The Fleet Air Arm figured most prominently in that abortive action, but for all their courage they remained a losing 'team' and it was hardly the time for the Senior Service to be parading its theatrical talent in Britain's principal Army garrison town. The concert proved a complete fiasco, quite the most unpleasant evening Olivier has ever known in any theatre. The men in khaki made life hell for those in blue, whistling and jeering and howling so that some acts were completely inaudible. And Olivier, with his comparatively highbrow turn, received the rudest reception of all. As soon as he stepped on stage in shining armour, he was greeted with raucous laughter, his words punctuated throughout by ribald comments. When he came to his supreme delivery of the Saint Crispin's Day speech, he was hooted down until not a single word could be heard. Yet he stubbornly stood his ground and finally, after many minutes of anguish, he made one last desperate bid to still his audience. It was an inspired theatrical gesture. He suddenly advanced to the footlights, sank to his knees, looked upwards as though to Heaven, clasped his hands together and said nothing. Momentarily the audience was puzzled. They hushed so that they might understand. And in that instance of quiet Olivier launched into Henry's prayer before Agincourt, his irresistible soul cry:

> *O God of battles! steel my soldiers' hearts;*
> *Possess them not with fear; take from them now*
> *The sense of reckoning . . .*

And it held them. They heard him out and at the end of that brief prayer, as the curtains closed, he actually won their applause. But it was meagre consolation in an evening that was otherwise total disaster.

Continually he found himself allotted dull, routine duties that kept him on the ground, and rarely a week went by without his being summoned to a special briefing by his Commanding Officer, who had received a message from the Admiralty requesting his release for some patriotic broadcast or charity show that was judged to be in the national interest. The B.B.C. wanted him for a recitation of contemporary poems by Flight Lieutenant John Pudney. There was a Ministry of Information film that required him to speak a 'Words For Battle' commentary taken from the writings of Milton, Blake, Tennyson, Browning, Kipling and Churchill. He was needed at the Albert Hall to deliver the final oration for 'Battle for Freedom', a dramatic and musical pageant. And could he spare a few days to speak the commentary for the official film record of Malta's heroic stand against the Luftwaffe? So it went on. Olivier despaired of ever getting into operational flying. Then he heard of one possible way: volunteers were being accepted to fly Walruses, a small flying boat designed to be catapulted from battleships. He applied immediately for a transfer and, much to his wife's horror, his request was granted. He could report for special training in about three months.

In the interim he had no strong objection to killing time by working at Denham on a film which, he was told, would have considerable propaganda value and serve Anglo-Soviet relations at a crucial time. It was called *The Demi-Paradise*, and Olivier, crew-cut and coached to an impeccable Russian accent, played Ivan Dimitrievitch Kouznetsoff, a Soviet engineer sent over to liaise with a British shipbuilding company. Produced and scripted by Russian-born Anatole de Grunwald, directed by Anthony Asquith, son of the one-time British Prime Minister, it was excellent pro-British propaganda and at the same time it subtly implanted the idea that the Russians, not so long ago known as the Red Menace, were not such bad chaps to have as allies after all.

Its completion was neatly timed to coincide with the 25th anniversary of the founding of the Red Army, an event celebrated in cities throughout Britain with colourful parades and fulsome speeches—the greatest expression of Anglo-Soviet solidarity to be seen during the war. In London the highlight of the celebrations was a massive 'Salute To The Red Army' pageant, held at the Royal Albert Hall on Sunday, February 21, 1943.

Routine service on the Worthy Down station seemed far away at this time. The Oliviers were back in the full flush of show business life, reunited with many old friends in London and in the country. While filming *The Demi-Paradise*, he had leased a house (previously occupied by Noel Coward) in the little Buckinghamshire village of Fulmer. It was close to Denham Studios; and it enabled him to spend far more time with Vivien, who now had a comparatively short journey to London each day. Almost one year after its opening at the Haymarket, *The Doctor's Dilemma* was still thriving, on its way to an unprecedented run of 474 performances. At Fulmer, the Oliviers had several friends nearby—the John Millses, Rex Harrison and Lilli Palmer, and a few miles off, in the village of Dorney, Major David Niven and his wife Primula. The severe handicap of food rationing did not prevent them from getting together for hilarious parties, and whenever a chicken could be obtained they delegated Olivier, with his low-budget parsonage training, to take on the carving. Niven recalls one occasion when he arrived at the Oliviers' house with Brendan Bracken, then Minister of Information, and confronted a bizarre sight on opening the door. 'There was Larry in some sort of rug singing the Messiah—that was something appalling; Vivien was draped in some extraordinary garment like a sheet and Bobbie Helpmann wore a leopard-skin jock strap with a kitten in it.'[5]

Olivier was now virtually at the end of his service career. He had agreed to star in *The Demi-Paradise* on the firm understanding that his absence from the Fleet Air Arm would not jeopardize his transfer to a Walrus training unit. But just as filming neared completion he suffered the final, disillusioning blow. He was informed that Walruses had been taken out of commission; it was back to Worthy Down for the familiar round of routine, non-operational duties. The news killed his last hope of ever getting into combat, and from that point onwards he abandoned his vain struggle to be a pilot first and actor second. If he was to be continually released for film and radio work he might as well give himself wholeheartedly to that end and produce something really worthwhile. And already just such an opportunity was at hand—the chance to take on the most challenging project of his entire career, a work destined to occupy all his creative energies for the next eighteen months: a film of *Henry V*.

14

★ The Making of a Masterpiece

It is entirely characteristic of the mad, miraculous world of the movies that some of Britain's most stirring, morale-boosting World War II films should have been made by an Italian who arrived in England as a penniless refugee unable to speak a word of English and who was arrested as an 'enemy alien' as soon as Mussolini accepted Hitler's invitation to the war. His name was Filippo Del Giudice. He was responsible for the making of such distinguished and archetypically British pictures as *In Which We Serve, This Happy Breed, The Way Ahead, Blithe Spirit* and *Odd Man Out*.

Just as the American film industry was founded mainly by immigrants and sons of immigrants from central and eastern Europe—pioneers like Sam Goldwyn and Harry Warner from Poland, William Fox and Adolph Zukor of Hungarian extraction, Louis B. Mayer, Joseph M. Schenck and Sam Katz from Russia—so, to a much lesser degree, the British film industry expanded and flourished through the drive and vision of immigrants such as Korda, Gabriel Pascal and Anatole de Grunwald. And of all of them, none was more extraordinary than Del Giudice, everyman's image of the big-time movie producer—a cigar-chewing, language-fracturing executive, dumpy, potbellied and masked by the inevitable dark glasses.

In the early Thirties he lived in a cheap basement flat off London's Cromwell Road, eking a living by teaching Italian to sons of Soho waiters. In the Forties he was a giant of the film industry, making the enormous box-office successes that raised flour millionaire J. Arthur Rank to the position of Britain's pre-eminent movie magnate. In the Fifties he retired to a monastery, and in the early Sixties he died. Del Giudice was a lawyer by profession, a financial wizard by instinct. In 1937 he found the financial support to set up Two Cities Films Ltd., and launch it successfully with Terence Rattigan's *French Without Tears*, starring Ray Milland. In June 1940 he was among 4,000 Italians with less than twenty years' British residence to be dispatched to an internment camp on the Isle of Man. When he was released four months later, his law practice was finished, his film company existed in name only, his bank balance was near zero. But one movie changed his fortunes, and the fortunes of many others involved in its making. He approached Noel Coward with the idea of filming a naval story about destroyers. Coward said, 'No,' then changed his mind when Lord Louis Mountbatten happened to tell him over dinner about the exploits of his own destroyer, *H.M.S. Kelly*. The result was *In Which We Serve*. The picture was given a special Academy Award, chosen by New York critics as the best film of 1942 and generally recognized as the most notable example of new realism in the British cinema. It advanced the careers of many relatively unknown talents: actors John Mills, Richard Attenborough and Bernard Miles among others, and an untried director called David Lean. Above all, its profit and prestige enhanced the reputation of Del Giudice. He followed it with more propaganda entertainment: *The Gentle Sex*, to encourage recruiting for the A.T.S., and *The Demi-Paradise* to promote Anglo-Soviet relations. And when Olivier came to work on the latter picture, the Italian was already planning the most daring project of his career: a film of Shakespeare's *Henry V*.

The link between Olivier and Del Giudice was writer-producer Dallas Bower, who had been an associate producer on the 1936 film of *As You Like It*. In 1938 Bower had prepared a television script of *Henry V* for the B.B.C., but British televison closed down on the eve of war and the project was shelved. Later, when released from the Army to become Supervisor of Film Production for the Ministry of Information, Bower rewrote his script for a film version. Again it came to nothing. The M.O.I. could not afford to become involved in full-scale feature production. Their interests lay in one-reelers about Careless Talk Costs Lives, Holidays at Home and Digging for Victory. The filming of Shakespeare's armour-and-longbow spectacular scarcely seemed as relevant to the war effort as a low-budget documentary aiding the recruitment of buxom Land Girls. So Bower abandoned the idea, until, in May 1942, he came to produce a fifteen-minute radio show called *Into Battle*, in which Sub-

Lieutenant Olivier had to deliver *Henry V*'s speeches before Harfleur and on the eve of Saint Crispin's Day.

In the fall of 1942 Del Giudice heard Olivier in a full-length radio version of *Henry V* and decided at once that he was ideal for the film. But Olivier's reaction was guarded. Recalling his unhappy experience in *As You Like It*, he stressed that he could never contemplate such a picture unless he was given complete control over it—producing, casting, editing, the lot. Normally, this would have been judged an impossible demand. But Del Giudice was not the typically vain, power-loving producer with artistic pretensions. The end product, not the means to that end, was his overriding concern, and his *modus operandi* was always to let the creative artist have the utmost possible freedom while he himself concentrated exclusively on the financial side. In precisely the same way, he had given Coward full control over the production of *In Which We Serve*.

. Suddenly Olivier found himself committed, his every condition surprisingly met; and when he began to analyse the full range of his responsibilities, the enormity of the undertaking made him tremble with misgivings. It seemed best to recruit an experienced director, and he immediately thought of William Wyler, who happened to be in Britain at the time, serving with the U.S. Air Force. Wyler declined. 'I told him that I didn't know Shakespeare well enough, and he said, "Never mind; I know Shakespeare, you know film-making. Together we'll make a fine picture." ' Having failed with Wyler, Olivier approached his old friend Carol Reed. But Reed was committed elsewhere. And so was Terence Young. Finally, rather than risk *his* film in the hands of any lesser director, Olivier decided that he would have to direct it himself. And he covered himself by appointing Reginald Beck, editor of *The Demi-Paradise*, to assist on technical matters, serve as cutter and take over direction of those scenes where he himself was required in front of the camera.

He chose well. Beck was to collaborate with him so intelligently that their shooting resulted in a mere twenty-five per cent wastage of film, compared with the average fifty per cent on British films and an extravagant ninety per cent on those made in Hollywood. But then Olivier, aided by Dallas Bower and Del Giudice, had an unerring touch in assembling his *Henry V* team. He brought in theatre critic Alan Dent to work with him on a masterly editing of the play. For the score he sought out William

Walton, whom he regarded as 'the most promising composer in England'. He called in costume designers Roger and Margaret Furse and scenic designer Roger Ramsdell, recruited art directors Paul Sheriff and Carmen Dillon, and was largely responsible for the well-balanced cast. In all this, through his wide knowledge of the theatre, he made use of much talent that professional film-makers had previously ignored. Del Giudice also made one invaluable contribution: he suggested the brilliant Australian lighting cameraman, Robert Krasker, who had never worked in Technicolor before.

Although Bower's script was no longer suitable for a project of this size, Olivier shrewdly had him on his team as associate producer. As such, Bower played a major part in the planning and organization, and he had the satisfaction of seeing some of his original ideas incorporated in the picture. For example, the sequence of the charge of the French knights was obviously inspired by the charge of the Teutonic knights across the ice of Lake Ladoga in Eisenstein's 1938 film *Alexander Nevsky*, of which Bower had produced a radio version.

In view of the wartime confusion it was remarkable how often Olivier was successful in obtaining his first-choice actors in casting. The services were now more reluctant to release men for filming, but Bower negotiated through the Ministry of Information and obtained the release of actors from Army, Air Force and Navy, among them Leo Genn, Robert Newton and Griffith Jones. In one notable case, however, Olivier failed to get the casting he wanted. The service chiefs might be moved by his overtures, but not David Selznick. The Hollywood movie boss still had Vivien under contract and he flatly refused to have his Scarlett O'Hara 'devalued' by appearing in the modest film role of the French princess Katharine. Instead the part went to Renee Asherson, who was then playing Vivien's original role in *The Mask of Virtue* at an obscure North London theatre.

Months of preliminary organization and planning went into the making of *Henry V*. For much of that time Olivier was haunted by one problem above all others: how to present the Shakespearean Chorus on the screen. Would the attention of cinema audiences be held by a disembodied voice? he wondered. If a visual presence was essential for a film, what would Chorus look like? And how could he appear on screen without detracting from the realism and momentum of the story? There was no problem, of course, in relation to Shakespeare devotees, but Olivier wanted to achieve what some Wardour Street executives held to be impossible: to get Shakespeare across to the masses, combining words with pictures and music in such arresting style that their attention could be held for more than two hours.

The answer finally came to him one day when he and film director Anthony (Puffin) Asquith were sharing a London taxi from the Ministry of Information building. 'We were talking about this problem of mine. Suddenly I saw the solution. I have always seen my films from the last shot backwards and was trying out on Puffin the idea that the first time we saw the Chorus, who up to now would have been merely an off-screen commentator, would be for the last speech, when we would discover that we'd been in the Globe Playhouse all the time. I had no sooner said this to him than I saw immediately that the Globe Playhouse was to be the frame—with its actors employing a highly rhetorical method that would most felicitously set the central idea.'[1]

In essence, Olivier was recognizing that he could not camouflage the theatricality of Shakespearean verse in adapting it for the screen—so why not wholly recognize its theatrical setting and use the theatre as the film's framework, with Chorus appearing at both beginning and end as an actor taking part in a stage performance of *Henry V* in the seventeenth-century Globe? It had the advantage of introducing the Shakespearean verse in an accustomed setting before moving out of the theatre into the broad spectacle. It gave the audience an orderly sense of being transported back to another time and place. And—one decade before the advent of CinemaScope and the device of widening the screen for panoramic emphasis—it helped to give an added dimension to the large-scale exterior scenes. In fact, it suited Olivier's purposes in every way. But it was a device that evoked harsh criticism from less original minds within the film company. Some said that the Globe Theatre prologue was blatantly theatrical and therefore sure to alienate cinema audiences from the start. Del Giudice ignored them. Olivier was totally in command; Del Giudice made it clear that he had complete faith in him.

Olivier now faced his greatest practical problem: the shooting of the Battle of Agincourt, the action highlight of the film. Today such an outdoor epic could easily be shot in Spain or the Balkans with the full co-operation of regular cavalry. But this was 1943. Where could open countryside of fifteenth-century simplicity be found in a land bristling with the hardware of modern war, the skies streaked with the vapour trails of defending Spitfires or marauding Luftwaffe? And where could Henry's English army and the Dauphin's soldiers be recruited when every able-bodied man in England was fighting the real war? Bower suggested the answer: Ireland. Neutral, peaceful, accessible and with the kind of 'really poetic countryside' that Olivier demanded. They toured the country and finally decided on the Enniskerry (County Wicklow) estate of Lord Powerscourt. It was exactly right for Agincourt, and it had the advantage of a permanent Boy Scouts' camp in the grounds, thus providing accommodation for Olivier's armies. More important, Ireland had plenty of cheap labour available. Henry's army numbered 30,000, the French 60,000, and it was estimated that, to suggest such forces, they would need at least 650 men and 150 horses. Men were recruited from all over Eire at £3·50 per week, with a bonus of £2 per week for any man who brought his own horse. Volunteers included such assorted types as a Dublin taxi-driver and an overweight jockey, but for the most part they were farm workers, with a stiffening of more disciplined men from the Irish Local Defence Force, and they all had to be paid, fed and accommodated irrespective of whether there was work every day. Since two weeks' shooting time was washed out by rain, the costs rose astronomically. But Del Giudice (or Mr. Del, as he was popularly called) never gave Olivier a hint of the grave financial troubles. 'Don't worry,' he would say with an expansive flourish of his cigar. 'I'll take care of theese leetel details. You are making a masterpiece.'

In May, Lieutenant Olivier arrived on his field of Agincourt to find his mock armies encamped in khaki tents amid an array of long marquees serving as bar tents, cookhouses and storerooms. His headquarters was a caravan within snorting sound of the stables, set on a hilltop from which he could survey his entire command. He had never before taken charge of such vast numbers of men. He felt unsure of himself as general; so, like Montgomery in the desert, he had his 'troops' assembled and then explained what he was trying to achieve in the great battle scene. He ended dramatically: 'I may ask some of you to do some dangerous things, but I won't expect you to do anything that I won't first undertake myself.' Some Irish film extras were only too ready to hold him to that promise, and soon afterwards the producer-director-star was hobbling around on a crutch to support a sprained ankle, and later appearing mandarin-like with both arms in a double sling—more sprains from personally showing his men how to leap from a tree on to an enemy soldier.

Ten days were devoted to the basic training of his raw recruits —farm workers and their hacks being schooled to gallop and charge and move in line abreast, members of the Defence Force being trained to handle the longbow and fire their *papier-mâché*, felt-tipped arrows in unison. Then a half-mile single-track rail had to be laid for carrying a car-mounted camera to film the French cavalry charge, and several more days were needed to equip the armies with uniforms and banners. Since genuine armour was in short supply, this endeavour required much ingenuity—such as having 'chain mail' knitted by blind Irish students in a crocheted heavy twine sprayed with gold or aluminium paint. Olivier would not entertain a stand-in except for sequences when he was wanted behind the camera, so he also took riding lessons. And soon, mounted on the Irish grey gelding he named Blaunche Kyng, he became the most dashing and ubiquitous figure on location, one moment riding as a king in his pudding-basin wig and glittering and cumbersome armour, the next charging about as a mounted director bellowing instructions through a megaphone strapped around his neck. But ironically, once filming began, this most physical of directors received his worst injury when neither on horseback nor involved in combat. He was scrutinizing a shot through the viewfinder when a horse charged into the heavy Technicolor camera. His mouth was cut through to the gum and streaming blood, but he made light of the incident and immediately fussed far more about the condition of the camera. At the time it was the only one of its kind in Britain.

The first shot was obtained on June 9. It had taken all morning to dress the men and horses, and by the time the camera rolled, the clear skies had passed and clouds were continually obscuring the sun at crucial moments. At times Olivier felt supremely elated at achieving precisely the shots he wanted; then, just as suddenly, everything seemed to conspire against him and he began to despair. In Ireland he was seeing inferior black-and-white prints of the Technicolor film and these were often discouraging. Worsening weather added to his gloom, and in a letter to Vivien, then entertaining the troops in North Africa, he confessed that he sometimes got 'panicky and nervous'. Yet he never knew of the real troubles surrounding *Henry V*.

In London Del Giudice faced a financial crisis that threatened to see the picture being abandoned altogether. It was already clear that the film was going to exceed its £300,000 budget, and when a leading financier withdrew his support, Del Giudice could save the project only by some hard bargaining with J. Arthur Rank. He persuaded Rank to provide the bulk of the £300,000 (in fact the total came to more than £475,000, then far and away a record sum for a British film) and in doing so he sacrificed control of Two Cities Films. His company had long been largely dependent for finance on distribution contracts from Rank. Now Rank formerly became chairman of Two Cities Films and Del Giudice lost his much-valued independence. But *Henry V* was saved.

On July 22, six weeks after they had begun, the scenes of Agincourt were completed. The Eire expedition had cost £80,000, resulting in film that would take up little more than 15 of the picture's 137 minutes of screen time. But those scenes were to prove the most vital ingredient in the making of what was to be hailed as a cinema masterpiece.

Back at Denham studios, shooting resumed on August 9. They were no longer plagued by the vicissitudes of the weather, but now the recruitment of able-bodied extras was a major problem, and when suitably virile-looking men came forward to hold swords, lances and longbows it was best not to ask why they weren't holding rifles and sten guns instead.

Albert Meltzer, a Kine Union official who spent several days as an English bowman serving the king before Harfleur, recalls:

There was something ironic about the stirring speeches of war and glory, and closing the wall with our English dead, when one was in a throng of people many of whom were American, Australian and English soldiers on the run from the military police. A less patriotic band would have been hard to find. For the most part they stood around listlessly—they were not professional extras, of course—and Olivier was sometimes irked by their unresponsiveness.

Quite bluntly, they were unprofessional and it showed out-rageously when they came to shooting the Globe Theatre scene where the French Ambassador (Ernest Thesiger) brings Henry a defiant and cheeky message from the Dauphin, together with a 'tun of treasure'. The King asks: 'What treasure, uncle?' And the Duke of Exeter (Nicholas Hannen) replies: 'Tennis balls, my liege'.

Well, in his sharp reply to the French insult, Olivier, as King, threatened revenge on the Dauphin with the line: 'When we have matched our rackets to his balls.' A ripple of laughter ran through the ranks of extras at this. And the shot was lost. Olivier went cold with contained fury, but said nothing. Instead he played it again, this time correcting the line—'matched our rackets to these balls'—and delivering it with a pronounced gesture towards the treasure chest so as to divert their attention from a vision of the Dauphin's testicles.

Because of difficulties of filming in wartime, it was February 1944 before Olivier completed the final shots of *Henry V*. They were taken on the golf links at Denham, where club members held up their tee shots and watched as he rode by, handsomely mounted on a pure white Irish thoroughbred. Vivien, soon to start work on Gabriel Pascal's long-projected film of *Caesar and Cleopatra*, was there as a spectator. Weeks of editing lay ahead; William Walton's music had still to be recorded. But Olivier's main task was done—an astonishing debut as a star-and-director, almost comparable in its way with Orson Welles' work on *Citizen Kane* three years before.

'That feat of actually directing and producing, as well as acting the leading part, was a staggering thing,' says John Laurie, who played a captain in Henry's army. 'Such a thing had never been known. And I don't think Larry could have done this without a certain amount of military training, and the status of being an officer. I am sure it was most valuable. At the end of the war I was already over the hill, but the young lions, Olivier, Richardson, Jack Hawkins and the rest, were coming back, and they'd all become officers, and no question about it, that gave them an authority which no actor could get by playing leading parts. It was like becoming the head of an organization, and from being just rogues and vagabonds, these men (*especially Olivier*) came back with great authority, and a sense of being able to command people.'

Olivier himself had no ready explanation of his sudden advance to this new pinnacle of achievement. 'Maybe it's just that I've got older,' he said. He also stressed that *Henry V* was essentially a triumph for teamwork—and so it was—but in the final analysis it remained overwhelmingly his personal triumph. His starring performance, in the face of so many unaccustomed pressures as director, was extraordinary; his conception of the picture and its direction, nothing less than inspired.

Not least remarkable was the way he and Beck experimented with filming techniques, particularly in their treatment of important speeches where they broke with the custom of moving in with the camera for dramatic emphasis and taking the bulk of the delivery in intimate close-up. Olivier explained: 'Filming Shakespeare required some new techniques or at least abandoning some old ones. You don't need tricky shots—you don't have to shoot up a man's trouser leg or photograph through keyholes or keep shifting from one angle to another. Hollywood developed those techniques to make up for bad acting and weak scripts. But if you have good actors—and I was convinced that we had a very good company—and if you have Shakespeare's lines, you don't need tricks to maintain interest. In many of the scenes the camera hardly moves. Another thing about filming Shakespeare is this: You have to reverse the usual film technique of getting closer and closer to the actor as a scene reaches its climax. I remember when Norma Shearer played the death scene in *Romeo and Juliet*, as she lifted the cup of poison to her lips, the camera moved in until when she finally drank it, all you saw was her face, the cup and her hand. That was all wrong, because it didn't allow for the fact that it isn't necessary in Shakespeare for the camera to create the climax. The verse does that. At the very time that the lines demanded broader and broader acting, the camera compelled Norma Shearer's acting to become smaller. Anything else would have looked grotesque in close-ups. In making *Henry V* we did just the opposite. The camera started close up and, as the climax of the speech neared, it drew back so that the actor could let himself go.'[2]

This reversed technique was especially telling in Henry V's

speech before Harfleur. A medium shot shows the king on horse-back and with sword drawn urging his men loudly:

> *Once more unto the breach dear friends, once more;*
> *Or close the wall up with our English dead!*

Then we cut to a close-up of Olivier as he speaks more softly:

> *In peace, there's nothing so becomes a man*
> *As modest stillness and humility . . .*

As the King continues—'But when the blast of war blows in our ears' . . . —the camera slowly starts to backtrack, effectively revealing more and more of the array of troops around him. Finally, as the speech comes to its battle-cry crescendo—'Cry "God for Harry, England, and Saint George!" '—the camera cuts back dramatically to a medium close shot of Henry on the word 'George', with the king's horse rearing at the point of climax.

From the first private viewing it was evident to everyone that Olivier's film was a technical and artistic revelation. When it was first shown to a group of Shakespeare pundits at Oxford, the only dissatisfied comment came from a woman specialist who insisted that all the war horses at Agincourt should have been stallions. But the all-important test would come at the box-office, and even in 1944, when the Normandy invasion had provided the picture with a neat historical parallel, there were serious doubts about its commercial value. These doubts remained in the Rank Organisa-tion even after rave reviews from the critics. First, despite past successes, Laurence Olivier was still not a name to guarantee success at the box-office. He was not among the top ten in popu-larity polls of international movie stars; and in the current *Motion Picture Herald* poll of money-making British stars, he was placed behind James Mason, David Niven, George Formby and Eric Portman! Second and more important, it had yet to be demonstrated that Shakespeare, however supremely interpreted, could be 'sold' to the great cinema-going public.

Henry V opened at the Carlton in London's Haymarket in November 1944. For several days business was slow; then, gradually, attendance picked up. The word spread that here was something extraordinary, an entertainment not to be missed even by those who dismissed Shakespeare as 'too highbrow'. After three weeks the daily queues were so long that the one-month lease on the cinema was extended for another four. After four months the demand was no less and the film was transferred to the Marble Arch Pavilion where it completed a remarkable eleven-month London run. But success in the metropolis was no guarantee of popularity in the provinces, as was demonstrated in parts of the North of England where fans, favouring standard Grable-and-Gable Hollywood fare, booed it off the screen. Yet the faith of Rank, who stood to make a colossal loss on Britain's costliest film, remained unshaken. 'I refuse to believe that this picture won't appeal to the masses,' he said. 'Anyone who affirms that, underestimates the intelligence of the people. I am certain that it will bring many thousands of new patrons to the cinema.' And he was right. Research revealed that more than half the paying customers in London were not regular filmgoers, and the pattern was repeated elsewhere.

The film went on general release in the summer of 1945. Rival cinemas offered the touching story of *A Bell for Adano*, the romances of Joan Fontaine in *The Affairs of Susan*, the taut, Cagney-style excitement of *Blood on the Sun*, the tough realism of *Dillinger*, a typical Betty Grable musical frolic called *Diamond Horseshoe* and twelve-year-old Liz Taylor's big winner, *National Velvet*. Soon to follow were such massive box-office hits as *State Fair*, *The Wicked Lady* and *Brief Encounter*. Yet, with the boost of special matinées for schools, *Henry V* survived; so well, in fact, that Del Giudice forecast that it would pay for itself by British showings alone.

There had, quite simply, never been a film like it before. With unparalleled success it brought Shakespeare to the masses for the first time, and a whole new generation was fed upon it as, in major cities all over the country, schools were paraded in great crocodiles to morning matinées under the escort of teachers who purred with delight that the cinema had suddenly become such a powerful medium for education. Appropriately it was Brighton, now Olivier's home town, that set the pattern. In July 1945, the local education authorities paid for the admittance of thousands of children during a one-week showing at the Odeon. Other local authorities followed suit and the movie-makers benefitted to such a degree that there were disgruntled letters to the Press suggesting that the State should collect royalties from the film. For the school children it was that glorious rarity in those austere days of rationing and black-marketeering—something for nothing. And if the great majority saw *Henry V* as little more than a welcome escape from classroom routine, one likes to think that a sizeable minority was enriched by the experience and encouraged to view Shakespeare with a less jaundiced eye.

The cinema profited, too, because that film won over so many of the unconverted. Olivier's old drama teacher, Elsie Fogerty, was just one of thousands whose attitude towards films was changed by *Henry V*. Until then she had never much cared for the cinema. After seeing the picture, she viewed the medium with new-found respect and willingly accepted an invitation to Denham studios to help supervise the speech for the film of *Caesar and Cleopatra*. 'Larry is the only producer who has created a real film for England,' she wrote in her diary.

After the removal of such profanities as 'bastard' and 'damn' to satisfy the Hays Office, *Henry V* had its U.S. premiere in April 1946 in Boston's Esquire Theatre. It won unprecedented praise for a British film. In a two-page review in *Time* the esteemed critic James Agee hailed the arrival of a masterpiece and a new cinema style—'this perfect marriage of great dramatic poetry with the greatest contemporary medium for expressing it'.

In Boston the film played to capacity audiences for eight months and Tufts University awarded Olivier the honorary degree of Master of Arts for his outstanding contribution to the art of the cinema. In New York it ran for eleven months, a new record for a British film. Within a year, after being shown in only twenty American cities, it had taken $1,018,000. In December the New York Film Critics elected Olivier as the best actor of the year, and only after a second ballot was *Henry V* displaced by William Wyler's *The Best Years of Our Lives* for the best picture award. Finally, in March 1947, came the supreme honour—a special Academy Award to Olivier for producing, directing and starring in a picture that had done more than any previous work to boost the British film industry's prestige abroad.

But by that time, three years after its making, *Henry V* had brought Olivier rewards enough. It had trumpeted his genius to the world, and he could never forget his debt to the one man who had made it all possible. Soon after returning from the Hollywood presentation ceremony, he wrapped his Oscar and personally delivered it to Filippo Del Giudice. 'Without you, dear fellow,' he said, '*Henry V* would never have been made.'

15

★

Zenith at the Old Vic

Cleopatra is to the screen what *Macbeth* is to the theatre. Seven film epics have been made of the life and loves of the enchantress of the Nile, and since Cecil B. De Mille's 1934 extravaganza with Claudette Colbert, she has proved the most costly, disaster-ridden subject in cinema history. Hopefully no motion picture will ever match the appalling production record of the 1963 *Cleopatra*, which saw the destruction of two marriages, the near-death of its female star, the sacking of two directors, the fall of the president of Twentieth Century-Fox and the leaping of a $5 million budget to a world record $37 million. But in its time the making of Gabriel Pascal's *Caesar and Cleopatra* (1945) came perilously near.

It was the most expensive British picture of its time. The director was bitten by camels. A German buzz-bomb fell close by the location site. There were technicians' strikes, endless script changes and delays, wild extravagances such as the shipping of an eighty-ton model of the Sphinx from England to Egypt, and eighteen months of feuding, fussing and general mismanagement. These were transient troubles, seemingly ruinous at the time, but eventually bringing compensation at the box-office by sheer force of publicity and ostentation. The real tragedy during its making was one of a strictly personal nature that properly received a minimum of publicity. In July 1944, six weeks after filming began, Vivien Leigh, the cinema's fourth Cleopatra, had a miscarriage and lost the baby that she and her husband had so much hoped for.

For Miss Leigh, as for many others, *Caesar and Cleopatra* represented a time of confusion and heartbreak. She went into it with tremendous enthusiasm, regarding it as her greatest screen opportunity since *Gone With the Wind*. But apart from the financial reward (£25,000 for sixteen weeks' work) and the oppor-

tunity of meeting George Bernard Shaw, the film gave her no
satisfaction. Indeed, six years passed before she could bring
herself to see the finished work. It was curious. In the summer of
1943 Vivien had sweltered for three months in North Africa as
she entertained troops from Cairo to Tunis to Tripoli. She
suffered bouts of illness and lost nearly fourteen pounds in
weight on what was otherwise a richly rewarding tour, memorable for its wildly enthusiastic audiences and meetings with King
George VI and Generals Eisenhower, Montgomery, Spaatz and
Doolittle. Yet, typical of the topsy-turvy world of the movies,
when it came to playing Cleopatra in Egyptian summer scenes,
she was sometimes left shivering with severe cold. In November
1944 Alexandrian scenes were being staged in the 'desert' of a
field at Denham, with Vivien wearing flimsy gowns and endeavouring to look serenely majestic while she was actually blue with
cold. It was unfortunate for an actress who had been prone to
chest ailments since childhood, and soon after finishing the film
she became ill and was ordered to bed.

Doctors advised a prolonged rest, but she insisted that work
was the best remedy. She had already chosen her own 'tonic'—
the role of Sabina, Mr. Antrobus's maid-of-all-work in Thornton
Wilder's morality play, *The Skin of Our Teeth*. With Olivier
producing, she began rehearsals in April 1945, and simultaneously she fought a legal battle to enable her to appear on the
stage.

Selznick was making one last bid to bring his Scarlett to heel.
During the war Vivien had consistently resisted his efforts to
have her return to Hollywood to make films. She argued reasonably that it was unthinkable that she should leave England and
her husband at such a time. But now the war was virtually over.
Selznick was getting tough. Vivien's seven-year contract had
two more years to run, so he applied for a legal injunction to
restrain her from appearing in *The Skin of Our Teeth*. Two top-
notch barristers—Sir Walter Monckton K.C. acting for Selznick,
and Sir Valentine Holmes K.C. for Miss Leigh—fought the
courtroom battle of wits, and Sir Valentine emerged the victor
by virtue of his subtle argument that if his client was forced *not*
to act, then she might, under wartime regulations, be drafted by
the Ministry of Labour into the services or a munitions factory.
And surely, he reasoned, not even Mr. Selznick would want that

for his so highly valued star.* Miss Leigh won by a technical
knock-out and she went on, as Sabina, to score one of the stage
triumphs of her career.

A curious feature of the situation—one not generally realized
at the time—was that while Selznick was virtually trying to
pressure Miss Leigh back into making films, her husband was
actually being paid for *not* making films. Six years later, by way
of another legal battle, it was revealed that Two Cities Films had
paid Olivier £15,000 to stay out of pictures for eighteen months
and so assist the exploitation of *Henry V*. The Crown contended
in court that he was liable to pay income tax on that sum; after
all, he wanted the film to succeed because he took twenty per cent
on the receipts. In reply, Olivier's counsel argued that his
client's profession was to act and that if payment was for *not*
acting then it could hardly be a receipt of his profession. Olivier
won the day, saving himself, at the current rates, something in
the region of £11,500 in tax.

Professionally as well as financially, the non-filming arrangement had suited him very well. For directly after making *Henry V*
he had been offered an opportunity that left him no time whatsoever for movie-making, one that opened the way to his most
spectacular successes in the theatre.

In June 1944 he secured a five-year contract as a director of the
revived Old Vic.

In 1941 the Old Vic theatre on Waterloo Road was reduced to
a bombed shell. It looked like the final curtain. But the organization was kept together, largely through the enterprise and energy
of general manager Tyrone Guthrie; and with some financial
support from the newly founded Council for the Encouragement
of Music and Arts (CEMA—later the Arts Council) it spread its
branches far and wide, taking roots in Bristol, Liverpool and
elsewhere and making provincial tours to factories and mining
villages and generally bringing drama to a great multitude who
had never seen professional stage productions before. Here was a
major step towards making the theatre a people's art and a

* Selznick is said to have received £50,000 for his share of Miss
Leigh's services on *Caesar and Cleopatra*, plus a share in the U.S.
rights.

people's pleasure, and it is a sombre thought that without the wartime circumstances that brought CEMA into existence, the prospect of state-aided theatre might never have been so swiftly advanced. In the mind, if not yet in fact, the Old Vic had initiated the National Theatre.

Early in 1944, unaware of the flying-bomb menace to come, the governors of the Old Vic decided that the company should end its provincial wanderings and return to London on a more or less permanent basis. Bronson Albery, joint administrator of the Old Vic with Guthrie, made his New Theatre available for their productions. Lieutenant-Commander Ralph Richardson was invited to help direct the new London company. He, in turn, requested the assistance of Olivier and John Burrell, a drama producer from the B.B.C. Since both Richardson and Olivier could look forward to service duties no more vital than the training of air gunners, they both agreed to join the Old Vic provided that they were formally released by the Admiralty. This release was granted immediately—as Olivier expressed it, 'with an alacrity that was positively hurting to both Ralph and myself'.

If Olivier was excited about returning to the regular stage, he gave no sign of it. When asked if he welcomed the opportunity, he simply replied: 'I am a man who does what he is told. A year and a half ago I was told by the government to make films. Now it is indicated that my place in the service is not, perhaps, so necessary as a place in the theatre.' In stiff-lipped military fashion he kept his true feelings about the mission to himself—and those feelings were mostly compounded of doubt and anxiety. His film of *Henry V* had not yet been seen. And after so many years out of the theatre, his distrust of critics and his fear of unfavourable audience reaction was more acute than ever. He and Richardson had the advantage of a strong company around them, including Sybil Thorndike, Harcourt Williams, Nicholas Hannen, George Relph, Joyce Redman and a nervous youngster direct from the Birmingham Repertory: Margaret Leighton. Yet they had no great faith in the plan to open with a nightly repertoire of three plays; and their pessimism seemed all the more justified when the buzz-bomb war started up in August and they found themselves rehearsing to the accompaniment of V-1 rockets droning overhead.

Nor was Olivier happy about their choice of plays. He was content to play the minute part of the Button Moulder in Richardson's main showpiece, Ibsen's *Peer Gynt*. But he disliked the character of the priggish Sergius Saranoff that he was to play in Shaw's *Arms and the Man*, and above all he was deeply apprehensive about his own star vehicle, *Richard III*. Donald Wolfit's Crookback, seen so recently in the Scala season, was still alive in his mind's ear. He could not free his memory of Wolfit's inflections; at the same time his actor's pride demanded that he find another approach to the part. His natural inclination was not to attempt it at all, but Burrell had suggested it, and he could not think of a suitable alternative without returning to a major Shakespearean role that he had already played.

Both Olivier and Richardson felt the need to flex their dramatic muscles elsewhere before returning to the London stage, and so they arranged a try-out of *Arms and the Man* at the Opera House in Manchester. There, Richardson was praised for a brilliant Bluntschli, but the local critics had reservations about Olivier's humourless Sergius, and suddenly he was reminded of all the pre-war agonies he had suffered in exposing himself to critical judgments. His private feeling at this time was that he could not face any more trials by ordeal and that he would prefer to be back in the Navy.

The following night Guthrie came to see the performance. Afterwards, as they were leaving the theatre, he observed by way of encouragement: 'Liked your Sergius very much.' Olivier growled back in a manner that clearly indicated his contempt for the part.

'But don't you love Sergius?' Guthrie asked.

'Look,' said Olivier. 'If you weren't so tall, I'd hit you. How do you mean, how can you love a part, a stupid, idiot part? Absolutely nothing to do but conform, to provide the cues for Shaw's ideas of what was funny at the time. How can you possibly enjoy or like a part like that?'

'Well, of course,' Guthrie told him, 'if you can't love Sergius you'll never be any good in him, will you?'[1]

And that remark, spontaneously thrown out, made an indelible mark on Olivier, striking so deep that he still rates it as the most priceless advice that anyone ever gave him. It at once reminded him how, in his first season at the Old Vic, he had struggled with

Henry V until he had shed his contempt for the character. Recalling Guthrie's remark many years later, he said: 'Well, it clicked, and something happened, I suppose, that gave me a new attitude, perhaps an attitude that had been completely lacking in me, up to that time, towards the entire work of acting.'[2]

The Old Vic opened at the New Theatre on August 31, 1944. Olivier had left the London stage as a triumphant Coriolanus; now, six years later, he was back in the ten-minute part of the Button Moulder. It was a shrewd choice, allowing him to ease himself back into the theatre and at the same time winning him praise for modesty in accepting such a role 'in the true repertory tradition'. His last-act appearance gave what was described as 'an unearthly glow'—a miniature high-quality gem of quiet but strangely disturbing power. The greatest praise, however, was deservedly for Richardson, giving one of the outstanding performances of his career as the poetic and finally pathetic Peer Gynt, and for Sybil Thorndike who, in her playing of Peer's mother, staked a further claim to recognition as England's foremost actress.

Next, in *Arms and the Man*, Olivier did not repeat his error of attempting to turn the caricature that was Sergius into a serious portrait. Plastic-nosed, he conformed by playing him strictly for laughs, and this time, though veering dangerously towards burlesque, he revealed his enormous flair for comedy in a performance praised as a 'joyous travesty' and a 'museum of invention'. In this way he neatly whetted the appetite for his appearance in a major role, but he had done nothing to ease his own anxieties. He was all too aware that his real come-back to the London stage had yet to be made—on a night when the critics would microscopically examine his performance in a play that he regarded as 'the poor relation' of their repertory. He prepared for his examination with the darkest forebodings.

In rehearsing *Richard III* Olivier had more difficulty in remembering his lines than he had ever known before. He put it down to advancing age and wartime rusting of the memory. But it went deeper than that. There was so much physical business to occupy his thoughts in trying to portray a man twisted in both body and mind. He still needed frequent prompting at the dress rehearsal, and on the night before the opening he was at Claridge's until four in the morning, going over his part with cues given by

Vivien Leigh and Garson Kanin. On the opening night his nervous tension and sense of impending doom were so acute that he telephoned John Mills and asked him to look in at his dressing room before taking his seat in the audience. When Mills arrived he confronted Olivier, dark and menacing in his grotesque make-up, and pacing up and down in a convulsion of anxiety. 'You are about to see the worst performance I've ever given,' he told his friend. 'I haven't even been able to learn the bloody lines. I'll be terrible, terrible. I want you to know as one of my friends. You can tell any of my other friends who're out there to expect the worst. If you're warned in advance you won't be too disappointed.'[3]

Perhaps, in some strange way, that exercise in dark despair helped him prepare to enter the black, satanic mind of Gloucester. If not, then no actor can have tortured himself with fears more needlessly. For that prophecy of doom was the prelude to a night of sheer theatrical magic—a night when a frightened, doubt-ridden actor took the stage as a shuffling, humpbacked figure and left it as a veritable giant. Out of the shadows he limped, very slowly making his way downstage to open with the most effectively atmospheric of all first lines. And from that arresting and supremely paced beginning—

> *Now is the winter of our discontent*
> *Made glorious summer by this sun of York . . .*

—until his final, convulsive death throes, he held his audience with an almost supernatural fascination. This Richard was, according to many of the *cognoscenti* privileged to witness it, a performance of such hypnotic power and sustained excellence that even now, thirty years later, they insist that Olivier has never surpassed it—nor, perhaps, has anyone.

Incorporated in that opening speech, seemingly unobserved, were some lines taken from Gloucester's long soliloquy in Act III, Scene II of *Henry VI*, and besides throwing additional light on Gloucester's make-up, it allowed the actor more scope to vary his pace from the start, more time to build up his initial image of a paranoiac with rather more sardonic humour than was usually suggested. It was a device that suited Olivier's purposes well, but then everything about this performance was painstakingly thought out to build up a Crookback essentially of his own design.

At the final curtain tumultuous applause indicated a memorable triumph. Olivier waited warily for the verdict of the critics. That night he stayed up till three in the morning, reading notices and having rather too much to drink. He never had more cause to celebrate. The reviews were sensational— 'a masterpiece' . . . 'the finest Richard III of our generation' . . . 'moments bordering on genius'.

Four days later the big guns of the Sunday critics fired another impressive salute. In *The Observer*, J. C. Trewin wrote:

Too often an actor of Shakespeare's *Richard III* has offered us the mask without the mind. When the brains are out a part should die, and there an end. Not so here . . . It is the marriage of intellect and dramatic force, of bravura and cold reason, that so distinguishes Mr. Laurence Olivier's study at the New Theatre. Here indeed we have the true double Gloucester, thinker and doer, mind and mask. Blessedly the actor never counterfeits the deep tragedian, the top-heavy villain weighted by his ponderous and marble jaws. His Richard gives to every speech a fire-new glint. His diction, flexible and swift—often mill-race swift—is bred of a racing brain. If, outwardly, he is a limping panther, there is no lameness in his mind. Other players have achieved the Red King, boar, cockatrice, bottled spider, and developed the part with a burning theatrical imagination; none in recent memory has made us so conscious of the usurper's intellect, made so plausible every move on the board from the great opening challenge to the last despair and death.

In the *Sunday Times*, Agate, true to form, contrived to prod and pick at petty details of Olivier's approach and delivery. But in his own time he came round to bestowing praise:

There was a great deal of Irving in Wednesday's performance, in the bite and devilry of it, the sardonic impudence, the superb emphases, the sheer malignity and horror of it. If I have criticism it is that Mr. Olivier takes the audience a little too much into his confidence . . . This Richard coheres from start to finish, and is a complete presentation of the character as the actor sees it and his physical means permit . . . But even if this Richard is not Shakespeare's, it is very definitely Mr. Olivier's, and I do not propose to forget its mounting verve and sustained excitement.

At the Thursday matinée, when making his second appearance as Richard III, Olivier experienced a strange and profoundly satisfying sensation. He had been on the stage for twenty years but this was the first time that he felt totally in command and totally at ease, lacking not even a fraction in self-confidence. Instinctively, he felt that he had the audience in his hands, even before he had delivered his first lines. He has described it as 'an overwhelming feeling, a head-reeling feeling', and confesses ashamedly, that it went so much to his head for a time that he didn't even bother to affect a limp on stage. He knew that he had the audience anyway. And it was the intoxicating moment when he knew that he had really 'arrived' as an actor.

Why did Olivier achieve true greatness in this particular role and at this particular time? In a sense his triumph owed something to Guthrie's gentle reminder about the need to 'love' a character; he was now all the more aware of the importance of sympathy in drawing a portrait and, in the case of a character too loathsome to love, of at least appreciating the circumstances and factors that contributed to the making of such a villain. But, above all else, Olivier attained Olympian heights as a result of having enormous pressures upon him at a time when he had both the maturity and the experience to rise to meet the challenge. Roger Bannister has conceded that he would never have broken through the four-minute mile barrier without three athlete friends snapping in turn at his heels. Indirectly, Olivier was no less *driven* to supreme effort. There was the haunting fear of so many critical eyes upon him for his come-back. Then, more significantly, there was the pressure of having to follow Wolfit's greatly admired Richard III. He felt compelled by pride to search and strive for something different.

In that search, Olivier began by looking back to Irving, or rather, he remembered imitations of Irving's voice by old actors. Gielgud, in much the same way, had looked back to Irving in preparing his first Macbeth. Also, he thought deep and long about the physical appearance of the character ('I work mostly from the outside in,' as he puts it). He thought about Jed Harris under whom he had suffered in New York, and of the physiognomy of Disney's Big Bad Wolf, and not far from his mind was the devil incarnate across the Channel, Adolf Hitler. From preliminary sketches and hours of experimentation before the mirror, there emerged his own evil creation—the long reptilian nose, lank black hair streaked with red and lying on the shoulders, warty cheeks of a pallidness that contrasted demonically with the bright, thinly drawn mouth. Harcourt Williams recalled that he achieved such a satanic look that actors gave him a wide berth in the wings. But that was just the façade. His real achievement, born of twenty years of practising the actor's craft, was the overwhelming sense of malignity that he conveyed from within.

Olivier was now being loudly hailed in some quarters as the greatest living actor, so ending the fifteen-year reign of Gielgud. And Gielgud responded with characteristic generosity. He made a gift to him of one of his most treasured possessions: the sword that Edmund Kean had carried as Richard III and which had been passed on to Irving when he first played the role in 1873. It bore the added inscription: 'This sword given him by his mother Kate Terry Gielgud, 1938, is given to Laurence Olivier by his friend John Gielgud in appreciation of his performance of Richard III at the New Theatre, 1944.'

For Olivier, who regarded 'great actor' comparisons as invidious and who never wished to have a friend for a rival, it was a deeply moving gesture. But then Gielgud, so distinctively different in style, would always have his champions in the great acting stakes. Unhappily, the actor who now suffered most by comparisons was the man whose Richard III had previously been so much admired. During the war Donald Wolfit had risen to great prominence and was unrivalled in terms of industry. In 1944 he was performing an astonishing feat of memory and stamina and versatility, presenting eight productions in repertory, each performance a different play, seven by Shakespeare and one by Ben Jonson. 'He is a National Theatre in himself,' wrote one critic. But largely as a result of the dazzling series of revivals at the New he became the victim of comparisons that did not always make sufficient allowance for the fact that he lacked the strong supporting talents enjoyed by Olivier and Richardson in the Old Vic company. Out of the situation would emerge that most biting witticism from Hermione Gingold: 'Olivier is a *tour de force*, and Wolfit is forced to tour.'

In the gossipy world of the theatre many smart anecdotes have been repeated and embellished to describe a rivalry between Olivier and Wolfit. In fact, the two men did not know each other well and there never was any personal hostility between them. Indeed, in April 1944, when a drama critic reported that Olivier had made a disparaging remark about Wolfit's Lear, Olivier wrote to the critic to say that it was 'completely untrue', that he had not even seen the performance and he had only respect for Wolfit's work. Furthermore he sent a copy to Wolfit, together with a letter explaining his distress and adding that he was 'looking forward to seeing your King Lear—as soon as I can get in'. Ronald Harwood, Wolfit's biographer, has written: 'The unsolicited action by Olivier endeared him to Wolfit, and from that moment on he regarded him with uneasy awe and admiration. Grudgingly, Wolfit acknowledged Olivier's position as the leading member of the theatrical profession.'[4]

At the beginning of the new year *Uncle Vanya* was added to the Old Vic repertoire, with Ralph Richardson in the title role. Olivier, as Astrov, felt miserable during rehearsals. 'I kept on worrying how I could make it real to myself. Then we came to the dress rehearsal, and suddenly seeing my face made up in the mirror and jabbing those pince-nez on my nose, the whole part fell into place in my mind.'[5] He certainly looked exactly right, but not all the critics were satisfied that he fully captured the rusticity and basic inner weakness of the man, and Harcourt Williams, who played the Professor, Serebryakov, had a feeling that Richardson and Olivier should have exchanged roles.

Compared with the three preceding plays, this production was a disappointment. Nothing, however, could dim the extraordinary success of that 1944–45 season. It was hailed as a living example of the practical possibilities of a National Theatre. For many people it was the most exciting and encouraging theatrical event of the war. 'We are seeing in London today the beginning of a golden age in the theatre,' wrote Beverley Baxter.

Olivier had firmly planted his flag on the summit of the theatrical profession. Now, in the last weeks of the war in Europe, he guided his wife towards a high plateau of her own, by directing her in *The Skin of Our Teeth*. The play, an extremely daring choice, is an allegorical extravaganza described by Wilder as a 'history of mankind in comic strip' and crowded with un-conventional tricks and symbolism. When it was first produced in New York, some theatregoers walked out during the inter-mission and did not return. This did not happen in England, where the drawing power of Miss Leigh always assured packed houses, but the play certainly baffled British audiences during its provincial run. And then, on May 16, 1945, in the warm after-glow of a million celebration bonfires set aflame on VE Day eight days before, the play opened in London at the Phoenix.

It was a glittering first night the like of which had not been seen since the Thirties. Fur coats and evening dresses came out of moth balls as London society defied post-war austerity for one unforgettable evening of glamour. The personal magnetism of the Oliviers had never been more evident. With his double involvement as producer and husband, Olivier found it an experience as unnerving as any he had known as an actor. In a sense, it was even more nerve-racking than his first night as Richard III, since now he had no control over events on the stage. He sat in the middle of the stalls, a bundle of nerves that became increasingly taut as he looked on helplessly at a second act badly disturbed by a succession of late lighting cues. Finally, after the second interval, he noticed something that made his blood boil over. James Agate, that doyen of critics, was returning late to his seat just across the gangway. He had missed no less than ten minutes of the third act—ten minutes that were arguably vital for a full appreciation of the play. Nervous energy erupted into impulsive action. Olivier crossed over to Agate and rapped him aggressively across the shoulder. 'You're late, blast you!' he rasped.

'Who's that?' asked the sixty-eight-year-old critic, startled in the theatre's darkness. Olivier hissed back, 'You know who I am all right.' Then, still livid, he stalked back to his seat.

He had not hit Agate hard, but for a producer to hit a critic at all on a first night was, as far as anyone could recall, unprece-dented in the history of the English theatre. How would Agate respond in his columns? No critic was better equipped to retaliate with pen dipped in acid. Olivier looked anxiously for a hint of personal injury in Agate's *Sunday Times* review. Instead, he read:

The play's comedy, farce, fantasy, what you will, can be

summed up in Joe Gargery's 'What larks!' On the visual side, owing to Mr. Olivier's ingenious, inventive producing backed by some brilliantly co-ordinated team-work, the play must be reckoned a complete success. Through it all, lovely to look at, flitted and fluttered Miss Leigh's hired girl, Sabina, an enchanting piece of nonsense-cum-allure, half dabchick and half dragon-fly. The best performance in this kind since Yvonne Printemps.

In rhapsodizing about *The Skin of Our Teeth*, Agate was for once in step with every other theatre critic. There was general agreement that Wilder had written an outstanding morality play and that Olivier had directed it with rare ingenuity. But it remained essentially Vivien's triumph. Her Sabina was, by common consent, her most brilliant stage performance so far— 'as sparkling as a diamond' and 'as volatile as quicksilver'. Beverley Baxter expressed the popular view when he wrote in the *Evening Standard*: 'Miss Leigh is startlingly good. Forget about Scarlett O'Hara, and her stiff performance of the artist's wife in *The Doctor's Dilemma*. We see her as she really is—part gamine, part woman, a comedienne, an artist.'

In a sense, 1945 was the Oliviers' Coronation Year—as the new 'Royals' of the entertainment world. And that year, in a style to match their stature, they acquired their own country 'palace': Notley Abbey, founded in the twelfth century for Augustine monks, and standing amid some seventy-five acres of land by the river Thame near Long Crendon in Buckinghamshire. This L-shaped building, where Henry V and Cardinal Wolsey are known to have stayed, is now officially listed as an Ancient Monument. The Oliviers first inspected it on a house-hunting tour in the winter of 1943 and came away with diametrically opposed opinions. Miss Leigh, seeing it in strictly practical terms, thought it was absolutely impossible. It was cold and draughty and damp, its garden an unkempt wilderness; and it would obviously cost a small fortune to provide adequate heating and make necessary structural alterations and repairs. Olivier thought it was absolutely perfect and saw it only in terms of what it could be made to be. It had history and a certain majesty that appealed to him, and when he heard that it had been endowed by Henry V he took it as a sure signpost of destiny. Vivien cajoled friends to look at the place and then bring him to his senses. David Niven was one who went down and agreed that it looked hopeless. Olivier stood firm. He reasoned that they could tackle it stage by stage, as building permits and money became available. Moreover, with so much acreage, they might even make it pay part of its own way, by some farming and market gardening. They could breed pigs and grow cabbages, and there could be greenhouses for Vivien to raise the hothouse plants and exotic flowers that she loved. And so it was done. He bought Notley shortly before the war's end, with the money received from *Henry V*. Builders were working on the structure at the time that Miss Leigh was appearing in *The Skin of Our Teeth*.

The Old Vic season had ended at the New Theatre on April 14, 1945, being followed by a four-week tour of the provinces and a six-week tour of the newly liberated countries of Europe. They were in Manchester on May 8, and as they joined in the wild VE Day celebrations, no one was more profoundly overjoyed than Sybil Thorndike. The news of peace had left her wondering and worrying about the fate of her son John, who had been a prisoner-of-war for so long. Then, on arrival at the theatre for the evening performance, she was called to the telephone. It was John and he was speaking from his home in Surrey. All at once the tension of many years of anxiety was released; with Olivier quietly cheerful at her side, she wept uncontrollably until it was time for her stage entrance, and professional self-discipline automatically took command. Five months later, still in uniform, John Casson appeared in the wings at the New when Olivier was leaving the stage in the role of Oedipus. The eyeless king saluted his senior officer and said, 'Reporting for duty, sir.'

In the meantime, Olivier had been abroad with the company, touring in the wake of the liberating forces. They were all in uniform (under the command of Basil Dean's ENSA), and they travelled by troopship, bus and plane to show the troops *Arms and the Man*, *Peer Gynt* and *Richard III*. After playing in Antwerp and Ghent, they flew from Brussels to Hamburg for their first performance in conquered Germany. Remarkably, amid all the ruins, the famous old *Staatliche Schaupielhaus* survived, and every night this vast theatre was packed by wildly enthusiastic audiences. Less happily, while appearing in Hamburg the company was asked to visit the notorious concentration camp at Belsen and give a special matinée for the military staff who were facing such a harrowing and deeply depressing time. It was an unforgettable experience that brought home to everyone the greatest horror of the war. Sybil Thorndike, who had been taken by a doctor to see the emaciated children in the camp, wept on the bus journey back to Hamburg, and that evening she wrote, 'I'll never get over today—*never.*'

Otherwise the tour was memorable thoughout for scenes of great rejoicing, and in July it ended triumphantly in Paris, with a week at the Marigny and then the unique honour (for a foreign company) of appearing for a fortnight at the Comédie Française. There, on the final night, after a rapturous reception for his Richard III, Olivier made a curtain speech in carefully rehearsed French. Dramatically, he kissed his finger and imprinted it on the stage. 'And now,' he said, 'I give back the Comédie Française to its rightful owners.'

For Olivier, those exciting weeks in Paris were overshadowed by grave anxiety. He had heard that Vivien was ill and, alarmingly, the only letter he had received from her simply stated, 'now that you know the worst', without giving any real information. She had, in fact, sent an earlier letter, explaining her medical condition and playing down its seriousness so that he would not worry too much. But that letter had never reached him. Finally, he learned the facts from his old friends Alfred Lunt and Lynn Fontanne, who had just arrived in Paris from London to entertain American troops. They told him that X-ray examinations had revealed a tubercular patch on the lung, and that Vivien had been advised to take a complete rest as soon as possible.

Months earlier, during the provincial tour of *The Skin of Our Teeth*, Miss Leigh had been coughing badly and was advised by a doctor to see a specialist as soon as the play reached London. But only after two months in the demanding role of Sabina did she act on that advice. By that time she was terribly thin and tiring very easily. Olivier hurried home to learn that her tubercular condition was less serious than was supposed at the first diagnosis, but a very long rest was absolutely essential. The play was taken off at the end of July and its star went into University College Hospital for six weeks' treatment before going to Notley to convalesce.

Meanwhile the Olivier-Richardson-Burrell triumvirate was launching another sensational Old Vic season. This time, primarily because Richardson wanted to play Falstaff, they began with the two parts of *Henry IV*, with Burrell producing. Olivier shrewdly took the non-star roles of Hotspur and Mr. Justice Shallow. They gave him generous scope to demonstrate his virtuosity, appearing as a virile warrior one night and a senile scarecrow the next, and he played them to extraordinary effect. Kenneth Tynan awarded that Shallow the highest marks of all of Olivier's work in this and the previous season, and Beverley Baxter raved over a creation that was 'like something devised by Grimm in collaboration with Dickens . . . fantastic yet as real as human vanity'. But it was his ginger-wigged Hotspur that commanded the greater praise—a masterly portrayal which he stamped with his own original mark by choosing to stammer on every word beginning with the letter 'W'. Lady Percy's reference to her husband 'speaking thick' was reason enough for a stage stutter. The device admirably fitted the character. But in choosing 'W' as the key to his impediment he gained new advantages. Most notably it enabled him to give added pathos to the death scene in which he expires in a vain struggle to get out that line: 'No, Percy, thou art dust, and food for —.' Now he could add a final 'w-w-w' to Shakespeare's lines before Prince Hal, his executioner, gave the telling finish, 'For worms, brave Percy . . .'

As in *Richard III*, Olivier staged a death of electrifying style and stunning realism. Mortally wounded by a sword blow to the neck, and delivering his dying lines—'O Harry, thou hast robb'd me of my youth!'—he stood erect for several seconds, grasping his neck in an effort to staunch blood that oozed through his fingers. And then, fully armoured, and with startling suddenness, he plunged down two steps, crashing forward on to his face. 'On paper one would say an anticlimax, or perhaps a sure laugh,' said Harcourt Williams. 'But no, the whole thing held the audience spellbound.' [6]

The next evening Olivier had replaced that most masculine and heroic of warriors with a spinsterly lecher, a wizened, white-haired figure, sharp-nosed and goatee-bearded. He was at his most heavily disguised since he burped on to the Old Vic stage as Toby Belch nearly nine years before, and though some malcontents thought he worked in rather too much comic business that had little relation to the dialogue, the overall effect of his Shallow was another performance that delighted its audiences and greatly enhanced the actor's reputation, even though he was playing in the broad shadow of a quite outstanding Falstaff.

But his most dramatic character switch in that Old Vic season was yet to come—in a brilliantly devised double bill of Sophocles' *Oedipus Rex* (the translation by W. B. Yeats) and Sheridan's *The Critic*. This time his transformation was not unveiled on alternate nights, but at one sitting of tragedy followed by burlesque, which had him leaving the stage with blood streaming from his eyes as the soul-tormented self-blinded king, and returning after a fifteen-minute interval as the absurd and foppish Mr. Puff, tossing snuff in the air and catching it in the nostrils of his comical retroussé nose. Some Old Vic traditionalists thought it was too blatantly showing off, too suggestive of a quick-change music-hall bill, but the verdict of the vast majority was that it represented an irresistible and quite extraordinary exhibition of virtuoso versatility.

Olivier's accursed king, achieving moments of stark terror and flashes of genuine pathos, was hailed as a *tour de force*. As Puff, there was some suggestion that he sacrificed audibility in his pursuit of physical antics and that he sought to introduce invented humour where Sheridan's sparkling wit needed no elaboration. But audiences left no doubt about their feelings. *The Critic* was a hilarious hit, and they adored the rollicking spectacle of a Mr. Puff who was borne up by a piece of scenery, lowered perilously on a rope, fired at by a cannon and catapulted on to the stage from the very top of the proscenium arch. Of all Olivier's many daring acrobatics on stage, none was more extravagant than this performance which had him hoisted into the flies on a painted cloud. And at one matinée it very nearly ended in disaster. The rope for his descent, inadvertently taken off its cleat, came away in his hands, and he saved himself from a thirty-foot fall only by grasping the thin wire that supported the painted cloud and hanging on until rescue came.

Here was Olivier at his zenith in terms of sheer theatrical excitement; outrageously ostentatious perhaps, but nonetheless supremely entertaining. Each night he received an overwhelming ovation, and when the season closed there were unprecedented scenes outside the New, with several thousand fans massed in the street and chanting 'We want Larry' and subjecting him to the kind of hysterical mobbing he had not known since his appearance on Broadway at the time of *Wuthering Heights*' release.

Baxter of the *Evening Standard* concluded: 'Laurence Olivier grows in stature before our eyes. His intelligence sheds radiance upon everything he touches. Here is an actor who refuses to repeat himself but brings to each role a freshness and an understanding that leaves us wondering if anything is beyond his reach.'

At the end of April 1946, immediately after their record-breaking season, the Old Vic company flew to New York to open a six-week run at the Century Theatre. Vivien, now fully recovered, accompanied her husband and in Manhattan they were met by Garson Kanin and Ruth Gordon, who had booked them in at the St. Regis. As with Olivier's 1940 *Romeo and Juliet*, the company arrived in the wake of massive advance publicity. New Yorkers understood that they were about to witness an extraordinary exhibition of ensemble acting, and the box-office was swamped accordingly. The critics were properly on their guard, preferring to err on the side of caution. They reacted with controlled enthusiasm to the two parts of *Henry IV*, but once Olivier had revealed his Oedipus, the battle was won, the flood-gates open for a Niagara of superlatives. John Mason Brown, in a brilliantly penetrating review of the five-role repertoire, was finally persuaded to use 'that precious, dangerous, final adjective —"great"'. 'This Oedipus,' he wrote, 'is one of those performances in which blood and electricity are somehow mixed. It pulls down lightning from the sky. It is as awesome, dwarfing and appalling as one of nature's angriest displays. Though thrilling, it never loses its majesty.' [7]

Before this short run was ended, the New York drama critics had voted Olivier as the best actor seen on Broadway in the 1945–46 season—this in a season that had seen the return of such talents as Walter Huston, Raymond Massey, Maurice Evans, the Lunts and Oscar Homolka. And in those six weeks of staggering success the large theatre was always packed, even for matinées in the high heat of summer.

At the beginning of that Broadway season Olivier was reported by the *New York Times* magazine to be 'in the pink of condition—tanned, rested, relaxed, eager for the fray'. Six weeks later the case was the reverse. He was now in his fortieth year. Out of financial necessity he had taken on Sunday radio work in addition to performing his incredible Hotspur-Shallow-Astrov-Oedipus-Puff pentathlon, and after two years of almost non-stop endeavour the immense physical and mental strain was clearly beginning to tell. It had reduced him to an intense, nervous condition that was reflected by a recurring nightmare in which he saw himself either falling when suspended high above the stage as Mr. Puff or being involved in an airplane crash.

Together, the Oliviers left New York for London aboard a Pan-Am Constellation Clipper. They were not long out of La Guardia Airport when the outer engine on the starboard side caught fire. Through the window they watched helplessly as the wing blazed. Then they saw the entire engine fall away. The plane was descending fast from 15,000 feet and the pilot, Captain Samuel Miller, was looking desperately for a landing spot. Providentially, a break in the clouds revealed a small airfield at Willimantic, Connecticut, but then, as they descended at about 300 miles per hour, the pilot discovered he could not work the undercarriage. He had to make a crash landing. Only his supreme efficiency saved the fifty passengers that day. After a half-mile, belly-scraping skid, he finally brought the plane safely to a halt. 'It was brilliant and almost superhuman,' said Olivier later. 'Such a brilliant piece of work that every passenger stood and cheered the pilot.' That escape did not fully discourage Olivier's superstition about flying, but it did serve to exorcize his nightmare.

After a long summer holiday at Notley—tennis parties, gardening and developing their small private farm—both the Oliviers returned to the London stage in September 1946. Vivien resumed where she had left off, in a revival of *The Skin of Our Teeth* at the Piccadilly Theatre. He prepared for his third Old Vic season in harness with Burrell and Richardson, this time not beginning quietly in a secondary role but making a storming start in the most ambitious style imaginable. As King Lear—and producer!

Lear is recognized as the most difficult of Shakespeare's characters to act; indeed, some actors have called it unplayable. In tackling this Everest, Olivier 'achieved the summit, . . . reached a dizzy height . . .' or 'never looked like bringing it off' —depending on which expert judgment you most value. Undoubtedly, the varied reactions owed something to the fact that other notable Lears still lived bright in the memory. It was, after all, only two years since Agate had described Wolfit's Lear as 'the greatest piece of Shakespearean acting I have seen since I have been privileged to write for the *Sunday Times*'. Harcourt

Williams could remember four Lears—Benson, Gielgud, Wolfit
and Olivier—and, while admitting to prejudice as the producer,
he thought that Gielgud at the Old Vic in 1931 came 'the nearest
to the titanic figure'. Some critics now found Olivier insufficiently moving in the later scenes of downfall and madness and
felt that his gifts were not especially suited to the role. Beverley
Baxter (London *Evening Standard*) wrote: 'King Lear floored
him almost as completely as if he were a British heavyweight.
Olivier's attempt to give subtlety to a role that is glorious but
completely "ham" was a brave but undoubted failure.' Others
praised the same performance to the skies. J. C. Trewin recognized it as 'the best Lear yet', faltering only in the hovel scene.
Alan Dent hailed a 'great' Lear—'nothing short of tremendous
achievement. It had everything that this hardest of parts should
have ideally.' 'Unfaltering! Unflagging!' thundered *The Times*.
'No actor that we can recall has matched the creative stamina
which enables Mr. Olivier to rise equal to the demands of every
phase.'

There can be no doubt about the popular success of Olivier's
King Lear. It had a limited run of forty-eight performances, with
never a seat empty. Kenneth Tynan, in a brilliantly measured
appraisal of what he called 'a moderate Lear', referred to the Old
Vic becoming a new myth and complained of the 'loud battalions
of ingenuous claqueurs who nightly mobbed the New Theatre'
and fed the players 'on nothing but cheers'.[8]

It may be, indeed, as one critic observed, that this production
told us nothing new either of Lear or of its star player, but it did
emphasize most tellingly one crucial aspect of Olivier's art—the
indelible vein of humour that lurks behind the actor's mask.
Even in Lear he found an element of humour. Some praised this
as an achievement; others did not. 'He is our model Richard III
and his Hotspur is unique,' wrote Tynan, 'but he has no intrinsic
majesty; he always fights shy of pathos; and he cannot play old
men without letting his jaw sag and his eye wander archly in
magpie fashion—in short, without becoming funny.'[9]

James Agate, who had reservations about a performance
'brilliantly imagined and achieved', also remarked on the grim
and unexpected humour with which this Lear was invested. And
this perception led Agate to his most illuminating insight into
Olivier's art: 'I have the conviction that Olivier is a comedian by
instinct and a tragedian by art. He keeps his sense of fun under

control in his tragic parts, but I can see him controlling it.'

'A comedian by instinct and a tragedian by art.' It is a fundamental statement about Olivier as an actor that one finds supported again and again by critics and players alike. As a succinct definition of the nature of his acting, it will never be improved upon.

16

The Film HAMLET

On January 1, 1947, the New Year's Honours List proclaimed a new Bachelor Knight of the Theatre: Ralph Richardson. Immediately everyone was asking: if Richardson, why not also Olivier? At the Old Vic, Harcourt Williams always replied with the story that the Prime Minister had wanted to honour the company but did not know which actor-director to choose. So the two stars had tossed up for the knighthood. But no one believed that. The widely accepted notion was that Olivier was yet another victim of the antiquated tradition that discriminated against divorced persons.

It seemed the obvious explanation at the time. Overlooked was the fact that Richardson was Olivier's senior by four and a half years and was the first of the triumvirate to have been invited to direct the Old Vic's revival. Moreover, to have had two actor-knights in one list (there had been only eighteen in the past half-century) would have been unprecedented generosity. So it was Sir Ralph and Mr. Olivier. In an earlier age, when dramatic duelling was popular sport, such distinction might have fired bitter rivalry. But never in this case. Richardson agreed to accept a knighthood only after satisfying himself that Olivier would not feel slighted. In the same way, when Olivier was knighted six months later, he promptly wrote to Gielgud expressing his embarrassment at being given prior recognition. A remarkable sympathy and understanding cemented these three pillars of the English theatre.

On that New Year's Day, as it happened, Olivier was pre-occupied with a project destined to win him a heap of honours. He telephoned Del Giudice in Zurich to say that he had decided to go ahead with the production they had tentatively discussed a few weeks before: a film of *Hamlet*. Fraught with difficulties in adaptation, Shakespeare's most celebrated play had been significantly neglected by the film-makers. Leslie Howard in 1940 had failed to realize an ambition to direct himself as a screen Hamlet. Alfred Hitchcock at one time canvassed in vain the idea of a modern-dress *Hamlet* starring Cary Grant! For Olivier, in 1947, it was a case of now or never. He would be playing the part at the age of forty when, even with blond-wigged make-up, a few critics were to judge him too old for the part.

It was a time in his career when he could seemingly do no wrong. In January another season at the New ended with extra-ordinary scenes in St. Martin's Lane—fans sleeping out all night to be first in line for tickets to *King Lear*, hundreds of bobbysox girls gathering outside the stage door every evening and chant-ing, 'We want Larry', and screaming so hysterically when he appeared that a national newspaper pompously complained: 'This actor is the first in the land. It is regrettable that he should be treated as another Sinatra.' Then, just before leaving for Northern Italy, he saw his production of *Born Yesterday* through a dazzling first night at the Garrick. There were rave reviews for the play and its dumb-blonde star Yolande Donlan. Most significantly, it spurred Olivier's aspirations in theatre management.

For the moment, however, all his creative thoughts centred on the formidable task of reducing and reshaping Shakespeare's *Hamlet* for the screen. When completed, his film would be severely criticized by those pedants who could not accept cuts and changes in a masterpiece, but a full treatment would have meant a film of four and a half hours and certain death at the box-office. So the cutting had to be drastic. Characters had to be eliminated entirely. This, in turn, made it necessary for scenes to be transposed. Also, it was necessary to excise obscure phrases and modernize a score of Elizabethan words no longer compre-hensible to the general public. Olivier did not relish the work. But it had to be done, and he believed that it was worthwhile, even if they could convey only a part of the original to the vast cinema audiences of the world.

Del Giudice booked a luxury five-room suite for the Oliviers at the Hotel Miramare in Santa Marguerita Ligure on the Italian Riviera. There, after a ten-day holiday, they were joined by Alan Dent, again collaborating on a Shakespeare film script, and later by other members of the *Hamlet* team, among them Regi-nald Beck, Roger Furse and Carmen Dillon, all with valuable experience on *Henry V* behind them. Preparation of the script occupied the bulk of Olivier's time. In the end, after much debate, it was agreed reluctantly that they would have to dispense entirely (as Miss Leigh suggested) with Rosencrantz and Guildenstern, thereby sacrificing some of the best tragicomedy. Voltimand and Cornelius inevitably went with them. Fortinbras was eliminated, too, part of his final speech being given to Horatio. They found it necessary to cut important soliloquies, including 'Oh what a rogue and peasant slave am I'. Hamlet's big scene with Ophelia ('Get thee to a nunnery') was switched so that it came immediately before rather than after his 'To be or not to be' soliloquy, and this planted the possibility of the Prince's madness earlier and arguably gave more immediacy to his reasons for contemplating suicide. But mostly the changes served three basic purposes: pace, length and comprehension.

There was precious little room for sentiment in this task; at the very last stage of the filming Olivier even left out his favourite soliloquy: 'How all occasions do inform against me.' On the film's release it was supposed by some critics that this notable omission, along with others, had been forced upon Olivier by structural changes in the text. A few called its absence unforgivable; others stressed how much heart-searching it had cost Olivier and how he had put off the final decision until the last possible minute because he considered it to be so illuminating in showing the development of Hamlet's character. In fact, rather mundane circumstance contributed to the loss of that soliloquy. The poignant speech *was* actually spoken, on horseback, shot on location by the sea. Unfortunately, as Olivier spoke ('What is a man if his chief good and market of his time be but to sleep and feed?'), the horse closed a weary eye and looked supremely bored, rather in the manner of Lee Marvin's nag in the final scene of *Cat Ballou*. If they had decided to keep in the soliloquy, a retake costing several hundred pounds would have been necessary.

They spent a month in Italy, completing the script and making technical plans for the shooting sequences, camerawork and lighting. Olivier had already decided that the sets should be bare of all but essentials, and similarly he judged that colour might be too 'pretty' for this dark tragedy. The tone had to be basically grey or 'death-black'; he saw *Hamlet* as an engraving

rather than a painting. And the great attraction of filming in
black and white was that it allowed the use of deep focus photography by which foreground and background can be made
equally sharp in definition. The deep focus technique had been
employed more than a quarter of a century before, but never
with truly telling effect until cameraman Gregg Toland went to
work on *Citizen Kane*. It greatly reduced 'tracking' and cutting—
eliminating, for example, the need to cut from one face to another
during dialogue and so allowing longer takes and avoiding dis-
tracting breaks from the poetry of the lines. It could also be
used, as Toland showed, to achieve unusual dramatic effects.

Meanwhile, in London, casting for Hamlet was proceeding
apace under the direction of Anthony Bushell. In the main, he
found it a straightforward task; after the impact of *Henry V*,
well-established actors were only too eager to be included, and a
host of talents came forward. Casting the two female roles
proved the main difficulty. The search for Hamlet's mother
ended with Eileen Herlie, a Scottish actress thirteen years
younger than Olivier. She could be made up to appear a queenly
mother and yet still look desirable enough to move Claudius to
fratricide. For Ophelia, Olivier's original choice was eighteen-
year-old Jean Simmons, who had greatly impressed him as
Estella in *Great Expectations*. But she was already working on a
picture at Pinewood, *The Woman in the Hall*, and shortly afterwards she was due to fly to Fiji and don a Lamour-style sarong
for a spectacular, unintended comedy called *The Blue Lagoon*.
Thirty other girls were tested, the runner-up being seventeen-
year-old Claire Bloom, who went on to play the part in the
Stratford Festival. But Olivier stood firmly by his first choice.
When he returned from Italy he insisted that there must be a
way to get Miss Simmons. Finally it was arranged. Her departure
to Fiji could be delayed, but her work on *Hamlet* had to be
completed within thirty days.

Jean Simmons came to Shakespeare totally fresh. She had
never even *seen* one of his plays. All her professional experience
had been in the movies. Now she was so overawed that she said
she could never play the part, and husband-to-be Stewart
Granger was advising her not to try. But Olivier had chosen well.
He found, as David Lean had advised him in advance, that she
responded quickly to direction. Of all the cast she was the one,

attuned to cinema technique, who gave the least 'theatrical' performance.

Shooting of *Hamlet* began in May, in an atmosphere of unusual secrecy. Olivier ruled that no visitors were to be allowed on the set at Denham studios. Sightseers, eager friends popping in to see 'Larry' at work, feature writers, reporters, photographers—all were indiscriminately barred. Inevitably, the ruling was criticized by the film publicity men and by the Press, but Olivier would not budge. He rightly guessed that his production would arouse all the more interest and curiosity for being veiled in mystery. Moreover, his behind-closed-doors policy was justified because the filming of *Hamlet*, for a variety of technical and artistic reasons, demanded intense concentration. Desmond Dickinson, director of photography, later said that in thirty years in the movie business he had never known a film to present so many problems.

John Laurie as much as anyone appreciated the burden under which Olivier laboured. He was the former Old Vic and Stratford star who had advised Olivier the fledgling actor on how to cross a stage and how to speak blank verse. Now their roles were completely reversed:

When Larry asked me to be in the film, I was engaged for a lead in *School for Secrets*. But then he found I had a week free from the other picture and so he invited me to play Francisco. 'Splendid,' I said. 'Lovely. Just to be in it. Anything.' Francisco was all right. Just ten lines. Then finish. But it wasn't quite that simple. As it happened, it took the whole week, with a perilous set—an enormously high drum, a thick mist, and dear Teddy Knight,* who could hardly see, about to fall over the edge at any moment.

It was in rehearsal that I suffered most. I started overconfidently. After all, I'd done the lot—*Hamlet*, *Othello*, both Richards and so on. Yet I had a really tough time getting those ten lines just as Larry wanted them, even though I knew my Shakespeare as well as he did. Perhaps I wasn't very good; anyway, I had a bad time for two or three days. And this is

---

* Esmond Knight, as a gunnery officer aboard the battleship *Prince of Wales*, was blinded in action against the *Bismarck* in May 1941. Two years later an operation partly restored sight to his right eye.

Larry. It was going to be *his* film, and no bloody nonsense about anyone coming in, thinking that because they'd played Hamlet they knew it all. It had to be done his way. And rightly so. But I am quite certain I resented it at the time. It was very difficult for me, though I accepted the situation with never a grouse because he'd proved his genius as a film-maker with *Henry V*. And that opening scene is one of the trickiest to direct in all Shakespeare—a *pons asinorum* right at the beginning of the play.

Mind you, I still think it took a pretty tough young man to do what he did to me. Olivier was an autocrat, no doubt about that. But in his position he had to be, because he was working from dawn, getting to the studio first to see that everything was ready as *producer*. Then, at half past eight, he assumed his role as *director*, provided that he was not required at the time as *leading actor*. We finished at about six o'clock, but Larry had to stay on to get ready for the next day, or to rough-cut what he'd shot the day before. God knows when he got back to Chelsea where he was living then. Really he had taken on the job of a superman. Two supermen. I don't know how he lived through it. In fact, I don't know how Larry has lived so long. His three Shakespeare films would have worn out anyone else I can think of. It made one forgive the autocracy, for one realized the weight the man was carrying when he would say, 'Don't argue! Do it as I want it!' And they were the best Shakespearean plays that have ever been filmed.

Because he knew so surely what he wanted, Olivier had accepted from the beginning that he would have to play the Prince himself. But he did so reluctantly. He wrote later: 'I feel that my style of acting is more suited to stronger character roles, such as Hotspur and Henry V, rather than to the lyrical, poetical role of Hamlet.'[1] His preference was for directing, and theoretically it would have been best to have another actor of sufficient stature to carry the role, one on whom he could impress his own interpretation. In practice this was impossible. He had very decided views on Hamlet's every line, movement and inflection, and no actor of the necessary ability would have tolerated a director acting out each inflection and gesture for him. Olivier rehearsed all other actors in the appropriate scenes, and for groupings he used an understudy as the Prince. Then he re-

hearsed himself with Beck and Bushell in attendance, and the
scene was shot. Years later, when asked for advice on directing
and starring in Shakespeare, both Olivier and Orson Welles
would independently give Charlton Heston the same tip: 'Two
things are absolutely vital. You have to get rehearsals ahead of
shooting. And you must get a very capable actor to stand in for
you when you are behind the camera.'

In July, Olivier took his one break from the filming to attend a
rather special engagement. As one of forty-seven new Knights in
the Birthday Honours List he was going to Buckingham Palace
to receive the accolade from King George VI. He went with hair
still dyed blond for Hamlet, looking immaculate in a morning
coat borrowed from Bushell and a waistcoat provided by Sir
Ralph Richardson. He came away the youngest actor ever to
receive the honour. Irving had been the first in 1895.

There could be no late-night celebration; both Sir Laurence
and Vivien (now Lady Olivier) had to be on the film set early
next morning. Miss Leigh was working at this time at Shepperton Studios, co-starring with Sir Ralph in *Anna Karenina*, an
overlong, unsatisfactory Korda film that was in one or two cases
appallingly miscast. She did not enjoy working on the picture
and was so depressed by the result that she could not face her
guests at a post-premiere party.

The filming of *Hamlet*, unlike *Anna Karenina*, was remarkably
free of grievances or personal feuds, but because of the technical
pressures and the film's brooding, tragic theme, it was a grimly
professional working unit that rarely knew the kind of joyful
moments experienced on *Henry V*. Esmond Knight can recall
one lighthearted moment, in the opening scene. 'A chap was
spraying mist around the Elsinore turrets, and an assistant
director was calling to him, "A bit more over there, some more
over there . . . and another little squirt just to the left of Sir
Laurence." And I called out, "Hey, are you referring to *me*,
sir?" And Laurence couldn't stop laughing at that. "Damn you
Ned," he said, unable to get into the mood again, "why don't you
keep your bloody mouth shut!" But it wasn't often like that. He
always maintained a sort of aloofness, never became one of the
chaps. And if he came and had a drink, a bit of a silence was
inclined to settle upon the company.'

Inevitably, Olivier had his physical misfortunes. By now this had come to be expected with almost any role that allowed him a degree of athleticism, and as with *Henry V*, he appeared briefly on crutches. He had cracked an ankle in his leap on to the battlements of Elsinore. Fortunately it did not interrupt filming since they had arrived at scenes exclusively between Gertrude and Claudius. And wisely he saved his most reckless piece of physical business until last. It was on the final day of shooting that he revealed precisely what he had in mind for the climactic death scene. Gertrude is dying of poisoned wine, Laertes lies stabbed with the envenomed blade and Claudius is unmasked for the villain he is. Now, with his cry of 'Then, venom, to thy work,' Hamlet stabs the king. Olivier proposed to heighten this drama by leaping from a high, raised platform—half-landing on Claudius.

Basil Sydney, then in his fifties, did not relish the idea at all. Even as a young man, playing Claudius before World War I, he had never gone that far towards realism. Once he realized that the camera was to be focused from below on Olivier, showing the king only from behind, he sensibly suggested that they use a stand-in. George Crawford, a professional strong-man, was brought in for the stunt, and the sight of such a sturdy frame beneath him only made Olivier more ambitious. He launched into an open-armed swan dive and landed directly on his victim. Crawford was knocked unconscious. And he lost two front teeth.

By mid-December *Hamlet* was off the studio floor and in the cutting and editing stage. It would finally have 155 minutes running time. Shooting had been completed in the scheduled six months and without exceeding the original budget. But its £500,000 cost still represented a huge financial risk and much depended on the film's success in the light of Mr. Rank's recent statement to Odeon shareholders disclosing a £2 million loss during the past six years. A special screening was now arranged for Arthur Rank and his chief executive, John Davis. Olivier watched it with them and, like any creative artist revealing his work, he was nervous and looking hopefully for some favourable reaction. But Rank, always conscious of his own very marked limitations when it came to art in the cinema, felt unable to presume to pass judgment on the film. It seemed to him that he had witnessed a rare artistic achievement but he considered that it might seem patronizing for him to say so. Instead he politely

said, 'Thank you very much, Sir Laurence,' as one might for any
small service rendered. Then he walked away, followed by Davis.
He had not given a hint by word or expression as to whether he
liked the film or not. Olivier felt severely deflated.

He had to wait until May the following year for the critics'
reaction. That month *Hamlet* was given a royal premiere at the
Odeon, Leicester Square—the most glittering mink-and-
diamond occasion of its kind since the war, one attended by the
King and Queen, together with Princesses Elizabeth and Margaret, and Prince Philip. Olivier, then in Australia with his Old
Vic touring company, was represented by his sister, brother and
stepmother. From that moment, despite the carpings of the
purists about 'unforgivable cuts', he was assured of a second
screen triumph for Shakespeare. The public reaction was immediate. The Odeon had its longest queues for years, the beginning
of a six-month run. It was the same when the film was premiered
in Australia; Olivier was so overwhelmingly mobbed by admirers
there that he briefly went into hiding near Brisbane.

Milton Shulman, the London *Evening Standard* critic, predicted that *Hamlet* would raise more controversy than any other film
made in Britain since *Caesar and Cleopatra*. 'To some it will be
one of the greatest films ever made; to others a deep disappointment. Laurence Olivier leaves no doubt that he is one of our
greatest living actors. His rich, moving voice, his expressive face,
make of the tortured Dane a figure of deep and sincere tragedy.
Arguments about his age and his blond hair cannot detract from
the personal triumph of his performance. His liberties with the
text, however, are sure to disturb many.'

Some critics were indeed deeply disturbed. But once they had
put on record their predictable disapproval of the more daring
surgical work, the great majority of the critics recognized
Olivier's extraordinary achievement in adapting so vast and
intricate a play to the screen. 'Masterpiece' and 'genius' were
words used again and again. The duel scene consisting of more
than 300 passes was generally accepted as being the cinema's
best-ever swordplay sequence. And in the United States the
film's impact was even greater, critics hailing it as the best
British production brought to their country . . . one of the
greatest pictures of all time.

Today it is fashionable to point to Olivier's pioneering film of

Henry V as much the greater achievement, while his *Hamlet* is less favourably viewed. Many voices have since echoed the complaint made by John Mason Brown that 'at least forty precious minutes are squandered in travelogues up and down Mr. Furse's palace. To sacrifice great language, to have innuendo dispensed with, and to lose key speeches, characters, or scenes merely because so much time is wasted getting the actors from one part of the castle to another, is to be a *Hamlet* dislocated by being on location.'

There have been harsh words, too, about Olivier's use of deep focus photography. As early as 1952, Alan Wood, Lord Rank's biographer, wrote:

The normal use of focus in films dictates the attention of the eye to whatever point the director desires; with deep focus the eye is much more free (apart from the overriding compulsion of following movement) to study any part of the screen: just as a man in a theatre can look at any part of the stage, and study any of the actors on it. So the use of deep focus for *Hamlet* was, in a way, unfortunate; it emphasised its main fault—its excessive theatricality. For it led me to the heretical opinion that Laurence Olivier is not a good screen actor (in later years at least: he was brilliant in some earlier performances before his acting acquired a touch of *amour-propre*). For screen acting, in contrast to the theatre, the supreme virtue is naturalness. In *Hamlet* the audience was conscious throughout of Olivier's acting . . .[2]

Such opinions, however, belie the quite sensational impact that Olivier's *Hamlet* really had in 1948, and how far it dramatically enhanced the reputation of its director-star. The New York reviews especially were nothing less than rapturous: 'The screen has come of age with *Hamlet*' (*Herald-Tribune*); 'the greatest show on earth' (*The Star*); '*Hamlet* puts Olivier at the top of his profession' (*Daily News*). *Life* magazine gave *Hamlet* more publicity than any previous picture and recognized Olivier as the greatest theatrical figure of his time. Even Olivier's old adversary, Sam Goldwyn, was hailing him as 'the greatest living actor on stage or screen' and describing his Hamlet as 'without question the highest spot on the drama of our day—perhaps of any day'.

James Agee (*Time*) did have certain reservations about Olivier's conception of the role, but he, too, joined in the resounding chorus of praise:

> With this admirable filming of one of the most difficult of plays, the whole of Shakespeare's dramatic poetry is thrown wide-open to good moviemakers . . . In its subtlety, variety, vividness and control, Olivier's performance is one of the most beautiful ever put on film. Much of the time it seems a great one . . . No other actor except Chaplin is as deft a master of everything which the entire body can contribute to a role; few actors can equal him in the whole middle register of acting . . . He is a particular master of the sardonic, of complex reaction and low-keyed suffering, of princely sweetness and dangerousness of spirit, and of the mock-casual. On the invention of business, he is equally intelligent and imaginative . . .
>
> Broad as his range and virtuosity are, it seems possible that Olivier's greatest gifts are for comedy, especially for comedy which works close to the tragic. Like every first-rate comedian's, his sense of reality is strong and cool; his understanding of 'the modesty of nature', and his regard for it, are exceptionally acute . . .
>
> A man who can do what Laurence Olivier is doing for Shakespeare—and for those who treasure or will yet learn to treasure Shakespeare—is certainly among the more valuable men in his time. In the strict sense, his films are not creative works of cinematic art: the essential art of living pictures is as overwhelmingly visual as the essential art of his visually charming pictures is verbal. But Olivier's films set up an equilateral triangle between the screen, the stage and literature. And between the screen, stage and literature they establish an interplay, a shimmering splendour of the disciplined vitality which is art.

From Venice to Hollywood, from Copenhagen to New York, *Hamlet* swept the board of prizes and records as no other film had done before. It was the first English-language film to be retained in the same New York cinema for over a year. It was the first foreign-made picture to win the Best Film Academy Award. It was the first British film to win four Oscars, the others being

Laurence Olivier as Katherine the Shrew, aged fourteen (*Radio Times Hulton Picture Library*)

In *Beau Geste* at His Majesty's, 1929 (*Radio Times Hulton Picture Library*)

Wedding Day of Olivier and Jill Esmond, July 25, 1930 (*Radio Times Hulton Picture Library*)

In *Private Lives,*
September, 1930, with
Adrianne Allen, Noël
Coward and Gertrude
Lawrence (*Radio Times
Hulton Picture Library*)

With Vivien Leigh in
Fire Over England, 1937
(*Pendennis*)

With Merle Oberon in *Wuthering Heights,* 1939 (*Sam Goldwyn*)

With Joan Fontaine in *Rebecca,* 1940 (*David O. Selznick*)

Richard III, 1944 *(John Vickers)*

Shallow, in *Henry IV*, 1945
(*John Vickers*)

Astrov, in *Uncle Vanya*, 1945
(*John Vickers*)

Oedipus, 1945 (*John Vickers*)

King Lear, 1946 (*John Vickers*)

Topsy-turvy exit (as Hotspur) — the piggy-back ride courtesy of
Ralph Richardson (as Falstaff) (*John Vickers*)

Olivier sings 'Triplets' with Danny Kaye and Vivien Leigh — the hit of an
all-star charity show at the London Palladium in 1951 (*Popperfoto*)

With Marilyn Monroe in
*The Prince and the
Showgirl,* 1957
(*Warner Bros.*)

As Solness with Joan
Plowright (Hilda
Wangel) in *The
Master Builder,* 1964
(*Angus McBean*)

Othello, 1965 (*BHE Productions*)

awarded to Olivier for the best performance by a man,* to Roger Furse for costume design, and to Carmen Dillon and Furse for black-and-white art direction and set direction. Rank's most rewarding year in films was completed by the award of two Oscars for his picture *The Red Shoes*. And Olivier's year of glory was crowned when he was invested by Denmark as a Knight Commander of the Order of Danneborg.

Awards and box-office receipts are not, of course, the true measure of artistic achievement. More often they indicate entertainment value and popular appeal, as the second most profitable of all motion pictures (*The Sound of Music*) shows. In the case of *Hamlet*, however, Olivier the director made a very real contribution to cinema art. He relied greatly on the technical know-how of his colleagues and he has acknowledged that debt. But his team, as with *Henry V*, were equally insistent that his inspired leadership and originality of ideas were the vital factors. Even Reginald Beck stressed that Olivier taught him much about his own business, often cutting through technical difficulties with his directness of approach. 'One has often accepted a point of technique out of habit, rather than reasoning. But Larry would sweep away the dust of established prejudice with the impelling question: "Why?" '[3]

One original line missing from the film was Hamlet's observation to the First Player: 'the play, I remember, pleased not the million; 'twas caviare to the general'. In the final analysis, Olivier's greatest triumph in films was in successfully serving caviare to the millions. The only sad footnote to the story of the film *Hamlet* is that Filippo Del Giudice, who set up the project, did not fully share in the glory. Before the picture was released, fundamental disagreements had caused him to part company with the Rank Organisation and Two Cities. With his idealistic, fast-dating extravagant approach to film-making, the colourful

---

* Ironically, Ethel Barrymore was recruited to announce the winner of the Academy's Best Actor Award. She had previously made it clear that she didn't care for Olivier's performance, regarding her brother John as a much superior Hamlet. After making the announcement, she said: 'I didn't sound too Sonny Tufts, did I?' She was referring to a famous radio incident when the master of ceremonies, handed the names of his guests for the programme, said in disbelief: 'Sonny Tufts?'

Italian was totally incompatible with accountant-trained John Davis, Rank's tough, super-efficient joint managing director. It was the beginning of the end for him. He formed his own company, Pilgrim Pictures, but the golden touch was lost. After unsuccessfully seeking financial backing in America, he retired to a monastery in Rome, later made an abortive come-back bid, then slipped into obscurity and died in 1961. For some conservative English tastes, he was rather too 'loud' in singing his own praises and those of people he admired. But he was a genuine character, imaginative and generous and kind; and he made a very real contribution to the development of the British film industry. Olivier, with every reason, would always remember him with affection.

17

★

Theatre Royals

With stylish living allied to dazzling artistic success, Sir Laurence and Lady Olivier achieved a social prominence in Britain that invited comparisons with the Barrymores and Lunts of America and eventually brought them recognition as the new theatre royals of the post-war world. And in February 1948 the temptation for the Press to project the Oliviers as 'The Royals' of show business became totally irresistible. That month the squire and his lady of Notley Abbey were embarking with a fifty-strong Old Vic company on a 30,000-mile tour of Australia and New Zealand. They left London in majestic style, with Euston's station master turned out in ceremonial top hat and tails, with flash-bulbs popping, movie cameras turning, bouquets being presented. As official ambassadors of the British theatre they would be expected to undertake official engagements on a scale previously associated only with members of the Royal Family.

The objective was to present to as many citizens as possible their repertoire of three major plays: *Richard III*, *The School for Scandal* and *The Skin of Our Teeth*. But on arrival they found themselves also committed to official functions quite divorced from the theatre: receptions by state governors and mayors; visits to hospitals, universities, museums, galleries, factories and war memorials. They were required to make speeches and give interviews. And the 'royal' flavour was at its most piquant when Sir Laurence was asked to take the salute at a march-past of the Royal Australian Navy!

The Old Vic touring party comprised ten administrative and technical staff and forty actors, including some of the Oliviers' closest friends, most notably George Relph and his wife Mercia Swinburne. Its success was extraordinary. In Adelaide over a hundred people slept out all night in a storm to line up for tickets, and in the morning the line multiplied to a thousand. In Sydney some £100,000 had to be returned by the box-office as supreme optimists mailed cheques and cash in the hope of reserving tickets. Wherever they went, the Oliviers were mobbed by passionate, sometimes near-hysterical fans. They drove themselves so hard in meeting the engagements thrust upon them that, towards the tour's end, Olivier was to tell a reporter, 'You may not know it, but you are talking to two walking corpses.'

By July the pressures had become so great that they were compelled to grab a few days' rest in a bungalow hide-out. Then they faced another formidable round of receptions and speech-making in Sydney, and for Olivier the strain became all the greater when he fell and damaged his right knee during his duel in *Richard III*. It was cartilage trouble.

The knee injury forced Olivier into the hospital for an operation before the tour was ended. Yet it was not the cruellest blow he suffered in Sydney; that came in the form of a letter from London. It was written by Lord Esher, chairman of the Old Vic governors, and after some preliminary words of praise it politely advised Olivier that his five-year contract as a director, along with those of Sir Ralph Richardson and John Burrell, would not be renewed on its expiration in June 1949.

The decision was ironic, ill-timed and nigh incredible. Olivier had sacrificed a fortune in Hollywood contracts in working for the Old Vic. He and his fellow directors had raised the company to an unprecedented peak of popularity and prestige, and here he was, 12,000 miles from home, conducting on their behalf an overseas tour of unparalleled success. Yet, with the tour only half completed, they were telling him that his services would not be required beyond the coming season. Why?

The internal politics behind this drastic and much-disputed change in Old Vic policy have never been fully revealed, but it was certainly not because the Old Vic was prospering very nicely without him. Quite the reverse. One suggestion is that a small but influential minority still clung to the tradition of the Twenties and Thirties, disapproving of any suggestion of a star system and feeling that the success of such a prestigious company, hopefully the National Theatre in embryo, should not be so dependent on the activities of two actor-knights. How far such an attitude prevailed, how far jealousy and resentment came into play, is entirely a matter of conjecture. But one factor most certainly influenced the decision: the unfortunate circumstance, entirely coincidental, whereby Olivier and Richardson were absent from the London Old Vic simultaneously. The latter was currently in Hollywood, working on *The Heiress* with Olivia de Havilland and Miriam Hopkins, and this double box-office loss served to emphasize dramatically how greatly the Old Vic had come to rely upon its two actor-directors for commercial success.

From the time of their appointment it had been clearly understood that Olivier and Richardson would absent themselves from time to time for film work. Yet now, apparently, there had been second thoughts among the governors, and a conflict of interests was seen. Tyrone Guthrie, who had originally agreed to the idea of an Olivier-Richardson-Burrell triumvirate, was to return to the Old Vic as director in 1951. He confessed years later that he had soon had misgivings about their appointment, and he was probably not alone in his opinion that Richardson and Olivier, by making films and radio appearances and travelling abroad, 'tried and failed, to have the cake and eat it'.[1]

Eventually the governors were to announce that the reorganization of the Old Vic and its administration was a step towards the long-promised establishment of a National Theatre. But that was also the overriding aim of Olivier and Richardson, and the real tragedy of the 1948 decision to change the directors was not so much that it robbed the Old Vic of two outstanding talents, but more, that it seriously arrested rather than accelerated progress towards a National Theatre. Olivier and his two co-directors had made no secret of their long-term plans in that direction. They wanted to establish a second Old Vic company so that one could always be playing in the provinces or abroad, thus making it a 'National' available to British audiences in general, not London in particular. The current tour of the Antipodes was seen in part as a move towards that end. They recognized, too, the need to encourage young actors and foster their growth so that new leading talents would always be pushing up to replace the old. And they had taken concrete steps to that purpose by sponsoring the foundation of the Old Vic Theatre School, the Young Vic Company, and a flourishing new branch of the Old Vic at the Theatre Royal, Bristol.

In 1949 Harcourt Williams paid a glowing tribute to the triumvirate in his history of the Old Vic.

Three men of cultural integrity and unquestioned ability in the art of the theatre gathered up the threads of the original organisation which the black hurricane of war had blown hither and thither and wove them into a pattern again, but a slightly different pattern. It was an undertaking that required great courage, foresight and patience. I sometimes think that it could never have been done but for the old friendship that existed between Richardson and Olivier.

Yet he concluded in his final chapter:

The task before us is to persuade the public that plays and the art of acting are more important than individual stars. The National Theatre would be doomed to failure if it pursued a policy of importing stars. It is the business of a first-rate theatre to make not stars but great actors. More than once I have known fine work done in a theatre associated with famous names—work which attracted a wide public; yet when the 'names' were withdrawn the attendance began to decline, although the work of the company as a whole was *just as good*.[2]

The irony was that Olivier and Richardson recognized the merits of that argument as much as anyone. It was never their wish or intention to command the Old Vic stage to the exclusion of other talents. Yet the fact remains that, without them, the Old Vic never fully regained the position in which they left it, and seven years would pass before it emerged from financial and organizational difficulties.

In July 1948 only Olivier, his co-directors, colleagues and friends were aware of his coming break with the Old Vic. The decision was not to be made public until the New Year. Meanwhile, he had to continue on tour for another four months, still representing the Old Vic and tackling a crippling schedule as professionally as ever. In September they arrived in New Zealand to give forty-four performances in less than six weeks. Olivier's cartilage trouble worsened, compelling him to use a crutch for some stage appearances and finally to give way to his understudy for the last three performances. Doctors recommended an operation as soon as possible and, seeing that the homeward sea voyage could be advantageously used to recuperate, he had the cartilage removed before they sailed.

It was a dramatic and rather sad end to a remarkably brilliant tour. They had given 179 performances, played to some 300,000 people and been welcomed by many thousands more. But there were no bands or bouquets, no vast cheering crowds, to mark their departure from New Zealand at seven o'clock on a miserably overcast October morning. At Wellington, as rain bucketed down, Sir Laurence arrived at the quayside in an ambulance, was taken out on a stretcher and then placed in a canvas sling to be hoisted aboard the liner *Corinthic*. He laughed as he was swung high into the air on the cradle, but he might well have reflected that it was hardly a 'right royal' exit in keeping with so much of the tour.

Recalling that tour with great affection, actress Eileen Beldon says:

They worked so tremendously hard, Larry and Viv. They had to go out every single day, to cocktail parties and to visit this and that, and they never went to bed until about two in the morning. I don't think they could have enjoyed it very much, and what it must have taken out of Vivien one can only imagine. She had very little stamina, was such a tiny thing, and of course she had this tuberculosis.

Before we set off for Australia, Larry said a lovely thing to all the company. He told us, 'We are going to be a long time away, in very close communication with each other, and we are all going to get miserable, and I want anybody with any kind of problems at all to please not bottle them up but bring them to us, and we'll try to sort them out. Furthermore, before we start I want everybody to let me know what day their birthday falls on, and we will act in *loco parentis*.' And they did. They gave a party for everyone in the company on their birthday, and they were marvellous in that way as host and hostess. When at last we got back home, Larry told us: 'We are the first National Theatre Company.'

A few weeks later the unbelievable news was made public: that the contracts of Olivier, Richardson and Burrell would not be renewed in June. It aroused severe press criticism of the Old Vic governors, and it seemed all the more senseless at a time when some £10,000 had poured into the New Theatre box-office. The bulk of that money was not for the current season; the public were paying in advance for the second part of the Old Vic season—when Olivier would appear.

He returned to the New on January 20, 1949, and once again hundreds of fans were sleeping out on the sidewalks of St. Martin's Lane. They were lining up to see a first night of special significance. For the first time the Oliviers were acting together on the English stage. In his own production of *The School for Scandal*, with sumptuous costumes and settings by Cecil Beaton, Sir Laurence was playing Sir Peter Teazle, a part that greatly appealed to him. Vivien Leigh, as the tinsel Lady Teazle, had a part that patently suited her but one which she rather disliked.

Conscious that he was working in an age 'when not to be original is not to attract notice', Olivier gave the comedy a treatment that boldly defied convention and surprised the audience. Harold Conway of the London *Evening Standard* commented:

This was scarcely the Sheridan—or, for that matter, the Olivier—they thought they knew. For Olivier, it would seem, has psycho-analysed Sir Peter Teazle. In that disillusioned, sore-tired ex-bachelor, he has found, not a figure of fun, but a creature of infinite (and inhibited) melancholy; not a verbal sparring partner for his spirited young wife, but a gentle spoken, sweetly smiling philosopher. 'How all occasions do inform against me!' this Sir Peter all but exclaims; and his wounded love, pride and hopes become the dominant focus of the play. On stage or off, his pathetic figure haunts us. It is a performance of masterly sensitiveness by Olivier; and it is matched by Vivien Leigh's Lady Teazle—exquisite to behold, beautifully modulating devilment into contrition by the merest flicker of her eyes, the subtlest inflection of the voice. But Sir Laurence really cannot have it both ways. His chosen way is to glimpse the tears behind Sheridan; and the structure trembles before his success . . .

Miss Leigh had profited from experience as Lady Teazle on the Antipodean tour, and although the critics' adjectives bore a strong suggestion that they found her more attractive to the eye than to the ear, the general tone of the notices was encouraging.

It was a first night that ended with six final curtain calls and a long speech by Olivier before he and Vivien left to face another mobbing by adoring fans. Safely, if not sensationally, they had taken the first step towards their dream of establishing a brilliant theatrical partnership that might eventually see them playing many of the great classical roles together.

Six days later Olivier reappeared as Richard III. Nearly four years had passed since he first electrified playgoers with this sardonic study in villainy, and again it was hailed as the best entertainment that the London stage had to offer. It was producer John Burrell's swan song as an Old Vic director. And this time its cast included Miss Leigh. As Lady Anne she had another part that she scorned, but she played it well—as one critic wrote, 'with a force of manner and voice unlike anything she has done before . . . an impressive performance and a brilliant contrast to her Dresden china Lady Teazle'.

She was now developing into a powerful dramatic actress at a pace that even her husband underestimated. And curiously it was in a role that he tried to dissuade her from playing that she made her greatest impression in this season of farewell to the Old Vic. Olivier doubted whether she was yet ready for the title role in *Antigone*, Jean Anouilh's version of the Sophocles tragedy. The part demanded more emotional and vocal power than she had hitherto revealed. But Vivien thrived on challenge and she had her way. Olivier directed the play (also Chekhov's one-act play *The Proposal* as a curtain-raiser) and appeared as the dinner-jacketed Chorus who outlines the story. The result was a notable hit.

Together, the Oliviers put the Old Vic box-office back on the gold standard with takings of approximately £60,000 in five months. The season perhaps did more for Sir Laurence's reputation as a director than as an actor; for Miss Leigh it represented an enormous advancement. She was no longer primarily a bewitching butterfly of star quality. She was being talked about as a potentially great actress. And soon, going far towards realizing that potential, she was to rise to new dramatic heights in the most sensational role of her career: as the tormented and doomed Blanche Du Bois of Tennessee Williams' *A Streetcar Named Desire*.

Actresses can have more difficulty than actors in shaking off a part, and some friends were alarmed at the idea of Vivien playing this harrowing, emotionally disturbing role. Olivier himself had reservations about directing her in it, though after her Antigone he had no doubt that it was within her range. There was also the question of physical strain; as Blanche she would be on stage for the best part of two hours. Yet she scorned suggestions that it might be too exhausting for her. Instinctively, as with Scarlett and Sabina, she recognized it at once as a part that she had to play.

Streetcar opened in October at the Aldwych—the most eagerly awaited first night of the year. There were fourteen curtains, and during most of them the audience was calling for Olivier. 'They don't want to see me all togged up in white tie and tails,' he said. 'I'd spoil the illusion.' So the evening ended without speeches, but with resounding cheers for Miss Leigh, now almost beyond recognition with dyed blonde hair and the haggard features of an ageing wanton. Outside some five hundred fans waited but the Oliviers did not pause to give autographs. Vivien was too exhausted after acting with rare dramatic power one of the longest female roles to be written for many years. For eight months of full houses, never missing a performance, she was to appear as Mr. Williams's lonely and decaying Southern belle, raped and driven to near suicide by her vicious brother-in-law and finally removed to a mental institution. And each night, for minutes after the final curtain, she would be left trembling in the lingering fever of self-induced hysteria.

Many critics, as Olivier feared, were not yet conditioned to stomach such gruesomely dramatic fare. One wrote: 'I feel as if I had crawled through a garbage heap.' Self-appointed arbiters of public taste called the play pornographic, immoral, salacious. And even when judged purely on dramatic merits, this production of *Streetcar* had its detractors. Kenneth Tynan, especially, has condemned it—as being 'a good illustration of the way in which a good play can be scarred by unsympathetic and clumsy direction'.[3] He thought that both Miss Leigh and (much more arguably) Bonar Colleano as Stanley Kowalski were miscast. But the public, perhaps enticed by the sensational publicity, made it a resounding hit. And it was on the strength of this performance that Miss Leigh landed the coveted role in the Hollywood film version—the movie that was to win her another Oscar and establish Marlon Brando as an international film star.

After leaving the Old Vic, Olivier did no more acting for six months. It was time, he felt, to gratify an ambition he had harboured for many years: the desire to launch out on his own as an actor-manager. Laurence Olivier Productions, Ltd., had come into being in 1947, making a triumphant start with *Born Yesterday*. In March 1949, while he was appearing at the New, he had been further encouraged by his presentation at the next-door Wyndham's Theatre of a new Bridie comedy, *Daphne Laureola*, with Dame Edith Evans and a young actor he had discovered in Australia: Peter Finch. That second L.O.P. venture, like the first, ran for nearly a year. But then in August the company had its first flop: *The Fading Mansion*, an adaptation by Donagh MacDonagh of Anouilh's *Romeo et Jeanette*, with its background shifted from France to Ireland. It starred a gifted, young Irish actress named Siobhan McKenna, and was produced by Anthony Bushell and designed by Roger Furse, both directors of Laurence Olivier Productions. It survived only two weeks.

In November 1949 Korda announced that his London Films group had taken a substantial shareholding in Olivier's company. He had lost money on two of his latest films, *Anna Karenina* and *An Ideal Husband*, and now, he said, it seemed an excellent arrangement that he should be associated with 'the two outstanding figures of the British theatre'. Three days later came the news that Olivier had taken over the lease of the St. James's Theatre for four years. His first production would be *Venus Observed*, a modern comedy in verse especially written for him by Christopher Fry. At last he had what he had always wanted—a theatre of his own.

The St. James's, opened in 1835 by Charles Dickens's friend John Braham, was one of the oldest and most celebrated of London playhouses, and there were now great hopes that Olivier would restore to it the eminent actor-manager tradition established in the Nineties when Sir George Alexander reigned supreme for twenty-eight years and launched such notable new plays as *The Second Mrs. Tanqueray*, *The Importance of Being Earnest* and *Lady Windermere's Fan*. Olivier certainly made an auspicious start. *Venus Observed* proved to be Fry's best full-length play to date. It opened on January 18, 1950, and ran for seven months. Yet this popular artistic success did not make a profit for Olivier's company. In his keenness to revive the former glories of the St. James's, he had refused to be cheese-paring over costs. The result was a production of great style, and one al-

together uneconomical for a play staged in this intimate, red-
and-gilt theatre with seating for less than a thousand.

Faced with the burden of entertainment tax and ever-rising
costs, Olivier was to find management of the St. James's fraught
with economic difficulties unknown in the days of Alexander or
even in the later time of Sir Gerald du Maurier's managership.
Not one of his productions there would make a profit. Some
would incur a very substantial loss. Yet he would persevere in
this ambitious vein, taking film work to subsidize his theatrical
ventures, and never lowering his artistic standards for the sake of
commercial gain. His profit was to be measured in terms of
wide-ranging experience that would prove so valuable one decade
later when he became the first director of the National Theatre.

Separately, both Sir Laurence and Lady Olivier were now
firmly established in long-running plays in London. Social life at
Notley began to flourish again. Weekend parties became elaborate productions planned by Vivien with infinite taste and care
from the moment that guests foregathered at Durham Cottage,
their town house in Chelsea. Lady Redgrave has recalled: 'It was
usually after the theatre on a Saturday night as we had mostly all
been working. There would be something small like delicious
little sandwiches and drinks. We would then split up into cars
and begin the hour-and-a-quarter drive to Thame. As most of us
were pretty tired it was a very pleasant way of unwinding. Arriving at Notley at midnight out of the dark was marvellous. All the
lights would be blazing, huge fires everywhere and masses of
flowers.'[4]

Vivien had come to love Notley with a passion she would
never have dreamed possible when she first moved there. The
house, with its old world atmosphere, its vast drawing room and
its high walled garden, was perfect for entertaining in grand
style, and here she revelled in her role of hostess, carrying it off
with exceptional style and elegance. She liked guests to dress
formally for dinner. She planned menus with flair and imagination, chose wines with discernment. Her attention to detail was
extraordinary, right down to placing at each bedside a new book
which she believed would appeal to that particular guest. Most
remarkable of all was her late-night vitality. She looked so delicate and yet she was invariably the last to show signs of tiredness,
and when her husband and guests were beginning to wilt and

yearn for their beds she had the ability to breathe new life into the fading festivities. All through the night arguments were liable to wax and wane over every topic imaginable. There would sometimes be charades, impromptu cabarets, brilliant take-offs of show business personalities; and often it was dawn before guests retired.

Stories of high jinks at Notley abound, and most often retold is the misadventure that occurred when Olivier took Sir Ralph Richardson into the loft to admire some old paintings. Earlier, when attending a house-warming party at the Oliviers' newly furnished Chelsea cottage, Sir Ralph had let off a firework that accidentally set fire to some curtains and caused considerable alarm. His introduction to Notley was no less fortunate. In the loft, he stepped back carelessly—and put his foot clean through the ceiling of the best bedroom.

On another occasion, Danny Kaye and his wife were guests, and Sir Laurence at once became Larry the vaudeville comic, slapping a cheesecake in his own face during lunch and afterwards joining Kaye in uproarious singing duets. Yet those weekends at Notley were not quite so 'madly gay' as embellished stories have suggested. Recalling days spent there, Peter Finch wrote in a woman's magazine: 'An attitude circulated that these weekend parties were in some way exclusive gatherings of a small and somewhat superior theatrical clique. It was never like that. Vivien adored her home and she was never happier than when she could share the peace and beauty of Notley. I think Larry would have appreciated their being on their own a little more. But Vivien was one of those people who must have people around her. They were not wild parties nor in any way particularly unusual—except possibly that they gave us a chance to relax and be ourselves far removed from the artificiality that surrounds much of life in the theatre. Larry, I remember, spent much of his time enjoying his hobby of tree-pruning. I spent one glorious afternoon employed in nothing more glamorous than cleaning out a stretch of clogged-up river.'

The Oliviers glowed with success at the dawn of the Fifties, a decade in which they dominated as the brightest twin-stars in the show business firmament. But their gold-glittering image was somewhat superficial, reflecting wealth in prestige and artistic achievement rather than in hard cash. To maintain their lifestyle, and more immediately to subsidize their theatrical ventures, they were compelled to turn back to the quick and enormous rewards of working in films. At the end of July Miss Leigh left *Streetcar*, which continued with Betty Ann Davies in the lead, and went to Hollywood to play Blanche in the film version. Ten days later, after directing a new comedy, *Captain Carvallo*, for the St. James's, Sir Laurence joined her to start work on the film of Theodore Dreiser's *Sister Carrie*. With him travelled Vivien's daughter Suzanne, who had completed her years at a boarding school at Sherborne in Dorset. She was now sixteen, already taller than her mother, and studying to be an actress at RADA.

The Oliviers were back in Hollywood for the first time in ten years, and Danny Kaye marked their return by throwing an all-night party attended by 170 of the film colony's top stars and directors. It was a grand reunion, and the beginning for them of new friendships, most notably with Humphrey Bogart and Lauren Bacall. But the star who spent the most time with Sir Laurence was Spencer Tracy. He had been Olivier's house-guest when in England to film *Edward, My Son*, and now he was giving his services free as 'American voice coach'. As usual, Olivier was at great pains to get his accent right. He also grew a moustache for his role as a middle-aged married man who ruins his life by running off with a young woman (Jennifer Jones), and he put himself on a diet for his final scenes as a meal-begging derelict of the Bowery. Director William Wyler observed how much more serious and respectful the actor had become in his approach to filming since they last worked together, on *Wuthering Heights*. But, in truth, Olivier did not have great faith in the film. He turned in a superlative performance ('the finest acting of his career', according to critic Richard Winnington) but he suspected all along that this study in obsessive passion and respectability tottering to degradation might be too overwhelmingly gloomy for popular tastes. Events proved him right.

Vivien was the one who profited greatly from this three-month sojourn in Hollywood. She won overwhelmingly favourable notices for her work on *Streetcar*—and an Oscar, as did supporting players Karl Malden and Kim Hunter. (Brando, in his second film, might have also taken an Academy Award if Bogart had not come along in *The African Queen*.) Tennessee Williams later told *Life* magazine that Miss Leigh had brought everything to the part of Blanche that he had intended, and much that he had never dreamed of. She would always fight for recognition as a stage actress first and film star second, but this performance reinforced opinion (one shared by Kazan among others) that she was superior on celluloid. Of Sir Laurence's acting, the reverse opinion increasingly applied.

On his first night back in London, Olivier went to the St. James's to see *Top of the Ladder*, with John Mills in the lead. This latest Olivier production had opened during his absence and it was not a lasting success, partly due to the mistake of having the author (Tyrone Guthrie) as director of his own work. Meanwhile, *Captain Carvallo* had enjoyed a good run after being transferred to the Garrick. But that modern comedy also failed to show a profit. Olivier badly needed another big money-spinner like *Born Yesterday*. Gambling, he presented Gian-Carlo Menotti's *The Consul*, a grim, lounge-suit opera about people in an Iron Curtain country, and a desperate young wife trying to obtain exit visas from an unimaginative, red-taped Western consulate. He brought over the original company from New York, and since his own St. James's was inadequate for a production demanding a large orchestra, he took over the Cambridge Theatre. *The Consul* had run for a year on Broadway. In London the first night brought tumultuous applause, and some enthusiasts returned to see the opera again and again. But for Olivier it was another sharp reminder of the unpredictability of public taste. After seven weeks he announced that the opera was closing. He estimated his loss at about £10,000.

London was now filling up with visitors for the 1951 Festival of Britain, and every theatre management was vying to stage the main attraction of the summer season. Gielgud was back from Broadway, planning his own production. Guinness was to direct his own Hamlet in the West End. Anthony Quayle and Michael Redgrave were to work at Stratford through the entire cycle of Shakespeare's historical plays. Something irresistible was needed for the St. James's, and the circumstances spurred the Oliviers to embark on a daring joint venture: a twin presentation of Shakespeare's *Antony and Cleopatra* and Shaw's *Caesar and Cleopatra*, staged on alternate nights.

The pairing of dramas separated by three centuries made exciting theatre—two brilliant productions by Michael Benthall in the best St. James's tradition. There was, however, a significant weight of critical opinion that judged Olivier to be well below his best as Caesar and as Antony. Certainly he himself was not very happy in either role. But what irritated most was the denigrating suggestion that he had deliberately 'played down' both parts to give greater emphasis to the acting of Miss Leigh. Kenneth Tynan wrote of *Antony and Cleopatra*: 'Miss Leigh's limitations have wider repercussions than those of most actresses. Sir Laurence with that curious chivalry which sometimes blights the progress of every great actor gives me the impression that he subdues his blow-lamp ebullience to match her. Blunting his own iron precision, levelling away his towering authority he meets her half way. Antony climbs down and Cleopatra pats him on the head. A cat in fact can do more than look at a king; she can hypnotise him.'

During the four-month run of the two Cleopatras, the Oliviers were in the high summer of their so-called Royal period. In May, Sir Laurence was seeing his forty-fourth birthday at a midnight supper given by Sir Winston Churchill. His June engagements included a midnight gala performance at the Palladium in aid of the family of the late Sid Field, a comedian for whom he had the greatest admiration. In July he was making a public speech on opening the London gardens round Henry Irving's statue ('He died two years before I was born, and yet I am conscious of him as if I had served as a member of his company'). And always Vivien, Lady Olivier, was at his side.

In November the Oliviers sailed on the *Mauretania* for New York. They were taking over their full company, plus twenty-five tons of scenery including the revolving stage, the queen's barge and the massive Sphinx, for a Broadway season of the two Cleopatra plays.

Their first night at Billy Rose's Ziegfeld Theatre was described as Manhattan's most glittering theatrical opening for years. It was also a night of sensational scandal. The celebrity-packed audience included Danny Kaye, Tyrone Power, David Selznick, Luise Rainer, Rosalind Russell, Margaret Truman, Sarah Churchill, Cole Porter, Richard Rodgers, Ethel Merman, John Steinbeck, Lewis Douglas, Ruth Gordon, the Lunts, and a bevy of business tycoons, bluebloods and political bigwigs. But one dapper little man in the stalls eclipsed all of them in attracting attention. That man was Billy Rose. With a typically outrageous sense of showmanship, he had chosen this night of all nights to force a showdown with his wife by appearing openly with his beautiful blonde paramour.

A few months earlier Rose had been headline news when his girlfriend attempted suicide. Ostensibly he was later reconciled with his wife, Eleanor Holm, the 1932 Olympic backstroke champion and one-time Tarzan's mate. But now he wanted to precipitate the marital break and he ensured maximum publicity by parading his illicit relationship in the limelight of the Oliviers' production, and so fired the opening shot in what America came to know as The War of the Roses—the long-drawn-out, no-holds-barred, scandal-ridden separation proceedings that for a time pushed the Korean War and the approaching presidential election off the front pages.

It was regrettable that Rose should use the Oliviers' showcase for his own personal devices, but then the brilliant, turbulent Billy hadn't clawed his way out of an East Side ghetto slum and risen to multimillionaire status by always acting the gentleman. In any event, his first-night stunt happily took nothing away from the impact of the twin productions. The plays were even more highly praised in New York than they had been in festive London. *The New York Times* said: 'There has not been an *Antony and Cleopatra* to compare with this in New York in the last quarter of a century, and there have not been many productions of any Shakespearean play that have approached this exalted quality. Everything about the production is glowing or crackling with vitality.' The *New York Tribune* thought that the Oliviers had performed 'a near miracle of pulling the sprawling canvas of Shakespeare's play into a coherent and increasingly exciting whole'.

Although the Oliviers were honoured by the American National Arts Foundation for 'the most exalted and memorable stage performance of 1951', the Broadway run was not quite so propitious as it seemed. Miss Leigh's health had deteriorated, and Wilfrid Hyde-White recalls that she often shivered with weakness while waiting in the wings for her cue. Nor was the season a financial success. They were taking more money than such hit musicals as *Guys and Dolls*, *South Pacific* and *Call Me Madam* ('What a dollar windfall for the British Treasury!' reported a London evening newspaper) and yet, in reality, the Oliviers barely broke even. High transport and running costs made it necessary to take a large theatre and charge the highest admission prices ever known on Broadway. It meant filling the

Ziegfeld every night for four months to ensure a worthwhile profit. And that didn't happen. The run began with tickets fetching $100 a pair on the black market and ended with rows of empty seats. The only person to make a real profit was Billy Rose. He received about $100,000 on a 'share' percentage basis for his theatre.

Of course, in terms of prestige the profit to the Oliviers was incalculable, but that was small consolation at a time when they were still losing money at the St. James's. In their absence, an American play, *The Happy Time*, with Peter Finch in the lead, had opened and soon folded. It was the twelfth play presented by Laurence Olivier Productions. Some had enjoyed long runs, and on the whole the selection would have done credit to a National Theatre supposing its dual purpose to be to encourage new works and maintain a standard with the classics. But the economics were always discouraging, and the Oliviers' financial position was such that they now began to talk about selling Notley Abbey.

Quite probably they could have made a far greater financial success of the St. James's by appearing in more of its productions, but this ran counter to Sir Laurence's idea of balanced theatre. As it happened, he was destined to appear in only one stage play (and a very lightweight one at that) in the next three years. Excluding his wartime service, the years 1952 to 1955 made up his leanest period on the stage. It encouraged the notion that he was losing interest in acting as he became more and more immersed in management and direction. There was a sad suspicion, too, that the theatrical excitement of those seasons of great roles at the Old Vic were gone forever, that the stage had seen the best of an actor who might otherwise, in his mid-forties, have been expected to be showing himself at the peak of his powers.

It was easy to misread Olivier's course when his interests were so diverse, ranging as they did over the entire spectrum of the entertainment media. Today, as we survey the vast tapestry of a career spanning more than half a century, an overall pattern is more clearly discernible—the questing progression of an actor-manager-director who has never allowed himself to stand still; who, for better or worse, has always sought out fresh challenges and moved from one new phase to another. Thus, theatregoers who wanted to sanctify Sir Laurence Olivier as the great classical actor of the age were due for a rude awakening in 1952. He himself had no intention of being enshrined in doublet and hose, of rescaling peaks already conquered. He wanted to attempt things refreshingly different, to indulge his personal delight in testing his own versatility. So it was that, while playing Caesar and Antony, he secretly trained his voice ('a frustrated bathroom baritone') for his first professional singing role since *The Circle of Chalk* in 1929.

Exclamation marks punctuated the news that Olivier was preparing to play Macheath in a film version of *The Beggar's Opera*. There were Shakespeare-starched devotees who regarded Gay's eighteenth-century comic opera as an unbecoming vehicle for so distinguished an actor. Later they would be even more horrified when he accepted the unrewarding role of the Grand Duke of Carpathia in Terence Rattigan's *The Sleeping Prince*. Why was their Prince of Players associating himself with such unworthy trifles? Intermittently, over the next two decades, the same question would be asked again and again. And the answer remained basically the same. By refusing to rest on his hard-won laurels, by avoiding monotonous repetition, by keeping in touch with contemporary drama, by sometimes taking work without altruistic motive and simply for his own enjoyment, he ensured that he would never become stale. Critics might say he was misguided, frivolous, impulsive. But no one was going to call him 'old hat'.

18

★

The Sleeping Prince

In the motion picture business of the Forties and early Fifties the making of an all-British musical was commonly recognized as the surest way to financial suicide. Cinema folk were no longer content with unimaginative trifles mixed to a standard recipe to show off the talents and personality of Jack Buchanan, Jessie Matthews, Gracie Fields or George Formby. Hollywood had encouraged a taste for richer fare; and it was the same on the London stage where a procession of entrancing shows—*Oklahoma, Annie Get Your Gun* and *South Pacific*—had completed the domination by America in the field of musical entertainment. The glorious failure of the Rank Organisation's *London Town* (1947) was seen as final proof of the folly of Britain's attempts to emulate the success of Hollywood musicals. And this defeatism was not dispelled by the triumph of *The Red Shoes* (1948), which, as a musical without song, stood in a category of its own.

In these circumstances, Olivier and Herbert Wilcox showed unusual bravado when they linked up in the summer of 1952 as co-producers to film *The Beggar's Opera*. Wilcox had been encouraged by the success of *Spring in Park Lane*, a light comedy with music rather than a pure musical, but most especially their optimism was founded on the assembly of so many outstanding talents: Peter Brook as director; Christopher Fry, screenwriter; Sir Arthur Bliss, music arranger; and a cast including Dorothy Tutin, Stanley Holloway, George Devine, Hugh Griffiths and Daphne Anderson.

Brook had never made a movie before. But that fact was dismissed. He was the twenty-seven-year-old whizz-kid among stage directors, and it was his involvement that most attracted Olivier to the project. This was ironic because once filming began, star and director were rarely in agreement. As Herbert Wilcox has vividly recalled, theirs was an almost unworkable oil-and-water combination of creative talents:

'Larry, with his wide experience of the stage and screen, and I, with nearly thirty-five years of continuous production behind me, endeavoured to combine Peter's experimental approach with our experience—and give him the best of both worlds. But Peter would have none of it. Stage genius though he had undoubtedly proved himself, and as Larry and I freely conceded, we could not get him to accept our practical suggestions—all of which he seemed to regard as criticisms. The insoluble problem was that Peter enjoyed a superiority complex that shone from his young blue eyes like highly polished brass buttons, insolently surveying and cocking a snook at the conventional; whereas long experience embracing success and failure had mellowed any suggestion of superiority Larry or I may have nursed in our early professional days.

'Larry bent over backwards to co-operate, and how he worked. Not even the usual lunch hour, of which he spent forty-five minutes with his Italian singing-master. Unlike most stars, Larry refuses to be doubled in any aspect—singing (a tremendous role), riding, swordsmanship, the lot. His riding alone—with cameras mounted on cars doing forty miles an hour—would have made most of the Hollywood western stars have a heart attack. On one occasion, he rode up "Dead Man's Hill", an incline of one in six, so many times that the horse had a heart attack!

'The sad thing was that Peter was fanatically keen to turn in the action film of all time, but he lacked the know-how.'[1]

At the start of filming Olivier was in ebullient form, making a welcome speech to cast and technicians and joking about the time, three decades earlier, when Wilcox had offered him a £100-a-week contract. But the gaiety soon died. By October, shooting at Shepperton was running seriously behind schedule. Then they came to the crisis point. Olivier was rehearsing a duel scene that required him to leap on to a gaming table. Four times he had vaulted on to it successfully, but in the fifth run-through he fell heavily and tore a calf muscle. In acute pain and unable to move, he initially cursed his opponent for having lunged at him as he jumped. Afterwards, realizing his mistake, he sent for the man and apologized. The injury put him out of filming for three weeks.

This delay, plus the differences between Olivier and Brook,

alarmed Wilcox's financial advisers. Already a quarter of a
million pounds had been spent on the production. Now they
recommended that either the star or the director should be
changed. Wilcox later recalled: 'Film Finances, a company
which guaranteed completion, demanded I change directors.
But I refused and I took over their potential liability of excess
costs and relieved them of all liability. This eventually cost me
personally £31,000. In three weeks Larry was back, and I had a
talk with him. "Larry," I told him, "we've both decided that
Peter might turn out something really great. Let's give him his
head." Larry agreed, and the film was completed without further
argument. Goodness knows what we had—the greatest film ever
or the biggest egg ever laid. However, it was completed.' [2]

After editing, they came to the surprising conclusion that they
had a great movie. But at least Wilcox had the good sense not to
take success for granted. When Korda, who had put up money
against foreign rights, received a $700,000 bid from Jack Warner
for the western hemisphere rights, Wilcox advised him to accept,
on condition that Warner bought 'blind' rather than with a
'subject to viewing' escape clause. The deal went through.
Korda's company made a healthy profit. But not Wilcox and
Olivier. In reality, they had laid a very substantial egg.

It was the beginning of a darkening time in Olivier's fortunes,
both artistic and personal. He had been making *The Beggar's
Opera* when *Carrie* was released to a cool reception. *Carrie*, like
Olivier's first musical, was thoroughly bad box-office. At the
same time he faced growing anxiety over Vivien Leigh's health.
He was taking a much-needed rest after the stresses and strife of
work at Shepperton when he learned that she was suffering
alarmingly from nervous exhaustion following location work in
Ceylon on the film *Elephant Walk*. He cut short a holiday in Italy
to join her at once.

Ceylon in February 1953 was oppressively humid. It rapidly
sapped Vivien's strength as she drove herself hard on the set by
day and fought insomnia by night. The breaking point came in
March when she was due to leave for Hollywood and face
months of studio routine. She had been nervous about flying
ever since that crash landing at Willimantic in 1946, and now, in
her state of extreme mental and physical exhaustion, the tension
of a long flight to Los Angeles pushed her to the brink of a complete nervous breakdown. Conscientiously, she reported for film-

ing on schedule. But she was in no fit condition to work. Her depression was total now. All self-confidence had drained away. She had a neurotic terror of meeting other people, periodically and inexplicably broke down in tears on the set, and at other times walked around distractedly reciting Blanche dialogues from *A Streetcar Named Desire*.

In her rented home she exhibited a strange compulsion to do housework, to sweep and dust and empty ashtrays even though plenty of servants were at hand. She eventually sank to the point of distraction where she could no longer identify friends and began to call co-star Peter Finch 'Larry'. The studios called in David Niven, one of the few very close friends with whom she could feel at ease. After talking to her, he agreed that they should assign a doctor and nurse to her and notify her husband at once.

On arrival, Sir Laurence agreed with doctors that it was imperative for her to leave the film immediately and return to England. Elizabeth Taylor was invited to take over her role. Meanwhile, the distraught and sadly confused star was put under sedation and accompanied by two nurses on the homeward journey. The flight back to London was completed with the greatest of difficulty. At New York airport there was a distressing scene as Miss Leigh argued and fought and wept while Olivier, Danny Kaye, nurses and stewards tried to persuade her to board the transatlantic airliner. Throughout the journey her husband remained constantly at her side, gentle, understanding, infinitely patient; but his position was largely one of depressing helplessness in the knowledge that only strictly professional medical care and treatment could help her for the time being. From London Airport Vivien was taken by ambulance direct to a Surrey nursing home, where doctors ordered three months of complete rest, and no visitors whatsoever. Later she was transferred to the University College Hospital to be attended by a specialist in tuberculosis as well as consultants in nervous disorders, for there was a recurrence of the lung complaint that had attacked her nine years before.

It was late April when Olivier finally drove Vivien home to Notley. He had been itching to get rid of the country house, but all thoughts of selling were abandoned now. The house on high ground would prove an ideal convalescent home. Vivien looked forward to resting there at least until July. Then, perhaps, she would be strong enough to return to the stage with her husband in Rattigan's new play, *The Sleeping Prince*. Memory of her living nightmare in Hollywood was now locked away in some dark recess of her subconscious.

By July she was back in London, seemingly fully recovered. She joked about her illness now, though privately she was deeply concerned about her recurrent fits of depression and their growing severity. In August she reappeared on the West End theatre scene, attending the first night of *Anastasia*. Sir Laurence had acquired the stage rights after seeing the play on television and, with a strong cast headed by Helen Haye and Laurence Payne, it ran at the St. James's for 117 performances. Vivien, in a black organza ballet-length dress, looked stunning at that premiere, and afterwards she was as vivacious and gregarious as ever when they went on to a late-night party. Now more than ever before, she was eager and determined to return to the stage and all the attendant theatrical excitement and glamour that had become her lifeblood.

Terence Rattigan had intended *The Sleeping Prince* as a Coronation offering to be staged that summer of 1953. The action was set in 1911 with the nobility of Europe assembling for the crowning of King George V, and the story centred on the Regent of Carpathia's romantic involvement with Elaine Dagenham, a flirty American chorus girl. The author wrote it with the Oliviers in mind, but then he became wary that it might be taken too seriously and so he styled it as 'an occasional fairy tale' and balked at the idea of casting the theatre royals in the leading parts. Yet Olivier could not be dissuaded from seeing it as a play eminently suited for himself and Miss Leigh. So they went ahead, with Rattigan remaining gloomy about the whole thing. 'It'll be a disaster,' he predicted. 'We'll all end up in the Tower.'

The *pièce d'occasion*, postponed because of Miss Leigh's illness, opened in Manchester in September. It was a complete sell-out. Vivien's dressing room overflowed with flowers, all of them white except for a posy of pink and white roses from Sir Laurence, and after the show, when they went on to a supper party at the Midland Hotel, the packed restaurant stood up to clap and cheer. They were saluting an actress of irresistible beauty and style who had pulled back from the brink of despair to re-emerge triumphantly, still glowing with star quality of rare and undiminished brilliance.

It was the same in London, though on a grander scale. The opening at the Phoenix coincided with Vivien's fortieth birthday, and the welcome accorded her transcended anything she had known before. The theatre was inundated with bouquets and good-luck messages. Afterwards John Mills led the singing of 'Happy Birthday' at a party in Rattigan's penthouse suite. And then the papers arrived, mostly with rapturous reviews. 'Miss Leigh is the most disarming little demon who ever upset a royal applecart,' wrote Cecil Wilson. 'She minces round the legation in a wide-eyed daze of innocence and guile and carried her American accent with a practised ease. It is the teasing sing-song accent of Blanche du Bois suddenly aware that all that neurotic nonsense was only a nightmare.'

On reading notices in a similar vein, Noel Coward turned to Rattigan and quipped. 'You see, the Oliviers have ruined your play just as the Lunts ruined mine.'

The Sleeping Prince was a brilliant commercial success. It ran for eight months and, if so desired, could have completed a year. The Queen, Prince Philip and Princess Margaret went to see it. Yet it did not represent a significant artistic triumph for Olivier the actor. Critics judged that his talents were wasted on such a trifling role as this Ruritanian grand duke; and it strengthened the plausibility of the suggestion that he was nursing Miss Leigh's lesser talents and underplaying his parts so that they might act together on equal terms.

Of course, the Grand Duke of Carpathia was a thoroughly dull fellow, and in his subtle efforts at characterization Olivier possibly made him a little too charmless. But any suggestion that he gave less than his utmost either as director or leading man is entirely refuted by the evidence of first-hand witnesses. Contrary to critical opinion, Rattigan thought that Miss Leigh was the one who was miscast, and that Sir Laurence gave a performance of sheer theatrical magic. 'What makes magic is genius, and what makes genius, we are assured, is the infinite capacity for taking pains, and if that definition be correct, Larry has it in abundance. The demands of "total acting" are indeed total. I would watch in rehearsal utterly spellbound as, over the weeks, he built his performance slowly and with immense application from a mass of tiny details, some discarded, some retained . . . Where

I had expected my flimsy little confection to be burst asunder by the vastness of his talent, it was in fact held firmly in shape by his quietly magisterial performance which, while remaining resolutely faithful to his author's frivolous intentions, succeeded in adding to the part those dimensions that one looks for from great acting . . .'[3]

In a curious way, Olivier's 'minor' performance in *The Sleeping Prince* provides a more readily understandable illustration of the greatness of his playing than do some of his major roles, whose subtlety and power tend to overwhelm the mind. Peter Barkworth, cast as a footman and understudying Jeremy Spencer as the Grand Duke's son, recalls Sir Laurence saying, ' "The public doesn't realize that in a rather lightweight play like this the amount of push I have to give it to drive it over is more than anybody could imagine. They don't realize the importance of *attack* in acting."

'I shall never forget those first rehearsals under Olivier. He called me to his dressing room afterwards and said, "You know, as far as acting is concerned you should really try to forget all about technique when you're actually acting during a performance. With this reservation, there are two things which I always try and remember. Relax your feet. And always have more breath than you need. Those two things never escape me. Other technical things I try and forget."

'Olivier is the only director I've ever known who sat on stage, beside the footlights, *behind a desk*! I used to have a recurring dream after that. I was acting alone on stage, not knowing the play—a proverbial nightmare—and in the stalls, the circle, the gods, there were a whole lot of desks. And behind each one sat Laurence Olivier!'

Olivier's too-easily-dismissed part in *The Sleeping Prince* represented his only stage appearance between 1951 and 1955. Yet he was not exactly idle in those in-between years. Besides starring in *The Beggar's Opera*, he recorded a long series of half-hour radio programmes entitled, 'Laurence Olivier Presents' for N.B.C., and presented two plays: *Waiting for Gillian* at the St. James's and *Meet a Body* at the Duke of York's Theatre. There were the usual wide-ranging engagements for charity, including a Palladium show that had him doing a stylish soft-shoe-shuffle with Jack Buchanan. Above all, in the winter of 1954 there was his one truly great achievement of the period: the making of his film of *Richard III*.

But Olivier's third Shakespearean movie was not unveiled until December 1955. In the meantime he could be judged only on work seen, and undeniably his record so far in the Fifties— the two *Cleopatras*, *The Sleeping Prince*, and films of *Carrie* and *The Beggar's Opera*—had done nothing to enhance his reputation as an actor. The judgment of his sternest critics was that he had sunk to the nadir of his post-war career.

Olivier's return to critical favour began in April 1955, when, amid a blaze of publicity, he reappeared on the stage on which he had triumphed anonymously thirty-three years before: the Shakespeare Memorial Theatre, Stratford-upon-Avon. He and Vivien Leigh were to play in *Twelfth Night*, *Titus Andronicus* and *Macbeth*. Their fame was so great that the season was an assured box-office success before a line had been delivered. But this was no longer Olivier riding the crest of a wave; it was Olivier, as some critics chose to dramatize the occasion, fighting to regain his position as the world's leading actor. The Stratford season was equally a stern examination for Miss Leigh. She had never acted there before, and she was taking roles (Viola, Lavinia and Lady Macbeth) that were all new to her.

John Gielgud's mannered and perhaps over-charming revival of *Twelfth Night* scarcely provided a spectacular beginning to the long-awaited come-back of the theatre royals. Despite an un-usually experienced cast that included Angela Baddeley (Maria), Alan Webb (Sir Toby Belch) and Michael Denison (Sir Andrew), the production was found to be strangely lacking in gaiety, and arguably this owed something to Olivier's shaping of Malvolio. He was as imaginative as ever in his comic invention—crinkly hair, heavy, high-raised eyebrows, pointed nose, light-footed walk and the faint nasal whine of a social creeper—but he sympa-thetically played down the arrogance. In the process he again demonstrated his rare talent for plumbing hidden depths of personality and causing a familiar character to be viewed afresh. 'He is, very simply, Malvolio,' wrote J. C. Trewin. 'He takes us back to the man's past, and makes us speculate about his future.' But some critics thought that his subdued Malvolio was so deeply thought out that it lost its spontaneity and humour and that it was rather out of tune with the story-line.

Whatever view one takes of it, Olivier's lisping major-domo fitted into a now familiar pattern. He could never be content with safely following a well-chartered course; each role was a fresh challenge to which, for better or worse, he had to bring something new. His originality ensured that the least important of his Stratford roles was not forgotten, but in going his own highly individual way he was always liable to disturb the traditionalists—and even to present added difficulties for other players.

Ivor Brown spotlighted both the advantage and disadvantage of such an approach when he wrote:

> He created a fresh Malvolio, not so much over-weening as under-weening, a dry vessel of petty vanity at first and then gradually filled by the conspirators with an unholy glee at his supposed promotion to a golden fortune. He affected a curious accent, foreign-sounding, with the r's softened into w's ('Some have gweatness thwust upon them') . . . The performance was exquisite in detail: Laurence really did create a credible individual at the summit of life below stairs . . . I came away with the feeling that I had now met a Shakespearan character whom I had never seen before: how often does that happen? But there is one difficulty about this less flamboyant reading of the role. It makes Malvolio's interruption of the drinking scene less easy for the other players. For this is no gaunt, gigantic champion of austerity that bids them stop drinking and singing and is therefore only to be defied with courage. He is no more than an ordinary fellow at whom fingers might be snapped without abnormal temerity.[4]

This Malvolio was, in a sense, strictly for the connoisseurs, or as one critic expressed it, 'a diverting exercise but hardly the substance of Sir L's vocation'. It was in the great roles that Olivier had won his spurs; only there could he reinforce his reputation as the great actor. Thus, almost two months after his first professional appearance at Stratford, the London *Daily Express* was running the headline: HAVE THE OLIVIERS LIVED ON TOO LITTLE FOR TOO LONG? Beneath it, theatre critic John Barber recalled how, one decade earlier, a crowd of 2,500 had blocked the entrance to the New Theatre and closed St. Martin's Lane for an hour; how hundreds of girls chanted 'We want Larry' and how, when he appeared, he was forced on to the roof of a taxi to make a speech of farewell. 'But for ten years now Laurence Olivier has done nothing that has added an inch to his stature. Once he had a reputation; now he has only fame.'

Concluding his lament for those stirring Old Vic days immediately after the war, Mr. Barber wrote:

I hate that phrase, 'The Oliviers'. It kow-tows to the most fashionable couple in show business. The titled lions of Mayfair salons. The pair royalty knows as Larry-and-Viv. Now look beyond the gloss. Olivier was a great actor. But since his gleaming, viperish Richard III, his fiery Hamlet, he has lost his way. Now, at 48, he is an aging matinée idol, desperately fighting to win back his old reputation. To young people, he is a name that attaches to no outstanding achievement. She is a great beauty—still, at 42. As an actress, excellent in a dainty waspish way that seldom touches the heart. It is time we saw them both as they really are.

And so, in June, the Oliviers came to their greatest dual test. *Macbeth*. Eighteen years had passed since Sir Laurence first played that title role in an Old Vic production he chooses to remember as 'utter disaster'. Agate had then suggested that he would play it twice as well when he was twice as old, and now, at least in terms of range and experience, he was twice as advanced —not only in experience of acting but also in experience of life, which he recognized as being even more important and essential for playing this part successfully.

Happily, however, he was not advanced at marked physical cost, as he showed in the banquet scene by a histrionic leap on to the table, with a great billowing of his scarlet cloak, to advance on Banquo's ghost. In 1937, painfully conscious of his too youthful baritone, he had relied heavily on make-up so exaggerated that Miss Leigh remarked, 'You heard Macbeth's first line, then Larry's make-up came on, then Banquo came on, then Larry came on.' He had no need of such artifice now. He sought no physical hint of a thane more monster than man, and he gave an unusually low-keyed performance to match, a masterly demonstration of villainy so refined that one critic called it 'restraint run amok'. Harold Hobson (*Sunday Times*) expressed his belief

that there was no actor in the world who could come near to him.
J. C. Trewin and W. A. Darlington both described it as 'the best
Macbeth of our time'. Kenneth Tynan judged that he 'shook
hands with greatness'.

The blood and butchery of this *Macbeth* was so subdued that it
was suggested Byam Shaw might have been influenced by all the
recent agitation against horror comics. No such suspicion could
be aroused by the next Stratford production. All restraint was
now fully abandoned for *Titus Andronicus*, that blood-chilling
anthology of atrocities which includes thirteen deaths, two muti-
lations and one rape, and concludes with a cannibal banquet at
which Tamora, Queen of the Goths, is served pie made of the
blood and bones of her two murdered sons. It was a Chamber of
Horrors that resulted in drink sales at the theatre's bars breaking
all records as patrons pressed for doubles to deaden shattered
nerves.

At least three members of the audience fainted every night;
one performance had twenty casualties, most of them falling as
Titus sacrificed his left hand to the axe with a sound-effects man
hacking a nice scrunch of bone offstage. It was history repeating
itself, for at the Old Vic in 1923 it wasn't considered a successful
evening unless a dozen people fainted at the horrors of *Titus*.
And, as at the Old Vic in 1923, Stratford now achieved the
distinction of having staged all of Shakespeare's plays.

Titus Andronicus, so popular an entertainment in Shakespeare's time, had become half-forgotten in modern times. But
at Stratford, in the care of Peter Brook, Elizabethan Grand
Guignol emerged from under the dust jackets to be boldly edited
and made into one of the most brilliant and breathtakingly
inventive productions of the decade. In cinema partnership with
Olivier, the young Mr. Brook had produced one of the least
memorable of films; together in the theatre, they worked a veritable miracle that more than redressed the balance. This *Titus* was
hailed as a masterpiece, a triumph essentially due both to Brook's
inspired theatrical sense and to towering performances by
Olivier and Anthony Quayle. But, above all, it will be remembered
as the production in which Sir Laurence, as the grizzled, war-
weary general, returned to full-blown greatness and dominated
the stage with his spellbinding command of acting on the grand
scale. This time his mastery of his art was beyond dispute,
without even the faint qualification that had heralded his

Macbeth. His performance was called by *The Times* 'one of the great things of his career', and described by Bernard Levin as 'not so much on the heroic scale as on a new scale entirely, the greatness of which has smashed all our measuring-rods and pressure-gauges to smithereens'.

The pathos he achieved was often overwhelming, and it was by his superbly timed silences as much as by his supreme delivery of the lines, that he reached down into the darkest depths of despair and fully conveyed the agonies of a tormented soul. Thus, after sacrificing a hand in ransom for his sons, he momentarily froze and, as Philip Hope-Wallace said, 'for an eternity of seconds withheld his howl of pain'. Again, after his severed hand had been returned, together with the heads of his sons, he made silence speak volumes and extracted the last drop of agonizing suspense from the moment when his brother Marcus asks, 'Now is a time to storm; why art thou still?' Another pause, another breath-freezing silence, and so all the greater was the effect as he finally erupted into his quavering, ghastly, nerve-shattering laugh.

'Sir Laurence Olivier's *Titus*, even with one hand gone, is a five-finger exercise transformed into an unforgettable concerto of grief,' wrote Kenneth Tynan in *The Observer*. 'This is a performance which ushers us into the presence of one who is, pound for pound, the greatest actor alive . . . One hears great cries, which, like all of this actor's best effects, seem to have been dredged up from an ocean-bed of fatigue. One recognized, though one had never heard it before, the noise made in its last extremity by the cornered human soul. We knew from his Hotspur and his Richard III that Sir Laurence could explode: now we know that he can suffer as well. All the grand unplayable parts, after this, are open to him—Skelton's *Magnificence*, Ibsen's *Brand*, Goethe's *Faust*—anything, so long as we can see those lion eyes search for solace, that great jaw sag.'

For Olivier, the only disappointment of that Stratford season was Miss Leigh's lack of a similar triumph. Her achievement was considerable, but far short of the highest standards that she set herself. Though some critics thought her lovelorn Viola lacked variety of pace and mood, she handled the part with the most charming lightweight touch and certainly did not fail there. Tynan scorned her Lavinia, ('Miss Vivien Leigh receives the news that she is about to be ravished on her husband's corpse with little more than the mild annoyance of one who would have preferred foam rubber'), but others felt that she did as much as could be expected with a miserable part that has the player without hands or tongue before the second act is through. Lady Macbeth was the role that really mattered, the one in which she most dearly wanted to succeed, and here she suffered some very harsh criticism indeed. 'The most monumental piece of miscasting since Arthur Askey played Shakespeare,' was Mr. Barber's sweeping judgment. And though no one else expressed it quite so bluntly, the majority opinion was that she was too greatly handicapped by her own physical attractions.

Sir Laurence himself strongly disagreed with the view that Lady Macbeth was outside her range. He said that her playing of the part meant to him 'a perfect and ideal stage partnership'. So eminent a critic as Ivor Brown thought that she exactly provided the qualities required of the character and that her vocal range was 'more than adequate to all the poetry'. Noel Coward was another who judged that she achieved greatness in the role, and Alan Dent, her most loyal admirer among critics, not only thought she was superlative but later wrote that he believed the Oliviers had never before or since been so exceedingly well-matched and well-partnered. But Miss Leigh, always her own severest critic, was never satisfied with her performance; and the barbs in some of the notices cut deep. Openly and often she conceded that her acting could never match her husband's, but she had an innate desire to achieve greatness and at times she gloomily reflected that both time and her health seemed to be against her.

Before the end of the 1955 Stratford season Sir Laurence gave the last lecture in the Shakespeare Memorial Theatre summer school. He talked most about Malvolio and how the part, however well played, had come to be acted in so traditional a style that, like Falstaff before George Robey played it, it was almost dead. On acting in general, he said: 'I have always tried to believe that my job was to make the audience believe in the story—believe that it was really going on. I have always thought that was the point of it.' In his early days, he explained, his ambition was always to look quite different in every part. It was true that certain parts, like Shallow, lent themselves to elaborate characterization so that you could play them without repeating yourself, but such parts must have in them 'a certain shallowness'. On the other hand, he had discovered that you could not play Macbeth without drawing on every single thing you had— 'You've got to give it everything you've ever done—Hamlet, Richard III, Malvolio, or Henry V. There's no hope if you're not repeating yourself.'

As Olivier delivered his lecture in the packed Conference Hall he was standing almost on the spot where, in the old fire-ravaged theatre, he had played Kate the Shrew as a fourteen-year-old schoolboy down from 'Teddy's' for the Easter holidays. In 1922 he had left the Stratford stage as a promising boy actor without name. In 1955, with a still boyish sense of the theatrical, he ensured that *no one* remained anonymous. On the final night of the season he made the longest curtain speech ever proclaimed in the Memorial Theatre and, in an astonishing feat of memory, he mentioned by name ninety-seven members of the company including wig dressers, property masters and stage carpenters. He was concluding a season of unparalleled commercial success: thirty-three weeks when 375,000 people paid £165,000 at the box-office and over a million applied for seats. And he was leaving with his reputation firmly re-established. If many had doubted before that he was the world's greatest actor, few doubted it now.

19
The Filming of
RICHARD III

It was late summer of 1954. Eleven years had passed since Sub-Lieutenant Olivier, riding his Irish grey gelding Blaunche Kyng, charged around the field of Agincourt, one moment Henry V in pudding-basin wig, the next an untried film director bellowing instructions through a megaphone. Now, aged forty-seven, he was back in the saddle as director, producer and fighting monarch. The Battle of Bosworth Field was being fought (rather improbably over the wooded acres of a bull-farm near Madrid) and the cast was tackling the scenes where Richard III twice has a mount shot from beneath him and finally stands alone to be hacked down in a circle of enemies.

Sir Laurence was a more commanding general now—self-assured, authoritative, at times even awesome. But in one aspect he hadn't changed: despite advancing years he still took manly pride in sheer physical endeavour, still chose to dispense with a stand-in except where his behind-camera work as director demanded otherwise. So now, garbed once more as King Richard, humpbacked, raven-wigged and tapir-nosed, he was galloping full pelt towards a camera mounted on a small hill. And master archer George Brown, who was reputed to be able to hit a sixpence at fifty yards, was stepping forward to shoot the king's horse from under him.

'That arrow was fitted with a real warhead,' recalls actor Bernard Hepton. 'On being struck, the horse was trained to roll over "dead". But the horse couldn't be harmed. He was protected by an armour suiting of half-inch cork covering hardboard, and beneath that a plate of steel. The cork ensured that the arrow appeared to really pierce the horse.

'At the crucial moment when George fired, Olivier was urging his mount up the hill. In the process he jerked his left leg forward.

His own armour was made of rubber and wouldn't stop a paper dart. The arrow sank deep into his calf. There, in the middle of a Spanish bull ranch, the whole location of warring soldiers gradually came to a halt. Everyone fell silent while Olivier just sat there, motionless, the blood gushing from his wounded leg. But when Tony Bushell, the associate director, ran over to him, he simply asked, "Did we get that in the can?"

"Yes," said Bushell. And Larry still sat there on his horse, discussing in matter-of-fact fashion how they might use the shot to best advantage. And not until then, after several minutes of business talk, did he finally say, "Now get me off this horse and find a doctor, will you?"

'He limped genuinely after that injury, and fortunately it was the same leg that he always used for his Richard III limp. He scotched the story from being released to the Press, judging it to be the wrong kind of publicity for his film. But I am glad to recount it now in total admiration of the way Olivier conducted himself.'

This was the third occasion on which Sir Laurence found himself directing, contrary to his original intention. Korda had asked him to film *Richard III*. Vivien Leigh and Carol Reed had persuaded him. But again he was disappointed to find that Reed (now Sir Carol, and Britain's most celebrated film-maker) was unavailable to direct. However, his problems as he came to 'Bosworth Field' were infinitesimal compared with those he had encountered at 'Agincourt'. He was surrounded by highly experienced aides, all conversant with his ways and needs, largely the same team of talents that had worked with him on both *Henry V* and *Hamlet*: Roger Furse (production designer), Carmen Dillon (art director), Alan Dent (text adviser), Sir William Walton (composer). Moreover, his old friend Tony Bushell, assistant producer of *Hamlet*, had become a full-fledged film director in his own right.

Collaboration on the making of a film is not the surest way of cementing personal relationships and it says much for Olivier's influence, and for the loyalty of his friends, that he was able to bring all these creative individuals together again and again. In fact, for *Richard III* he excelled himself in assembling outstanding artists. This fact was succinctly summarized when two Cockney lads were studying a poster and one was heard to remark: 'Cor, look! Four Sirs in one picture.' The quartet of actor-knights were Olivier, Hardwicke (the diseased and in-effectual roué, Edward IV), Richardson (a roly-poly, crafty Buckingham) and Gielgud (Clarence, the trusting brother drowned in a butt of malmsey wine).

On one occasion three of the quartet were riding in a car that was stopped for a traffic offence. Sir Ralph leaned out and said to the policeman, 'I am Sir Ralph Richardson. Seated next to me is Sir Cedric Hardwicke and behind me is Sir Laurence Olivier.'

The policeman replied, 'I don't care if it's the whole of King Arthur's ruddy Round Table—you're getting a summons.'

In addition, the remarkable cast included such prominent players as Claire Bloom, Pamela Brown, Helen Hayes, Andrew Cruickshank, Stanley Baker, Timothy Bateson, Alec Clunes and Patrick Troughton. Two actors, Norman Wooland and Nicholas Hannen, had worked under Olivier's film direction once before. Esmond Knight, John Laurie and Russell Thorndike shared the distinction of having been cast in all three of his Shakespearean films.

As with *Hamlet*, his most formidable task preceded filming: the challenge, shared with Dent, of editing and reshaping one of Shakespeare's less distinguished works into an entertainment of sufficient pace, style and, above all, intelligibility, to appeal to mass audiences. After preparing the film *Hamlet*, Dent re-marked, 'One had to choose at the outset between making the meaning perfectly clear to 20 million cinemagoers and causing 2,000 Shakespearean experts to wince.' The same applied with *Richard III*, though more so, since the story was less familiar to the general public, the background of political intrigue and inter-relation of characters that much more confusing. Half a dozen characters were eliminated, including, most controversially, the fishwife-tongued Queen Margaret. Entire scenes were aban-doned. Richard was made to woo Lady Anne (Claire Bloom) over the coffin of her husband Edward, not of her father-in-law Henry VI, so making the young widow's seduction even more daring and revolting than it is in the original, and giving Anne's capitulation—emphasized on the screen by a passionate kiss unforeseen by Shakespeare—a new and neurotic twist. Mistress Shore (Pamela Brown) was given an entrance, and this added weight to the picture of corruption at court and further compensated for the loss of Margaret the murderess.

More important, Olivier incorporated the coronation of Edward IV from *Henry VI, Part III*. It helped to elucidate the complex political situation in England and it reinforced the crown imagery, a valuable unifying device which, like the Globe Theatre in *Henry V*, served as a central pillar of the revised structure. Just as *Henry V* begins and ends at the Globe, so *Richard III* opens and closes with the screening of an ornamental crown. The coronation of Richard III brings the crown sharply back into focus, and when the king has his horse shot from beneath him, the prize-symbol of the story rolls symbolically in the mud, kicked aside by horses' hooves and finally recovered from a bramble bush by Stanley, who places it reverently on Richmond's head.

Beyond all this, for the sake of cinematic expediency, there were numerous alterations to the text. Olivier explained later:

> If you are going to cut a Shakespeare play, there is only one thing to do—lift out scenes. If you cut the lines down merely to keep all the characters in, you end up with a mass of short ends. This is one of the problems with *Richard III*.

The filming—in VistaVision and Technicolor—began not unusually at the end of the story, with the climactic battle scene and Crookback's horrific death. Olivier did not relish this part of direction. 'How the hell can one shoot another medieval battle?' he remarked with some exasperation to Esmond Knight. 'The Americans have done it over and over again in so many films.' He had no intention of trying to compete with Hollywood epics. Perhaps mistakenly, he did not even aim to repeat the breath-taking spectacle of his Agincourt. Rather he sought to achieve the stylized look of a tapestry as a visual counterpart to the poetry. At the same time, he demanded savage realism for the hand-to-hand fighting. As Hazlitt wrote of Edmund Kean's Richard III, Olivier's Crookback 'fought like one drunk with wounds' before thrashing and twitching on the ground in animal convulsions, finally extending his sword in a deformed hand and staring momentarily at the cross formed by the hilt. The action leading up to that memorable scene was to be played out with relentless, fast-moving ferocity, and the responsibility for making it convincing was largely the responsibility of two boyish-looking actors, Bernard Hepton and John Greenwood, recruited to take charge of the swordplay.

'The main problem was one of communication,' says Hepton. 'The opposing armies were, for the most part, composed of Spanish extras who understood no English. Olivier wanted us to arrange a battle scene with 800 extras, with the camera on a twenty-foot tower pointing down on to archers, panning over foot soldiers, then across to Lord Stanley's men deserting to the side of Richmond at a crucial point of the conflict. We organized the armies into groups of three and four, and taught them four sword cuts and parries which they did at different times during rehearsals while instructors called out through loud hailers, "one, two, three, four". At one point Olivier came bounding down the tower steps and slapped me on the back. "That's good," he said. "Just right. Now Willie Walton's got to write some music to this, so could we have them do it all again—in rhythm?"

'Tony Bushell warned us at the start not to expect Sir Laurence to react to suggestions, but he explained that he was always alert to the good idea and would absorb what you said to him even if he didn't appear to. What irritated him was people trying to press ideas upon him. Well, I had boned up on Richard III and knew that his favourite weapon was a battleaxe that he used with his right arm and with all his strength. When I suggested this to him he seemed to look right through me, paying no attention. But two days later he came back enthusiastically. "Lovely idea. Get a battleaxe." So we had one made in Madrid, and when it arrived it was terrible—like a toy tomahawk. Sir Laurence was livid. The only time I saw him lose his temper.'

Esmond Knight, who likes to refer to Richard III as 'Dickie Three Eyes', was one actor not greatly impressed by the filming of the battle sequences. 'One terrible mistake was the armour—made of rubber so that you could see it bend in close shots. All Richard's men were in dark, blackish armour, and Richmond's men were in whitish armour that made them look rather like the Tin Man in The Wizard of Oz. And then there was all that pantomime with the horses. Once Olivier was sitting on his white mare—Richard surveying the drawn-up forces of Richmond. From some trees behind him, three gauleiters ride up to the king: Catesby, Ratcliff and Lovel, you know—"The Cat, the Rat and

Lovel the Dog, rule all England under the Hog." Well, Laurence was worried because we were about to lose the light as the sun neared the mountain range. He shouted orders to us to get on with it, ride through the trees and pull up behind him. So we thundered up immediately behind him. But my horse was a stallion, and being possessed of its natural instincts he promptly mounted Laurence's white mare, practically engulfing the king in the act.

' "Get off, Ned, you bloody twit," he shouted.

' "It's not me," I protested. "It's this randy stallion."

'Then the grooms rushed in to pull the stallion off. And as I fell off backwards, somebody shouted, "Castrate that damned horse." '

Olivier is an accomplished horseman. Unfortunately, he was not always working with riders of equal experience. Even John Laurie, though married to a fine horsewoman with her own stables, was no horseman. Dressed as Lovel, with sword dangling at his side, he was instructed to have a few trial rides so they could see how the sensitive Spanish horses reacted to a rider in gaudy, medieval costume. After cantering a short distance, the actor's horse broke into a spirited gallop. Mrs. Laurie had advised her husband to saw on its mouth in such an emergency. He did. The horse only went faster, leaping over ditches with the frail-looking fifty-seven-year-old actor hanging on for dear life. Finally it stopped short at a wide ditch. Laurie didn't. He somersaulted over the horse's head and crashed on to rock-hard ground. Unconscious, he was carried back to camp in a jeep. 'Afterwards I discovered what went wrong. A Spaniard explained that their horses have very sensitive sides. The hanging sword was the cause, gently tickling the horse, and the faster it went the more strongly the irritation spurred it on. After that, we all thrust our swords through our belts so they stayed solid.'

As in his first (1944) stage appearance in the role, Olivier played Richard III as a paranoiac of reptillian appearance—the same hard, thin lips, lank, jet-black hair, stalactitic nose; a skulking, smarmy-voiced, sardonic villain with scuttingly spider-like walk and a deformed, two-fingered hand that some-one likened to a shrunken haggis. His make-up took him three hours every day. But then he had long been known as the most painstaking of actors. 'What really astounded me was his energy,' said Douglas Wilmer, who played Lord Dorset. 'His work programme was exhausting; yet he could just sit down in a chair and close his eyes for a short time, then walk straight on to the set and act a long scene perfectly despite the enormous burden he was carrying in his three roles as producer, director and leading man . . .

'And he's got a mind like a vacuum cleaner. If there's something you've got that he wants, he'll draw it out of you. We were walking around the set on *Richard III* and I remarked that a bit of heraldry wasn't correct. Heraldry is a hobby of mine. "What?" he said, and then started on me as if he was drilling for oil, pumping every bit of information out of me. His precision and concentration are enormous. Like a diamond drill. He is a very formidable man, and I know some actors find him a frightening man. I certainly do.

'Sometimes he cuts with a bluntness that is really amusing. I remember Esmond Knight wanted to make more of his lines where, as Ratcliff, he comes into Richard's tent at dawn on the day of the Battle of Bosworth. ("The early village-cock hath twice done salutation to the morn; your friends are up, and buckle on their armour.") And he said to the director, "Larry, suppose I loosen my sword in the scabbard, then look over my shoulder through the flap of the tent towards the horses, and then say it." And Olivier just sat there and looked at him, sucking his teeth. Then he said, "No. Just say the line and piss off." '

Laurence Naismith, who distinguished himself as the turncoat Lord Stanley, remembers Olivier in much the same light. 'He never spares anything. And the things he did in Richard were extremely gutty—not only like the time that arrow was shot in his leg. It was the same in sword-fighting. He really expects you to have a "go". No quarter is given, and he expects none in return. You hit him, or he hits you.'

It was now more than thirty years since Naismith had been with Olivier as an All Saints' choir boy. 'I had letters from Larry when I was working on *Richard III* and he was exactly the same in his manner as I remembered him at school. The letters were like directives from a theatre manager; "Thank you, dear Laurie, for an excellent day's work. Please note that tomorrow I shall be changing the line to so-and-so . . . Yours, Larry O." He always had this kind of incisive, commanding regimental style.'

By Olivier's decisiveness born of experience, and by his refusal to dwell on tiny or imaginary imperfections at the cost of pace and mood, an astonishing new tempo of production was achieved. *Henry V*, largely because of wartime conditions, was more than a year in the making. *Hamlet* was six months on the studio floor. Unbelievably, *Richard III*—165 scenes involving thirty featured players, forty actors in bit parts and hundreds of crowd artists—was filmed in just seventeen weeks. And that included the two weeks' rehearsal time and one month on location. Not once did shooting fall behind schedule.

Contrary to all expectation, *Richard III* was not chosen for the annual Royal Film Performance. Alfred Hitchcock's *To Catch a Thief*, starring Cary Grant and Grace Kelly, was preferred, possibly because the selection committee shied away from another unsavoury royal subject after the showing of *Beau Brummel* the previous year. Nevertheless, it still had a Royal premiere, attended by the Queen and Prince Philip, in aid of the King George's Pension Fund for Actors and Actresses, and for the third time in succession Olivier won overwhelming critical acclaim for a Shakespearean film.

C. A. Lejeune (*The Observer*)

Olivier may have savaged the play's text, but he has cut deep and true to the play's spirit. As a director he grows in stature film by film. *Richard III* is full of moments one will remember ... The more I consider it, the more highly I regard this film.

Dilys Powell (*Sunday Times*)

A huge, stirring, splendid, sardonic version of Shakespeare's historical melodrama. To fear disappointment, with Olivier's stage Richard in mind, is unnecessary. I found this screen Richard even more spellbinding ... Of his stage performance one remembers both how funny it was, and how ferocious. Nothing is lost of those qualities; perhaps something is gained by the intimacy which the cinema permits ...

Paul Dehn (*News Chronicle*)

... To see it so mounted on the screen makes one almost cry with gratitude for having been born at a time when such talent co-existed.

Alan Brien (London *Evening Standard*)
Richard III embalms in celluloid one of the greatest Shakespearean performances of our day. Olivier plays his Richard
for laughs. And he raises the grisly humours of the horror
comic to the level of genius.

Milton Shulman (*Sunday Express*)
A more exciting *Richard III* than anything that the stage has
ever done, or is ever likely to do, with the same material . . .

Only *The Times* had strong reservations about the film: 'Somehow this *Richard III* never, with pennants streaming and trumpets sounding, storms to decisive victory.'

In the United States the critics were unanimous in hailing it as
a great production. The Bijou Theatre premiere made front-
page news in the *New York Times*, and a few hours before that
premiere *Richard III* made entertainment history, as the first
full-length feature film ever to be televised in advance of its
cinema showing. N.B.C. paid half a million dollars for one
screening, and it was estimated that this Sunday showing—146
stations in 45 states—was watched by upwards of 40 million
people, the largest number ever to witness a daytime television
programme, excluding certain political and sports broadcasts.
Many schools used the production for a homework assignment,
and for viewers in general it was a case of the economically
impossible coming to pass. Without charge they were seeing a
major new film that could cost a top fee of $2·80 a person to
witness in a New York motion picture house.

But artistically Sir Laurence viewed the TV experiment with
complete dismay. Varying long shots and close-ups were almost
lost on the small screen, the colour was available only to a wealthy
minority, and much of the blood and gore had been cut out for
the 'benefit' of children. But what appalled him most was the
use of commercial breaks. General Motors, sponsoring the
experiment, generously gave part of the first interruption to an
American professor explaining some of the background of
Shakespeare's drama. But this was followed by a full-blown
commercial for a car battery, and Sir Laurence, not yet conditioned to television treatment of modern movies, later found it a
little disconcerting to be told that a certain automobile had 'more
power than all the horses in *Richard III*'.

Olivier's third Shakespearean film brought him three British Film Academy awards (for the best British actor, best British film and best film from any source), and although, unlike *Henry V* and *Hamlet*, it earned him no more than a Best Actor nomination in the Oscar stakes, a number of critics still judge it to be the finest of his trilogy. *Henry V* was arguably the greater achievement because he was then breaking entirely new ground. But *Richard III*, especially difficult to adapt for the screen, was no less a personal triumph for him both as actor and director. Just as his sensational Stratford season had reinforced his reputation as the greatest living stage actor, so this film now re-established him as the foremost interpreter of Shakespeare on the screen.

If fate had not intervened, Olivier might well have added to his extraordinary record. In the fall of 1955 Sir Alexander Korda announced that his future plans included another such picture with Olivier, most probably *Macbeth*. But a few months later the colossus of the British film industry was dead, and without his vision and shrewd business sense the project was doomed to remain a dream. When the final heart attack struck Korda down on the evening of January 22, 1956, Olivier lost one of his greatest friends and his most valuable ally in the movie business. He was the only star who had ever worked with Korda on a co-producer basis. And when hundreds of cinema celebrities packed St. Martin-in-the-Fields for the memorial service, it was appropriately Sir Laurence who followed Sir Ralph Richardson to the pulpit to deliver the final and most moving tribute. After describing Sir Alexander's poor and gallant youth, his magnificent generosity and personality, he concluded by adapting Hamlet: 'Take him for all in all, we shall not look upon his like again.'

When Korda died in his sixty-third year, his empire, London Films, died with him. And soon afterwards Olivier wound up his company, Laurence Olivier Productions, which had presented plays at the St. James's and had linked up with London Films to make *Richard III*. Korda had been the principal shareholder. Sir Laurence, chairman and director, was to form a new company to produce his next picture. But, as it happened, *Richard III* now represents his last great achievement as a film-maker.

In more ways than one, Korda's death marked the end of an era. In the emerging world of the cinema, desperately developing new techniques, madly trendy and ever more blatantly commercial in the fight to live with television, Olivier would not again discover the kind of unhesitating support that Korda had so generously given.

20
★ *Marilyn*

SIR LAURENCE TO STAR WITH MARILYN. The story broke with the dawn of 1956—front-page news that provided a tasty conversational titbit for suburbanites over their coffee cups, a matter for sly winks and approving grunts in the public bars, and an arsenal of cannon fodder for the gossip columnists for many months to come. Marilyn Monroe, supreme sex symbol of the Fifties, was planning to co-star with Olivier in the film version of *The Sleeping Prince*, playing the role created by Vivien Leigh.

The prospect of a Monroe–Olivier alliance inevitably intrigued both press and public. It was seen as a new peak in the extraordinary success story of the girl born Norma Jean, illegitimate, fatherless, and later abandoned to an orphanage and a succession of foster homes. Only five years had passed since Marilyn, the wartime parachute-packer, had flitted across the screen in *All About Eve* as the dumb-blonde in a film dominated by Bette Davis; only three years since she had first riveted men's eyes with her accentuated wiggle through *Niagara*. Yet here she was now with her own Marilyn Monroe Productions Incorporated, proposing to employ the theatre's most lauded knight as her co-star.

It was seen, too, as a daring departure for Olivier. In a sense, by fraternizing with Monroe, he was stepping down from the Royal Grandstand of his profession to join in the passing parade that represented movie commercialism at its loudest and brassiest. After three years of dedicating himself exclusively to Shakespearean art, he envisaged it as a refreshing and lucrative departure before he faced the heavyweight task of filming *Macbeth*. But there were obvious dangers. Years ago it had been judged unseemly for the Old Vic's most celebrated player to be mobbed by bobbysoxers in the style of a young Sinatra. Now, as partner to Miss Monroe, he was exposing himself to precisely that kind of frenzied scene, to movie-fan hysteria and all the excesses of publicity and frivolous reportage that is peculiar to pop entertainment idols.

It had a certain appealing gaiety at first. The Press talked about a double act that would rival the appearance in Britain of Bulganin and Khrushchev. Olivier and Monroe became the Knight and the Garter. And when Sir Laurence went even more commercial and lent his name to a new brand of cigarettes, they dubbed him Sir Cork Tip. A bit of harmless fun. Good. Like the time zany Salvador Dali ('I see Sir Laurence as a rhinoceros') had come over to paint him as Richard III. It could be healthy to deflate from time to time the image of the theatrical dignitary that tended to isolate him from the mainstream of show business.

But surely working with Monroe was rather more than a breezy exercise in public relations. He was moving back into the peak-voltage glare of film fame that he had not known since *Wuthering Heights*. He had not liked the intensity of the fan-fever he generated as Heathcliff, yet soon he would be embroiled in the ballyhoo that attended his playing Prince Regent to Hollywood's queen of seraphic sex. Not for the first time, as an introversive Englishman who cherished his privacy and a perfectionist actor who worked by the axiom that to be dull is to be dead, Olivier was to be the victim of the strikingly schizophrenic element in his life.

The proposed union of the Knight and Garter came at a time when circumstances assured a riot of publicity. Miss Monroe had not made a movie since November 1954 and her appearance in *The Seven Year Itch* as the sweetly tantalizing girl upstairs who sends the staid summer widower below into a confusion of frustrated infidelities. It personified her image as every married man's jackpot dream, as the candyfloss girl of super-ripe physical charms who miraculously combined the contradictory qualities of carnality and innocence, and it left film fans hungry for more. At that strategic point, complaining of being underpaid and ill-cast, Marilyn had walked out on Hollywood in open breach of her contract with Twentieth Century-Fox. She had since lived in New York as a non-working rebel, guided in business by ex-photographer Milton Greene, and in artistic matters by Lee Strasberg, founder and director of the Actor's Studio and principal exponent of the controversial 'Method' school of acting.

For over six months Marilyn had studied under Strasberg. In her desperate bid to improve her mind ('I want to be an artist, not a freak') she developed extravagant cultural aspirations, talked of tackling Aristophanes' *Lysistrata* on television and playing Grushenka in Dostoyevsky's *The Brothers Karamazov*. She also became romantically involved with Arthur Miller, the intellectual, Pulitzer Prize-winning playwright who was already prominent in the news by virtue of the witch-hunt of the House of Representatives' Un-American Affairs Subcommittee and his persistent refusals, on grounds of conscience, to name people he had seen at Communist meetings seventeen years before.

Greene, Strasberg and Miller were all well-intentioned influences on Marilyn. They by no means worked in harmony. After a tentative suggestion that Olivier might be employed as director as well as leading man for *The Sleeping Prince*, Marilyn mentioned that Strasberg had said the possibility was 'a good idea'. Greene promptly cabled Olivier a firm offer. But later it was explained to him that Strasberg had merely said that it *might* be a good idea and was worth exploring. If there had been full consultation before taking action, it is by no means certain that Strasberg, as Marilyn's artistic mentor, would have approved the idea. After all, Olivier's approach was quite unlike that of the 'Method' school, choosing as he did to work 'mostly from the outside in', making some physical detail, a peripheral characteristic, the starting point to his search for the inner man.

But since they were all agreed that Olivier was desirable as leading man, it was decided that they had no alternative but to let the cabled offer stand. The deal was made. In February Sir Laurence flew to New York for preliminary talks that received almost as much press attention as the New Year discussions between President Eisenhower and Sir Anthony Eden. They first met at Monroe's New York apartment. The appointment was set for noon. Marilyn postponed it until six. Sir Laurence arrived at six. Marilyn emerged from her bedroom at seven—wearing the simplest of dresses and no discernible make-up. She apologized. 'I just didn't know what to wear,' she later explained. 'Should I be casual or formal? I went twice through my entire wardrobe but everything I tried on wasn't kinda right.'

Sir Laurence was eager to be punctual because he had booked a transatlantic phone call to Vivien. However, he accepted the delay gracefully. He was to learn the hard way about his co-star's

notorious tardiness. Being late had become an instinctive response to any event that made her nervous. A psychiatrist suggested that her unpunctuality, procrastinations, phobias and
frequent headaches were all symptomatic of a typical hysteroid
personality—a person who, as a result of lack of love and affection in early youth, suffered a marked subconscious feeling
of insecurity and constantly craved sympathy and attention.
Rattigan, who attended the New York meeting, simply described
her as 'a shy exhibitionist; the Garbo who likes to be photographed'.

On February 9 Milton Greene arranged a noon press conference in the Hotel Plaza's Terrace Room for the anticlimactic
announcement that filming of *The Sleeping Prince* would begin
in London in August, with Olivier as both director and leading
man. As much had been rumoured for weeks; still, 200 reporters
and photographers turned out for the show. After all, this was
Monroe's first large-scale conference in more than a year. She
purred that Sir Laurence was her favourite actor and her hero.
He, in turn, came out with the right kind of ingratiating publicity
talk: 'Marilyn is a brilliant comedienne, which means to me she
is a very fine actress. She has the extremely cunning gift of being
able to suggest one minute that she is the naughtiest little thing
and the next minute that she is beautifully dumb and innocent.
The greatest effect on the audience is that they are gently titil-
lated to a sense of excitement in not knowing which is which.'
And yes, he did think she could play Shakespeare.

Pressmen jostled for advantageous positions. Sir Laurence
accepted the uproar with good humour. Finally he called a halt.
'No more leg pictures. From now on she is too ethereal.' But he
could not play the ringmaster in this kind of cheesecake circus. A
reporter asked Marilyn if she was continuing to take dramatic
lessons. 'Oh, yes,' she replied, inhaling deeply. 'I'd like to continue my growth in every way possible.' Flashbulbs exploded.
And then the predictable happened: the breaking of a flimsy
shoulder strap on her black velvet gown. A coat, conveniently at
hand, did not cool the situation. The shifting mass closed in. The
love goddess was trapped against a wall. More popping of flash-
bulbs and inane questions. A great titter at the teasing suggestion
that the other strap may have busted. And finally the stars were
released. Sir Laurence had had his introduction to what Marilyn
liked to call 'the zoo'.

Back in London, Olivier had five months to prepare for the coming of Monroe. He gave much of that time to charity work—organizing, producing and appearing in a midnight revue on behalf of the Green Room Club and its charities, busying himself as the newly elected president of the Actors' Orphanage in succession to Noel Coward, who had held office for twenty years. Coward, now living in Jamaica, still contributed to the charity's annual midnight spectacular *Night of a Hundred Stars*, but more and more the main burden fell upon the Oliviers, organizing endless rehearsals and, most important of all, securing the added support of such American headliners as Jack Benny, Bob Hope and Tyrone Power. And Vivien had a further commitment at this time. In April, after a five-week provincial tour, she returned to the London stage as Lady Alexander Shotter, the governor's lady in Coward's colonial romp *South Sea Bubble*. The play was a hit, destined to run at the Lyric for 276 performances.

The Oliviers had sold their Chelsea home and were now living in the backwaters of Belgravia in an elegant cottage rented for nine months from Sir William Walton. But soon after the opening of *South Sea Bubble* something occurred that set them hunting for a new London home and arranging for Vivien to be replaced in the play. At the age of forty-two Lady Olivier had discovered to her great surprise—and with mixed feelings of joy and apprehension—that she was expecting a baby. Twenty-two years had gone by since the birth of her first and only child.

Sir Laurence was delighted. His son by his first marriage was nineteen, currently in Germany doing his National Service as a second lieutenant in the Coldstream Guards. Now he hoped for a daughter, and they had already chosen a name: Kathryn. Although Vivien had suffered a miscarriage in 1944 during the filming of *Caesar and Cleopatra*, she was reassured that there was no reason to suppose that she could not still have a strong and healthy child. All the same, she would be advised to give up her stage work early in August. The baby was expected in December.

This happened to be a time of great theatrical excitement in London, and Vivien determined to make the most of it before being condemned to temporary retirement. First, with typical zest, she prepared for the glittering *Night of a Hundred Stars*. The Oliviers and John Mills put thirty-four hours of rehearsing into their four-minute act, 'Top Hat, White Tie, and Tails'. The

song and tap-dance routine ended with Bob Hope cutting in and
waltzing off with Sir Laurence, the high point of an unforgettable
June night at the Palladium. Then, two weeks later, Vivien
joined her husband for the most extravagantly publicized event
of the year: Britain's welcome to Marilyn Monroe.

Since Olivier's meeting with her in New York, Marilyn had
dominated the show business and gossip headlines to an extraordinary degree. As Hollywood's most coveted out-of-work star
she held Fox by the tail, and in February she returned to the
studios in triumph, all her demands met: veto power over roles
and directors, freedom to make one independent film and four
television shows a year. Under the terms of her new contract she
could expect to earn at least $8 million in the next seven years.
Above all, Marilyn was now front-page news because of her
probable third marriage to recently divorced Arthur Miller,
the solid, quiet, pipe-smoking, bespectacled intellectual who had
survived the McCarthy purge. Only two weeks earlier, in sensational circumstances (a White Russian princess, reporting for
Paris-Match, accidentally crashed to her death while pursuing
them by car) Monroe and Miller had followed a quickie civic
wedding with a religious ceremony in Westchester County. With
some difficulty Miller had obtained a limited-period passport.
Now they were arriving in Britain as a honeymoon couple.

The Millers landed at London Airport on July 14—one hour
late, with twenty-seven pieces of baggage (three of them his).
Immediately they were embroiled in a press conference more
frenzied than the one in New York. Reporters clambered over
chairs and on to tea counters. Photographers were thrown to the
floor. The two couples, Oliviers and Millers, were backed into a
corner. Finally, from behind a soft-drink stand, they proceeded
to answer questions. Miss Monroe, born to chaos, said it was
'very orderly'. She was fluent but hardly audible. Sir Laurence
was kept busy relaying her answers in a supremely penetrating
voice. Lady Olivier remained calm, cool and uninterrogated.
Mr. Miller occasionally wore a teeth-gritted smile. He came
through this ordeal, and so many similar public appearances,
with a kind of tortured dignity, like a reincarnated Abe Lincoln
on a pre-emancipation tour of the Deep South.

Later, a more formal press conference was held at the Savoy
Hotel. Olivier conducted the affair with authority and in a style
likened to that of a benevolent uncle assisting a gifted niece

through a difficult examination. More inane questions poured forth: Was it true that Miss Monroe slept in Chanel No. 5? Did she believe in the seven-year itch? How did she define an intellectual? Was she serious about Dostoyevsky? Sir Laurence repeated them through a microphone, with a gravity that subtly made them sound even more banal.

Until the novelty wore off, the presence of Monroe in Britain engendered extraordinary public interest. Her every move, whether going to the theatre or riding a bicycle, was photographed in detail and reported in purple prose. Only *The Times* failed to accord her the attention of a State visitor. This prompted the London *Daily Mirror* to launch an editorial assault on the Top People's newspaper for 'suppressing notable news' and 'giving twenty inches to a review of the bulb growers' catalogue but not a blooming word about Miss Monroe'.

The honeymooning Millers hid from prying eyes at a cost of £125 a week, the rental for Parkside House, Lord Moore's eleven-bedroom country mansion at Englefield Green in Surrey. They had two weeks' holiday, then filming began at Pinewood Studios with the scene where the American chorus girl is presented to the Grand Duke Charles of Carpathia and invited back to the London Embassy for supper. Monroe reported for work accompanied by her own vice-president, make-up man, hairdresser, cook and bodyguard. Olivier introduced her to the rest of the cast, then suggested: 'Why don't we go on to the set, because they're just building the ballroom scene, which might interest you.'

'Hey, wait a minute,' said Milton Greene. 'How many security men have you got on the floor?'

Sir Laurence replied, 'In this studio we don't really need a security man on the set while they're building.'

'Ah, but you never know,' said the Monroe executive. 'There may be a sex-mad carpenter at work.'

'Yes,' chirped in Paul Hardwick. 'And you never know— Dickie [Richard Wattis] or I might be a sex-mad actor.'

Hardwick recalls that Marilyn was 'practically paralysed with nerves' on the set. 'And sometimes her work was quite dreadful. She had one very short scene where she was supposed to be in Westminster Abbey, a five- or six-second "take" that simply required her to raise her eyes and appear strangely moved. Well, she simply couldn't do it. Larry had a loop of "Air on a G String" playing for a good hour, over and over again, trying to coax that look out of her. At the end of the hour he switched it off and said, "Look, how can I help you? I don't know what more to say to help you to get this look. You love 'Air on a G String,' don't you?"

' "Yeah," she said. "But I think I could do it better if I had 'Danny Boy' playing." '

The first weeks of shooting progressed reasonably smoothly. Then, more and more, Marilyn arrived late for work—late in the morning, late coming back from lunch. And unpunctuality was not the only problem. Marilyn had a disconcerting habit of suddenly breaking off work if she spotted some friend on the set and calling out, 'Hi there!' As often as not this was liable to happen just when an elaborate scene had been set up and Olivier was about to call for action. In later stages, when Mr. Miller appeared on the set almost every day, she would never hesitate to drop everything and rush over to embrace him. Beyond this, Olivier's patience was strained by the disturbing presence of Paula Strasberg. In continuing with the exercises and study set by Lee Strasberg, Marilyn had become more and more dependent on guidance from his wife, finally reaching the stage where she regarded her as indispensable. Now, as the leading lady's paid drama coach, Mrs. Strasberg inevitably encroached on the director's territory, and her advice ('Think of cold sausages and Coca Cola', she said when Marilyn struggled to achieve a certain facial expression needed for a scene) did not always concur with Olivier's ideas.

In his triple capacity of producer, director and leading man Sir Laurence now found himself working under as much mental strain as he had ever known when filming Shakespeare. Every morning he had to rise at five thirty, rarely could he leave the studios before seven thirty in the evening; and the pressures were increased because, without complete control over events, he could not always cut through difficulties in his usual decisive manner. Monroe was a law unto herself, and one could hardly take a firm line with her tantrums and tardiness when she was the financial boss and virtually paying the bills.

On Saturday, August 12, Vivien Leigh left *South Sea Bubble*, handing over her role to Elizabeth Sellars so that she could rest through the final four months of pregnancy. The following day she was feeling unwell. Doctors were called. But it was too late.

She had had another miscarriage.

Friends have since said that Vivien only wanted the baby 'for Larry's sake'. He adored children, was very much a family man at heart, and a child of their own was the one powerful bond missing in the Oliviers' marriage. By coincidence, on the day of Vivien's miscarriage, Hesther Olivier, wife of Sir Laurence's brother Dickie, who lived in a cottage at Notley and managed the farming estate, gave birth to a baby girl.

Once again Vivien found herself confined to her bedroom at Notley and advised to take a long rest before returning to work. In so many ways it was a cruelly frustrating time for her. As she learned about her husband's growing difficulties at the studios, she regretted that she herself had been unable to recreate her stage role in the film of *The Sleeping Prince*. Ironically it was Vivien who had first recommended Marilyn to Sir Laurence. She later recalled: 'I saw Marilyn Monroe in *How to Marry a Millionaire* and I thought, heaven help me, that she was very funny. I said to Larry, "This girl is wonderful in comedy." I suggested that she star in the film . . . and I added that I thought I might be too old for the part. They believed me, and Terry Rattigan and Larry went crazy over Monroe, and when I changed my mind and suggested I might play the part after all, they said, "Oh, but you're too old." '[1]

Late in September, when Miss Leigh returned from ten days' holiday on the Italian Riviera at the Portofino villa of Rex Harrison and Lilli Palmer, she found that Sir Laurence was the one more in need of a rest. Early in the month, because his work was so 'exceedingly arduous and nervously exhausting' he had missed the presentation ceremony at the Edinburgh Film Festival where he was to receive the 1956 Selznick Golden Laurel Trophy for outstanding screen work. Since then work at Pinewood had come to a complete standstill on the increasingly frequent days when Monroe failed to appear.

'Sir Laurence was always the gentleman,' recalled Marilyn's make-up man, Whitey Sneider, 'but after a while there were tensions and tightness. Looking back, I remembered that Marilyn did much better when there was no dramatic coach around. But Sir Laurence had to accept the presence of the dramatic coach on the set . . .

'Often while I was making her up she would be on the verge of hysterics. She was scared of the day's work with a brilliant, talented man. Sir Laurence tried to help. He would say, "Well, it was perfect for me." Then, in a kind of resignation, he would say, "All right, we'll do it again."

'Marilyn slowly ran down in energy. She became ill more frequently, more nervous. But I never noticed any change in Sir Laurence. He was always ready for the day's work. And obviously disappointed that production did not go according to schedule.'

Joshua Logan, who had directed Marilyn in *Bus Stop*, recalls: 'From the time Larry Olivier was announced as her director and co-star I began to write him every few days about the things I had discovered about Marilyn. I remember saying, "Don't allow her to get your goat. It is the only thing that can spoil the picture—if you ever lose whatever calm you have and blast away out of frustration and anger." At one point Larry wrote me and said, "I will try to follow your advice. I will force myself to be calm. I will iron myself out flat and creaseless every morning like a newly washed shirt."

'Mostly, I explained how talented Marilyn was and what a natural creature she was to have in front of a camera. She seemed to know exactly what to do and think the moment the film was rolling. Olivier wrote back, "She wants a dialogue director on the set—Paula Strasberg. What do you think of that?"

'By this time I had found Paula Strasberg most co-operative, even though I never allowed her on set, and I wrote that to Larry. Months later when I visited Larry on the set he came at me with a venomous rush and said, "How dare you tell me to have Paula Strasberg on the set! She's a bloody nuisance." I said, "I told you that she never appeared on my set." And suddenly he looked at me, aghast, and said, "You did? How did I get the idea she was there all the time? Oh, I am sorry—that was a slip on my part."

'Then I asked, "Are you getting along well with Marilyn?"

'He looked rather hurt. "What did *you* do when you were demonstrating how the scene should be played and she walked away from you as though you weren't there and went over to the other side of the stage and started talking to one of the hair-dressers?"

'I answered, "The way I handled that, Larry, was by never demonstrating how a scene should be played." '

From all the evidence, Sir Laurence clearly did his best to follow Logan's advice about keeping cool. Though he can swear most picturesquely,* his language usually became a perfect knight. But there had to be limits to the amount of confusion such an efficiency-loving director could take. 'The things he had to put up with were terrible,' recalls actor Douglas Wilmer. 'She was always late, and one day when we were shooting the Coronation scene it meant that Dame Sybil Thorndike was kept waiting for ages in her heavy robes. Laurence told her, "Don't you think you ought to apologize to Dame Sybil?" And Marilyn exploded. "Apologize!" And she turned on her heels and flounced off. But she was good enough about half an hour later to apologize very nicely and Sybil said very grandly: "Not at all, my dear. I'm sure we're all very glad to see you. Now that you *are* here."

'But Laurence had to learn patience because really it was useless to get annoyed with her. It was just water off a duck's back. One morning he finally stormed at her, "Why can't you get here on time for fuck's sake?" And Marilyn just replied, "Oh, do you have that word in England too?" '

Esmond Knight believes that Olivier's own performance suffered as a consequence of his difficulties with his co-star. 'Laurence, who is punctilious about his lines, was his usual self in the early part of shooting, but when one came to Take 32 or 33 of a scene, and Marilyn finally got it right, it was a case of saying, "Cut! How was that for sound? . . . All right for camera? . . . Okay. Print it." Well, by that time even the great Laurence was beginning to look a bit strained. But Marilyn, photographic par excellence, would be looking absolutely splendid, perfect. And they had to use that take because it was the first one she had got right.'

Dame Sybil recalled: 'Larry had awful fights with her, and I said to him, "Why do you bother? She knows how to do it, just as you knew how to do things. She's an intuitive actress. Leave her alone." He replied, "I don't care. There are one or two things I *will* have right." But he didn't get his way with Marilyn, not entirely. She could not take direction really. She knew what she could do and that was it.'

---

* Olivier once mentioned to Noel Coward, in almost apologetic tones, that Oxford University was about to make him a Doctor of Letters. Coward's automatic riposte was: 'Doctor of four letters, I presume.'

For three months filming continued at Pinewood. Sir Laurence did not endear himself to the Press by strictly enforcing a locked-door policy, but it was necessary to avoid additional delays and diversions. Even then Marilyn remained prominent in the news, especially when she was invited to attend the Royal Film Performance and be presented to the Queen. The stars were advised to dress with due modesty, but Marilyn knew only one sure way to stand among a crowd of celebrities. She squeezed into a tight sheath of gold lamé with a low-slung neckline that defied decorum in the most appetizing way. It made curtsying an intriguing adventure, and it ensured that she got the measure of such a generously endowed star as Anita Ekberg who stood by, somewhat cheated, with her best-known attributes discreetly veiled.

The last shots of *The Sleeping Prince* were taken in mid-November. Amazingly, after all the revised shooting schedules, the picture had been completed marginally ahead of time. Marilyn, relaxed at last, was all wide-eyed innocence, sweetness and charm. She told the cast: 'I hope you will all forgive me. It wasn't my fault. I've been very, very sick all through the picture. Please, please don't hold it against me.' And, of course, they did forgive her, because one could no more sustain hostility towards this child of nature than one could take offence at a butterfly going berserk on the wing. All the same, filming with her had been for Olivier an exhausting experience that he would not wish to endure again. Only Billy Wilder ever came back to make a second film starring Monroe, for which he said, 'It behoves the Screen Directors Guild to award me a purple heart.'

Because the original title did not refer to Marilyn's involvement and because they considered the word 'sleeping' to be negative, the American backers renamed the film *The Prince and the Showgirl* ('It sounds like an old Betty Grable musical,' Olivier grumbled). In mid-1957 it had a gala premiere at Radio City Music Hall in New York, and it subsequently received some quite outstanding reviews on both sides of the Atlantic. It was not a commercial success, due in the main, perhaps, to the frailty of the story-line. But there was no disputing its elegance and charm. Olivier's performance was called impeccable, his direction skilled and tasteful. As for the wayward Marilyn, she came across with a natural, irresistible freshness that totally belied the mental anguish with which it was achieved; again she radiated that unique Monroe quality, inadequately described as 'flesh impact', on the screen. Through her role in *The Prince and the Showgirl* she won her only acting award of any consequence, the David Di Donatello statuette from Italy.

Five years and only three films after the release of *The Prince and the Showgirl*, the star born Norma Jean was dead, a neurotic and tragic casualty of the Hollywood system that created her. She was thirty-six. Her bequest to the film colony was a giant guilt complex. And at once there was wide support for Olivier's statement, quoted all over the United States, that she was 'the complete victim of ballyhoo and sensation . . . exploited beyond anyone's means'.

'Sir Larry and I belong to a special club, the Directors of Marilyn Monroe,' says Josh Logan. 'I don't think either of us will ever know what made her almost jump through the screen into the arms of the audience, while her co-stars, brilliant as they were, never quite achieved that quality. I think of all the miracles that were performed by Sir Laurence Olivier, but she was the one that got there by herself.'

21

★

The Entertainer

In the sunset of a supremely distinguished film career Spencer Tracy expressed one deep regret: that he had never realized his ambition to work with the actor he most admired, Olivier. They had come close to it in the casting of several pictures (*Judgment at Nuremburg* was one), but each time one or the other proved unobtainable. The most exciting opportunity of pairing the colossus of the theatre with the consummate artist of the cinema had come in February 1957, when the Oliviers flew to Los Angeles to discuss a prospective film of *Separate Tables* to be produced by the Hecht–Hill–Lancaster triumvirate. There was a suggestion that Sir Laurence might star in the picture and direct, but eventually he withdrew, reportedly because of a disagreement over structural changes in adapting Rattigan's play for the screen. According to Tracy, however, another factor contributed to the breakdown in negotiations.

'Larry asked me to be in the picture. "Won't Burt Lancaster want the part?" I asked. "No." Larry said. "He's agreed that you do it." We had a party to celebrate, and then the Oliviers flew home. When they arrived, a call was waiting from Hollywood. Lancaster had decided he wanted the role. "Either Tracy does it or you can't have us," Larry said. But Lancaster was determined. Larry rang me that night. "Well, old cock," he said, "we've all been fired." I said, "That'll teach you to ask for me." '[1]

The decision to withdraw from *Separate Tables* cost Olivier something in the region of $300,000. Immediately afterwards he signed up for the lead in a new contemporary play, at a salary of less than £50 a week. It was another demonstration of the man's steely artistic integrity, unbending to purely commercial interest. And far more extraordinary than his modest wage was his choice of play: *The Entertainer*, another provocative work by twenty-seven-year-old John Osborne, currently the most discussed playwright in Britain and commonly labelled The Angry Young Man by virtue of the savage rhetoric poured out by his anti-hero in *Look Back in Anger*. Here was a professional alliance even more improbable, and certainly more significant, than the pairing of Olivier and Monroe. This time the prince of players was proposing to go arm-in-arm with the young radical most popularly identified with the new anti-Establishment revolution.

The rumblings of rebellion had been heard before the petulant Jimmy Porter launched into his tirades against a society without a soul. But *Look Back in Anger*, by the immediacy and topicality of its impassioned language, struck the first truly resounding chord, echoing the mood of a whole generation so knowingly that 'angry young man' grew from a publicist's catch-phrase into a cult. It also, in effect, set off a great revival in British drama, since its success encouraged a host of new writers to attempt plays whereas previously they would have been more inclined to express themselves through the novel. Not that there was anything new in rebellious youth sounding off in open defiance of their elders. Most generations had thrown up angry young men of distinction. Indeed, when *Look Back in Anger* exploded on to the London theatre scene in May 1956, it probably created no more shock impact than Coward's *The Vortex* in the 1920s.

But there was a difference. The young intellectuals who questioned values between the world wars tended to be drawn from within the Establishment itself, sons of privilege nobly seeking social justice for the underdog. Now the underdog was yapping quite effectively for himself. It heralded the emergence of a new generation of non-U intelligentsia drawn for the most part from the regions of the lower-middle class and developed through the marginally improved hand-outs of state education. They had varied grievances, but they shared a common enemy: the so-called Establishment, everything in 'the system' that so efficiently preserved wealth and power and influence in the hands of a privileged minority.

To people with a rigid sense of social order it seemed illogical that Sir Laurence, public school product, officer and gentleman member of the Beefsteak, Buck's and The Other Club,* the

* The Other Club had only twenty-five members, including Sir Winston Churchill, and with the exception of Olivier and attorney Sir Hartley Shawcross, it was made up exclusively of politicians and service chiefs.

actor-knight most strongly identified with the Establishment, should consort with the likes of Osborne, a Redbrick failure scornful of Flag and Empire and the playing fields of Eton, and capable (as he later proved) of describing the British Royal Family as 'the gold filling in a mouthful of decay'. But then it was no more illogical or incongruous than the involvement of Lord Harewood, the Queen's cousin, who, along with George Devine and poet-dramatist Ronald Duncan, had founded the English Stage Company in 1956, so giving Porter a platform he could never have gained initially in an established West End theatre.

From the start it was the avowed intention of the company's founders to emphasize modern work and encourage new playwrights. *Look Back in Anger*, the only interesting work submitted after they had advertised in *The Stage* for new plays, was the financial shot in the arm that enabled the company to prosper with Devine as artistic director and the Royal Court Theatre as a permanent home. And it so happened that Devine was a close personal friend of Olivier (they had worked together as long ago as 1935, in *Romeo and Juliet* at the New, and were associated professionally after the war when Devine became director of the Young Vic). It was through Devine that Sir Laurence sounded out the possibility of playing in Osborne's next play and subsequently came to accept the role of Archie Rice, a broken-down, third-rate music-hall comic.

Olivier had seen *Look Back in Anger* the previous summer. He had loathed it. After a second visit, in the company of Arthur Miller, he changed his mind. It was easy to say (and some critics did) that he was joining with forces he couldn't beat, that it illustrated his pragmatism. Nevertheless, his decision to go into *The Entertainer* undeniably took courage. He had been warned against risking his reputation in the hands of comparatively inexperienced talents (Tony Richardson, the same age as Osborne, would be directing a major star for the first time). And by going into a non-Establishment play (one that contained some scathing comments on political figures, the Royal Family and Suez invasion, that had Patriotism represented by a Britannia going naked except for her helmet, and that indirectly sustained Jimmy Porter's cry that there were no good causes left to die for) he was very conceivably inviting the disapproval of friends in high places. But he was essentially an actor by profession and in the final analysis he had to be guided by his professional instinct. By association, his name lent a certain respectability to Osborne's art if not to the 'angry young man' cult as a whole. And most importantly, his presence gave impetus to the breakthrough in contemporary drama that was being achieved at the Royal Court in Sloane Square.

In one sense Olivier was not gambling quite as recklessly as some people imagined. There was a suggestion that an actor of his power and presence was ill-fitted for the shabby jacket of a third-rate vaudeville comic performing in a seaside holiday show called *Rock 'n' Roll New'd Look*. But he knew otherwise. As he later explained it: 'There's a morbid fascination in thinking what might have happened to me if I'd made good as a chorus boy. Because at one time I would have been glad to take a job in a concert party if it had been offered. I'd have called myself Larry Olivier, and been as happy as a lark. That's why I feel I can play this Archie Rice quite intuitively. There must have been something of Archie in me all along. It's what I might so easily have become . . . because I'm always thinking that I've never had the opportunity to make people laugh as much as I would have liked. *I'd like to make them die with laughter*. There is to me a tremendous attraction in being a general entertainer, and to bridge the lines of demarcation in the theatre.'[2]

Often enough there had been sardonic devilment in his playing of great roles. He had revealed his flair for comedy in strictly eccentric parts. But until *The Entertainer* he had never had a major opportunity to show himself on stage in full flush as a comedian. Archie Rice, the pathetic and lecherous song-and-dance jester of twice-nightly nude revue, was unlike any character he had played before. Yet he knew the man well. He had met him in his early years of cheap boarding rooms in London and Birmingham—the artificial funster ever cracking atrocious jokes while behind the professional façade was a gin-soaked failure, aware of his own degradation but incapable of dragging himself out of the mire. Olivier knew that he could play the part, but would the public accept him in the role of such a common man? He recalled the reverse case of Sir Gerald du Maurier, who, at the height of the naturalistic Twenties, was asked why he had never played Richard III. 'Good God!' the matinée idol had exclaimed. 'I couldn't embarrass the public like that.'

As an exterior actor, choosing to work 'from the outside in', Sir

Laurence began by visiting the century-old Collins' Music Hall, Islington. He sat through a variety bill that included nudes and rock 'n' roll numbers and then, while Vivien and their party of friends remained in the front stalls, he tripped backstage to quiz the showgirls. Collins' management were so flattered that they put up a commemorative plaque. A few days later came the first rehearsal. Olivier was so consumed by nerves that he could snatch only a few hours' sleep beforehand. But the first run-through went well, and at lunchtime he was all smiles and warmed with nostalgia. He was working in the Royal Court theatre for the first time since his Birmingham Rep days almost thirty years before. Osborne, too, was beaming at everyone and saying, 'It's a dream'—for the present not at all living up (or rather down) to the Angry Young Man tag that he had come to loathe.

At one time it had been suggested that Miss Leigh, by wearing a rubber mask* to conceal her good looks, might play Archie's blowsy, cinema-addicted wife. Wisely this ludicrous idea was dropped. Brenda de Banzie, who had previously worked with Olivier in *Venus Observed*, took the part, and she played it with a brilliance verging on greatness. But inevitably it was Sir Laurence—in natty check suit, black bow-tie, white socks and grey bowler, and chattering with the forced heartiness of an over-the-hill Max Miller—who was made the main focus of critical scrutiny. Although suffering from gout ('psychosomatic in origin') on the first night of *The Entertainer*, he came through the examination with first-class honours. John Barber's judgment in the *Daily Express* fairly represents the critics' reaction: 'Olivier is tremendous. Not because of that hilarious music-hall act. It is the man backstage who counts. Olivier has it all. The puffed cheeks and uneasily refined accent. The gurgling, leering funny stories. And the too-hearty laugh that conceals the pang of shame. For there is more to this man than you think. "Old Archie," he boasts, "is dead behind the eyes." Then he hears his soldier son has been killed. And the man's agony shows naked. Before your eyes, you see how a body crumbles as the heart cracks within.'

---

* Miss Leigh had worn a rubber mask once before—as the ageing Emma in *Lady Hamilton*.

The view would eventually take firm root that Olivier, as Archie Rice, achieved his greatest performance outside the classics. In his scholarly book *The Player Kings*, critic Richard Findlater writes: 'This masterly performance (later recreated in the cinema) was acting *about* acting, its shams and realities; it was the personification of a dying theatre and (less certainly) a dying society; but it was also the incarnation of one man's suffering and despair, nonetheless overwhelming in its theatrical truth because the man was a third-rate comic rather than a Shakespearean king.'[3]

William Gaskill, who later took over as director of the English Stage Company, has expressed the opinion that all Olivier's qualities as an actor were seen at their best in *The Entertainer*. 'Larry had a complete understanding of the role. In an odd way he knew it was about him. I remember we had an evening at the Old Vic for the George Devine award when various actors came along to do their pieces. Naturally enough, Larry's was from *The Entertainer*. People were sitting around in their costumes as they do on those occasions and suddenly right behind us in the stalls there was the face of Archie Rice—that peculiar mask—and Larry was leaning forward saying: "This is really me, isn't it?" And it was him absolutely. That kind of heartless clown's mask is very much part of Larry Olivier. I don't mean that he's cold and unemotional, but at the same time I think it's sentimental to expect him, because he is an outstanding actor, to be a man of great feeling and emotional depth. Not many actors are.'[4]

The play itself was not at first received with the same accord. There was some carping over its structure, pace and content, and in praising Olivier's 'superb virtuosity' *The Times* added that 'less expertly played, the part would fall all over the place in the last quarter of an hour'. At the same time, no one could deny the sheer vitality of the work, blazingly contentious and contemporary. Osborne's Archie Rice offered acting opportunities rarely equalled in modern drama, and arguably these were taken so brilliantly that the master's performance tended to dazzle at the expense of the lesson—i.e., the author's intention of making the seedy showman symbolic of the decaying edifice that was present-day England. One first night, with Olivier in full flood, switching from breathtaking versatility from cheekie-chappie patter to moving pathos, was really inadequate for a studied appraisal of the play. Like *Look Back in Anger*, it would be more deeply appreciated on revival.

The Entertainer closed after a limited season of five weeks. Immediately Olivier was switching from grey bowler to laurel wreath and plunging back into the disturbing horrors of *Titus Andronicus*, a revival of Peter Brook's sensational production being taken on a 5,000-mile tour to Paris, Venice, Belgrade, Zagreb, Vienna, Warsaw and finally London. The Oliviers, together with sixty actors of the Shakespeare Memorial Theatre Company, left in mid-May for Paris, where the play served as Britain's contribution to the International Theatre Festival, and though some of the more gory business had been eliminated, the effect was much the same as it had been at Stratford. People fainted. Michelle Morgan screamed. Jean Marais bit his tongue. Douglas Fairbanks swallowed his chewing gum. And Françoise Rosay, after witnessing the surprise cannibal banquet, swore she would become a vegetarian. For ten days they played to full houses at the Theatre Sarah Bernhardt.

In Paris Sir Laurence celebrated his fiftieth birthday, and on the last night Vivien Leigh was presented with the Legion of Honour. During the ceremony on stage a Minister from the French Foreign Office made a speech in praise of Miss Leigh's services to art; then, as he came to the presentation, he posed a question that was obliquely directed to Sir Laurence. But Olivier was not fluent in French, and he remained blissfully unaware of the situation. Finally Vivien hissed across to him in a stage whisper, 'He wants to know if he can kiss me, darling.' Language difficulties were frequently encountered on that tour. At Warsaw station the company was mistaken for a delegation of post office workers and presented with a bouquet. Then, on the first night, Polish electricians and stagehands hopelessly misunderstood instructions. Lights came on unpredictably, chairs ghosted on and off stage to no purpose, and the stage itself sagged so much under the weight of scenery that one of the cast likened it to walking on foam rubber. At the final curtain the company prepared to take a bow; Sir Laurence stood ready to deliver a carefully rehearsed speech in Polish. But they were promptly plunged into darkness and without the curtain rising the audience escaped into the night.

'Larry had his curtain speeches translated into the various

languages,' recalls Paul Hardwick. 'He learned them all phonetic-
ally and he managed in France and Austria quite well. But when
we reached Yugoslavia he had to speak in Serbo-Croatian and, of
course, none of us knew that language. The audience gave us a
tumultuous reception, and during the twenty minutes of curtain
calls they were shouting, "Long Live Sir Laurence!" Then
Larry stepped forward and with one of his great gestures began
his speech: "Ladies and gentlemen, thank you all . . ." And
suddenly, after a stunned silence, the house erupted for about two
minutes with applause and shouts, and none of us had the faintest
idea why. Later someone from the Embassy explained to Larry
that he had got one of the words wrong, and that he had actually
said, "Ladies and gentlemen, *fuck* you all." Apparently it was
one of the most endearing things he could have said.'

When they came back to London, booked for a five-week
season at the Stoll, Olivier ended the first night by thanking the
audience in six languages immaculately spoken. Some critics,
now seeing the production for the first time, condemned the play
itself. 'WHY TRUNDLE THIS HORROR COMIC ACROSS EUROPE?' was
one national newspaper headline. But the reaction to Brook's
original treatment and Olivier's acting was again overwhelmingly
enthusiastic and *The Times* hailed Sir Laurence's piteous playing
of Titus as one of the great things in his career.

Professionally, in the summer of 1957, things continued to go
very much Olivier's way. He was prominent on stage and screen,
booked for a return in *The Entertainer* and for the film of *The
Devil's Disciple*. Furthermore, he was profiting from one of the
big smash hits of the West End stage: his presentation of *Summer
of the Seventeenth Doll*, the first Australian play with an Australian
cast ever seen in London. Yet, in other ways, this was a distinctly
uncomfortable time for him. Following the year of the Suez
invasion and the Hungarian revolution, it was very much the age
of protest and demonstration, and the stage had causes of its own
to fight, most notably campaigns for the abolition of the entertainment tax and for new legislation to ensure that no theatre
was pulled down unless another went up in its place. Sir
Laurence naturally lent his support. But he had no real appetite
for offstage 'performances'; as he said when Dorothy Tutin took
his place in leading a delegation to the House of Commons, 'I'm
not sure that I am very good at this sort of thing.'

Miss Leigh was not very good at it either, but true to her nature she plunged into battle with spitfire determination, her passion roused by the news that the St. James's Theatre was scheduled to be demolished and replaced by an office block. Her first 'Save the St. James's' demonstration was a mini-fiasco: a forlorn little procession from Fleet Street to Westminster that comprised actress Athene Seyler, critic Alan Dent bearing a sandwich board and Vivien clanging a handbell borrowed from a pub while her chauffeur-driven limousine cruised along behind. No one took it seriously. But her next protest commanded massive publicity. She was escorted from the House of Lords after she had dramatically interrupted the debate by getting up in the gallery and proclaiming: 'My Lords, I want to protest about the St. James's Theatre being demolished.'

One hour later she was at the Stoll (also scheduled for demolition) preparing to go on stage and have her tongue cut out as the tragic Lavinia. She agreed that she had given the least effective performance of her career. But she was unrepentant. Backstage she became even more passionate: 'If the St. James's Theatre goes, I go, too. I will quit the English stage and this country—I really mean it. I feel that I have no place in a country that has no use for art, and by pulling down theatres is slowly killing one of the branches of art.' Sir Laurence, robed as Titus, kissed her when he heard of the incident. His only public comment: 'I think it was a very sweet and gallant thing to do.'

At first he had hesitated to take part in the argument because he knew full well that the St. James's was in many ways an unsatisfactory theatre, especially with so many lines of sight blocked by pillars. But now he argued in a letter to *The Times*: 'There are many other London theatres which are disadvantageous from this point of view, and the present fever of demolition makes it better to have an imperfect theatre than no theatre at all.' Battle was waged for one week more. Miss Leigh revealed that Sir Winston Churchill had offered to contribute £500 to a Save the Theatre Fund, though he had added in his letter: 'As a Parliamentarian I cannot approve of your disorderly method.' She had talks with the principal property developer, organized another procession, this time on such an impressive scale that Olivier joked, 'I'm thinking of changing my name to Mr. Pankhurst.' Sadly it was all too late. On July 27 the Oliviers attended a farewell champagne party at the theatre. There was one last desperate bid to raise enough money to buy out the developers and modernize the theatre. Huntington Hartford, the American grocery store millionaire and art patron, offered to contribute £35,000. But the total sum needed had now risen to £500,000, an impossible target. In October the demolition squads moved in.

Today the Oliviers' association with the St. James's is perpetuated in marble, with plaques of their profiles in the entrance hall of the great glass slab that replaced the 122-year-old playhouse of Braham, of Charles Dickens and of Irving—the theatre that presented Wilde's greatest successes and served Sir Laurence the actor-manager through seven years of considerable artistic achievement. It was there, in the Cleopatra plays, that 'Larry and Viv', the darlings of the Festival of Britain season, had achieved one of their most memorable triumphs in theatrical partnership. And ironically, as it happened, the final curtain at the St. James's now coincided with their last experience of acting together, on either stage or screen.

On August 4, the season of *Titus Andronicus* closed. Two weeks later the Oliviers' personal life was harshly spotlighted in the most obtrusive manner. They had made no secret of the fact that they were taking separate holidays that summer—Sir Laurence motoring in Scotland with Tarquin, his son by his first marriage; Miss Leigh joining her first husband, Leigh Holman, in taking their daughter Suzanne to Italy. To ordinary folk it may have seemed an unusual arrangement, but it was certainly not extraordinary to the people involved. Miss Leigh had always remained on the friendliest terms with her ex-husband. Sir Laurence and Jill Esmond had also maintained the warmest regard for one another and they were soon to get together to celebrate their son's twenty-first birthday with a party at Notley. It was, to them, a civilized and adult way to behave. In any event, how they chose to organize family holidays was strictly their own affair. Unfortunately, Mrs. Jean Mann, a Labour Member of Parliament, and mother of five, thought otherwise. Addressing the National Conference on Social Work at Edinburgh, she riveted the attention of her audience by declaring: 'There is a woman who took the House of Lords by storm and she has gone off on holiday with her first husband. Her second husband is on holiday elsewhere. I do not know of any protest about it . . . It is a terrible example for people who occupy high places in life to place before our young children today.'

Local reporters could scarcely believe their shorthand. A dull, routine assignment had suddenly produced the bonus of a sensational personal attack by one woman castigating another; they had a front-page story for the nationals. From that point on, the state of the Oliviers' marriage became a subject for frequent discussion and speculation in the gossip columns; rumours of an impending break-up were to blow hot and cold for almost three years. Unlike some well-known film stars who have revelled in headlines secured by frank and open discussion of their marital problems, the Oliviers never at any time sought or wished for such intimate attention. But it came nevertheless—the severe penalty of their particular brand of fame as the most celebrated couple in show business.

Exactly what goes into the break-up of any marriage is something that only the two participants can ever truly know. Similarly, the private anguish and torment that the disintegration of a long-standing partnership involves is something that can only be experienced to be appreciated. The rumours and counter-rumours, the evidence of vicissitudes in the relationship of the Oliviers, are not to be catalogued here. It need only be said that no person or single event was responsible for their growing estrangement. The ultimate breakdown was to be the result of a long-drawn-out process of deterioration in their relationship, partly arising from pressures in their work, partly from obvious incompatibilities in their temperament that became accentuated as they advanced in years. Their friends were well aware of these difficulties long before Mrs. Mann cast the first stone.

Despite the gathering clouds of disturbing publicity, Olivier and son had one of the most enjoyable holidays that either could remember, simply motoring about 150 miles a day in Scotland and setting up easels to paint wherever the fancy took them. And on arrival back in London Sir Laurence was kept far too busy to concern himself for long with busybody gossip. Above all, his time and energy were occupied by two professional ambitions. First, he wanted to make a greater success of *The Entertainer*, which was about to have an eight-week season in the West End before transfer to Broadway. Second, he was determined to start filming *Macbeth* the following summer. The latter project meant more to the Oliviers than anything else. With Miss Leigh as Lady Macbeth, they would be starring in a film together for the first time since *Lady Hamilton* in 1940.

In his first ambition Sir Laurence was eminently successful. The critics were now far more generous in their praise. They preferred Joan Plowright ('more earthily sincere') in the part of the daughter previously played by Miss Tutin. And at the end of the year Olivier and Brenda de Banzie won the coveted *Evening Standard* Drama Awards for the best performance by an actor and actress respectively.

On Broadway, Olivier dazzled again. But the play only puzzled—even though the programme provided theatregoers with a glossary of such un-American phrases as draught Bass ('highly popular brew of ale consumed by many devoted adherents'), slewed ('drunk'), and Warrington and Widnes ('minor industrial towns in the north'). In the foyer on opening night members of the audience were heard to say that they couldn't understand a word that Olivier was saying but that they loved his performance just the same. The critics mauled the play. But Sir Laurence, back on Broadway after six years' absence, remained unscathed, his greatness still beyond dispute, and the outcome was a sell-out and an extended run.

Olivier's failure in his second ambition was a bitter personal disappointment, and a sad commentary on the state of the film industry. His proposed film of *Macbeth*, originally with a £400,000 budget but more likely to cost half a million, had been abandoned by the Rank Organisation, which was frightened into harsh economics by a new bank rate of seven per cent. But his resolution never wavered. Somehow he would find the money. After all, he alone had proved three times in three attempts that Shakespeare on the screen could be both commercially and artistically rewarding. So he went on preparing his script, made several safaris to Scotland in search of a suitable location, sounded out his familiar production team of Roger Furse, Carmen Dillon and Anthony Bushell.

But the one old friend he needed most at this time was dead: Alexander Korda. There was, of course, Fillipo Del Giudice, and on January 1, 1958, it was reported that he had come out of monk-like seclusion in Rapallo, Italy, to make a secret trip to

London. It was ten years to the day since he and Olivier had agreed to film *Hamlet*. But the ageing financial wizard no longer had influence in Wardour Street. Moreover, the combination of Olivier and Shakespeare no longer worked its open-sesame magic. British film backers were strictly interested in low-budget movies and quick profits.

Sir Laurence saw no alternative but to seek support in the United States. But there, during his months on Broadway, he found the reaction was very much the same. It was as though his three previous Shakespearean films belonged to some long-lost age. *Henry V*, *Hamlet*, *Richard III*—all that profit and prestige counted for so very little now. Yet memories were not so short in recalling that *The Beggar's Opera*, *Carrie* and *The Prince and the Showgirl* had been commercial let-downs. He was recognized as the Titan of the theatre, but in the film industry he was curiously branded as suspect box-office. It was an attitude soon to be strengthened when a national film magazine asked its readers if they would queue to see Olivier in a film. The majority answered: No.

Late in 1959 there were reports that he had actually been offered all the necessary money ($1·5 million) by Huntington Hartford. But apparently there were a few catches to the deal, not least being the fact that the American millionaire was quietly hoping Olivier might appear on the London stage in a play he had written from Charlotte Brontë's *Jane Eyre*. Hell-raising Errol Flynn, drinking hard and unable to remember the lines, had caroused his way out of this play on tour. Eric Portman, at enormous expense, had been persuaded to star in it on Broadway, where it folded after two difficult months. It was beyond imagination that Olivier would become a third puppet on a purse-string.

In retrospect, it was both shameful and absurd that he should have been cold-shouldered month after month as he went around, cap in hand, trying to raise money. Business is business, but his $1·5 million *Macbeth* would surely have been a safer and more worthwhile investment than, say, Twentieth Century-Fox's *Cleopatra* (1962), originally given a $5 million budget and ulti- mately consuming $37 million. But then it was typical of the values of the movie industry that Elizabeth Taylor could com- mand a million dollars for playing a role outside her dramatic range while Olivier, with unrivalled experience, could not raise as much for a project that had an excellent chance of producing a cinema classic.*

---

* A new version of *Macbeth* was finally made in 1960—shot on location in Scotland as Olivier had planned, but on a modest scale with TV sales in mind. Lady Macbeth was played by Dame Judith Anderson, who had taken the same role opposite Olivier at the Old Vic in 1937 and who had appeared with him (as Mrs. Danvers) in *Rebecca*. Macbeth was Maurice Evans, the actor who had died in Olivier's arms so long ago in *Journey's End*.

22 ★ *Separate Lives*

The success of Laurence Olivier rests on a God-given talent harnessed to extraordinary dedication. One searches in vain for vast flukes of fortune. Like the champion rock-climber he has moved on the dizzy peaks with consummate skill allied to a carefully calculating approach. Margaret Leighton has recalled that as long ago as 1946, when he directed *King Lear*, she was astonished to find that he had everything plotted in advance, right down to her every single move as Regan. It has been the same with his career. Occasionally, as with *Romeo and Juliet* on Broadway, he has miscalculated and taken a fall, but the pattern of his adult years has always remained the same: cautious forethought, decision, then all-out attack.

The unrealized film of *Macbeth* was a significant milestone in this career pattern. As he later expressed it, 'I don't think I'd ever given up on anything before.' It shook him profoundly, so much that he halted to reconsider his aspirations in the light of radically changed circumstances. He was now fifty-one years old, no longer eligible for dashingly romantic leads on the screen, and he concluded that, with Shakespeare denied, he was not suddenly going to re-establish himself as a top box-office movie star. Nor would he again be able to work on a film in the triple capacity of producer, director and actor. It was time to set his career on a rather different course.

For the moment, however, he had no choice of action. He was already committed to playing General 'Gentlemanly Johnny' Burgoyne in the film of Shaw's *The Devil's Disciple*, with Burt Lancaster (Pastor Anthony Anderson) and Kirk Douglas (Richard Dudgeon) in the leading roles, and he went into it still smarting from the rejection of his *Macbeth* and rather resenting having to work on what seemed a less worthy project. Unlike him, Mr. Lancaster had had no difficulty in setting up his own

production to be filmed in England; the former circus acrobat
and army private had amassed a personal fortune of three and a
half million dollars in the movies. But then his approach to the
business was rather different. 'I like to think of myself as a
craftsman rather than an artist,' he said. 'It is not my ambition
to be a great actor like Mr. Olivier, nor would I be capable of
becoming one.'

'Mr. Olivier', as his employer called him, did not enjoy working
on *The Devil's Disciple*. Indeed, according to Harry Andrews,
now playing Major Swindon as consolation for losing the part of
Macduff, Sir Laurence was 'treated disgracefully' and for once
seemed lacking in confidence. If so, his uneasiness never showed
on the screen. When the picture was released one year later his
performance won rave reviews, and remarkably the London
Evening Standard accorded it front-page treatment under the
headline: THE GREATEST ACTOR IN THE WORLD.

It is a film to see. Just because Laurence Olivier gives the
performance of his life. And because, in his superb self-
confidence, he dared to take the third lead. Knowing that he
would steal the film from Burt Lancaster and Kirk Douglas,
the two male leads. And he does. Those two able actors look
like stupid oafs who have wandered back from a 'Western'
into the world of the American War of Independence.

The curious thing about *The Devil's Disciple* was that Olivier
had grown his Macbeth beard a month before playing the
beardless Burgoyne, yet the American producers had firmly
proclaimed all along that he would take the part of Shaw's
urbane and efficient commander. They were in close touch with
the film industry and quietly confident that their star would never
raise the money for his own project. Olivier, who even tried to
secure financial backing from the garment trade in New York,
was apparently less well-informed—a situation that further
emphasized his need to recognize the change in climate and take
fresh stock of his career. He did so at once, and in consequence
he decided to try his hand at something entirely new: television.

To some minds it seemed extraordinary that the man acclaimed
the greatest actor in the world had never acted for television—
that is, discounting his one appearance in a production of *Macbeth* made in the experimental days of 1937 when receiving sets

were limited to a few thousand viewers, all in the London area. But in this respect Olivier was in excellent company. Of all the theatrical knights only one had busied himself with television: Sir Donald Wolfit. By way of explanation, Wolfit said, 'Perhaps they do not wish to risk in one evening reputations built up over the years in the West End.' Olivier recognized the dangers and he warily agreed to try 'just a taste' of the medium, limiting himself to one television play in Britain, then one in America.

Unfortunately, in the first instance his judgment was not so admirable as his ambition; he chose for his debut Ibsen's *John Gabriel Borkman* and so saddled himself with an impossible handicap from the start. Borkman is a notoriously difficult part to interpret, so arguably a worthy challenge for Olivier. But that is beside the point. Pertinently, the play is overwhelmingly sombre and humourless and, horror of horrors, costume drama as well—a sure-fire combination to send the Philistines stampeding to another TV channel.

The 'curtain' went up at eight thirty on November 19, 1958, and never was a television performance subjected to closer critical scrutiny. The *Daily Express* alone had five writers assigned to making individual appraisals. An American critic (John Crosby) was flown over specifically to cover the event. The professional opinions were hopelessly divided: he was 'boring', 'stagey', 'remote', 'uninvolved'; he was 'compelling', 'powerful', 'faultless', 'immaculate'. But there was no doubt about the verdict of the viewing public *en masse*. According to audience-reaction measurements, *John Gabriel Borkman* was one of the biggest television flops of the year, and though these ratings can be deceptive it remained abundantly clear that the play was caviare only for the connoisseur.

It was a baptism of smoke without fire and Sir Laurence came out of the experience saying that television needed more concentration than anything else and that three weeks of rehearsals had not been as much as he would have liked. He hoped for more time on the next attempt. His second essay was an adaptation of Maugham's *The Moon and Sixpence*, but unhappily rehearsals in New York were interrupted by a great personal loss. Late in November there came news of the death of his brother, and he flew home at once. Gerard Olivier, always known as Dick or Dickie, was fifty-four. In recent years he had been living with his wife and two children in a cottage adjoining Notley Abbey and working as manager of the estate's sixty-nine-acre farm. He had been ill for about a year, though only aware in the last few weeks that he was suffering from leukaemia. The previous summer the two brothers had had their last holiday together, on Spain's Costa Brava.

Back in New York, Sir Laurence applied himself to his television role with a relentless concentration that astonished even such as experienced actress as Jessica Tandy, who had worked with him almost a quarter of a century before. She recalls: 'By then I expected nothing else from him but brilliance, and I was not disappointed. What was amazing then was the incredible stamina which enabled him to shoot the first day for about sixteen hours (there were interminable technical difficulties), sleep for about five hours, shoot the second day for about twenty hours, sleep for two or three hours on the set (there was no time to go to his hotel) and then shoot the third day, another gruelling eighteen hours with actors with less responsibility falling apart all around him.' Quite a tribute considering that the cast included such formidable talents as Judith Anderson, Denholm Elliott, Hume Cronyn, Cyril Cusack and Geraldine Fitzgerald!

The ninety-minute colour production of *The Moon and Sixpence* was hugely expensive. Olivier alone receiving a $90,000-plus fee, and difficulty followed in finding sponsors for so costly a project. As a result ten months elasped between the filming and the public screening. Then, in his first television role of obvious popular appeal, Olivier earned notices of a richness that even he had scarcely known before. The *New York Times* called it 'a towering accomplishment'; for the *New York Herald-Tribune* critic it was 'the closest thing to dramatic perfection ever known on television . . . adjectives alone cannot describe the haunting beauty of the production and particularly the performance by Sir Laurence Olivier, a towering craftsman, whose portrayal of the Gauguin-like hero had a brilliance and magnetism unmatched in the annals of television'. He also earned several awards, including an 'Emmy', television's equivalent to an Oscar, for the best single performance of the year.

It was a gratifying success for an actor relatively new to television techniques. Unfortunately, the encouragement of those reviews and prizes remained a long way off at the end of 1958, and the first 'taste' of television had certainly not whetted the actor's appetite. Meanwhile his antidote to disappointment over *Macbeth* was to keep as busy as possible. The outcome was a great flurry of activity which, with the exception of the British television performance and a promise to appear at Stratford in the New Year, was strongly commercial. He responded to Kirk Douglas's invitation to the gladiatorial uprising of 72 B.C.—a supporting role in a film extravaganza called *Spartacus*. He agreed to recreate his Archie Rice for the cinema. And coincidentally both he and Vivien Leigh were reaping a surprise bonanza from their investment in *Roar Like a Dove* which, despite a panning by the critics, was now moving into a second year of packed houses in the West End.

In November 1958 they could well afford to celebrate Vivien's forty-fifth birthday by buying a £7,000 Rolls-Royce, and two days later to throw a lavish Mayfair party for a hundred friends, with Lauren Bacall as guest of honour. Miss Leigh at this time was having a notable stage success as Paola in *Duel of Angels*, Christopher Fry's adaptation of Jean Giraudoux's *Pour Lucrèce*. She had dearly wanted to play Lady Macbeth on the screen, but without that opportunity her film career had now fallen into abeyance—nothing between *The Deep Blue Sea* (1955) and *The Roman Spring of Mrs. Stone* (1961). The star who shone so brightly from the screen, who more than anyone else had the ability to give pleasure as an irresistible *soubrette*, continued to hunger for loftier achievement on the stage. 'I would rather be an Edith Evans than a Greta Garbo,' she said. The vast majority of her myriad fans would have happily settled for seeing her be her own incomparable self—pert and sprightly and totally feminine.

The Oliviers, who had previously dovetailed their engagements quite effectively, were now, for the first time, committed to work programmes that involved very long periods apart. When he was in America, she would be tied to a long West End run. When he was at Stratford she would be returning to the London stage in *Look After Lulu*, a Noel Coward play based on Georges Feydeau's famous French farce, *Occupe-toi d'Améilie*. When he was back in London she would be on tour abroad. It was the beginning of an emotionally painful time for both of them, a year of trying to adjust to that strangely unreal half-world of marriage without a partner.

Spartacus, or rather the reported fee of $250,000, lured Olivier back to Hollywood for his first extended stay since *Carrie* eight and a half years before. He was there for almost six months and, but for the proximity of a few old friends such as Max Adrian and Roger Furse and his wife, he would have found the isolation nearly unbearable. There were a few parties, and at an all-star welcome-home party for Ingrid Bergman, Olivier danced so energetically with Anita Louise that John Wayne was talking about starring 'Sir Larry' in his production of *The Fred Astaire Story*. But such carefree nights were exceptional.

The night after the Bergman party saw the annual Oscar ceremony, and Olivier could have been forgiven an ironic smile as his great pal David Niven ran up (so eagerly that he fell flat on his face) to accept his first Best Actor Academy Award after a quarter of a century in the movies. Attending a different prize-giving, Sir Laurence once quipped to reporters: 'I don't really approve of all these awards for actors unless I'm receiving them.' But on this occasion he was genuinely pleased for Niven, even though his friend had won with Rattigan's bogus major, the part originally intended for him.

Meanwhile the British star who was called the greatest actor on earth had not taken the Oscar since *Hamlet* (1948) and was condemned to a mere supporting role in a Hollywood spectacular. Some critics thought it ludicrous for such a distinguished actor-knight to be playing the modest role of the Roman general Marcus Crassus. And when Richard Burton, the one-time idol of the Old Vic bobbysoxers, came to be asked what was the most important lesson he had learned from pictures, he replied: 'Just this. If you're going to make rubbish, be the best rubbish in it. I keep telling Larry Olivier that. It's no good playing a minor role in an epic like *Spartacus* which he's just done. Larry had a dressing room half the size of Tony Curtis's on that film. And he got about half Curtis's money. Well, that's ridiculous. You've got to swank in Hollywood. When I go there I demand two Cadillacs and the best dressing room. Of course, I'm not worth it, but it impresses them.'

There was almost an element of masochism about Olivier putting on another false nose to play in *Spartacus*. Having failed to raise $1·5 million for *Macbeth*, he was working on a gigantic pre-Christian saga of very dubious merit, one involving a cast of 8,000 and costing over $10 million and an inordinate amount of time to make. The interminable working schedule prompted

Jean Simmons to remark: 'Making *Spartacus* was enough acting
to last anybody a lifetime. You know, after we had been filming
a year Kirk Douglas sent me a magnum of champagne with a
little note saying, "I hope our second year will be as happy as our
first." '

And the film packed so much banal dialogue into its three
hours and thirteen minutes: glorious verbal anachronisms such
as Olivier the patrician general saying to Miss Simmons the
slave girl: 'Will you have some squab?' (squab being American
for spring chicken). It had galloping gladiators giving out
shrills of 'Yippee', and Miss Simmons crying out, 'Spartacus,
put me down, I'm going to have a baby.' And then the *coup de
grâce*: Miss Simmons approaching Kirk Douglas (Spartacus),
nailed to a pole on the Appian Way, and holding up his baby for
him to see while a Roman centurion calls out to slave-dealer
Peter Ustinov, 'Tell the lady that no idling is allowed on this
road.' One critic said he hadn't laughed so hard since seeing the
Marx Brothers in *The Cocoanuts*. Yet *Spartacus* was not *ipso facto*
a bad film. Rather it was highly entertaining hokum, a bonanza
of bunk graced with a remarkable array of talent and imagina-
tively directed by Stanley Kubrick.

Olivier was more fortunate than some, since Dalton Trumbo
had given him one of the best-written scenes, that in which the
wealthy, cold-lipped Crassus conveys obliquely to a slave his
sexual predilections. Even so, his contribution to this picture far
transcended all-round competence. He breathed life into seemingly routine lines like a bellows on lukewarm ashes, hinted at
effeminacy by a pettish pulling at his necklace, conveyed ruthlessness by a curiously glazed look out of foxy eyes, and generally,
by manner and make-up, achieved an authenticity that made one
all the more aware of cheap Roman reproductions around him.
He alone, one critic observed, suggested the sort of patrician
that Plutarch might have recognized.

On *Spartacus*, Kirk Douglas was filming with Olivier for the
second time within a year. 'I had no feeling of awe *before* I
worked with him,' he says. 'But there was certainly a feeling of
awe *after* working with him. I remember one scene, on the eve of
battle, where he had to say something like, "Never have I faced a
battle with such confidence." And incredibly he took that line
and made it mean exactly the opposite. He started off with a great

firmness and ended hesitantly—"Never have I faced a battle with such . . . confidence"—and in one line he had transformed from complete self-assurance to complete insecurity. Extraordinary. And that has always amazed me. Not only how he achieved it, but the actual concept of doing it.'

In June 1959, after their longest period apart, the Oliviers were united at London Airport. But they had no appreciable time together. The next day Sir Laurence was back at work, rehearsing at Stratford, while Miss Leigh was preparing to play Lulu D'Arville at the Royal Court. This year, by way of celebrating its hundredth season, Stratford had a concentration of headliners ranged over its programme of five plays in thirty-four weeks: Paul Robeson (Othello), Sam Wanamaker (Iago), Charles Laughton (Bottom and King Lear), Dame Edith Evans (Volumnia and the Countess of Rousillon), Olivier (Coriolanus). It seemed to Kenneth Tynan that the five guest stars were remote from the rest of the cast and that the general result was a stylistic chaos ('like an all-star benefit show run in doublet and hose and lacking for the most part, either unity or purpose').

But if no one production was wholly satisfying, there was no question about the outstanding individual performance. Olivier's Coriolanus dominated this centenary season. Twenty-one years had elapsed since he last played the role under the firm direction of Lewis Casson, who steered him towards the more traditional style. Casson was now eighty-three years old. The new production was in the hands of a twenty-eight-year-old: Peter Hall, Stratford's heir-apparent following Glen Byam Shaw's decision to relinquish the directorship of the Shakespeare Memorial Theatre in favour of a younger man.

'Sir Laurence Olivier turns Coriolanus into something new,' wrote Bernard Levin (*Daily Express*). 'He is a man interested only in war, unhappy when he is not fighting, and taking pleasure only in the sight of blood, even if it is his own . . . This Coriolanus does not hate the common people, he is bored by them . . . The danger of this kind of interpretation is dullness. Sir Laurence, covered in blood and armour, skirts the danger commandingly . . . and once again confirms himself as our greatest actor when it comes to playing on his audiences' sympathies.' *The Times* recalled that his Old Vic Coriolanus had carried a clear intimation of acting greatness in the making.

'The acting of Sir Laurence Olivier has since then grown marvellously in power and beauty; and returning to the part at Stratford he does with it precisely what he likes: that is to say, he plays it just as well as it can be played.'

Laurence Kitchin, whose *Mid-Century Drama* provides the best detailed study of this performance, was also fortunate in being able to compare it with the Coriolanus of 1938 vintage.

Two decades had scarcely dimmed my memory of his 'You common cry of curs!' in Casson's production. Now the delivery was changed. Just before this speech Olivier leaned against the masonry high up on Aronson's set, head rolling from side to side, eyes mad as those of a Sistine Chapel prophetess while he listened to the tribunes. The head movement, I was amused to notice, was one recommended by Elsie Fogerty to her students for relaxing tension in the neck; Olivier was preparing himself. Advancing to the Tarpeian projection on which we had first seen him, he made the speech with less volume than in Casson's production, but with a terrifying concentration of contempt. People who think him a prose actor, because he so often breaks up lines, overlook his sustained power in a passage of invective like this. Only the lyrical escapes him. Here, cursing the plebeians, he gave the phrases such a charge of emotion that he gathered them into a single rhetorical missile, so that the speech had an impact like jagged stones parcelled together and hurled in somebody's face. There was a bizarre impression of one man lynching a crowd.[1]

In that last single phrase Kitchin caught the spirit of this newly fashioned Coriolanus by the throat. Sir Laurence, weightier in voice and body, was obviously better equipped at fifty-two, as opposed to his thirty years at the first attempt, to give the military commander the necessary stamp of authority and arrogance. But the difference in this portrait went far beyond its smouldering physical power and electrifying voice; to a far greater degree it was a performance praised for its intuitive intelligence, the subtleties of timing and delivery by which Olivier brought the noble Roman down from his plinth, especially in his stressing of the spoiled only-child aspect of Caius

Marcius. He brought out the humour, too, and once again, in humanizing a rigid larger-than-life personality, he secured an unusual amount of sympathy for a largely unsympathetic character. This, in the words of Kenneth Tynan, was 'all-round Olivier'.

At the first night party (attended by Vivien Leigh, Terence Rattigan, Lauren Bacall, John Osborne and Leslie Caron, among others) Olivier chuckled to himself at the way everyone talked in exclamation marks about the death scene in which he had fallen head downwards from the twelve-foot-high Tarpeian platform, dangling there while two soldiers, who had grabbed him by the ankles, held on. Inspired by Mussolini's death, it had startling effect, but as he well knew, it was much less dangerous and hurtful than his original death-fall at the Old Vic. It gave him personal satisfaction to know that, in his fifties, he could still produce awe-inspiring acrobatics, but, of course, this was strictly theatrical stuntmanship. For fellow players on stage, watching and studying him night after night, it was his sheer all-round mastery of technique, the enormously wide range of subtle detail crammed into every performance, that left an indelible mark on the memory. 'His technique is second to none.' says Paul Hardwick, who played Cominius in this production. 'Even Alec Guinness doesn't touch him. When I first started working with him I used to stand in the wings and just watch. One tried to copy his marvellous effects, but, of course, you can't do it. For example, he will find the strongest light and he will look up straight into it so that it catches his eyes and makes the whites gleam bright. But you couldn't imitate him. So many people have tried and failed.'

The cast of that *Coriolanus* included a twenty-two-year-old newcomer to the Memorial Theatre company: Vanessa Redgrave, playing Valeria. In acting alongside Olivier for the first time, it amused her to recall that she had attended one of his performances before she was born and that she had been lucky to survive the experience. It had happened in January 1937, when Rachel Kempson, eight months pregnant, went to the Old Vic to see her husband (Michael Redgrave) playing Laertes to Olivier's Hamlet. As Miss Redgrave retells the story: 'My father played the duel scene in a wild way with Olivier, and suddenly his sword flew out of his hand and came spinning towards the box where my mother was sitting. Lilian Baylis flung herself in front of my mother, crying, "Oh God, not the dear child?" '

When filming *Spartacus* in Hollywood, Olivier had developed the habit of working out regularly in the gymnasium, mostly repetitive exercises with light weights. He continued the practice at Stratford, and with good reason. He was driving himself at a fearful pace. Besides playing Coriolanus he was intermittently making trips to London to rehearse for another *Night of a Hundred Stars*, to Nottingham where his production company was presenting an Australian play, *The Shifting Heart*, to Shepperton Studios in Middlesex and to Morecambe in Lancashire to film *The Entertainer*.

Why was Olivier sprinting furiously at the end of a marathon that had already earned him the title of the busiest actor of the year? During a break in the filming at Morecambe he explained to an interviewer: 'Well, there's so little time, you see. I feel I've got what, fifteen years if I'm lucky, and so very much left to do. I really couldn't stop now. I enjoy acting today even more than I did during the first twenty years. It's my driving force. In fact, it's my life. I've always worked hard. I've had to force myself to take a holiday when the enthusiasm fails. And that is the hardest part of all . . . You see the only time I ever feel alive is when I'm acting. That sounds a strange paradox doesn't it . . . Oh gosh, that sounds damn silly and pretentious. What I mean is the feeling of being vitally alive when one is actively exploring and creating something new in terms of performance.

'Why do I drive myself so hard? Enjoyment? Satisfaction? They're not the reasons. An artist isn't supposed to get satisfaction from a performance, you know. I don't know why I do it. I just don't know . . .'[2]

Olivier had four weeks of shooting at Morecambe, and four times he had to dash back to Stratford to play Coriolanus. He hired an ambulance to enable him to sleep on the way. On the first September day of filming he surprised everyone by turning up on the set at eight o'clock in the morning, even though he was not needed for scenes until many hours later. 'I thought I'd see how you all were,' he told director Tony Richardson. His mood was decidedly more buoyant than it had been on his previous film. He looked tired and worn, but at least he was playing one of his favourite roles ('the most deeply absorbing part I have ever played with the exception of Macbeth') and he felt more at home here than in Hollywood—working in the invigorating air of Morecambe, and in the company of many old friends.

By necessity, *The Entertainer* was considerably expanded for the film version. Scriptwriters John Osborne and Nigel Kneale developed Miss Plowright's stage part so that it became a central theme, and for more obvious cinematic appeal they wrote in a part for twenty-one-year-old starlet Shirley Ann Field as the local girl who takes second place in a bathing beauty contest emceed by Archie Rice and ends up in the seedy comic's bed. Miss Field, after a childhood in a Lancashire orphanage, actually had won a beauty contest a few years earlier, using the prize money to help pay her way through drama school. She had a provincial background in common with Joan Plowright, who was the daughter of a local newspaper editor and hailed from Scunthorpe in Lincolnshire, but otherwise the two actresses were strongly contrasting types. The former, with her pin-up good looks and an apprenticeship in films like *Horror of the Black Museum* and *Beat Girl*, was readily identified with the gloss-and-glamour side of showbiz. The latter, a comparatively demure personality with a beauty shining more from within, was schooled in a more classical mould and was now recognized as the queen of the contemporary drama exemplified by the Royal Court work of Osborne and most especially Arnold ('Roots') Wesker. Miss Plowright, elfin-faced, with engaging frank eyes and copper hair tightly cut into curls, had had the perfect training for an actress—studying at the Old Vic Theatre School under such outstanding producers as Michel Saint-Denis, Glen Byam Shaw and George Devine, then years in repertory, touring and playing one-night stands before achieving fame with the English Stage Company. Now she was almost thirty years old, a complete professional, with a brilliant future assured.

It was just over two years since the day (August 26, 1957) that Sir Laurence and Miss Plowright had first met on the stage of the Royal Court. On that occasion she confessed to being terrified at meeting her new leading man. He simply said, 'Delighted to have you with us,' and then disappeared upstairs to rehearse his song-and-dance routine in private. Now, while filming at Morecambe, they spent more and more time together.

Years later, when talking about the terrible sense of loss he felt after his mother's death, Olivier said that he had been 'looking for her ever since. Perhaps with Joanie I have found her again.' Miss Plowright had no desire to pursue a career in the commercial film world ('I do not look upon acting as a glamorous occupation, but as a job'). She had a great sense of responsibility in her work ('I hate the word dedication, but I've got to feel I'm doing something I was intended to do, something that is a contribution to humanity'). Most importantly, she came across as a very practical, home-loving woman with down-to-earth values ('I don't see the need for a great deal of money. I like expensive food and I like expensive wine to go with it. But I am not interested in a social life. I just like to go out occasionally and then really enjoy it'). In many ways her sentiments echoed Olivier's. They thrived on each other's company.

As Sir Laurence came to the end of this year of endeavour and achievement, only one thing clouded his horizon: the persistent and nagging rumours about his marriage. For a man of his sensitivity it was loathsome to see his private life openly discussed in the gossip columns. It was certainly no less agonizing for Miss Leigh, who night after night had to drive herself on stage to play comedy when all she felt was tragedy. During this most delicate time in their lives, when it was common kowledge that they had been separated for the best part of two years, they both maintained a discreet silence about their personal affairs. But there was no escaping the spotlight that clung to them relentlessly, off stage as well as on. Long ago they had achieved a public prominence that denied them the freedom of ordinary mortals to suffer in privacy.

When Olivier was appearing at Stratford, it had been his custom to live at Notley Abbey, since it was within reasonable commuting distance. During his season as Coriolanus he stayed at a near-by hotel. The 'Sandringham' of the theatre royals, their country home since 1945, would never again be the scene of stylish weekend parties. Following the death of brother Dickie, the Notley farm had been allowed to run down, most of the livestock sold. And since July 1959, the Abbey itself, now scheduled as an Ancient Monument, had been up for sale. Sir Laurence later referred to it jokingly as the end of his 'baronial period'. It was also the end of an era in the theatre world, the end of what Lady Redgrave once described as 'the last age of elegance'.

23

The Third Act

A silver-haired ghost from the past came back to haunt Olivier in the winter of 1959: Walter Wanger, the quietly persuasive film producer who had played a key part in luring him to Hollywood for the great non-event of co-starring with Garbo. Wanger was now sixty-five, distinguished-looking, and with a sober elegance and style that made it difficult to believe that this was the top movie executive who had served a prison sentence in 1952 for armed assault on the agent of his wife, film star Joan Bennett. Since then he had made a gritty climb back to power and now he was in London on behalf of Twentieth-Century-Fox to prepare for the making of the most extravagant motion picture of all time.

Radiating goodwill that belied a sharp business brain, Wanger said he had always felt rather badly about the way Olivier was treated on the film of *Queen Christina* and now, twenty-seven years later, he welcomed a chance to make amends. He was offering Sir Laurence a leading role in his new movie. Again the director would be Rouben Mamoulian. Again Olivier would be cast opposite the reigning movie queen of the day. The part: Julius Caesar to Elizabeth Taylor's Cleopatra. Of course, the fee would not rival Miss Taylor's unprecedented deal of $1 million against ten per cent of the gross; nevertheless it would represent one of the biggest pay-days the English actor had ever known, and it would give him a rare opportunity to regain star billing in a film he envisaged as the greatest box-office block-buster since *Gone With the Wind*.

Olivier turned him down. It was Wanger's great loss; it was the theatre's most significant gain.

By concentrating on his wide-ranging activities as stage actor, director and impresario, Olivier was to consolidate his position as an all-round man of the theatre without peer. And when, on

August 9, 1962, he was named the first Director of Britain's National Theatre, the news surprised absolutely no one. It was what he had always wanted and had been working towards, was so obviously the logical culmination of his efforts and achievements: those executive years at the Old Vic and the St. James's, long-term service on National Theatre committees, election to the board of trustees in December 1957, and then, in 1962, a finishing burst of experience in theatrical administration as director of the newly established Chichester Festival Theatre. Yet the impression of absolute inevitability is false. Olivier's emergence as head of the National was very probable, but it could never be certain so long as that theatre remained no more than a politician's promise.

The 1949 National Theatre Bill (passed by Parliament 101 years after the first concrete proposal for the project) had allotted £1 million for the theatre. When the grant would be made was never specified. It was uncertain when Queen Elizabeth, now the Queen Mother, laid the movable foundation stone on Friday the Thirteenth in June 1951; still uncertain in 1960 when Sir Laurence and his fellow trustees were dreaming of a National Theatre company being in operation for Shakespeare's Quatercentenary four years hence. Meanwhile, building costs had doubled, and supporters of the project were marking time before the locked doors of the Treasury. At any time those doors might be thrown open at the discretion of a Chancellor of the Exchequer. But when it happened, would Olivier still be first in line?

With the advantage of hindsight, the turn of the decade may now be seen as the most critical point in Olivier's marathon progress towards his ultimate goal. It was no time for the front-runner to stumble disastrously in theatrical ventures nor to digress by committing himself far ahead to the kind of protracted film work that Wanger and other Hollywood producers were offering. Providentially he had neither the desire nor the immediate financial need to become tied down by film contracts. But the other danger loomed very large indeed. In fact, he made such a stuttering start to this period of concentrated stage work, aroused such suspicion about his judgment of plays, that there was a brief moment when his fitness to direct a national theatre might have been cast into serious doubt.

In January 1960 he went to the United States to direct Benn Levy's new verse play, *The Tumbler*, with Charlton Heston,

Rosemary Harris and Martha Scott the leading players. It was a veritable disaster, surviving on Broadway for only five performances. 'I alone profited from that play,' recalls Heston. 'Because I had worked with Olivier . . . with the world's greatest actor . . . Unfortunately the play never had a chance. In the midst of it all, Larry had the most trying personal problems with the end of his marriage, and I marvelled at him coming back to face all the difficulties of this moribund play with total commitment, giving the play, and me, his very best. I never worked with a more professional man.'

Olivier's professionalism was, of course, never in question. But what of his judgment of plays? True, he was profiting greatly from *Roar Like a Dove*, now coming up to its one thousandth performance, but Miss Leigh had picked that particular winner. In the past year he had backed two West End flops—*The Shifting Heart* and *One More River*—and now critics wondered how a man of his experience could become involved with such a torpid 'psychological melodrama' as *The Tumbler*, concerning a young girl who discovers that her lover is her stepfather and may have murdered her father. 'Is Sir Larry losing his touch?' they asked—a cry echoed in the spring of 1960 as Laurence Olivier Productions presented two more losers, *Over the Bridge* and *A Lodging for a Bride*.

When these productions failed, Olivier was not in the least surprised. Then why put them on? He once explained: 'The life of a theatrical manager is one in which hope is constantly at odds with better judgment.' His aim was to stage plays that seemed to be interesting or important or entertaining on a certain level of accomplishment. His failing was not in missing major weaknesses in plays but in being too generous in excusing faults because he had discerned some overriding virtue.

Now it was one thing for Olivier to fail nobly as an impresario encouraging new writers, quite another for him to fail when directly involved with a production, and after such a disaster as *The Tumbler* it would have been understandable if he had sought refuge in the classics, where he had not tasted serious failure in twenty years. The record showed that there was no decline in his professional standing that a good dose of Shakespeare could not put right. But this was 1960, the end of a decade in which his proposed film of *Macbeth* had been roundly rejected and the public had flocked to see two decrepit tramps in *Waiting for Godot*. The wind of change had long been howling through the London theatre from the Royal Court in the west and from Joan Littlewood's Theatre Workshop in the east, and in such dominant fresh breezes doublet-and-hose was hardly the trendiest gear. Olivier responded to the changing climate by choosing to take the leading role in a contemporary work that made *The Tumbler* seem downright conventional by comparison: a surrealistic play in which everyone else on stage was required to sprout the horned forehead of a rhinoceros. His decision was greeted with jibes of 'pathetic', 'a stunt', 'absurd', and was openly interpreted as a sign of a great actor slipping and clutching at gimmicks to stay in the limelight. Yet it proved absolutely right.

Sound logic lay behind his decision to enter the Theatre of the Absurd and play the Chaplinesque figure of M. Berenger in Eugene Ionesco's *Rhinoceros*. The play was already a smash hit in Paris. The London production was to be directed by Orson Welles. It had a suitable part for Joan Plowright. Beyond this, Olivier was attracted by the prospect of doing something that was different and surprising and refreshingly new. As early as 1929, when he had leading roles in six plays, all conventional and yet short-lived, he had learned that an absolutely safe bet in the theatre was virtually impossible to recognize, and his career ever since had been a series of calculated risks, if not in his choice of parts then usually in his interpretation of them. However, his willingness to live dangerously had a stronger element of urgency now. In the fall of 1959 he explained:

'I suppose my life is my early dreams come true, but I can never think about it like that. I haven't arrived. One must keep moving for the sake of living life, for the sake of not retiring from it. Because if you stop, you stop. There is nothing else I want to do except to work. I do not want to play golf. I thought at one time that I might like to retire to a country life, but now I don't want it. Variety is the thing—to do both plays and films, always to try to do something new, hoping that people won't think it's just Olivier trying a new stunt . . . And the worst danger of growing old is that you become more difficult to cast. It's that which makes you go out and look for new things to do. You must ward off that terrible series of farewell tours in your favourite parts, because, by heaven, there's nothing left after that. And I don't want to sit back and make records and have them laughing at my interpretations in twenty years' time, as they'll be bound to. It's up to the John Osbornes of this world to see that it will never happen to me—to write parts that will make farewell appearances a Thing of Never . . .'[1]

Olivier was now fifty-two years old. He could never again memorize Romeo in two days as he had done a quarter of a century before, and yet acting was his life-blood and he had to maintain the struggle to survive. It was Mr. Everyman's dilemma, the fight to sustain personal achievement by making growing experience compensate for declining physical and mental prowess. But the key to Olivier's continued holding of the centre stage lay in much more than the remarkable energy and drive he carried over into advanced middle-age; it rested equally, if not more, upon his chameleon-like ability to blend in with his background and to keep pace with the great burst of new vitality that swept through the English theatres in the late Fifties and early Sixties. He embraced revolutionary developments at a time when a man so steeped in tradition might have been expected to stand Canute-like against them. And none of his leading contemporaries could have done so with the same facility. Sir John Gielgud, for example, once defined his style in relation to Olivier's by saying quite simply, 'Olivier is a great impersonator. I am always myself.' By nature, too, Gielgud could not change with the tide. So much of the new-wave drama, especially the Theatre of the Absurd, was anathema to his well-ordered sense of dramatic form—*Waiting for Godot* ('sordid and utterly pessimistic'), *Rhinoceros* ('endlessly driving home a point it has already established'). Olivier's taste was not wildly more catholic; his willowy capabilities in the face of variable winds were infinitely greater.

In 1950, as actor-manager of the St. James's, Sir Laurence was criticized for his reluctance to experiment, accused of being successful and impressive without ever being original or significant. He then stood firm in his view that contemporary problems were ill-suited to the theatre, tending to be dull and depressing. 'All plays should have a beginning, a middle and an end,' he said. 'Plays about contemporary problems have no end.' Ten years later, however, he had the wit to recognize the truth in Osborne's remark that there was no longer a third act in life, no final scene where all loose ends are neatly tied together, sending the audience home with all questions answered, no problems lingering on. He recognized, too, that with television's coming of age, with every family having a baby proscenium arch in the living room, it would seem wise to offer people a rather different kind of experience when they went to the theatre. These observations required no great powers of perception, certainly not on the part of an actor who had seen the theatre weather the competition of radio, the silent film and the talkies. But Olivier, always the conjurer at heart, was *technically* better equipped than any other actor of his generation to keep in touch with a new generation that thrived on controversy, novelty and surprise.

Rhinoceros more than satisfied the new theatre public's appetite; it was a sell-out from the moment the Royal Court box-office opened, and again on its transfer to the West End. Arguably its weird blend of realism and fantasy alone was enough to excite the curiosity of theatregoers—the prospect of seeing all but Olivier transformed into rhinoceri as Ionesco satirized the herd instinct, man's willingness to convert himself into the ugliest of creatures rather than bear the ridicule of being different. Even so, the play had rather more to offer than sheer physical gimmickry, and Olivier's performance was more notable for its subtle restraint than its dramatic fireworks. In *The Observer* it was described as the most perfect of his career. 'In the ordinary sense, it is not a "triumph". The range is deliberately limited, and those who wait for obvious sensation wait in vain. But it is a performance that dramatic students will see as often as they can, the first time in sheer admiration and thereafter with notebooks on their knees.'

M. Berenger was a peculiar success for Olivier in that he has rarely scored high marks in the role of the 'little man'. Here were no obvious opportunities for the master of great physical and vocal effects, of flashing pyrotechnics and menacing thunder. Until the intermission Berenger is not even a major character. Yet, by a 'rainbow of nuances', he artfully contrived to command the stage in an uncommanding role—to such effect that critic Bernard Levin (*Daily Express*) proclaimed: 'Sir Laurence is still our most daring actor. He can do things that in anyone else would be trickery and quackery—double-takes, falling over, flapping his hands about—but that in him are refined into the quintessence of the character he is playing.'

Rhinoceros won even more enthusiastic acclaim when it reopened at the larger Strand Theatre. Meanwhile, Joan Plowright (replaced by Maggie Smith) had left the cast to remain at the Royal Court for a revival of *Roots*, and it was confirmed at this time that she and Sir Laurence hoped to marry as soon as they could obtain divorces from their respective partners. Miss Plowright was then married to television actor Roger Gage, whom she had met in 1952 on the Old Vic company's South African tour. Miss Leigh was on Broadway in *Duel of Angels*. On May 22, Olivier's fifty-third birthday, she announced that her husband had requested a divorce and that she would not oppose his wishes. A few days later the American entertainer George Jessel made a ludicrous attempt to bring them together by offering them, most indelicately, co-starring roles in a film tentatively entitled *Mary Todd*, *Kentucky Belle*, about Abraham Lincoln's naggingly ambitious wife. But all chance of reconciliation had now passed. Divorce proceedings went ahead and were to be completed before the year's end.

That summer Olivier continued to decline lucrative film offers in favour of the theatre. So, more remarkably, did a film star who hadn't walked on a stage in ten years. When Anthony Quinn was offered the chance of playing opposite Sir Laurence in Jean Anouilh's *Becket* on Broadway, he reacted like Heston before him. 'He's the greatest! I can learn a lot just being on the same stage with him. I figure with the pictures I've turned down to take this play I'm paying a quarter of a million dollars just for an acting lesson from Mr. Olivier. And at that price he'd better damn well give me one.'

Generously Sir Laurence agreed to play Becket although he was obviously more suited to the showier part of Henry II. Quinn would never have been right for Becket, and even Henry was a curious adventure for him. In the circumstances, he acquitted himself reasonably well, but it was a fearful struggle on his part. During the first week of rehearsals his voice began to fade. A voice specialist advised him to leave the play. Instead he saw a psychiatrist, who told him: 'You're acting opposite the world's greatest actor. He's got one of the finest voices in the world. Subconsciously you're trying to compete. That's why you've lost your voice.' Quinn went back and played the king and gradually regained full vocal power.

Today the film actor recalls that chastening experience in the theatre with mixed emotions. And Mr. Quinn is a very emotional man. 'The terrifying thing about working with Larry was hearing that clarion tone of his. It becomes an obsession to you because on the stage he has such fantastic authority that if you try in any way to match him vocally he can kill you. You find yourself reaching for notes that aren't in your repertoire. The first two weeks I had a terrible case of laryngitis trying to stay up with him. I really went through hell and many times I wanted to give up. But then Larry has such an amazing way of making you feel that he's depending on you, when actually he's not at all. He is so disarming, in the sense that everybody drops their guard. "You will carry me tonight, old boy, won't you because I'm terribly nervous?" he would say. But, of course, the minute you are on stage you realize you've taken on a cage full of lions.

'I identified so strongly with Henry in relation to Becket that I used that as the relationship between myself and Laurence Olivier. This way I could avoid any danger of falling in awe of my co-star. I wasn't working with the great Olivier. I was working with Becket. It was very much part of my kind of subjective approach as opposed to an objective method of working. But it wasn't necessarily Olivier's approach. He once made a brilliant observation to me on the difference between the American actor and the English actor: "You American actors are like football players. You wait until you have the truth in your arms before you start running. We English actors start running when the curtain is up and hope that the truth will catch up with us." '

The Olivier–Quinn *Becket* was too inappropriately cast to qualify as a significant achievement. Yet, measured in terms of rave reviews, it must be counted as a triumph for Olivier. Indeed, it was his week of triple triumph on Broadway, since the hosannas for his Becket were accompanied by critical acclaim for his acting in *Spartacus* and especially for his starring role in the film of *The Entertainer*. Moreoever, with a climactic cosiness worthy of a Hollywood musical of the Forties, his success coincided with Joan Plowright's triumphant Broadway debut, a haunting prize-winning performance in *A Taste of Honey*.

They shared only one disappointment: that *The Entertainer*, despite all the superlatives lavished on Olivier's contribution ('the pearl in this very bad oyster') was not a commercial success. Tony Richardson's direction suffered much of the blame, but the basic problem was that such an essentially theatrical work could never transfer satisfactorily to the film medium.

For almost six months *Becket* ran on Broadway—Olivier's longest period on the American stage—and in that half-year he had the rare good fortune to find that life can sometimes provide a 'third act' after all. For now, all at once, out of the confusion of his personal and professional life, a clear and wholly satisfying pattern began to emerge. There was growing optimism about the go-ahead for the National Theatre. In February 1961 he was offered responsibility for full artistic direction of the Chichester Festival Theatre that would be opening within reasonable distance of the new home he had bought at Brighton. And the following month, on St. Patrick's Day, ten days after their divorces became final, he and Joan Plowright were married in the small New England township of Wilton, Connecticut, fifty miles north of New York.

Edward S. Rimer, a fledgling Justice of the Peace, was examining land deeds in the town hall when someone asked him, 'Can you do a wedding in half an hour?' It was only his third ceremony since taking office. 'They don't marry much hereabouts,' he explained later. 'Anyway I was keen for more experience. When the wedding party arrived, I thought the man's face looked familiar. I asked for the marriage licence and read the name—Laurence Olivier. Then I caught on. They didn't muff their lines once, and finally I kissed the bride and said I hoped they would be very happy.' Bride and bridegroom had to be back on separate stages that same night. Afterwards they celebrated at a midnight champagne party given by Richard and Sybil Burton, with Lauren Bacall and Jason Robards the only other guests.

The following month Broadway had its annual prize-giving—the Tony awards. Joan Plowright was the best actress, *Becket* the outstanding drama. The best actor award went to Zero Mostel—for John in *Rhinoceros*! But the benevolent spell of this continuing 'third act' was not to be disturbed, and when Olivier returned with *Becket* after a six-weeks tour it was no longer in Archbishop's robes and projecting soul-searching torment; he was now free to unleash his emotions as the roistering Plantaganet king. Quinn had left the play for a movie role, and with Arthur Kennedy in the quieter role, *Becket* took on a new dimension. Tynan described the new playing of Henry II as 'a major act of interpretation . . . the actor implied what the character never suspected, namely, that his attachment to Becket was homosexual'. And the New York critics loved it enough to vote Sir Laurence (with Joan Plowright as his elected female counterpart) the best leading actor in a straight play on Broadway that season. The success of the Oliviers was complete.

And so was the chagrin of Anthony Quinn, who had been shattered by his ex-partner's switching of roles. On location in Rome he growled: 'I'd never have left if I'd known he was going to do that. Never! Then when I arrived here to make *Barabbas* someone showed me a magazine review of his performance in my part. "Against Quinn's clod-like vigour," it read, "Olivier's Henry has an easy swagger, a skipping verve." I felt quite sick.'

On June 2, immediately after Sir Laurence had completed work as Graham Greene's whisky-sodden priest in a U.S. television production of *The Power and the Glory*, the Oliviers sailed from New York on the *Queen Elizabeth*. Ahead of them was a new way of life, the kind of settled, family-anchored life that Olivier had often yearned for but had never really known. Home for the itinerant actor-knight was now No. 4 Royal Crescent, an elegant, four-storey Regency house on Brighton's seafront. The social scene remained predominantly showbiz (John Clements and Kay Hammond for neighbours, Dora Bryan, Terrence Rattigan, Anna Neagle and Herbert Wilcox living near by), but the atmosphere was decidedly more domestic. They had the basement converted into a nursery, hired a Hungarian nanny, and in December their first child was born—a boy named Richard Kerr. Later came daughters, Tamsin, Agnes Margaret and Julie-Kate.

Two years after settling in Brighton, Olivier conveyed the spirit of his changed life-style when he told theatre critic Harold Hobson: 'I know nothing more beautiful than to set off from home in the morning in a taxi and to look back and see your young held to a window and being made to wave to you. It's sentimental and it's corny, but it's better than poetry, better then genius, better than money.'[2]

Words of a man who had discovered fulfilment in his private life. But there was no corresponding sense of contentment and security in his professional life. The actor-director, now looking anything but the thespian as he strode out briskly in city-executive pinstripe to catch the 9.25 *Brighton Belle* to London each day, was as ambitious and adventurous as ever, a coil of nervous energy wound tight for the challenge that has resulted in what history may remember as his most enduring achievement.

24

The Shaping of the National

In 1930, shortly before his first marriage, Laurence Olivier had reluctantly accepted a disagreeable stage role for £50 a week. In 1961, eight days before his third marriage, he enthusiastically accepted the offer of a £5,000 a year job on one extraordinary condition: that his salary was reduced to £3,000. The job was the directorship of the Chichester Festival Theatre, and some prominent actors would not have touched the appointment at twice the salary. Sir John Gielgud, for one, thought the new theatre was a 'harum-scarum idea'; so much about the project smacked of experimentation and uncertainty. It was the brainchild of a man without any expert knowledge of the theatre—one Leslie Evershed-Martin, an optician and ex-mayor of Chichester, who saw a television programme about Sir Tyrone Guthrie's Festival Theatre at Stratford, Ontario, and promptly seized on the notion of raising funds by public subscription for a similar theatre in his own cathedral city. The Theatre Building Fund was still far short of its £105,000 target. The foundation stone had not yet been laid. No attempt to form a theatrical company had been made. Yet Olivier, then in America, accepted the directorship, and he did so without meeting his prospective employers beforehand.

In the light of subsequent events, it appears an obvious and logical move. It provided a perfectly timed dress rehearsal for his performance as the first director of the National Theatre, and subsequently, during the formative years of the National, Chichester was to be of immeasurable value as a proving ground for N.T. productions. Its value, however, was far from assured when Olivier signed on in March 1961. He was satisfied that the building would materialize; plans were well advanced for an elaborate hexagonal amphitheatre to be set on concrete stilts amid a horseshoe of elm trees in Chichester's Oaklands Park. But two key imponderables remained: Would this 1,360-seat theatre, on the fringe of a mini-city with only 20,000 residents and no theatrical tradition, find sufficient public support? More pointedly, would playgoers accept an amphitheatre of such revolutionary design, a cross between theatre-in-the-round and an Elizabethan playhouse, with a stage that was thrust from one wall, placing the audience on three sides? The theatre itself would be on trial. So, as the man most likely to run the National, would he.

Olivier had accepted because, next to producing and directing his own films (a luxury now denied him), nothing in professional life offered him greater pleasure and satisfaction than forming a new theatre company, fostering its growth and hopefully seeing it flourish and achieve permanency. At Chichester he was assured of complete artistic control—over the selection of plays, directors, designers, actors, everything. But to be a hired dictator was not enough; he wanted to enter fully into the spirit of the enterprise, hence his self-imposed cut in salary, followed by his transfer of a £500 television fee to the Building Fund.

In the spring of 1962 he completed work in Dublin and Paris on a film in which he played a schoolmaster accused of criminal assault by a girl pupil. His co-stars were Simone Signoret and an eighteen-year-old 'unknown' named Sarah Miles, and the picture was called *Term of Trial*. His own term of trial was about to begin. He was now obviously the outstanding candidate to run the National Theatre; the first Chichester festival would provide timely evidence of how well he could combine the duties of administrator, director and actor, of his judgment and imagination in the selection of the plays, of his ability to assemble a company of high proficiency. On this last count he immediately scored full marks. Who else could have lured to Chichester so many distinguished players: Sir Michael Redgrave, Dame Sybil Thorndike, Sir Lewis Casson, Athene Seyler, Fay Compton, Joan Greenwood, Kathleen Harrison, John Neville, Rosemary Harris, Nicholas Hannen, Andre Morell, Timothy Bateson? In addition, though expecting their second baby, Joan Plowright appeared in every production. Three plays were performed in repertory in the inaugural season. Olivier directed all of them, acted in two and finally carried the festival to enduring success. In fact, he came through his examination with distinctions in every department save one: his choice of plays.

Two-thirds of the Chichester programme comprised pieces from the Jacobean era, both long-neglected, and with good reason. The first, a bawdy Fletcher-and-Beaumont romp called *The Chances* received a resounding raspberry from the critics, but did at least pull in satisfactory audiences. Not so the second play. John Ford's lurid melodrama, *The Broken Heart*, was a dreadful flop that played to half-empty houses despite having an alluring cast that included Olivier, as the madly jealous husband Bassanes.

The most sweeping and significant indictment of that production came from Kenneth Tynan in the shape of an open letter published in *The Observer*. 'Who put the hex on the hexagon?' he asked Sir Laurence. 'Does the fault lie in the play, in the theatre, or in you, its artistic director?' The critic's main argument was that in a large theatre like Chichester's the promontory stage simply did not work. He adversely criticized Olivier's production style and his individual performance, and he concluded that directing three plays and appearing in two leading parts was too much for one man. He suggested that, in running the National, Sir Laurence might return to the triumvirate arrangement so successful in the Old Vic's 1944–46 seasons— a joint directorship perhaps consisting of Olivier, Peter Brook and Anthony Quayle.

According to publicist Virginia Fairweather, later to be press representative to the National Theatre, Olivier erupted into a blistering ten-minute rage on reading that open letter. Then he turned to his wife and said, 'Darling, in my most silky, throwaway tone I would suggest that I employ Mr. Tynan at the National. In the time-honoured phrase, "If you can't beat 'em, join 'em," and at least he would not be able to write notices about the theatre again.'[1] When Tynan did eventually join the first National administration it suggested the old cliché of many a true word being spoken in jest. As he chose to express it: 'They would probably rather have me on the inside pissing out than on the outside pissing in.'

But that open letter did not immediately bring about the improbable actor-critic partnership. Indeed, Mr. Tynan's acid outburst appeared at the time to have no significant impact, since the very next day his judgment was made to look somewhat premature by the festival's saving grace: a supremely distinguished production of *Uncle Vanya*, a palpable hit that cancelled out the gloom of two misses. It attracted full houses throughout the season.

Again Olivier played Astrov. It was an evening full of stars (Sybil Thorndike, now eighty, Lewis Casson, no less amazingly vigorous at eighty-seven, Misses Compton, Greenwood and Plowright among others) and dominating this crowded night-sky were Olivier and Redgrave, each brilliant in his own fashion, the latter, in his tragi-comedy creation as Vanya, giving one of the outstanding performances of his career. With few exceptions the critics adored it. Some talked of near-perfection. Most important, in view of Olivier's forthcoming appointment to the National, that production was seen as a miracle of team acting, stars seamlessly woven into the ensemble.

The long-awaited appointment officially came on August 9, shortly after the Queen's first visit to the Chichester Festival. Olivier's directorial work was analysed more closely now. His organizational ability had been proved. Administrative pressures had not detracted from his achievement as director or actor. But one richly cast revival of *Uncle Vanya* could not veil a certain capriciousness in his choice of plays. In fairness it must be stressed that he was largely influenced in his selection by a desire to offer three entirely different styles in demonstrating the amenities peculiar to this Chichester stage. *The Chances* certainly showed off the virtuosity of the open stage to striking effect. *The Broken Heart*, he freely admitted, was a major error of judgment—'I was trying to be too clever and over-anxious in not wishing to be thought to be recondite.'[2] But rather more disturbingly, in a prologue to Mr. Evershed-Martin's *The Impossible Theatre*, he revealed that he felt betrayed by the senior critic who first suggested this play to him and then, on production, proceeded to condemn the play, the performance—and even the choice itself!

Sir Laurence, as he continued to prove, was entirely capable of making errors of judgment without any mischievous help from outsiders. Worse, he was capable of making the same mistake twice. For example, there now came the lesson of his experience as Graham Weir, the misused and miserable North Country teacher in *Term of Trial*. In the climactic court scene, where Weir defends himself against the charge of indecent assault, Olivier launched into a long tirade of heart-rending power. It was supremely moving, and remarkably he had achieved it in the first long 'take'. But otherwise he gave a necessarily low-key performance and some critics thought that the film failed because he was miscast. Thomas Wiseman (*Sunday Express*) was one: 'Sir Laurence seems to have a taste for playing insignificant little men, but his noble looks, his commanding personality, and his natural authority are against him. He can play a king, but he cannot play a mouse.' Alexander Walker (London *Evening Standard*) was another: 'If there is one role that Sir Laurence Olivier cannot play well, it is that of the little man . . . I beg Olivier to refuse any more roles like the one in *Term of Trial*.' So what role did he take next? Almost immediately after those reviews he agreed to return to the London stage in slacks and cricket sweater as Fred Midway, the obsessively social-conscious insurance agent in David Turner's *Semi-Detached*.

Perfectly cut for audiences in the industrial Midlands, this new satirical comedy had been a popular success at Coventry's Belgrade Theatre, but it was ill-suited to an actor of Olivier's proportions and the London production wavered too uneasily between realism and farce. Tony Richardson, who directed, feels that Olivier's conception of the role was basically wrong from the beginning, that the only point of such an individual actor taking this kind of part was that he should play it with tremendous gusto and a certain spivishness. But Olivier, as was his wont, rejected the obvious and stubbornly clung to the steeper path, one of restraint lest Midway, with his excessive, snob-ridden cupidity, should appear a character too far removed from the common herd.

Richard Burton wickedly told me how Olivier, in striving for the glutinous Nottingham dialect, stayed for a while in the Midlands. 'Finally, he tried out his splendid accent in a tobacconist's. The shopkeeper looked oddly at him for a moment. Then he asked, "Been in the country long, sir?" Larry was absolutely shattered.' It is one of several apocryphal stories spawned by Olivier's suffering in *Semi-Detached*. In fact, the actor polished his accent in a room at the top of his Brighton home, practising there for days with the help of tape recordings. The reward for his pains: J. C. Trewin thought Midway's voice 'a master-piece', Philip Hope-Wallace described it as a 'terrible amalgam' of accents that rang 'completely false', and most other critics didn't much care either way since a precise accent was never crucial to the play anyway.

Although, in fact, a fair portion of the notices were excellent, Sir Laurence soon regretted his decision to play the balding and bespectacled Mr. Midway, and his discomfort in the part mani-fested itself in a recurrence of his psychosomatic gout. 'I was miserable doing it,' he admitted later. 'They hated me. The critics. The audience. I could feel it coming over me . . . It was eighteen weeks of sheer torture. I was sad because I wanted it so much to be a success for the young author.' And of course the stakes were relatively high. Bernard Levin (*Daily Mail*) put it the most forcefully: 'If this is the kind of play the Director of the National Theatre thinks worth putting on I can only say that it were better that a Foundation Stone be hanged about his neck and he be cast into the uttermost depths of the sea.'

This was the double price of fame that Olivier now had to accept: always to be judged in the future on two counts, as actor and as the National Director. And it was especially hard on him at this particular time. Christmas was near. His wife was expect-ing their second baby within the next month. He himself was alarmingly over-extended. His day started at 8.00 a.m. with an hour of reading the papers and morning mail before dashing to catch the *Brighton Belle* to London. He worked on correspond-ence on the train; then, at his office in Hamilton Place, he had a full working day dealing with the affairs of the National Theatre, the Chichester Festival and his own production company. In the evening it was on stage at the Saville as Midway before catching the midnight train home. It was a crippling routine, but basically the kind of total involvement in the present and the future that he wanted. He had always dreamed of establishing a real theatre, an enduring institution with a permanent company; but it was more than this dream that spurred him to greater effort at an age when most men look forward to increasing leisure. Also involved was his constant guarding against an excess of nostalgia, what Noel Coward once defined to him as 'vague longings for things half-remembered'. Sir Laurence had a great deal to be nostalgic about; he was also acutely aware of the dangers in looking back to golden days long ago and beyond recall. Allowed out of proportion, it could be an unhealthy form of self-indulgence; and in this context he described the National Theatre as his 'present check', something that looked entirely forward.

Olivier's perennial fear of seeming old-fashioned was now a key influence on his preparations for running the National Theatre. Early in 1963 he began to shape his team, and in electing his chief aides he did not look to the mainstream of classical drama but almost exclusively to the English Stage Company, which had been responsible for fostering so many contemporary plays and which, as he later acknowledged, had 'altered entirely the colour and tone of my career at a time when it was becoming dangerously a little bit staid and a little bit more predictable'. He saw the value of harnessing the strong creative energy that had been building up at the Royal Court, and ideally he would have liked his old friend, George Devine, as his right-hand man. Devine gave him 'priceless advice' on running a subsidized company, but was unsure that he could ever work as a second-in-command; so instead Olivier took on two Devine-trained directors, John Dexter and William Gaskill. Both had first achieved prominence at the Royal Court. Their appointment as associate directors was the first clear indication that the National would not be neglecting modern plays.

Olivier was equally forward-looking in his choice of players. His policy entailed putting sentiment on one side and completely disregarding the 'old pals act', and inevitably it was not designed to win himself popularity. Esmond Knight, who had played on Olivier's team in all those Shakespearean screen triumphs, is one of a number of actors who recalls this period with a certain melancholy. 'When those films were over and Larry went to the National Theatre it was a bit like *Henry V*—the king casting off all his old chums, Falstaff and the rest. We all tried to get into the National, but none of us succeeded. I don't know why. I wrote to him two or three times suggesting it, but I think he thought, "I'm through with all those chaps. Perhaps they're a bit second-rate. I don't want them any more." There's that famous story about Robert Atkins who found that leading members of his company were being invited to read the lesson in the church at Stratford-upon-Avon where Shakespeare is buried. But Atkins was never invited to do so and one day he taxed the vicar with this. He said, "I understand that various members of my company are invited by you to read the lesson on a Sunday." The vicar said this was absolutely true. "And can you," Atkins glowered, "advance any cogent reason why I should not read the fucking lesson?" Now everyone in the profession knows the story. So when I wrote to Larry I said, "Can you advance any cogent reason why I should not become a member of the fucking National?" He wrote back with a quotation out of *Twelfth Night*: "I have no exquisite reason for't, dear Knight, but I have reason good enough." I shouldn't have done it. He never used any of that crowd, not John Laurie, nor Norman Wooland, nor any of them.'

When Olivier started planning for an October opening of the National, George Devine told him: 'You're a fool. You can't do it. Tell them you must have another six months.' He replied that he felt duty-bound to start on time, but, profiting from Devine's experience (the strain of running the Royal Court virtually killed him in the end), he did have the sense to delegate important work as much as possible. For the first year, Stephen Arlen was to be on loan from Sadler's Wells as his administrative director. He had Dexter and Gaskill as associate directors. And, most controversially and forward-looking of all, he appointed Kenneth Tynan as his literary manager.

Tynan's title (coined by Harley Granville Barker in his pioneering book on how a National Theatre should be run) gave no real indication of the extent of his influence. He saw his job as one of planning in advance a programme of plays drawn not just from national classics, but internationally, so that at any time there would be a balance of comedy and tragedy, ancient and modern, in the repertoire. (In press conferences Olivier would repeatedly talk about the aim of presenting 'a spectrum of world drama', a usefully all-embracing and ambiguous phrase coined by his literary manager.) Besides this, Tynan described his task as being to seek out new playwrights, advise on the commissioning of new works or new translations, and act as a resident critic who sits in on rehearsals and a few weeks before the opening writes a review in great detail, commenting on lighting, costume, interpretation, casting, everything, and so serving as an early-warning system. If not quite Olivier's *eminence grise*, Tynan could be seen as becoming the second most important figure at the National.

In the latter years of their partnership, Tynan's influence over Olivier in matters of National Theatre policy was to be strongly criticized—by John Osborne, William Gaskill and Jonathan Miller among others. In 1963, however, two facts were incontestable: it was absolutely essential that Olivier should have such an adviser, if only to relieve him of an enormous time-consuming load; in terms of experience and ability, Tynan had outstanding qualifications for the job. His appointment to the National was entirely consistent with Olivier's vigorous, some might say too drastic, forward-looking policy. On a more personal level it was, to say the least, a surprising alliance.

Kenneth Peacock Tynan once summed up the story of his life as 'the effort of a Birmingham bastard to become an apostle of international hedonism, and to do that without having owned anything other than books and a typewriter'. He was speaking literally, being the illegitimate son of Sir Peter Peacock, owner of a chain of Midland drapery stores and six times elected Mayor of Warrington. Tynan was the surname of his Irish mother. After winning a demyship at Magdalen College, Oxford, the gifted son served a brief apprenticeship as a theatre director; then, without warning, his genius for drama criticism immediately burst into spectacular life with a remarkable first book, *He That Plays the King* (1951) favoured with a preface by Orson Welles. From the beginning Tynan had proclaimed his profound admiration for Olivier as an actor in the heroic mould. At the same time no critic had been so supremely scathing about some of Olivier's work, particularly on the production side. (For example, his judgment of the film *Hamlet*: 'Technically pedantic, aurally elephantine, the film plods thunderously to its conclusion . . .')[3] He was the first drama critic to whom Olivier had ever written a letter of complaint.*

Olivier's decision to have Tynan on his team may be interpreted as evidence of the man's extraordinary flexibility and determination. His entire approach to running the National

---

* It had happened in 1957. Olivier was not complaining for himself but at the request of Donald Wolfit who felt injured by a review of *Malatesta* in which Tynan said that Wolfit's title role needed Olivier to make it truly effective.

Theatre was ambitiously venturesome, whereas he could so
easily have taken a more traditional line. The latter might not
have achieved his ideals; it would certainly have made life more
comfortable for him. Instead, by choosing to work in harness
with a stridently progressive anti-Establishment intellectual,
he ensured that the daily routine at the National was anything but
cosy. It created a tension which arguably spurred creative work
during the early years but which later made life exceedingly
difficult for its director. Within two years, partly because he
disapproved of the range of Tynan's influence, William Gaskill
was to leave the National and succeed Devine as director of the
English Stage Company. More disturbingly, there was almost
from the start an uneasy relationship between Tynan and Lord
Chandos (formerly Oliver Lyttleton), chairman of the N.T.'s
board of governors.

In the Forties, when Olivier and Ralph Richardson were co-
directors at the Old Vic, they found the board meetings fairly
stuffy affairs, the members including a retired bishop who did
not remove his hat but used it to pull down over his eyes and go
to sleep. It was different now. The National had a vigorous and
conscientious board, with Lord Chandos taking an active part
in the running of a theatre which he had made possible by persuading the government, through his long friendship with
Chancellor of the Exchequer Selwyn Lloyd, to make available
the long-promised cash for its building. His interest in the new
enterprise went as far back as Olivier's since his mother, Dame
Edith Lyttelton, a great friend of Bernard Shaw and Mrs.
Patrick Campbell, had been a leading campaigner for a national
theatre: it is now a fair measure of his contribution that one of
the two auditoria that make up the new National Theatre
buildings is named the Lyttelton Theatre, with the other, and
larger one, dedicated to Olivier.

In June 1963 the Old Vic closed with *Measure for Measure* and
Olivier took over the theatre in which he had first appeared as a
Freudian Hamlet a quarter of a century before. Gone were the
golden years when Lilian Baylis could defiantly proclaim: 'I
don't care about the National Theatre. When I think of all the
work that has been done by our three companies—drama,
opera and ballet—I know that WE are the National Theatre.'
Since the peak seasons of the Olivier–Richardson–Burrell tri-

umvirate, the Old Vic had fallen into rapid decline, with a large-scale exodus of directorial talent—Michael Saint-Denis, George Devine, Glen Byam Shaw. Now, under the National banner, it would again lure hordes of playgoers across the river to the unfashionable South Bank, and this revival was coming at a time when it was most needed—as a counter to falling standards on the English stage.

By July, Sir Laurence had organized the second Chichester Festival, including a production of *Saint Joan* with his wife in the title part. Free to concentrate exclusively on the National, he now moved into the most unpretentious offices imaginable: three long Nissen huts joined end to end on a bombsite some 300 yards from the Old Vic. He cheerfully accepted his drab and primitive quarters on the understanding that it was strictly a 'temporary' arrangement. It was expected that the National Theatre complex would be ready in four years. He should be moving in soon after his sixtieth birthday. He had no way of knowing that the sisyphean struggle of his life lay ahead, ten years of continually meeting Kipling's two impostors and endeavouring to treat them both the same.

If Olivier started out with any model in his mind's eye, it was the Moscow Art Theatre, a company recognized abroad after the war as a perfection of ensemble playing and the last word in realism. More than any company of the period, it presented a sense of stylization, of smooth all-round assurance and efficiency, and it was this supreme team-work, above all else, that he wanted to reproduce at the National.

Initially, of course, with an ensemble in embryo, he had to recognize the need for a guest star if the National was to be launched in champagne style. *Hamlet* was chosen for the inaugural production in October, and the first National Theatre star was Peter O'Toole, returning to the London stage after two miserable years in the broiling African desert as Lawrence of Arabia, followed by a thirst-quenching partnership with Archbishop Burton on the filming of *Becket*. Olivier had declined a part in the *Lawrence* film. O'Toole, in turn, at first declined to appear in his *Hamlet*. But as he explains: 'Have you ever tried to argue with Olivier? He's the most charming, persuasive bastard ever to draw breath. I said "No", but then I said "Yes". Then I said I wanted to play it in a very cut version

—"I'll only do two and a half hours," I told Larry. A week later I was doing the uncut version which takes five hours. Then I wanted to play it with a beard because I said why should I be the only man in Elsinore with a razor blade. Three weeks later I'm standing on the stage clean-shaven in a Peter Pan suit with my hair dyed white. Such is the power of Olivier.'[4]

His presence ensured that the National Theatre had the encouragement of playing to packed houses from the start; also his breezy personality relieved some of the nervous tension. He was the joker in a dignified pack. He put ice in the dressing room showers, and during one matinée this myopic Hamlet set the audience tittering by neglecting to remove his horn-rimmed spectacles before returning on stage. It was, however, a disappointing production, memorable only for Sir Michael Redgrave's definitive portrait of Claudius as a villain with no small measure of charm, and it was fortunate that the National's reputation in its first season did not have to rest on this work in particular.

Hamlet, given only twenty-seven performances, was rapidly joined in repertory by the distinguished Chichester productions of *Saint Joan* and *Uncle Vanya*; then, in December, came the National's first real adventure: a revival of George Farquhar's *The Recruiting Officer*, a Restoration comedy that had not been performed professionally in London for twenty years. It was seen as a move in precisely the right direction, the fulfilment of what should be a prime function of any national theatre, that is, to take an indigenous, much neglected classic and present it with exciting new vigour and updated style. In this the new company was remarkably successful, but of greatest interest here is the manner in which Olivier, so individually inventive, responded to the challenge of playing a secondary role (Captain Brazen) in the first production that was absolutely fresh to all concerned.

Because he faced so many other pressures, Sir Laurence came late to rehearsals, for once without any preconceptions of how his part should be played, without any artful physical business worked out in advance. This was just as well since William Gaskill, in his debut as a National director, was taking unusual pains to arrive at a collective understanding of Farquhar's characters. He had begun by devoting the first morning of rehearsals to improvisations entirely divorced from the text— exercises in spontaneous mime that were akin to children's party games. One exercise had the cast, seated in a circle, passing an imaginary object from one to another, each actor having to transform it by way of mime into something else. Another required each actor to use a chair for anything but its usual purpose; one rode it, another made love to it, a third combed his hair with it. Each day there was to be an optional half-hour 'movement class', a limbering-up before rehearsals proper, and Gaskill explained that the principal aim was to help the actors 'relate to each other's imaginations'. There was also a great deal of discussion about the social background and the motivation of the characters, and in this preliminary stage the accent was essentially on emotional rather than physical make-up—a method of preparation directly in opposition to Olivier's own approach.

When, after a few days, Sir Laurence joined in rehearsals, he was asked by a director half his age to improvise in the part of Brazen. Gaskill wanted 'the boss' to feel the sense of ensemble. The rest of the group waited in breathless anticipation to see how the maestro would respond to an invitation to a five-finger exercise. According to Tynan, who edited a fascinating but strictly official record of this production, the expected tension did not arise, and Larry plunged in 'with zest and great inventiveness'.[5]

Zest? Gaskill has since expressed the belief that Olivier, while playing the game, really hated it and 'thought it was a load of rubbish'.[6] And Gaskill is surely right. In days of youthful self-indulgence, as when shaping his first Hamlet and Iago, Olivier had treated himself to some psychological exploration in conjunction with a few friends, but he had never been attracted by the kind of group discussion and therapy (much popularized by the Method school of acting) that placed great emphasis on improvisation and exercises to develop the actor's gifts of empathy. While working on *The Tumbler* in the United States he had confessed to being driven wild by American actors' habit of theorizing. 'Instead of doing a scene over again when it's giving trouble they want to discuss, discuss, discuss.' On the filming of *The Moon and Sixpence* he had known five-minute scenes to be debated for over forty minutes. 'I'd rather have run the scene eight times than have wasted that time chattering away about abstractions. An actor gets the thing right by doing it over and over. Arguing about motivations and so forth is a lot of rot. American actors encourage that sort of thing too much. Personally, I loathe all abstract discussions about the theatre. They bore me. I assure you I shall never write a book about my theories of dramatic art.'

The Recruiting Officer thus provided the first test of how far Olivier, without a leading role, would be willing to keep in tune with the ensemble, possibly sacrificing self-promoting opportunities for the sake of the common cause. So often in the past he had been a law unto himself in his interpretation of a part, going his own unpredictable way to great personal advantage but sometimes at the expense of the production as a whole. As director of the National Theatre, Sir Laurence could hardly keep stressing the 'hot breath of unity' and at the same time, when taking a lesser role, embark on dazzling opportunist solo runs. On the other hand, he was the master player, always to be judged by the highest standards, and a lifetime of experience and instinctive ego precluded him from surrendering the spotlight without some show of strength.

His solution appeared to be a partial compromise. He entered into the spirit of Gaskill's character-proving rehearsals, allowed the young director to guide him away from a Brazen more of a dandy than the text would bear. However, by introducing subtle minutiae, he did not tone down his performance perhaps as much as Gaskill would have liked. Brazen could be seen as a distant relation of Sergius Saranov in *Arms and the Man* and for a time Olivier toyed with the notion of repeating the irresistible comic invention he had first introduced as Sergius during the war: a clicking of heels that led to his spurs becoming entangled. In the end he abandoned the idea, but if he was not falling back on such a blatant piece of scene-stealing, he still had plenty of other tricks up his sleeve: invented muscular twitches in his cheeks, a shortsighted squint and specially built-up calves that arrested the attention of the audience before he had even spoken a line.

Gaskill thought this was one of Olivier's less successful performances. It satisfied almost everyone else. For a supporting player Sir Laurence took an unusually large share of the bouquets with his rococo portrait of a bleary-eyed and lecherous recruiting officer; one leading critic, Philip Hope-Wallace, went so far as to say that his performance outshone all the rest. Yet it was not achieved at the company's expense; the production itself was widely acclaimed and still remains recognized as one of the National Theatre's most praiseworthy achievements.

Thus both director's honour and actor's ego were served. At the same time the message behind Olivier's performance was clear: promotion to the super-executive ranks had not robbed the great actor of his instinctive urge to outshine others on the stage. Though he talked of personal ambition fulfilled, of the unity of a permanent ensemble being more important than the star system, when it came to a major test of dramatic power, this proud and ageing Sampson would never enter the arena with a self-imposed crew cut to be on a scale with lesser talents.

25

'Acting for Acting's sake'

Less than two years after Olivier's appointment to the National, his role as director was deplored by Sir Tyrone Guthrie as follows: 'He was the right figurehead for its inception. He is doing a fine job. But it is not the job he does best. Much of what he is at present doing could be done equally well by several other people, none of whom could play Othello, Macbeth, Lear, Faustus and a dozen other great parts which, at present, he has no time to think about. The years are passing. I suppose it is idle to wish it, but I'd like him to be less celebrated, less distinguished, less important and more free. I want to see him abdicate . . .'[1] It was a sentiment of obvious emotional appeal. Here was the colossus of the English stage, an actor already assured of a place alongside Garrick, Irving and Kean in the valhalla of theatrical giants, devoting the greater part of his time and energies to directing and to administrative duties. True, the public could see the infinite subtlety of his Astrov and the comic flamboyance of his Brazen, but for many it was not enough to know that Vesuvius was still rumbling with life; they had to hear the full crescendo of thunder, see the great sparks fly.

On April 21, 1964, encouraged by Tynan's flattery and lured by the bait of Shakespeare's Quatercentenary, Sir Laurence responded. Blackskinned and barefooted, sniffing effeminately at a red rose and gently chuckling to himself, he padded to the front of the Old Vic stage to embark, in a deceptively relaxed style, on the one great role he had been 'funking for years': Othello.

Olivier had nervously committed himself to this part seven months before. 'I've put it off because I think it's pretty well unplayable,' he said. 'It's a terrible study and a monstrous, monstrous burden for the actor. I think Shakespeare and actor Richard Burbage got drunk together one night and Burbage

said, "I can play anything you write, anything at all." And
Shakespeare said, "Right, I'll fix you, boy!" And then he wrote
Othello.' But not even Olivier could have foreseen just how
monstrous the burden would be. By the time he came to rehearsing *Othello*, he was appearing in *Uncle Vanya* and *The Recruiting
Officer*; he was also planning for the next Chichester Festival
and facing ever-increasing work in the day-to-day running of the
National, which was about to embark on its first provincial tour
while still keeping the repertory moving at the Old Vic. In the
end the load proved too great for him and it had to be lightened
by reducing the number of performances of *Othello*, but the
miracle was that the load was successfully carried at all, and that
miracle was worked by the actor's extraordinary self-discipline
in preparing for the role. Six months in advance he went into
training for the part. His two pre-rehearsal objectives: peak fitness and greatly increased depth of voice.

It has often been said that no English actor in this century has
completely succeeded as Othello. One man, in Olivier's estima-
tion, could have achieved it—Orson Welles.* 'He had everything for Othello, everything except the breath. He didn't go
into training, and after "Like to the Pontic sea" he had to pause
. . . When all is said and done, for Othello you need the breath,
the lungs . . . You need the self-discipline and the rhythm. At
the basis of everything is rhythm.' Sir Laurence did not intend
to fail on that same score. He worked out in the gym twice a
week, bought a track-suit and started jogging along the Brighton
sea front. He wanted breath and stamina, and agility, too, since
he saw the Moor as moving gracefully, 'like a soft, black leo-
pard'. For half a year he also kept up daily vocal exercises with
the aid of a professional teacher. After four or five months he
could get his voice down an extra five notes in the bass, eventually
almost a full octave. Occasionally, when the pace quickened
sharply or the poetry had to soar, he was liable to slip back to
near-baritone, but for the greater part he could sustain the blue-
black voice he wanted.

One could argue that Olivier, for once in his life, had rather too
much time to think ahead. The outcome was a characterization

* In 1951 at the St. James's Theatre, Olivier had presented Orson
Welles in the American's own production of *Othello*. It was Welles's
first appearance on the English stage.

crammed tight with technical inventiveness—a highly controversial portrait, arguably over-elaborate in style, but undeniably
a fascinatingly detailed exhibition of this actor's distinctive art
and craft. Being fearful of failure, he resolved to attack his canvas
with bold, positive strokes, to draw not a romantic, dark-brown
Arab but an uninhibited jet-black Moor, negroid in every movement and gesture and physical detail. He developed the easy,
swinging lope of the African and such general looseness of the
limbs that it seemed as though he had altered the very assembly
of his joints. His make-up was shaped with the same meticulous
care. Beginning with the feet, he covered himself from toe to
head with a first coat of liquid stain, then a layer of make-up
up containing some grease which he polished all over with a
chiffon cloth to give a fleshy sheen. The palms and soles and
thickened lips were incarnadined, the fingernails varnished a pale
blue transparent, and a black moustache and crinkly wig completed a self-transformation that took him two and a half hours
before each performance and an additional forty-five minutes for
the undoing.

In direct contrast to his work as Captain Brazen, Sir Laurence
came to rehearsals (under John Dexter, who was directing his
first Shakespearean play) with his homework fully done. He
knew all his lines in advance and at the first reading he went full
out while other actors, clinging to their scripts, looked on in
wonder. Moreover, his interpretation was this time prede-
termined. There would be no Iago kissing him full on the lips
as he had done to Ralph Richardson a quarter of a century before; long ago he had abandoned the theory of a homosexual
relationship between the Moor and his Ancient. ('That was before
I went into the services,' he explained. 'It's very easy to understand Iago's feeling towards Othello if you've ever had half a
stripe less than someone else.') Now he took as his psychological
guideline the belief that a tendency towards self-deception was
Othello's underlying weakness. So often, he explained, Shakespearean tragedy is based on the concept of a near-perfect statue
of a man, a statue perfect except for one fissure that widens
under pressure—the over-ambition of Macbeth, the pigheaded-
ness of Lear, the excessive pride of Coriolanus, the indecisive-
ness of Hamlet. In Othello it is highly inflammable jealousy,
but now his interpretation was to be based on a companion fault.
He was attracted by the much-disputed view of T. S. Eliot and

F. R. Leavis that a flaw of self-dramatized egotism and conceit in Othello contributed to his downfall: the notion that the Moor is kidding himself as well as those around him in his narcissistic picture of himself as a noble hero of great dignity and sophistication, a black emperor among the whites whom he serves.

Olivier explained: 'In Shakespeare I always try to reassure the audience initially that they are not going to see some grotesque, outsized dimension of something which they can't understand or sympathize with. If you have succeeded in the initial moments, either by a very strong stamp of characterization so they recognize you as a real guy, or by a quiet approach, then I think there's no end to where you can lead them in size of acting. God knows, you have to be enormously big as Othello.' In his initial moments at the Old Vic, sniffing at a flower fresh from his Brighton garden and fetishly fondling the large Christian cross hanging around his neck, he certainly achieved that strong stamp of characterization. Whether in the long run he made his audience sufficiently sympathetic or caring is less certain. But he had another declared ambition: 'to lead the public towards an appreciation of acting—to watch acting for acting's sake'.[2]

The majority of critics judged his Othello to be a stupendous achievement, and most especially they saw it as a dazzling display of virtuosity. Herbert Kretzmer (*Daily Express*) was in distinguished company in stressing the actor's embodiment of blackness: 'Sir Laurence has managed, by heaven knows what witchcraft, to capture the very essence of what it must mean to be born with a dark skin . . . It is a performance full of grace, terror and insolence. I shall dream of its mysteries for years to come.'

Richard Findlater capsuled its essential significance when he wrote:

The Othello created on that April night in the Waterloo Road seemed to combine all the qualities whose conjunction, at his best, had set Olivier through the years apart from other actors who made do with some of them: magnetic, masculine force; technical inventiveness: charm; emotional intensity and variety; a rare impersonative skill; pathos; a vein of humour; wide vocal range and attack; fury; a sense of tradition, blended with a readiness to experiment; the talent to surprise; a penetrating intelligence; gusto; a capacity for making the most of a character's humanity; the ability to make an audience frightened, make it laugh, bring it close to tears; eyes that spoke, grew, mesmerized; audacity; and something more as well—that intangible ingredient in a performance which prompts a grateful public to call it 'great'.[3]

Othello stands out as the most extravagant example of Olivier —seemingly unrestrained by his director—going his own outrageous way to achieve a great solo performance and stamp a production with his own individual trademark. It was his Moor, not necessarily Shakespeare's, and the unprecedented demand for National Theatre tickets that ensued was inspired strictly by a mass desire to see a one-man exhibition of acting on the grand scale. Let no one pretend that the public stampeded to see a great production by a well-knit ensemble or even to see, as Shakespeare wrote it, a play offering *two* great dramatic roles of equal opportunity. They were clamouring to see a spellbinder at work. They wondered at his magic in its execution and afterwards many wondered even more.

Technically, it was a stunning display; as Franco Zeffirelli* expressed it, 'an anthology of everything that has been discovered about acting in the last three centuries. It's grand and majestic, but it's also modern and realistic. I would call it a lesson for us all.' But was it great acting within the context of the play?

Alan Brien (*Sunday Telegraph*) wrote of 'a kind of bad acting of which only a great actor is capable . . . Alone so far among critics, perhaps alone forever among audiences, I find Sir Laurence Olivier's Othello the most prodigious and perverse example of this in a decade. Sir Laurence can move every muscle at will— I regret he could not move me . . . He is the romantic gymnast of our stage, the noblest Roman wrestler of them all. He can press his own weight in blank verse and hurl a soliloquy like a javelin until it sinks up to the haft in the back row of the gallery. But he is now in danger of becoming overtrained.' In fact, Brien was never alone. There were others no less unmoved; and even today, whenever critics or actors are joined in discussion

---

* Three years before, at Stratford, Zeffirelli had directed a disastrous production of *Othello*, with Sir John Gielgud and Ian Bannen as Moor and Ancient respectively.

of great Shakespearean performances, one will encounter more
fierce debate about Olivier's Othello than any other. Some
praise it to the skies; others talk of a horrifying 'caricature'. It
may come as no surprise to find John Osborne describing it as
'unspeakably vulgar'.[4] Less predictably, Olivier's longest admirer, Dame Sybil Thorndike, reacted with an expression of
saucer-eyed Grand Guignol when she was reminded of it. 'Oh,
his Othello! Well, I couldn't bear it. That awful Negro!'

There is no real difficulty in seeing how and why this Othello
divides opinion so sharply. When discussing the role, Olivier
stressed the importance of the colour difference: 'the whole play
seeps through with it . . . it's tremendously, highly sexual . . .
I'm sure Shakespeare meant there to be a great splash of shock.[5]
In stressing this aspect so vividly on stage, he gave an interpretation of enormous appeal to a new generation of theatregoers
who looked more for physical excitement than lyrical beauty, who
were not so greatly concerned that his bursts of accelerated
speech—especially in the last scene that demands seven climaxes
of the actor—sustained power at the expense of poetry. For
others, however, it seemed that he had concentrated perhaps too
much on the external image, too little on the emotional make-up
of the man; also that he had stamped this Moor with such massive authority from the onset that the facile undermining of his
supposedly immortal love failed to move one close to tears.

As long ago as 1950 Olivier told a critic: 'I have done everything but Othello and I have no burning desire to go into black-
face and have the stage stolen from me by some young and
brilliant Iago.' In 1964 those words were thrown back in his coal-
black face, harshly perhaps, but understandably since it was
difficult indeed to escape the suspicion that he was protecting
himself by entrusting Iago, one of the longest roles in all Shakespeare, to an actor (Frank Finlay) who had played only one
Shakespearean part before, that of the First Gravedigger in
Hamlet. Olivier described Finlay as having the best technical
equipment he had seen for years, and naturally enough the
director and his associates were keen to encourage the development of one of the National's most promising actors. Nevertheless, Finlay's sudden advancement to the heavyweight rankings,
pitching him into the ring with a champion trained to his peak,
did suggest something approaching the mismatch of the
century.

Finlay rose bravely to the occasion; by all accounts he steadily gained strength in his part, and in general, as an actor, he has since then more than fulfilled Olivier's high opinion of his potential. But at the time he could not hope to match Olivier's Moor on the histrionic level. One critic saw his interpretation of Iago as the fatal flaw that robbed the production of greatness. Equally, however, the blame could be thrown at Olivier's door, since his interpretation of Othello hardly permitted Finlay's rendering of Iago to carry conviction. Could one believe that this Moor, so sophisticated and debonair, a sharp step above the traditional slow-witted warrior, was having his mind poisoned by this rasping, unpoetic whipper-snapper of an ensign; and if he was, then could one deeply sympathize at his fate? Actor Robert Speaight goes to the core of the matter in his prodigious history *Shakespeare on the Stage*: 'There was no risk of anyone stealing the stage from this Othello, but an added dimension would have been given to the play if Michael Redgrave had been asked to share it.' [6]

The National's *Othello* did not have the perfectly balanced casting of *Uncle Vanya*; nor did it go so far towards the ideal of an ensemble to match the teamwork and strength-in-depth that had been achieved at the Moscow Art Theatre. But then did it really matter so very much? What was so wrong with a supreme athlete dominating an event to the exclusion of all others so long as he thrilled the crowd by a devastating exhibition of sustained pace that carried him through something equivalent in drama to the sub-four-minute mile barrier? Pundits might complain that this was not Shakespeare's *Othello*, that the dramatic balance was destroyed, but if nothing else, it was dramatic entertainment on the most spectacular and daring scale. Many loved Olivier's performance. Many loathed it. None could ignore it.

Sir Laurence was once asked what was his most important function as director of the National Theatre. He answered swiftly, 'Filling seats with the largest number of bums is my business.' His *Othello* succeeded in that aim to an embarrassing degree. In 1964 a ticket to this production became the piece of paper most difficult to obtain in Britain. Lord Snowdon had to stand during a matinée. Arthur Schlesinger, Jr., then one of President Kennedy's closest aides, failed to get in. Every day *The Times* 'agony column' carried advertisements begging for tickets at any price. The production became a kind of novel theatrical myth, the biggest Shakespeare box-office draw of modern times, and the greatest compliment of all to Olivier came in the shape of a batch of letters from leading actors engaged in current West End shows. They asked for a special matinée performance to be arranged so that they might have an opportunity of seeing *him*.

All-night queues outside the Old Vic were now the norm, and the theatre's total seating capacity of 878 never looked more absurdly inadequate. Olivier gave three performances a week during the first season and though the public cried out for more he found it too exhausting and could only give them less, limiting himself to two appearances a week in the following season. The case for filming the production became overwhelming. Sir Laurence himself had no enthusiasm for it. His larger-than-life performance was bound to be seen to less advantage under the close-up of the camera. The role was so essentially theatrical; also he was apprehensive about entombing himself in a film that could be revived constantly on television ('Myself, I could do without the laughs in the drawing rooms in twenty years'). But not to have filmed it would have been indefensible, denying not only the public of an opportunity to see great acting on the most extravagant scale but also the National Theatre of a most lucrative source of income. So he agreed. In three weeks in July 1965, under studio conditions, a Technicolor, Panavision production was filmed under the direction of Stuart Burge, who had previously made a film recording of the National's *Uncle Vanya*. Nothing was cut from the stage version; no exterior shots were introduced.

According to the producer the aim was 'to recreate completely, the atmosphere, effect and immediacy of the theatre performance, using the basis of film technique'. But the effect was *not* the same. Much of the high voltage generated by Olivier's stage presence was lost, though this was compensated by gains elsewhere. Othello and Iago were no longer on a completely different scale: Finlay profited enormously from the camera's magnifying lens. In close-up his quiet, often remote and mumbling Iago came across much more tellingly, the twisted cunning as evident in his face as in his words and deeds. In this sense, dramatic balance was restored. Significantly, the film won international best actor awards for *both* its leading men. The *New York Times* critic Bosley Crowther complained that this Othello looked like a Rastus or the end man in an American minstrel show ('You almost wait for him to whip a banjo from his flowing white garments or start banging a tambourine'), but the film version did not divide opinion as sharply as the stage production had done. In America especially it was hailed as 'a masterpiece'. Such reservations as there may have been were well expressed by John Simon, critic for *The New Leader*, who saw it as the best filmed *Othello* so far, vastly preferable to Orson Welles's, and, as filmed Shakespeare, surpassed only by Olivier's own *Henry V* and *Richard III*. 'Even so, with talent such as Olivier's and the British National Theatre's, what a chance was here for a definitive version of this tautest, swiftest, most concentrated of Shakespeare's major tragedies. The production, however, is "one whose hand,/Like the base Indian, threw a pearl away/ Richer than all his tribe." Still, it is throwing away in the grand style. The thing is worth watching—not so much for the pearl as for the technique of the throwing hand.'

The departure of Redgrave, leaving to launch Guildford's new Yvonne Arnaud Theatre was a grave loss for the National. As Olivier admitted, it meant that the autumn season was too firmly centred on himself; with Othello and Solness (replacing Redgrave in *The Master Builder*) he held both the ace and king of trumps—almost a grand-slam hand worthy of an old-style actor-manager. Inevitably, his first appearance as Solness prompted comparisons with Redgrave's performance. Some critics thought that his master builder was less strong in poetic insight, others that he scored more points with his wealth of naturalistic detail. What remained beyond dispute was the sustained brilliance of Maggie Smith as Hilde Wangel; at times she almost acted both these master builders off the stage. Unfortunately, she was so severely overloaded (playing in three National productions and rehearsing a fourth) that it was necessary for another actress to share the role with her. Joan Plowright, who had recently suffered a miscarriage, was brave enough to take on the unenviable task, but it was much less happy casting and the production lost some of its impact.

By now, the National had established a repertoire of impressive content and range, one including Peter Shaffer's successful epic *The Royal Hunt of the Sun* (first done at Chichester) and a memorable revival of Noel Coward's *Hay Fever*. It was therefore agreed that the director should have a short leave to make a film. The picture, shot on location in Hampstead, was Otto Preminger's *Bunny Lake is Missing*, and only a need to improve his bank balance can explain Olivier's involvement. He seemed content to plod through the part of a police inspector with a mechanical competence that any middleweight actor might have achieved. Remarkably, Noel Coward was also persuaded to take a modest and absurdly eccentric part in this thriller that cried out for the Hitchcock touch. When he and Olivier first met on the set they both fell about in a giggling fit reminiscent of their far-off days in *Private Lives*, but really it was no laughing matter to see two master craftsmen sporting on the nursery slopes.

Sir Laurence, as it happened, had every reason to conserve his dramatic power at this particular time. Directly after *Bunny Lake* he faced the formidable task of filming *Othello* in three weeks, and immediately after that he had to prepare for the National Theatre's first overseas tour, seventeen days in Moscow and Berlin, presenting three plays: *Othello*, *Hobson's Choice* and (new to the repertoire) William Congreve's *Love for Love*. Two weeks before the tour he was confined to bed with a virus infection. He missed rehearsals of *Love for Love*, in which he was playing Tattle the half-witted beau, and briefly it was feared that the tour would have to be cancelled, so much did its success depend upon his Othello. But he recovered in time, and on departure he was in such high spirits that he borrowed a B.E.A. cap and jacket and masqueraded as a steward to welcome his sixty-four-strong company aboard their Vanguard flight.

In Moscow the National Theatre became the first Western company to perform at the Kremlevsky Theatre inside the walls of the Kremlin. *Othello* opened to a tumultous reception, ending with fifteen minutes of unbroken applause that started up all over again when the blacked-up Olivier came forward to deliver a short speech in impeccable Russian. Harold Brighouse's *Hobson's Choice*, with its recognizable proletarian background, was almost equally well received, but the third play, an absurdly fancy dish to set before the Muscovites, was really beyond their comprehension. Congreve was unknown to them; his Restoration comedy, so elegantly stylized and fastidious, was totally alien to Russian life. They applauded generously at the end, but most of the humour was met with an innocent silence that played havoc with the actors' timing and prompted them to overact outrageously. Olivier was more fortunate; his best comic moments did not depend on the spoken word, and as he minced about, falling flat on his face in clambering out of windows, he finally won over the audience with sheer slapstick. After seeing his Othello, they were now all the more impressed by his variety. Olivier also had advantage in being the one member of the company with a ready-made reputation in Russia; not least, he discovered, his popular esteem rested on the enormous success of *Lady Hamilton,* which had run for months in Moscow during and after the war and had resulted in Vivien Leigh's adoption as the Pin-Up Girl of the Red Army.

On returning to London, Olivier was immediately involved in preparing the National's autumn season. By now it had become painfully obvious that he needed to cut back on his wide-ranging activities. Something had to be sacrificed and it was the director-ship of the Chichester Festival. Over gin-and-tonics he per-suaded his Brighton neighbour, John Clements, to succeed him at the year's end. Nor, in view of the growing financial need to film outstanding N.T. productions, could he afford any longer the time for major film work in a private capacity. So Sir Laurence turned to cameo film work in December 1965, when he had to black-up for his stage Othello one day and the next day black-up all over again to appear as the Mahdi opposite Charlton Heston's General Gordon in *Khartoum.* For the Mahdi he switched from the Moor's *basso profundo* to a sing-song counter-tenor, and spent three hours each morning in the Pine-wood make-up department to get every physical detail as accur-ate as possible, including even the V-shaped gap in the Moslem leader's front teeth. It set the pattern for a series of fine minia-tures rooted in meticulous preparation and, though not so financially rewarding, they were to serve his reputation better than ill-suited leading roles in films like *Term of Trial* and *Bunny Lake.*

During the following year Olivier became more involved with the overall running of the National Theatre than with the creative side of production. He directed not at all, his stage ap-pearances were exceedingly few. For once in his life he was keep-ing fairly conventional working hours and it enabled him to see more of his family at a particularly rewarding time. His children, Richard and Tamsin, were now in nursery school; a third (Julie-Kate) was to be born in July. In the same year, incidentally, he became a grandfather. His son Tarquin, now married and working on a sugar plantation for the Commonwealth Development Corporation in Tanzania, had a boy named Tristan. But if there were any fears that the 'old man' had mellowed in his sixtieth year and was prepared to forsake acting in favour of a more settled executive life, such fears were soon swept aside in the most positive manner. On February 21, 1967, Olivier added a new masterpiece to his gallery of definitive stage portraits: Captain Edgar in Byam Shaw's sombre and meticulous production of *The Dance of Death*.

Following *Miss Julie* the previous year, the National Theatre was taking a second plunge into the dark misogynist world of Strindberg, and it afforded Sir Laurence a role that vies with Archie Rice as his favourite. The embittered Edgar is a retired soldier who has never ceased from marital fight and even now, as their silver anniversary approaches, he and his younger ex-actress wife (Geraldine McEwan) are still waging total war, both captives of their corrosive, hate-infested relationship. As usual, Olivier contrived to look his part exactly—a severe-cropped Prussian head, a snarl of a moustache, reddened face, belligerent jutting jaw; and he played it with a towering intensity. He had to be arrogant, cunning, pompous, evil, brutal, vulgarly convivial; he had to erupt with volcanic force in his uncontrollable hatred, whimper like a sick child in the face of death, collapse pathetically into periodic comas and at one point clumsily break into a little quick-stepping to the *mazurka*. It could all have dissolved into grotesque caricature, and yet it never did. This Edgar was firmly contained within the realms of reality—a loathsome, miserable creature much larger than life but never beyond the reach of human pity. And remarkably there was a comic quality, too, but interwoven into the dark-grained fabric with such finesse that it only accentuated the sense of appalling menace.

This rare gem of characterization has since been recorded for the cinema, and although the play—so essentially theatrical—transferred uneasily to the screen, it does preserve, without too much loss of the intensity, the performance of a great actor at the peak of his powers. It was a portrayal that won for Olivier the *Evening Standard* Best Actor Drama Award, and the gold medallion of the Swedish Academy of Literature for his outstanding interpretation of Swedish drama. With few exceptions, the critics hailed its true greatness. Some people, notably Sir John Gielgud, rate it as Olivier's greatest non-Shakespearean performance.

The Dance of Death arguably represents the high-water mark in Olivier's fortunes as director of the National Theatre. His creative genius would surge again to burst the banks of dramatic excellence, as with his Shylock and especially with his James Tyrone in *Long Day's Journey Into Night*, a veritable tidal wave of histrionic art, but during the Sixties that cherished 'hot breath of unity' would never again blow quite so freely through his company. Very soon Sir Laurence was to be engulfed in a succession of crises that would see him fighting with extraordinary self-sacrifice for the future of the National and, with his own stubborn brand of courage, for life itself.

26
The Year of Crisis

The National Theatre had been launched by executives each with different temperaments and persuasions, with a keen-edged rivalry that was constructive only insofar as it kept creative minds at full stretch and so heightened artistic endeavour. It was always a sensitive superstructure and, under stress, some disturbing cracks began to show. In 1965 William Gaskill departed because he disapproved of Kenneth Tynan's influence and the way the National was developing. Early in 1967 more serious signs of 'metal fatigue' appeared. John Dexter, producer of such notable successes as *Othello* and *A Royal Hunt of the Sun*, left following a disagreement over the timing of his long-planned, all-male production of *As You Like It*. His departure left Olivier without both of his original artistic directors and with an added executive burden at a time when he was already heavily committed as an actor. At this point of vulnerability the most menacing situation in the National's brief history came to the boil: the divisive controversy over the proposed staging of Rolf Hochhuth's *Soldiers*.

Sir Laurence was preoccupied with rehearsals of *The Dance of Death* when Tynan began lobbying on behalf of this provocative play, which reaches its climax with Bishop Bell of Chichester launching a passionate attack on Churchill for 'terror raids' on German cities. The proposal now spawned a gigantic row that consumed more of Olivier's valuable time, and by April he found himself enmeshed in a full-scale boardroom battle that he could not hope to win. The board overruled the director in his wish to present the play and issued an official statement: 'Some of the characters, in particular Sir Winston Churchill and Lord Cherwell, are grossly maligned by the play, and the board unanimously considered that the play was unsuitable for production at the National Theatre.'

Once before the board had blocked Olivier and Tynan in the choice of a German play: Frank Wedekind's *Spring Awakening*. No great public debate ensued. After all, the Lord Chamberlain's office was never likely to approve such a disturbingly progressive play (written in 1891) that condemned a repressive attitude towards sex education through its story of adolescents responding to mysterious impulses and ending in lethal abortion and suicide. *Soldiers* was different: a matter of national concern because it dealt with national figures and national policy. In dramatizing an attack on Churchill over the bombing of civilian targets, Hochhuth was expressing a defensible viewpoint just as he had done in his play *The Representative* over the failure of Pope Pius XII to condemn Nazi atrocities against the Jews. This time, however, the author went beyond argument based on established fact; he suggested that the death of the Free Polish leader General Sikorski in an air crash in 1943 was the result of sabotage arranged by Lord Cherwell, chief scientific adviser to Churchill—with Churchill's passive connivance!

It was inconceivable that Lord Chandos, who had served his country with great distinction through two world wars, would permit this play to be presented at the National Theatre. In opposing it he was not simply acting out of loyalty to the memory of Sir Winston, a great personal friend. As a member of Churchill's War Cabinet, he had been closer to events than either Hochhuth or Tynan, and he knew of absolutely no justification for the conspiracy charge. Hochhuth insisted that he had evidence to prove his theory. But where was it? Locked up, so he claimed, in a Swiss bank where it had to remain undisclosed for another half-century! On the other side, there was the available testimony of the Czech pilot of Sikorski's plane and of members of the security guard in Gibraltar at the time of the crash. They all swore that the aircraft which exploded after take-off had not been sabotaged. How then could a state-subsidized theatre possibly be expected to propagate an unsubstantiated and scurrilous allegation against its country's most celebrated statesman?

The wonder was not that the battle to present *Soldiers* was lost, but that it was fought so hard and so long. For this the credit must go largely to Tynan. As an undergraduate at Magdalen College, he had been deeply fascinated by the brilliant manner in which C. S. Lewis, the Oxford don, would defend the

seemingly indefensible. He himself showed considerable aptitude in that same direction. In the Sixties—the decade of the
Profumo *affaire* and the Lady Chatterley court case, the decade
that saw the abolition of the Lord Chamberlain's power to censor
plays and a generous relaxing of film censorship—he came into
full flower as the progressive anti-Establishment intellectual
constantly challenging old standards and values and striving for
total freedom of thought and of artistic expression. He was
completely in his element in an age when unorthodoxy was made
fashionable and everything—mores, dogma, history—was being
brazenly challenged; and in such topsy-turvy times there was a
certain ironic appropriateness in the fact that Tynan the consummate wordsmith eventually became best known to the general
public as the first man to have said 'fuck' on British television. It
happened in 1965 during a serious B.B.C.-TV discussion when
he was arguing that sexual intercourse could be shown on the
public stage, and the ensuing publicity brought him instant
notoriety. Highbrow had met lowbrow on common ground, an
acquaintance later to be resumed through Tynan's pioneering
work in the field of 'elegant erotica' as the deviser and part-author
of *Oh! Calcutta!*, a revue he judged necessary, 'because it
occurred to me there was nowhere for a civilized man to take a
civilized woman for an evening of erotic stimulation'.

Tynan's activities were by no means confined to the arts, or
indeed to his missionary work as 'an apostle of international
hedonism'. In this decade of relentless war on gullibility he
became an energetic member of the 'Who Killed Kennedy?
Committee'. Later he was also to show much interest in a play
that expressed suspicion about the death in an air crash of U.N.
Secretary-General Dag Hammarskjold. This is not to suggest
that an obsession with conspiracy theories attracted him to
Soldiers. The Sikorski sabotage theory was of relatively minor
importance in the play. Nevertheless it was in keeping with the
thought-provoking spirit of the work. Tynan believed passionately that Hochhuth had something worth saying and that no one
should deny him the freedom to say it, and never did a playwright find himself with a more zealous champion. The literary
manager proclaimed: 'I believe that one of our functions as a
national theatre should be to create a place where the gigantic
historical issues as the Greeks and Shakespeare understood them
should be raised. This is the most imposing new script I have

ever read.' He went further. 'Larry,' he said, 'had been grievously humiliated by the board, and Hochhuth grossly maligned.' If Olivier was to resign, then he would certainly do so also.

Resign? Needless to say, Sir Laurence at no time contemplated such drastic action. Indeed, without Tynan, one cannot honestly believe that he would ever have allowed a clash of opinions over a foreign play of debatable artistic merit to reach such a crisis point. But it had happened, and to his credit, once he had accepted that *Soldiers* merited production at the National, he stood by his adviser. He would abide by the board's decision, but he went on record as being 'unhappy' about it and justifiably complained that the board was at fault in not respecting his request for more time to have the play revised. Soon afterwards he stated his position unequivocally: 'I think this play gives Sir Winston Churchill a new dimension as a great man. It adds to him the nature of a tragic figure and this does no harm. I think he would say let people see it. He would not like to see it performed in every other country of the world but England. That would be contrary to the principle of free speech for which we were fighting . . . I could not have anything to do with the play if I thought it decreased Churchill's stature. Like all Englishmen I admire this man and in my case there is a sense of worship.'[1]

The real issue at stake here was not whether *Soldiers* was material fit for the National but whether an artistic director should have complete artistic control. Some argued that Olivier should never have accepted the position without the complete authority granted him at Chichester. He himself put it in a nutshell when he explained: 'It is essential for a lay board to recognize that the theatre must be run by professionals, the artistic director in particular. But as more and more theatres are supported by public money, the governors become trustees of the public interest. The problem has not yet been solved . . . My choice when I joined the National Theatre was cloudy but simple. Do we have a National Theatre with a *faute de mieux* ambivalent contract between its Director and the Board or do we not have a National Theatre at all?'

Significantly (in view of his subsequent appointment as Olivier's successor) Peter Hall, managing director of the Royal Shakespeare Company, came out strongly on his side. 'It is a black and miserable day for the English theatre. I am appalled by the National Theatre's decision to treat their director like this.

Theatre companies have never been run by committees and never will be. This action against one of our greatest actors and directors will lead the subsidized theatre in this country towards the state of censored theatre in East Europe.'

Ultimately the controversy served no useful purpose. What it did achieve was irreversible damage to relationships at the National. The triumvirate of Chandos, Olivier and Tynan was no longer finely balanced. Moreover, the pressures on Olivier were further increased at a time when they were already too great. On April 28, while still embroiled in the *Soldiers* debate, he flew 3,000 miles to Montreal to deliver six minutes of verse at the opening gala of the Expo '67 World Fair. He returned to a crippling work load. He was now appearing in *Dance of Death* and *Love for Love* both in London and on provincial tour. He was rehearsing his new production of Chekhov's *Three Sisters*, and he was recasting and preparing for the company's autumn tour of Canada when he planned to appear in three plays: *A Flea in Her Ear*, *Love for Love* and *Othello*. Moreover, he and Tynan were exploring the possibility of staging *Soldiers* under their independent management.

Stubbornly, Sir Laurence continued to shoulder this burden even though he had been secretly enduring physical discomfort for several months. In mid-June, three weeks after his sixtieth birthday, the cause of that discomfort was diagnosed. An investigation under anaesthetic revealed a neoplasm ('new growth' or tumour) of the prostate gland. A form of cancer. Fortunately it had been detected at an early stage. By an established form of treatment it could be arrested for a time; and there was a newly developed treatment that might eradicate the cancer altogether. Olivier opted for the latter—hyperbaric oxygen radiotherapy carried out in a special hermetically sealed chamber in which the temperature was lowered to near freezing-point and the affected part then bombarded with X-rays. He would need to undergo this treatment twice a week for three weeks, and it was strongly advised that he enter the hospital at once.

At first he responded with almost too much spirited resolution. He accepted that he would not be strong enough to keep up his stage appearances on treatment days, Tuesdays and Fridays, but otherwise he aimed to carry on working as usual, both at the office and at the Old Vic. After a preliminary stay in St. Thomas's Hospital he would be returning only as an out-patient, and the treatment would not be allowed to interrupt his work as the director of *Three Sisters*. For once his ambition outmeasured his physical capability. After his initial treatment in the hospital, he sent out for a bottle of champagne and he went home for the weekend with every intention of continuing life as normal. There was no hint of sickness on Sunday as he took the family to Brighton beach for the afternoon. By the evening, however, he was feverish and weak. He had mild pneumonia. The set-back served one useful purpose: it convinced everyone around him that he needed to be protected from himself. 'He insists on working like mad,' said Lady Olivier. 'That is the kind of life he likes, and there is no point in stopping him. But we have all made a pact at the National Theatre to keep him in the hospital for at least a week or two. It is now obvious that he must rest up a bit.'

Olivier reluctantly agreed, but it did not stop him from working. He remained constantly in touch with the National by telephone, convened production meetings in his private room at the hospital and ran through scenes of *Three Sisters* with leading members of the cast. Anthony Hopkins and Derek Jacobi took over from him in *Dance of Death* and *Love for Love* respectively, but the Chekhov play, which marked Joan Plowright's return to the stage after two years' absence, remained essentially his own production, and the company pulled together all the more because they knew how important it was to him. *Three Sisters* was hailed as one of the finest achievements at the National, and the highest praise was reserved for the production style.

The following day, July 5, Olivier left the hospital. After so many difficult months, the future seemed to be 'set fair'; he looked forward to taking a recuperative holiday abroad when the National season ended on the 22nd, and afterwards he would be returning to his triumphant role as Captain Edgar and preparing for the Canadian tour. But then, almost immediately, all sense of relief and growing optimism was cruelly shattered. In the early morning of July 8, while resting at Brighton, he received the news that set him immediately hastening back to London. Vivien Leigh was dead.

For several weeks Sir Laurence had known that Vivien was unwell, confined to bed at her home in Eaton Square, Belgravia, while receiving treatment for tuberculosis, but the knowledge did not lessen the indescribable shock. Until the end she had been so vitally engrossed in the future, so confident that she would recover quickly and return to the stage in August in the Edward Albee play *A Delicate Balance*. Now, at age fifty-three, she was gone, and it was as though a star had suddenly fallen from the sky. That night, in tribute, all West End theatres extinguished their exterior lights for an hour.

Miss Leigh died as she lived—with a kind of perverse courage that continually impelled her beyond her physical limits. There had been no let-up in the later years, indeed she had only accelerated the pace. In 1961, after playing an ageing actress in *The Roman Spring of Mrs. Stone*, she embarked on an exhausting Old Vic tour of the Far East and South America, playing Viola in *Twelfth Night*, Paola in *Duel of Angels* and the doomed Marguerite Gautier in *Lady of the Camellias*; then, still making no concession to her own frailty, she plunged into her first musical, a Broadway production of *Tovarich*, the most strenuous acting-singing-dancing role she had ever tackled. She had five songs, a madly physical Charleston number, innumerable costume changes. The show ran successfully for six months. When the management failed to find a suitable replacement for her, she agreed to forego the holiday allowed to her by contract, working on through the dreadful heat of a New York summer until she finally collapsed and was compelled to rest.

After so many years of never-fading ambition and intermittent fits of depression, Vivien seemed to find a measure of peace and tranquillity at Tickerage Mill, a country home recommended to her by Dirk Bogarde. It had an idyllic Sussex setting beside a lake overhung by weeping willows, and there, having accumulated a considerable personal fortune, she could have settled for a life of graceful semi-retirement. But half measures were never her style. Always she yearned for the bright lights and social gaiety of London's theatreland, to be at the centre of things. She was one of life's compulsive workers, with the stage her over-riding passion. Sir Laurence, of course, was the most profound influence on her acting and her attitude towards acting, but it was much more than his example and standards that lifted her aspirations in the theatre. Only four days before she died, Brian Aherne was one of many friends to visit her when she was holding court in bed. He remarked to her closest companion, Jack Merivale, that he had seen one of her old films on television and that he had always felt she was at her best on the screen. Merivale agreed. But Vivien cried, 'You boys are crazy! I don't want to be a movie actress . . . I am dedicated to the theatre, and always will be.'

Speaking at a memorial service for Vivien Leigh at the University of Southern California, Aherne recalled their last conversation. He concluded: 'I think we should not grieve for Vivien. As I came into the University this evening, I saw a young man taking a surfboard from a car, and the thought came to me that Vivien had ridden through life like a brilliant surf-rider. All of us who knew her had watched, spellbound, while she rode the crests of the greatest waves with grace and skill, and when, as often happened, she fell off and then disappeared from sight, we shook our heads sorrowfully. "Poor Viv!" we said, "She's gone this time!" But no—even as we turned to look, there she was, up again in the sunshine, riding another great comber, as we gasped with astonishment, admiration and relief. I don't think she could have borne to feel the great wave of success break under her, to be washed up, like a bit of flotsam on the shore, and to find herself an old and perhaps unwanted actress. She had been too long on the crest, and her temperament was too fiery. It was not surprising that she gave such a superb performance as Scarlett O'Hara; they were very much alike, Vivien and Scarlett, and particularly, I suspect, in their relationships with their men.

'We should not grieve for her, but nobody who ever knew her will forget her, for she was, as Shakespeare's Enobarbus says of Cleopatra, truly a wonderful piece of work.'

By mid-August, looking bronzed and fit after a holiday in Switzerland, Olivier was back at the National Theatre, starting with a long and tiring day during which he rehearsed the company in *The Dance of Death* and held a series of executive meetings. Doctors had warned him to expect more spells of sudden tiredness and depression following his cancer treatment; nevertheless he insisted that the gruelling 8,000-mile tour of Canada would be going ahead in the autumn as planned. Moreover, since he was taking on the small role of Etienne the butler in Georges Feydeau's farce *A Flea in Her Ear*, he would be appearing in all three plays on tour—forty-eight performances in six weeks. He made just one concession: instead of playing Othello he would appear in the less arduous role of Captain Edgar. Even before his illness he had found that each performance of Othello left him shattered, 'as if I had been run over by a bus'. Now he was thankful to be rid of the role. He later explained: 'With all the preparation it became like a sort of pontifical midnight mass, it became so sacred it was awful. Putting on make-up, playing and taking off make-up was a seven-hour job, a dreadful punishment. You knew the audience had been waiting all night long out in the street, and your sense of responsibility was heightened to an extent it should never be. It became an obsession. When I did get cancer and they said, "No more Othello for you," I was secretly relieved.'[2]

Early in the New Year, after an enormously successful Canadian tour and then a brief visit to Rome for another bread-and-butter film role (Soviet Premier Kamanev in *The Shoes of the Fisherman*), Olivier spoke for the first time about the weeks he had lived with the doctor's diagnosis of cancer. 'Oddly enough it was good for me in a way. Because this kind of experience makes you count your blessings, makes you take a lot less for granted. It has changed my values a lot. Certain things I just won't tolerate any more—like being separated from my family. I won't accept that again. When you are my age and you have a young family, you must make the most of it—and during that time of illness they became extra precious to me. It has not been easy to bear. Richard Dimbleby was a real example—I learned from him. After all, he knew the certainty and carried on. I knew I had a seventy-five per cent chance. And Helen Keller too. Once she said to me, "Blindness is a thing to be resisted." When you find yourself with some fell disease, that is how one should instinctively react. I said to myself, "I will beat you, you bastard," and I think I have.'[3]

One month later he was in Edinburgh, midway through a performance of *The Dance of Death*, when he felt a spasm of pain in his stomach. The pain worsened; the following day a specialist diagnosed appendicitis. Because he wanted to be near his family, Sir Laurence was flown back to London for the operation. In St. Thomas's Hospital he underwent a routine appendectomy and at the same time the surgeon took the opportunity of carrying out a laparotomy, the opening of the abdomen, to make a thorough investigation. There was no trace of the cancerous condition. The 'bastard' was beaten.

27

The Second Term

In January 1970, on the National Theatre company's first visit to the United States, Olivier surprised the American press with a statement that seemed tantamount to heresy: 'It does seem sometimes that acting is hardly the occupation for an adult. False noses, lots of make-up and gum on my face. I can't stand it any more. I hope I'll never do another West End play . . . Directing is more important. I don't know of any elderly actors who enjoy acting very much. I don't think I have ever enjoyed it very much. One is too conscientious to enjoy it. But without it I would die, I suppose.'

Had the Grand Panjandrum of the twentieth-century theatre, after forty-five years in the business of make-believe, lost a measure of his dedication? It was beginning to seem so. In two years he had not played one major new role, although in 1969, besides reappearing in *The Dance of Death*, he did briefly take on modest parts at the National—the solicitor A. B. Raham in a revival of Somerset Maugham's *Home and Beauty*, and the old doctor Chebutikin in *Three Sisters*—plus cameo roles in three films. He was playing smaller parts, he explained, 'just to keep my hand in. I have this terrible fear that I will no longer be able to act, play my part on the stage'. Those malcontents who complained that he was too much the actor-manager at the National were unusually silent now. It was the turn of their opposite numbers to grouse that he was too rarely seen on the boards. Nor was he making a great impression on the production side. In those two years he had directed only two plays. The first, co-directed with Donald MacKechnie, was *The Advertisement*, basically a one-star vehicle with Joan Plowright giving a performance of vast technical skill as a neurotic woman alone in her city flat. The second, a production of *Love's Labour's Lost*, one of

Shakespeare's thinnest and most exasperating comedies, proved soporific.

Olivier was now sixty-two. His enormous creative energies had not really withered; rather they had been blunted as he became increasingly bogged down in a directorial role that tried his patience, enthusiasm and stamina beyond all reasonable limits. By 1967 he had done everything that was demanded of him and more. The company was firmly established, at its highest peak of success and prestige. Yet the day when he could lead the company into a permanent home designed to meet all its needs seemed further off than when he had started.

On February 1, 1968, he was thrown a fresh carrot. The government at last officially approved financing of the project at a cost of £7·4 million to be divided between the state and the Greater London Council. Olivier called it 'the best news for me in my professional life', wisely adding that he would not be cracking open his personal bottle of champagne yet. He had not served on building committees for the National since 1945 without learning something of the slow-grinding processes of bureaucracy. Even so, he could not have guessed in his darkest hours how much longer he would be kept waiting in the wings. During 1968, as building costs continued to soar, he was still suspended in doubt as to whether the theatre would be completed in the Seventies. In 1969 the first cement was poured for construction. It was said that the theatre would be ready in 1973. Yet its opening was still being delayed in 1975—almost thirteen years after his appointment as director.

It has been said by men with directorial experience that five years is about the limit any one man can be expected to run the same theatre and maintain his initial enthusiasm and freshness. In July 1969 it was just six years since Olivier held his first press conference in 'temporary' Nissen hut headquarters. His hair had turned grey. Some of his original zest seemed to be gone. He still hoped to be director when the National finally moved into its new home but, he said, he wouldn't insist upon it. 'I do get dreadfully tired at times, but I remain addicted to the idea of getting the National launched as an actor's theatre . . . In any case I wouldn't go on with this job if I thought I was losing my nerve or anything, if I thought I was losing the confidence of the public.'

He had accepted the job on the tacit understanding with the board that he would hold office for five years or until the new theatre was built, and with his phenomenal energy and tenacity he was altogether capable of completing a second five-year term. In the long run, however, not even a man of his iron will could be expected to sustain unflagging enthusiasm and ambition over a seemingly never-ending course on which two new hurdles appeared for every one he cleared and the finishing post continually moved further away. He saw production costs rise while subsidies remained static for three successive years; he helped the company expand and diversify its activities while all the time it remained restricted to the same antiquated offices and stuffy, low-ceilinged rehearsal room.

Following his fight against cancer, Olivier was belatedly relieved of some work by the appointment of Mr. Frank Dunlop as administrative director, and actor Robert Stephens as an associate director, but his work load was not appreciably lessened. Fresh problems arose as the building of the new theatre entered the advance planning stage. There were more meetings with the Arts Council, the Treasury and the G.L.C.; also, without increased subsidies, there was greater need to seek additional revenue from recordings, television, films and the sale of subsidiary rights on plays. Olivier played his part in this, starring in a film of *The Dance of Death* and later directing the film of *Three Sisters*, but inevitably his enthusiasm for acting waned when he had to give so much time and thought to business affairs. 'It is awful,' he said during the 1970 U.S. visit (yet another venture designed to keep the National out of the red). 'I wish I had more time to be at grips with the company. There seems to be so much day-to-day business. There is a limited opportunity for creative vision and Frank Dunlop and I regret it firmly. But we are beginning to get organized. I have never been a businessman or a chairman of the board.'

More than ever there was truth in those words of Tyrone Guthrie: 'He was the right figurehead for its inception. He is doing a fine job. But it is not the job he does best.' The job he did best was now being pushed farther into the background by preoccupation with problems more suited to the skills of a business efficiency expert. He himself played down this loss on the National's artistic side by insisting that the biggest successes of the last seven years had been plays in which he had not appeared.

This was not strictly true, yet he seemed determined to encourage the impression that he was essentially a working director undistracted by personal ambition, a part-time actor no longer with any burning desire to put on grease-paint and give a performance. 'I'm reaching an age,' he said, 'when I have to be cajoled, caressed, persuaded, stroked, before doing anything on the stage.'

Fortunately, in 1970 Olivier was cajoled and caressed into taking on a major new stage role—his first in three years. Jonathan Miller was to direct *The Merchant of Venice* with a late nineteenth-century setting. Two actors were unsuccessfully approached to play Shylock. Finally, under pressure from Tynan among others, Sir Laurence agreed to take it on, and he came back characteristically with a portrait worked out with infinite care and attention to detail. He wore a shiny top hat over his skull-cap and a Disraeli-style curl on his forehead; the not quite immaculate cut of his striped trousers and the affected dropping of his final g's gave subtle evidence of the pseudo upper-class gentility of this frock-coated Jew; and the slightly protruding upper teeth that showed when he smiled was another touch neatly designed to give the man an unsavoury visual image. Nor had Olivier lost any of his penchant for physical invention, though one most striking piece of business—an infernal dance of triumph based on Hitler's *schadenfreude* skip at the signing of the armistice in the Forest of Compiègne—was, in fact, suggested by the director. 'One rather needed to throw in this kind of contribution in exchange for concessions on the other side,' says Jonathan Miller. 'Some measure of give-and-take was essential; after all, at the beginning there was a real danger of Olivier shaping a too grotesque caricature, a full-blown hooked nose and all the rest. You can only go so far in seeking to restrain an actor of such stature and individual technique. He is so experienced at building up a strong characterization of his own design, and he is naturally wary of suggestions that seem to be incompatible with his own strong ideas.'

Predictably, critical opinion of that characterization is sharply divided. Michael Billington called this Shylock 'the best of its generation', especially because of its 'high intellectual power' and 'sheer interpretative originality'.[1] Richard Findlater thought it suffered to some extent from the implausibilities of the 1890s setting, 'yet in spite of that obstacle Olivier demonstrated once again the abyss that separates good acting from great acting, even when a great actor is below his summit'.[2] Herbert Kretzmer (*Daily Express*) was among critics who rated it less highly: 'Not even the genius of Sir Laurence Olivier can bring life sour of substance to Shylock . . . It is a performance of awesome technique, as one would expect, but it is lacking in both pity and truth.' And Harold Hobson (*Sunday Times*), whose profound admiration of Olivier goes back as far as *The Rats of Norway* (1933), was unusually blunt: 'Dancing with glee at Antonio's misfortunes, coming to court to cut off a pound of flesh with a briefcase more prominent than a knife, and after sentence apparently falling down stairs offstage, Sir Laurence will not be remembered for his Shylock. Or if he is, he will be singularly unlucky.'

Yet here again Olivier was running absolutely true to form. He had presented another fascinating demonstration of the actor's art; at the same time, he had given an interpretation that for some unyielding purists was too often at variance with the lines Shakespeare wrote. It was, needless to say, another overwhelming success in box-office terms, indeed a double Olivier triumph since Joan Plowright also came across effectively with a Portia of striking authority.

Shylock may never be rated among Sir Laurence's truly great characterizations. It was nevertheless one of his most important successes since it renewed his confidence at a crucial time. Joan Plowright recalled: 'On the opening night of *The Merchant of Venice*, Larry said, "I've got to have some tranquillizers, because if I don't have something, I'm going to walk out of that stage door and get on the first bus that comes." His reputation is so big and vast now that to have to live up to that . . . and when you're head of the National Theatre and you've got all those young actors looking up to you saying, show us the way . . . And then his roles always seem to have special moments that everybody's read about, and he fears terribly that he will dry up at those moments—or they won't be what people expected.'[3]

The stampede to the box-office set off by *The Merchant of Venice* proved conclusively that he had not lost any of his magnetic intensity. Indeed, at the time of its opening, both the Oliviers veritably glowed with realized ambition and recognized achievement. One month before, Lady Olivier had attended an investiture at Buckingham Palace, together with her husband

and their two older children, to receive the C.B.E.* Two months later, on June 13, 1970, Olivier and Dame Sybil Thorndike were exchanging congratulatory telegrams. At eighty-seven, she had been made a Companion of Honour in the Birthday Honours List. He, at sixty-three, was the first actor to be made a life peer. In social terms his honour was comparable to the knighthood conferred on Henry Irving in 1895, twelve years after Mr. Gladstone had wondered whether it would not be 'too audacious' to elevate the stage to such a level of respectability. Now, after forty-five years in what his grandmother had called 'that monstrous profession', Sir Laurence had cloaked the occupation of rogues and vagabonds in finest ermine.

At this point the National Theatre seemed well poised for a revival in its fortunes, and whether Olivier liked it or not this upsurge in the National's popular appeal owed more to his work on stage than off. Besides Shylock, he was due to reappear in *The Dance of Death*, and later in the year the new-style Lord Olivier was planning to take on the most unlordly role of Nathan Detroit, the crap-shooting king of the Brooklyn underworld in a revival of the 1950 hit musical *Guys and Dolls*. It promised to be the National's most refreshingly lighthearted and commercial production yet, directed by Garson Kanin, with Edward Woodward as Sky Masterson, Robert Lang as Nicely-Nicely Johnson and Geraldine McEwan as Miss Adelaide the night club canary. But it never happened. In August Sir Laurence was admitted to a London hospital following an attack of bronchial pneumonia. A few weeks later he suffered a mild thrombosis that ruled out any more stage appearances for the next few months.

Within a month he was back at his office desk, but now the Press openly asked: Has the final curtain fallen on one of the greatest acting careers? The actor, instinctively responding to a dramatic situation, told his audience of reporters: 'I cannot appear for about twelve months. I get puffed—too puffed to do an emotional scene or a long speech. Also, in the theatre an actor needs that little something extra—adrenalin perhaps, or heart— and just for the moment I haven't got it any more. For the first time in my life I'm having to accept the fact that there are roles I shall never be able to play. King Lear, for instance, which I've

* Maggie Smith was also awarded the C.B.E. in the New Year's Honours List.

had in mind for some time. It doesn't hurt an awful lot, because I don't really enjoy acting. I don't really know why. Perhaps one's sense of responsibility becomes exaggerated as one gets older. One gets more nervous. But, of course, when I'm told I can't do something, I start screaming.'

Fortunately, the actor was indulging himself histrionically. In fact, he would gently resume acting three months later, with the minutest of cameo roles in the film *Nicholas and Alexandra*. In the New Year he was to direct Giraudoux's *Amphitryon 38* with Christopher Plummer and Geraldine McEwan, and reappear as Shylock. Nevertheless, his illness could not have occurred at a more awkward time in the affairs of the National Theatre. The repertoire was in urgent need of major revision. Moreover, the company had taken on extra commitments, most notably the operating of a second theatre, the Cambridge.

The blow of losing Sir Laurence's services as an actor had been cushioned by news that Paul Scofield would be joining the National as an associate director and appearing in three plays in the 1970–71 season. But Scofield appeared in only two N.T. productions before taking his leave. It was one of many disappointments in a year of confusion at the National. By May 1971, the company was being subjected to an unprecedented wave of attacks in the Press. One national newspaper critic condemned its activities under the headline, PANNED, PAMPERED AND HALF-EMPTY; the theatre critic of a weekly magazine implied that the National was falling apart. The charges were many and varied, but basically they could be divided into three categories: (1) The choice of plays. The company was afraid of doing the obvious. Too many productions, especially of foreign plays, were 'curiosities' more suited to an experimental theatre, and the English classics were poorly represented. (2) The acting. There was inadequate ensemble playing by substandard actors poorly recruited, and the National had failed lamentably to attract actors of the highest class. (3) Box-office receipts. The company had received more public money (last year £260,000 from the Arts Council and £120,000 from the G.L.C.) than any other theatre, yet it had ended the past financial year with a deficit approaching £100,000. There were too many bad notices, too many bad nights when it did not even play to 800 people (ninety per cent of the Old Vic capacity).

The general view among the National's executives was that the present attack was rather out of date. So it was on current facts and figures. Unfortunately the worst was yet to come. In June the company ventured into the West End again, this time taking over the New with the idea of operating two theatres until it moved into the new N.T. buildings with three auditoriums. Those critics who had predicted that the move would lose the National money were proved absolutely right. In the West End the company made the fundamental error of ignoring the well-known need to cater to the tourist trade in summer. They put on plays unfamiliar to overseas visitors, staged productions without players well known abroad. Early in September, rather than lose more money, the N.T. board decided to withdraw from the New as soon as possible, and partly because of that disaster the Arts Council later made them a substantial supplementary grant.

This was the lowest ebb in the National's fortunes, and as Olivier witnessed four flops in succession, he was reminded of his experience in 1937 when the Old Vic's successful production of *Macbeth* was transferred to the West End and promptly ignored by the public. By November the situation was so grim that, for the first time, his leadership was questioned in the Press together with predictions that Peter Hall, former director of the Royal Shakespeare Company, would be taking over from him. No one, however, suspected for one moment that there was any possibility of Olivier's being replaced as director before the opening of the National on the South Bank.

Where had Olivier gone wrong? Kenneth Tynan, no longer literary manager (a post abolished in 1969) but now the National's chief literary consultant, denied that the reason for half-empty houses at the New was due to plays that were too highbrow. He denied, too, that top stars had left the company because they were not happy with the way they were being treated, and he argued that the loss of £50,000 for the year 1970–71 was hardly as catastrophic as some reports suggested. 'Our track record over the past eight years is better than that of any West End management. We had seven really great years and now we have had a bad year. I am only surprised that the slump didn't come sooner. There is nothing wrong with the National Theatre that a couple of hits will not put right.'

Tynan's conclusion proved absolutely correct. One month later Olivier returned to the West End in Michael Blakemore's unforgettable production of *Long Day's Journey Into Night*, and in this dreadnought's wake came a procession of solidly built vessels including Blakemore's revival of *The Front Page*, Jonathan Miller's production of *The School for Scandal* and Tom Stoppard's *Jumpers*. For the West End in general 1972 was an unmemorable year, so many theatres presenting shoddy goods dressed up (or more often undressed) to pander to the lowest popular tastes. For the National it was a year of distinction; and while many talents contributed to the revival in its fortunes, it was undeniably Olivier's personal triumph. All his genius as an actor, together with industry as an administrator, was called upon to spur the great upsurge in the quality of productions. It began with months of the most arduous preparation of Eugene O'Neill's modern classic—four weekly readings (an unusual procedure) before seven weeks of rehearsals, and when those rehearsals ended at five every afternoon Sir Laurence still had to attend to office chores as well as appear in *The Merchant of Venice*. Yet he succeeded in rising to his full height in the challenging role of James Tyrone, achieving a performance hailed by some critics as 'stupendous' and 'heart-stopping' and recognized by all as a work of extraordinary brilliance in technique. No less remarkably, he for once shaped a masterful portrayal without dwarfing all those around him. This production really was a triumph for teamwork, certainly no more a success for Sir Laurence than it was for Constance Cummings, who gave the performance of a lifetime as his morphine-addicted wife.

Olivier's Tyrone was admirably restrained until a titanic third act in which the actor opened up his full bag of tricks for a display of human emotions breathtaking in its range, riveting in its power and pathos. It won him his third *Evening Standard* Best Actor Drama Award. Most significantly (as an Irish-American in Connecticut) he won, via the video-tape film of the production, the top U.S. television award (Emmy) for the best single performance of the year. For the first time the small screen had done justice to one of his major roles in the theatre.

In recent years, however, it had seemingly become impossible for Olivier to satisfy all the critics at any one time, and even this now-legendary performance proved no exception. The first night (December 21, 1971) at the New Theatre earned him rapturous praise and, it must be noted, a surprising number of prickly notices, too. Robert Brustein (*The Observer*) disapproved of

Olivier's treatment of the part—'he attacked the elder Tyrone like a character in classical comedy, speaking the lines as if they were verse, and displaying ease only with the miserly side of the character'. Similarly, Frank Marcus (*Sunday Telegraph*) thought that Olivier came dangerously near to giving a comedy performance.

Was Sir Laurence, the 'comedian by instinct', a shade too self-indulgent in capturing the humour as well as the compassion and penny-pinching bigotry of a character trapped in an essentially tragic situation? Perhaps. But then inevitably, in portraying the miserly, guilt-ridden ex-actor, he was influenced by his own first-hand knowledge of the man. Just as he had been with Archie Rice. 'That chap wasn't a stranger to me at all,' he later explained, reflecting on childhood days when he used his father's bath-water and learned from him to carve a chicken in razor-thin slices. 'I didn't have to invent for his eccentricities. I knew them all. On the first night of the play I had a message from my darling lovely elder daughter (Tamsin, aged nine). She said, "Darling Daddy, now we know why you have been so strict about turning lights off at home. It's because you were practising for your play." It's just that I hate waste; petty economy, not sensible economy, is my sin.'[4]

Whether Olivier did, in fact, overplay the comic eccentricities is a question open to endless argument. Here, confessing to prejudice, I am content to put on record the judgment of one critic with whose opinions I heartily concur—Mr. Irving Wardle of the London *Times*:

Although Olivier's Tyrone is scaled down to the surrounding company, it is a performance of intense technical and personal fascination. Personal in the sense that James Tyrone was an actor with the kind of career which Olivier had spent his life avoiding: a strong young talent destroyed by years of imprisonment in profitable type casting. We see Tyrone at a stage where he is all too well aware of this; and the dejection that settles on Olivier's frame from the start—his body hunched and his mouth cracked into a small crooked line—expresses a sense of defeat that encompasses the whole of his life and not merely his family. There are touches of the old ham: as where he smugly intones a few of Prospero's lines and turns to his son in naked appeal for applause; and where Olivier pulls out a

pair of his own incomparable physical tricks in staging two
contrasted descents from a table. But what marks out this
performance most from the others is its breadth; all the com-
ponents of the man are there simultaneously—the tight-wad,
the old pro, the distracted husband, the ragged Irish boy—
and there is the sense not only that O'Neill is showing off the
different sides of the character, but that Olivier is consciously
manipulating them for his advantage.

From that opening of *Long Day's Journey Into Night* the graph
of the National Theatre's fortunes registered a sharp upward rise
that was to be sustained throughout the following year, when it
had record takings, enabling it to clear the financial deficit of
some £150,000 carried forward from the year before. The so-
called 'bad patch' was over; the signs indicated a healthy
strengthening of the company and its repertoire in preparation
for the South Bank opening. Yet, ironically, it was in the spring
of this year of revival that positive moves were made towards
choosing a successor to the main architect of the National's
success.

It was supposed to be confidential, but within the profession
most everyone had heard the rumour that Peter Hall would be
replacing Olivier at the end of 1972. Inevitably this rumour
became embroidered by actors in the retelling, dramatized in
terms of Ides of March treachery and boardroom intrigue, and it
took such firm root that Olivier called a meeting of sixty members of the company in the Old Vic's rehearsal room and reassured them that there was no question of his leaving before
they moved into the new buildings in 1974. On April 13 the
board issued an official statement to the same effect. They were
considering a successor in consultation with Olivier, but this was
strictly a far-sighted measure. Productions needed to be planned
more than a year in advance and so it was desirable that a successor should be consulted from the summer of 1972 onwards and
phased in gradually. He would certainly not take over as director
before the theatre made its long-awaited move.

In principle, this was both sensible and proper. In practice,
however, it proved wholly unfortunate for Olivier. Throughout
his years in office he had been frustrated again and again by
building delays, and in the end those delays denied his ambition
to lead the company into its luxurious and monumental new

home. By the end of 1972 it was obvious that the building would never be ready in time for the 1974 transfer. Mid-1975 was the new forecast. Olivier, on completion of a second five-year contract, was virtually compelled by circumstances to step down in favour of the director-designate.

On April 1, 1973, Hall arrived as co-director prior to assuming full directorial responsibility in November. Lord Olivier had led the most taxing of positions in the theatre for a whole decade. 'Time has marched on a bit,' he explained. 'Some of us feel the cliff-hang a bit of a strain. Also, it was reducing the glory, the pride and the term of office of Peter Hall, who could lose two and a half years of his five-year contract in the waiting.' It was an exit made with grace and dignity; his successor replied with a heart-stirring tribute, spoke humbly of being 'a caretaker for him until the new theatre is ready'. Yet the sense of an elegy remained—as though a famous Hamlet had been replaced by a brilliant understudy at the start of the climactic Act V.

In dramatic terms the summer of 1971 may be seen as the turning point in Olivier's reign at the National. In July of that disastrous season he had offered his resignation to Sir Max Rayne, the new chairman of the N.T. board. His offer was not taken seriously. At this time, however, Lord Goodman, chairman of the Arts Council, first 'sounded out' Mr. Hall, and in late 1971 the former Royal Shakespeare Company director had his first contact with the N.T. board. However tentative these discussions, it meant that the process of finding a successor had been set in motion *before* Olivier so impressively forged a revival in the National's fortunes. But the politics behind the change in leadership are of no great consequence. Time and the uncertain pace of building the South Bank complex were always heavily loaded against Lord Olivier; the longer the delays, the more pressing became the need to think in terms of a younger man for the job. When he finally relinquished his post as director he was sixty-six, his successor, a boyish-looking forty-two.

Fortunately, there was no sense of finality about Olivier's departure from the National; indeed, the end seemed more like a beginning since his last day as director coincided with the first night of Eduardo de Filippo's *Saturday, Sunday, Monday*, another National hit. He had only a minor part—the mischievous grandfather possessed of a kleptomanic obsession with hats—but his study of a retired hatter on the brink of senility was so artfully devised that even without lines to speak he held the eye as surely as Chaplin in a silent movie, a gentle reminder of the fact (so heavily obscured by identification with great tragic roles) that this actor is, above all else, a born comedian.

It was a reminder, too, that here was one kind of role he could never play in life. No gold watch and pension for him, no autumn of leisure in which to indulge that old enemy, nostalgia. He would see his years of service recorded for posterity in the naming of the National's largest auditorium, an intimate, open-stage 1,165 seater of ingenious design. But he would not retire. 'After all, what would I do?' he once asked. 'Dig my garden? Play golf? That's not for me. As long as I can stand, I will do my job.' It was the only way of life he knew or ever really wanted to know.

★
Post Mortem

        When Noel Coward and Binkie Beaumont
died within days of one another, the lights of Shaftesbury
Avenue were dimmed in their honour and theatre scribes wrote
finis to an era of refined and glossy drama. It was March 1973.
Arguably that era of refinement had already ended, its fate
merely sealed by the passing of a staccato-tongued genius of
consummate style and a theatrical entrepreneur of unrivalled
flair. Nevertheless, the sense of a closed chapter in the history of
the English theatre was immediate; and that feeling of an era's
end was reinforced in a year when a trio of knights (Olivier,
Clements, Daubeney) retired from the National, from Chichester
and from the World Theatre Season. A new generation had come
to the fore, in a theatre far removed from the glamorous West
End that Olivier had known in the Twenties. Revivals apart, this
was a radically different scene, transformed by a mid-century
social revolution, by freedom from the Lord Chamberlain's blue
pencil, and not least by rocketing production costs that pro-
hibited a Basil Dean from daring to mount a succession of
spectaculars and that encouraged commercial managements to
stage spicy, low-budget trivia.
    Among the myriad changes, for better and for worse, none was
more dramatic or ironic than the immediate transformation
brought about by the abolition, in 1968, of the Lord Chamberlain's power to censor plays. How much it changed the climate
was illustrated by the last production to be prepared during
Olivier's reign at the National: Trevor Griffiths' *The Party*, in
which he effectively played John Tagg, a sixty-year-old Glas-
wegian Trotskyist. This political play opened with a naked
couple copulating in a luxurious bed in the centre of the Old Vic
stage, and furthermore, lest the well-to-do customers in the stalls
should miss the voyeuristic treats available to those in the

gallery, a slanted mirror was strategically placed above and behind the performing pair. The scene aroused not a whiff of controversy. Yet it is easy to imagine the squall of scandal that would have been puffed up if Olivier and Tynan had proposed to stage such natural goings-on only four or five years before!

In 1969, when Tynan was demoted from literary manager, the late Lord Chandos, undoubtedly thinking of *Oh! Calcutta!* said: 'As a consultant he will be free to pursue his interests as an impresario without embarrassing the National Theatre.' Where was the embarrassment now? In 1970 a Tory M.P. (Mr. John Biggs-Davison) tabled a motion calling on the Commons to condemn *Oh! Calcutta!* as 'an insult to human dignity and a disgrace to London' and recommending that Tynan should leave the National Theatre and any other cultural enterprises receiving taxpayers' money. The following year saw the Young Vic treating the kiddies to a production of *Byron—The Naked Peacock*— with sodomy as its theme.

Enter Peter Hall. In May 1974 he revealed his programme for the next ten months in the run-up to opening on the South Bank. The first play on his list was Wedekind's *Spring Awakening*, relating to the problems of adolescents struggling to cope with the onset of sexual awareness and including a masturbation scene. It was the same play that the old N.T. board had prevented Olivier from staging prior to their ban on *Soldiers*. How did Hall get it past the new-formed board? The answer was that he didn't have to. He was restricted only in the sense that, like any hired hand, he could be sacked any time he overstepped the mark in courting his bosses' displeasure.

It was Olivier's misfortune to be the first and last director of the National Theatre to carry shackles before the general amnesty was granted. Like Olivier, Hall was also to 'feel the cliff-hang' as the grand opening was postponed again and again, but never did he experience the artistic restrictions imposed on his predecessor, and he enjoyed far greater financial freedom as he prepared to inherit the South Bank complex that he describes as 'the most extraordinary bombshell to hit the English theatre since the Globe'. Thus, comparisons between the Olivier and Hall regimes are largely meaningless, if not invidious.

The commonest charge levelled against Olivier is that his unchallenged pre-eminence tended to make the National Theatre a one-man band, too far an actor-manager's company, and that the box-office was subsequently too dependent on the magnetism of his name. Confronted with that charge in May 1971, he replied: 'I have had only six real parts out of our fifty-odd productions. Some of our best successes have been with the company, that is without well-known stars, for examples, *Rosencrantz*, *The Royal Hunt*, *A Flea in Her Ear*, *The Three Sisters* and *The National Health*. I have tried desperately to create an ensemble. It is no use basing your company on stars; it has been tried often in the past. In three years you always run out of stars.'

By the end of his ten-year reign he could make this point even more strongly; his total score was only seven significant parts—in *Uncle Vanya*, *The Recruiting Officer*, *Othello*, *The Master Builder*, *The Dance of Death*, *The Merchant of Venice* and *Long Day's Journey Into Night*.* Nevertheless, that list represented a very sizeable helping of the cream, including N.T. productions that could have played to capacity houses *ad infinitum*. In only one of them (*Uncle Vanya*) did he ever share the National stage with an actor approaching his own stature.

Where were the other giants of the English stage? Richardson and Guinness never appeared at the National during the Olivier administration. Redgrave played in four productions. Albert Finney in five, Gielgud and Scofield in two, but not one of these stars remained with the company for any appreciable length of time. But then this was not a situation peculiar to the N.T. There was no company in Britain able to hold on to players of such calibre in the face of the powerful inducements from films and television and the West End.

It is a fact of life that more people go to the theatre to see players than to see plays. Olivier recognized this as much as anyone, but idealistically he hoped in his years at the National to take a major step forward towards encouraging in the public an urge to see drama for drama's sake. Discussing the unity of a permanent ensemble, he said, 'Ultimately it is more important to an audience than the star system, though goodness knows how many years it's going to take us to make that clear to them.'[1] At his first press conference as director he suggested it might take forty or fifty years to make the company what it should be. Six years later, in July 1969, he accepted that his present ensemble

---

* Seventy productions were presented during Olivier's ten-year reign at the National. He appeared in nine, directed eight.

was not yet perfect, admitted that it was not easy to recruit or keep the established middle-aged player of less than star quality who might be chary of eager young directors and attracted by television fees. But he had not abandoned his main objective. 'I am still determined that the one drawing power at the National shall be the company, as with the Moscow Arts in its heyday. If you can get that reputation, that is the healthiest thing you can have in the theatre. When you have got that reputation you can put in some stars, but it is the ensemble which is the all-important thing.'

A high-minded objective, but whether it was realistic or even correct is fiercely debatable, depending on what one imagines the primary purposes of a National Theatre to be. Some N.T. productions did enjoy enormous success without marked dependence on star names. But not one of these rivalled the excitement and interest aroused by such Olivier showpieces as *Othello* and *The Dance of Death*. The crowds were not merely flocking to see Olivier for Olivier's sake, but to see acting on the grand scale—a scale that was never possible on the small screen in their homes. Confronted with a choice between the sheer thrill of seeing great actors stretched to their dramatic limits and the satisfaction of seeing drama precisely presented by a solid, totally professional cast without stars, the great bulk of theatregoers would surely opt for the former. Ideally, of course, one would wish for the best of both worlds. This was achieved in some productions at the National but by no means as often as one would have liked.

In retrospect, it seems inevitable that Olivier should have fallen between these two stools—the creation of an actor-manager's company and the encouragement of ensemble playing. He was resisting the star system, but he was himself the theatre's greatest star. In a sense he was striving to create at the National the kind of ensemble into which he himself could not fit.

In some ways, too, Olivier was the victim of the system he had contracted to establish. The whole concept of a permanent company with an ever-expanding repertoire created for him problems he had never faced as an old-style actor-manager. For example, while new productions were being prepared, the company was also bringing back successful old ones and this involved continual recasting and rehearsing, with returning players having to readjust their performances in relation to new-comers. Geraldine McEwan recalled: 'I was in *A Flea in Her Ear* for five years, and I think we must have rehearsed it almost more than we played it, with all the changes of cast. It would be nice if they could work it that when a production was a great success, after a time you could have a complete cast change. Unfortunately, it all comes down to a question of money in the end.' In fact, most of Olivier's problems boiled down to a shortage of money.

The repertory system had another drawback: it made it more difficult to encourage successful native playwrights—an obviously desirable function for a national theatre. As Peter Nichols (*The National Health*) observed, 'If you have an enormously successful play like *Saturday, Sunday, Monday* which is doing incredible business at present, is it sensible to take it off to make room for other plays in repertory?' By the same token, not every leading playwright was likely to be attracted by the distinction of having a hit at the National where it might be given two or three performances a week, as opposed to a long, uninterrupted run, producing far bigger royalties, elsewhere.

This does not, of course, answer the broad criticisms that were made of Olivier's choice of plays, and it is true that his judgment of unfamiliar works could be decidedly suspect at times. In the circumstances, Olivier was right to acquire a literary manager. Whether Tynan was the right man for the job is an entirely different matter, a question that has aroused more bitter argument than perhaps any other aspect of Olivier's reign at the National.

No one has been more outspoken on this question than John Osborne. In 1973 he talked of the 'disastrous influence' of Kenneth Tynan as follows: 'Whatever his qualities as a writer and a critic, he has, I think, absolutely the wrong attitude to running a theatre. It's a sort of intellectual spivery that Olivier mistakes for up-to-date awareness and flair. He's so afraid of being thought old-hat that he's allowed himself to be sadly misguided by Tynan.'[2] Osborne, however, cannot be considered an impartial witness; he made his prejudice abundantly clear as long ago as 1960, three years before Olivier and Tynan went to work. He then declared: 'The suggestion of creating a so-called National Theatre is like building a theatrical Albert Memorial. If it is ever built, I only hope someone sets fire to it.'

On the other side, we have Tynan's reply in a letter to the *Sunday Times*: 'What can I do but point to the record? And the record of the National reveals a higher percentage of critical and popular successes over a ten-year period than any other British theatre company in history has ever achieved (except perhaps Shakespeare's Globe, for which I have no attendance figures).' Of course, there were mistakes. After the 1967 peak Tynan arguably promoted too many obscure works and over-encouraged the import of plays from abroad, together with foreign guest directors. But the early achievements of his partnership with Olivier were undeniably great: in four years they saw the National firmly established as a living theatre, eclectic and empirical in its policy, and never in danger, as originally feared, of becoming a cultural mausoleum.

At the beginning Sir Laurence pledged himself to 'strive to my utmost to lay the foundation of a National Theatre that will finally justify its long wait for existence and be a source of pride to my profession and to the country as a whole'. He fulfilled that pledge. Sir Michael Redgrave has expressed the view that no other man in the country could have done the job. Just how well he had done it, however, was not fully appreciated until after he left. Then, with the passing of time, it became evident that the National (temporarily at least) had lost a large measure of its glitter. It developed into a greater hive of artistic activity, but somehow it was a much duller and less prestigious place without the excitement and inspiration generated by his presence.

On leaving the National, perhaps with a hint of wistfulness, he said, 'I am really quite happy to go. I have done the job. Whether it is good or bad I could not tell you yet; only life will tell. I look forward to a little lull, then no doubt something will turn up that I am bound to feel responsible about. Although I am dreading the depression that is almost bound to come upon a retirement, a few sneaking advantages are beginning to show their dainty little heads through the window.'[3]

But there really was no need of sadness on his abdication. This compulsive worker was now free to concentrate on the work he did best, and the advantages that showed were anything but dainty. One showed immediately as he thundered back to the cinema's front rank with his devastating portrayal of detective-writer Andrew Wyke in Anthony Shaffer's *Sleuth*—his first screen triumph outside the classics since leaving Hollywood in 1941. It won him the Best Actor Award from the New York critics in competition with Peter O'Toole, Burt Lancaster,

Marlon Brando and James Mason, and Best Actor Oscar nomi-
nations for both himself and film partner Michael Caine.

Sleuth was an important success for Olivier. It ended his procession of trivial cameo roles on the screen and served as a timely
reminder to millions who could never see him at the National
that here was an actor of still unrivalled virtuosity. It demonstrated again his meticulous attention to detail, and, above all, his
intuitive sense of comedy. Here was a role perfectly orchestrated
for his special talents, one that allowed him to plunge his gifts of
mimicry up to the hilt, skipping with imperceptible effort through
a bewildering assortment of impersonations—here a sheriff in
a Western, now a Fu Manchu character, suddenly a Cockney
charlady. He could be comic one moment, sinister the next; he
could jest, rage, tease, quiver with fright, be waspish, cruel,
devious, sternly masculine, fastidiously feminine. In romping
through this actor's decathlon he set a record in versatility that
seemed far out of reach, and even in silence, whether preparing
himself a caviare snack or skilfully manipulating a snooker cue,
he brought a stylish realism to every gesture that was always
fascinating to behold. Director Joseph L. Mankiewicz, in forty
distinguished years of film-making, said he had seen nothing to
equal this actor's 'Comstock Lode of experience'.

In playing the gloriously theatrical Wyke, Olivier indulged in a
rare flight of nostalgia. Amid the vast conglomeration of props on
the set of *Sleuth*, the observant cinemagoer could spot concrete
relics of his far-distant past—snaps of old screen colleagues
Douglas Fairbanks, Jr., and Leslie Howard, photographs on
Wyke's desk and around the walls of the young 'Larry O'
posing with Gertrude Lawrence, Noel Coward, Maurice
Chevalier, Jean Harlow, and (a fitting touch) Agatha Christie.
And two years later more memories of his pre-war Hollywood
days were to flood back as he found himself at Pinewood, working
for the first time with two of his oldest friends, Katharine Hepburn and veteran director George Cukor, filming *Love Among the
Ruins* for American television.

Anatomy of an Actor

The growth of your career should be like that of a tree, a simple, steady, all-round growth. You are now about, I hope, to sink your roots deep into the fertile ground of this institution, in order to assure yourselves of as strong a stem as possible, so that however gloriously your branches may flourish they shall not want for resourcefulness and poise. There is plenty of wind, torrents of rain and no end of thunder about, so don't get too tall too quickly. There is no more invidious state in a career than that in which one finds one's reputation outgrowing one's experience . . . All I ask, as an audience, is to believe what I see and hear. An actor, above all, must be the great understander, either by intuition, observation or both, and that puts him on the level with a doctor, a priest or a philosopher. If I can get more from him than just belief, then I feel both fortunate and overjoyed . . . there are many dimensions in the art of acting, but NONE of them . . . are good or interesting . . . unless they are invested with the appearance, or complete illusion of truth. The difference between the actual truth and the illusion of the truth is what you are about to learn. You will not finish learning it until you are dead.

Those words were spoken by Laurence Olivier in January 1947, when addressing drama students at the ceremonial opening of the Old Vic School. Since then, in the husbandry of his own career, he has practised what he preached supremely well—an evergreen achieving the strength of an oak, the stature and durability of giant sequoia.

Dedication has probably been the single most important key to his spectacular growth, and what makes this dedication so remarkable is the fact that, in a strange way, acting for him is rather more a labour of duty than a labour of love. Noel Coward said, 'In acting I give pleasure to myself and to the audience—in that order.' Olivier says: 'For me, this is simply not true. If I don't give pleasure to the audience it's just a waste of time. I very rarely give pleasure to myself. It's something to do with the distrust of pleasure in me. A puritan streak. It could be that because I am playing painfully arduous roles I find enjoyment of them very difficult. I challenge anyone to *enjoy* acting Othello. Don't think, though, that because I rarely *enjoy* acting I do it against the grain. Acting is natural for me; a task, a yoke that I have learned to love and work under. I could not live without it . . .'[1]

What else explains Olivier's pre-eminence in the theatrical profession? What qualities, emotional, intellectual and physical, have gone into the making of the most distinguished actor of this century? In writing about Olivier's Othello, Kenneth Tynan listed seven attributes of greatness: 'complete physical relaxation, powerful physical magnetism, commanding eyes that are visible at the back of the gallery, a commanding voice that is audible *without effort* at the back of the gallery, superb timing which includes the capacity to make verse swing, *chutzpah*—the untranslatable Jewish word that means cool nerve and outrageous effrontery combined—and the ability to communicate a sense of danger'.[2] Except that Tynan omits sharp interpretative intelligence, the list sums up the *basic* strengths of Olivier rather well. But considerably more may be said.

Let us, then, examine the strengths of this actor in greater depth, while recognizing at the outset that everything about great art may be analysed *except* the quality that makes it great. In discussing the attributes of Olivier's art—whether the small hard points of technique or such larger and more elusive matters as feeling and perception—we can only enter the antechamber to a mystery. Beyond lies something magical, something that can be known but not defined.* Still the effort to understand is worthwhile even if only to bring us in proximity to the truth. The catalogue that follows is the result of my efforts to comprehend exactly *why* Olivier is the greatest of actors.

* In her autobiography *On Reflection*, Helen Hayes retells the story of how Olivier, as Othello, gave one performance that transcended all others. His fellow actors were stunned by it, recognizing true genius at work. They were accustomed to being thrilled by his playing, but this was something else. As he made his way to the dressing room, with the audience still cheering, they formed two lines either side of the

COURAGE. Of all the personal qualities that have contributed to the making of Olivier the legend, courage rates highest by far—not the physical courage needed to perform reckless acrobatic feats, but courage in consistently backing his own judgment and never taking the surest and safest way ahead. The courage, when dreading first-night examination by the critics, to defy the purists and play a classical role against the traditional grain. The courage, when also playing the leading role, to plunge into grand-scale film direction. The courage, when stamina and powers of memory are diminished, to tackle a gigantic, nerve-devouring role like Othello and then play it in the boldest, most blazingly individual style imaginable.

Ralph Richardson has described an actor tackling great classical roles as being rather like a jockey. 'You know you have a famous horse which many great jockeys have ridden. You make all possible preparations, but then there is always a twenty-five per cent chance that you won't get it over the jumps. You know that and you are frightened. What makes you a professional is that you are used to being afraid. You accept fear.' Olivier not only accepted the fear, he also greatly increased the risks.

Without this boldness and originality, Olivier would never have become the unique theatrical star that he is today. Courageous individuality is a hallmark of genius and what distinguishes the true immortals of the stage. Kean was much the same: an audacious Iago bestowed with a worldliness that shocked the traditionalists, a black-wigged Shylock daringly projected as a human character rather than a cruel caricature. He was sometimes savaged for displaying a marked disregard for the text; so, too, was Irving. Critic Henry Arthur Jones referred to Irving's 'frequent habit and method . . . of getting his greatest effects not in, and by, the text and obvious meaning of his author, but in his own extraneous bits of business'.

Similarly with Olivier. At risk of being crucified by the critics he has been unpredictable in his interpretations, but invariably clear-cut in his definitions—the strongest Hamlet, the proudest

---

passage and applauded him all the way. He swept past in silence and slammed the door behind him. Someone knocked and asked, 'What's the matter, Larry? It was great!' He growled back loudly: 'I know it was great, damn it, but I don't know how I did it. So how can I be sure I can do it again.'

Coriolanus, the most anguished Macbeth, the most demonic Richard III, the most coal-black negroid Othello. Always he has given the critics something positive in his performances to describe, and though he has been severely mauled, he has never been ignored. His success supports every cliché ever coined about attack being the best form of defence and fortune favouring the brave.

INTUITION. Olivier's career has very largely been played out in the spirit of a high-stakes professional punter who scorns the obvious favourite and goes boldly for the long shot—with the prospect of high reward for success and no great disgrace in failure. Like the big-time gambler he must rely to a degree on intuition, and in his case, excepting a few disasters such as his 1940 *Romeo and Juliet*, that intuition has been uncommonly sound when it really matters. He has this gift for timeliness. As he once explained: 'The real impulse behind *Henry V*, filmed during the war, was to make a patriotic picture. With *Richard III*, the impulse was to suit the audience of the day by showing a paranoia with something Hitlerian in it.' Years later he was quick to respond to the changing climate by appearing in plays by Osborne and Ionesco. He never became an anachronism like Sir Donald Wolfit, that great virtuoso and dazzling soloist who remained out of fashion for the greater part of his career. For the most part Olivier has displayed an acutely developed instinct for divining in what direction the theatre was moving, and has possessed the courage to act upon it accordingly.

SHOWMANSHIP. That ability to keep up with, and very often ahead of, the times has enabled Olivier to avoid what he has always dreaded most—becoming 'old hat'. Equally, his durability rests on his acute sense of showmanship. This shows most obviously in his penchant for striking physical effects: his complete somersault down a staircase as the dying Coriolanus and, in a later production being suspended from the ankles in a Mussolini-style death, his writhing on the floor as a cripple in *The Ringmaster*, his epileptic fit in *Othello*, and so many memorable inventions. Even in his sixties he could not resist introducing some applause-winning physical feat: his mounting of a table in the last act of *Long Day's Journey Into Night* and then light-footedly stepping backwards to land gracefully on his toes.

The primary purpose of Olivier's showmanship is to surprise and astound, to keep an audience ever-alert, never relaxing into a semi-limbo of looking and listening in the unconscious belief that they know the shape of things to come. His method is as much vocal as physical. What makes a great actor? he was once asked. 'The trick of making the audience think you're good,' he replied. 'Yvonne Printemps told me years ago of the advice Chaliapin gave her: "Never do what the audience expected." Always be anticipating what the audience are expecting and don't do it . . . Yes, there's a certain amount of showmanship, though that's easier said than done . . . I rely greatly on rhythm. I think that is one thing I understand—the exploitation of rhythm, change of speed, change of time, change of expression, change of pace in crossing the stage. Keep the audience surprised, shout when they're not expecting it, keep them on their toes—change from minute to minute. And you have to study when you must put in your attack—at this point in this scene, at this point in this act: where is the weak link in this part of the author's chain? . . . What is the main problem of the actor? It is to keep the audience awake, and not let them go to sleep, then wake up and go home feeling they've wasted their money.'[3]

THE VOICE. Many times it has been said that Olivier cannot speak verse, that he has no sense of the architectural structure of long speeches. Others argue that he speaks verse more finely than any other actor. He has a capacity to seize on a single phrase in which he perceives the essence of emotion, to isolate it and, by subtle change of pace and tone, make it instantly light a torch of appreciation that plunges deep into the inner ear and illuminates a whole world of experience and feeling—for example, his 'troops of friends' in *Macbeth,* a telling chord so artfully struck as to make incomparably poignant the tragedy of a lifetime passed without love. As Coleridge said of Kean, to see him can be 'to read Shakespeare by flashes of lightning'.

At the same time it is true that he tends to gabble some of the longer speeches in Shakespeare where the melody has more importance than the meaning, and he has confessed to feeling unsure of himself in lyrical parts. ('Again, it's this old conflict between the Real and the Beautiful. I didn't really believe Keats when he said Beauty is Truth, Truth Beauty. And I've only been sure of myself in trying to play what is real. I would like to have been able to play the lyrical roles with more self-confidence; then I would have played them better. Though I think I can tell other people how to do it. I think I'm associated more with trumpets than with strings.'[4])

But the fact that Olivier has been accused of lacking poetry does not significantly diminish his stature as an actor. After all, the same charge was often made against Irving and Kean in their time. Other voices in the theatre are far more mellifluous; none is more expressive and flexible and distinctive. Tyrone Guthrie captured the transcendent qualities of the Olivier voice when he wrote:

He had been severely faulted by the drama critics for what they regarded as bad verse-speaking. I thought he spoke with marvellous clarity, energy and variety. What more can you want? He has, it is true a tendency to rant; to make rather exaggerated contrasts of pace, pitch and volume. But these were excesses of ardent, youthful temperament. Time would cure them. And, anyway, how rare it is to hear someone who really can blow up a storm, whose voice explodes like a bomb, crashes like breaking glass, screams like a macaw ... I will confess that to me the Voice Beautiful is all too often the Voice Dull. Laurence Olivier is never dull. The voice, however, has more the quality of brass than that of strings. And even now, after many years of intense cultivation and ceaseless practice, it is the vigour and brilliance of his tone that impresses. Sweetness does not come so easily. I have never been able to understand those critics who are not aware of the immense musicality that infuses all his performances—a rare sensitivity to rhythm, colour, phrasing, pace and pitch.[5]

Olivier has treated his voice as an instrument, never regarding it as an organ with only one stop, but constantly working on it to vary the tone and extend the range, so enabling him to achieve the bird-like trill of Mr. Justice Shallow or the *basso profundo* of Othello; and in playing on this instrument, what Trewin called a 'darting, searching, twisting blade', he has made his own kind of music without great regard for traditional form.

'What strikes me most about him,' says Athene Seyler, 'is that he so effectively combines the visual effect and the vocal effect to make his whole performance. Now I can think of two famous actors whose performances would be quite intelligible and almost as beautiful—one if you couldn't see him, the other if you couldn't hear him. But Larry—everything he does compliments his use of his voice. Yet he hasn't got a very beautiful voice at all. He's got that curious Olivier shout at the end of a line. But no matter. I remember my husband (the late Nicholas Hannen) saying to him once over the Crispin speech, "Larry, why do you send your voice up in this shout at the end?" And Larry thought for a moment and then said, "*It's me*." And that was the real answer, what he really feels, and that's how it must come out.'

'He was the first actor to bring in the rising inflection at the end of a line,' says Paul Hardwick. 'Not the shout, but simply going up at the end of a line and so making the next line sound more interesting. If you get a long, dull speech—like the first Claudius speech, "Though yet of Hamlet our dear brother's death the memory be green"—and go down at the end of the lines, it all sounds very boring. But if the actor takes a rising inflection you're kidded into thinking something interesting has been said, that something exciting is going on. Larry was one of the great exponents of that technique.'

'At drama school,' says Michael Jayston, 'we used to do the "Once more unto the breach" to a strict vocal pattern. Now Olivier breaks all the rules we were taught in saying that speech. He does it like an aria, and the way he moves up and down the scale is, strictly speaking, all wrong. If you try to do it his way it sounds bad. Yet somehow he makes it sound the most effective way to do it. He's like that in his approach to so many things; he tends to go for what is most interesting and exciting, and he will quite happily break up a rhythm in the process. It ties in, too, with his habit of aiming to be different, to do the unexpected. In *Nicholas and Alexandra*, for example, everyone said, "Sar". He said, "Ts-Sar". And it sounded great.'

Olivier once said that, as an actor, he would rather lose his voice or his arms than his eyes. The fact remains that when the final curtain has fallen it is his incomparable voice that lingers on, a capacity to strike unique chords that once heard are never forgotten. The impression he stamps on the mind's ear may owe something to gimmickry—the 'w-w-worms' stutter of Hotspur, the socially inhibiting accent of Malvolio ('Some have gweatness thwust upon them'). It may come through his supremely distinctive delivery of a single line, the crescendo roar of 'Cry "God for Harry, England, and Saint George"'. It may stem from ability to seize even on a single word and impale it upon one's memory—in *The Party*: 'You bite the hand that feeds you, but you'll never bite it OFF.' It may arise from an elemental sound—his harrowing, sobbing moan as James Tyrone, his dreadful animal howl as Oedipus. But what matters is that the impression is indelible, everlasting; and so many of his performances are definitive in the sense that actors preparing for Othello or Richard III or whatever have, whether they like it or not, Olivier's own interpretation echoing in a back chamber of their minds.

The voice of Olivier will be imitated for as long as there are actors. It will be remembered for its power and strength, its subtlety and range, and perhaps not least for its menace—such menace that one almost pitied the cowardly sneak-thief who invaded the actor's Brighton home in 1973 and was pursued by an injured Olivier brandishing his *Long Day's Journey* drama award and roaring for the intruder to come back. ('He had the full benefit of my most heavy invective, but I'm afraid he ignored me and carried on running. I can't blame him.') Olivier has always appreciated the capabilities of his most powerful weapon. He has exploited them to maximum possible effect.

OPTIC POWER. The eyes come a close second after the voice as the most vital part of the actor's equipment. When his vocal cords were gone, Jack Hawkins could still command attention and convey feeling through highly expressive eyes—the one organ that speaks volumes in silence and transmits emotion as profoundly as words. Olivier, like any true professional, has taken pains to develop his range of optic expressiveness—the wide-eyed horror of Titus, the narrow-eyed plotting of Crookback, the eyeball-rolling of Othello, the glint-eyed randiness of Shallow. He has, as Tynan demands of the great actor, commanding eyes that are visible at the back of the gallery. Characteristically, however, he did not rest content with wide-ranging use of the eyes as nature intended. He went still further and learned to dilate and undilate them. Kean, renowned for his brilliant use of the eyes, possessed this ability—'his eyes dilate and then lose lustre', wrote Leigh Hunt of his death in *Hamlet*. In the same way, Peter Glenville, who directed Olivier in *Becket* and *Term of Trial*, has remarked on the extraordinary effect he achieves by 'a sort of tragic anaesthetization of feeling when the eyes go balefully dead'.[6] Jayston is more specific. 'He can dilate and undilate the pupils of his eyes in a second. I've tried it—and you can do it by looking into a mirror, into the distance, and then looking back again. But he can do it at any time and at will. It's a marvellous effect—for example, when you're getting angry —and though it wouldn't mean anything on stage it is a very useful device on film. I've never seen anybody else do it. Also I've noticed that the pupils of Olivier's eyes are bigger than most people's; they seem about half as much again.'[3]

PHYSICAL FITNESS. Through his uncompromising quest for realism and his delight in extravagant physical effect, Olivier has sustained a catalogue of injuries unequalled in show business except by stuntmen and circus artists who make danger their business. That catalogue includes a full-thrust sword wound in the breast as Hamlet, untold sword slashes about the hands and arms and head, innumerable falls from horses including being thrown headlong into a lake, a broken ankle in *Theatre Royal*, a torn calf muscle in *The Beggar's Opera*, an arrow between his shinbones when filming *Richard III*, a torn cartilage as Crook-back on stage and an electric shock through a scimitar entering a studio dimmer. Only luck saved him from more serious injury when he dived into a net on the filming of *Fire Over England* or when he was left hanging by one hand from a piano wire some forty feet above the stage in *The Critic*. Unlike Gielgud, who suffered agonies simply learning to hammer a nail into his ark as Noah, who even had difficulties with the billiards scene in *The Cherry Orchard*, Sir Laurence has always responded readily to any physical endeavour—not because he is a natural athlete, but because he has always recognized a measure of athleticism as being essential for the truly protean actor. As a young man, Irving, the first actor-knight, showed all the dedication of a professional athlete in his regimen of daily exercises to condition his body for speed, strength and endurance. The first actor-peer followed his example. He wanted the ability to achieve Fair-banks-style physical effects, and later maximum lung power and stamina for playing great roles.

Physical glamour rather than fitness was his original aim. Reasonably handsome good looks, though not an essential for star status, are obviously a major asset, something that virtually all the giants of the English stage have had in common. So Olivier, starting out as a beetle-browed youth of frail physique, worked purposefully to improve his appearance. He was thirty-eight before he was prepared to venture on stage (as Oedipus) in tights without padding, but there was never a time when he was prepared to admit to physical limitations in giving a performance and he actually rejoiced in injuries that enhanced his reputation for stiff-lipped gallantry. It was physical self-discipline that made possible so much athletic business that arrested the eye; in later years—by weekly gym workouts, weight-lifting and training runs —it enabled him to work on with astonishing vigour after a series of strength-sapping illnesses that might otherwise have compelled him to retire. More generally, he has always needed a strong physical constitution to keep pace with his extraordinary creative energies. As John Laurie observes: 'You couldn't stretch that man too far, and the further he was stretched the better he was. That is why his films were so good. He was a man who demanded to be used to the full. He wants to be stretched. He's unique.'

PHYSICAL PRESENCE. Olivier's performances have so often been much larger than life that one expects to confront a veritable giant in the flesh. In fact, he stands only an average five foot, ten inches. Like Garrick and Kean, midgets by comparison, he has the stage ability to make himself appear tall or short at will, and not only bigger but stronger. And in a manner shared by very few of his contemporaries he can rivet an audience merely with his physical presence, whether projecting the strength of the virile warrior, the strength of a Hercules in chains, or strength weighed down by disillusionment and failure.

During a B.B.C. interview, Gielgud recalled Olivier's fundamental physical presence when playing his controversial Romeo in 1935. 'I remember Ralph Richardson saying to me, "When he stands under the balcony you know the whole character of Romeo in a moment because the pose he takes is so natural, so light, so animally correct, that you feel the whole quality of Italy and of the character of Romeo and of Shakespeare's impulse." That is an extraordinarily true criticism of his performance, and everything he does is based on that assumption: it gives him enormous power to be able to make his body obey him so well that he can almost characterize straight away.' So with his Othello; his assuming of both sinew and soul of a Negro was so much more than a transformation achieved by hours of painstaking make-up and practised movements. The frame as well as the canvas was reshaped, with a God-given impersonative skill most stunningly demonstrated in those Old Vic years, with his outrageous double bill of Oedipus and Mr. Puff, and his switching from the virility of Hotspur to the wizened impotency of Shallow.

Here is one asset not acquired by years of dedicated training and practice—a natural stage presence. 'He always had it,' says Laurence Naismith. 'If Larry O. walks on the stage now—boy, that's an effect. Something's arrived. But it was the same at All Saints' when he was an amateur child actor. That physical presence has lasted. All the other things have grown, through careful study and work and the widest possible experience.'

PERSONALITY. The late Spencer Tracy once recalled how George M. Cohan told him to read the *heart* into a play. He went on to explain: 'I try to do that. But I don't try to invent a personality, because you *can't* do that. Personality is what you *are*. Personality, I suppose, is "star quality" if anything is. I have not seen a good actor give a performance in which part of the personality didn't emerge. Olivier is the best, and damned versatile . . . but when I see him I know it's Olivier. Personality. It's all that an actor has to give . . . that, and his instinct.'

Raymond Massey has said much the same thing: 'Basically one's own character and personality surmount everything else—they must do. In all the great ones—look at Larry Olivier—something comes through and you can't miss it.' With Olivier, the real man shows through in much of his playing: the chilling remoteness and dignity of his Max de Winter, the sullenness and ruthlessness of his Heathcliff, the quiet sensitivity of his Astrov, the impish humour of his Archie Rice, the self-digust of his Tyrone. His acting range is extraordinary partly through exhaustive training and development but also because the range of the man's own nature is extraordinary, a kaleidoscope of moods and colours.

The late Sir Tyrone Guthrie perceptively stressed this aspect of Olivier's art when he wrote under the heading of *What Is Good Acting?*:

It is only theoretically possible to separate the actor's skill from his personality. Theoretically, however, there is a difference. I suppose the skill of acting lies largely in the fact that the performer is able to suppress certain traits of his personality and to emphasize others, to get the results that he wants. Theoretically, then, the most skilful actor should be the most protean, the actor with the widest range. It so happens, however, that the actors with the widest range do not usually go very deep. I have known many protean actors who could achieve startling changes in their appearance, voice and mannerisms, but their performances were apt to be superficial . . . some of the greatest actors have no protean quality at all. In every part, though the make-up and costume may vary, the performance is almost exactly the same. John Gielgud is a case in point: matchless in declamation, with extraordinary intelligence, insight and humour, he commands almost no skill as a character actor. Like many other eminent players, he is 'always himself'. Absolutely this is not to derogate the skill, imagination and taste with which such actors 'present' themselves. It is, however, to admit that every artist has his limitations, and to imply that protean range is not the ultimate in theatrical accomplishment. Of the actors whom I have seen, the two who, in my opinion, best combine protean skill with 'star quality' are Laurence Olivier and Sybil Thorndike. Both are more than equal to the long haul and are able, when required, to assume immense nobility, majesty and grandeur. Both excel in the expression of powerless passion. Both can be hilariously funny. Both take almost too much pleasure in the farouche and grotesque, and an endearing, almost child-like delight in looking, sounding and behaving as unlike their 'real selves' as possible.[7]

Guthrie, however, omits one important reach in Olivier's range: the fact that he can be positively feminine as well as blazingly virile. On stage and screen, even without resort to athleticism, he has projected tremendous male sexuality. Yet, remarkably, he also retains an ability, by word or gesture or movement, to project in an instant some strikingly effeminate quality. In his book *The Modern Actor*, Michael Billington examines in detail 'the androgynous, bisexual quality that invariably underpins great acting' and begins with a discussion of 'the strong masculine streak' to be found in all Garbo's work, and most especially in *Queen Christina*. He continues:

Among male performers I can think of no one who makes more positive and creative use of his femininity than Laurence Olivier. I remember once hearing Peter Hall asked what he thought Olivier's great quality was, the one that makes him such an astonishing actor to watch. And he replied, 'His sheer sexiness.' But the charm of this sexiness is that it is equivocal, shifting, sometimes a bit camp . . . Olivier is a great actor partly because he shows us so much of himself in all his performances, partly because he is unafraid to reveal those elements in his personality that most of us are trained to keep hidden. Men are taught from childhood to be ashamed of their femininity. Olivier exploits his brilliantly and therefore enables all of us to come to terms with a part of ourselves.[8]

OBSERVATION. Asked to define acting in a single sentence, Peter O'Toole described it bluntly as a 'matter of farting about in disguises'. Olivier, more constructively, describes it as the art of persuading:

The actor persuades himself first, and through himself, the audience. In order to achieve that, what you need to make up your make-up is observation and intuition . . . you've got to find, in the actor, a man who will not be too proud to scavenge the tiniest little bit of human circumstance; observe it; find it, use it some time or other. I've frequently observed things, and thank God, if I haven't got a very good memory for anything else, I've got a memory for little details. I've had things in the back of my mind for as long as eighteen years before I've used them. And it works sometimes that, out of the little things you've seen somebody do, something causes you to store it up. In the years that follow you wonder what it was that made them do it, and ultimately, you find in that the illuminating key to a whole bit of characterization.[9]

As a young man Olivier 'imitated absolutely unashamedly'— silent screen stars Rod la Rocque, Lars Hanson and Vladimir Gaidarow, as well as Hawtrey, du Maurier, Barrymore, Tom Douglas, Coward, Colman, Fairbanks, Chaplin, Sid Field, Alfred Lunt, Rex Harrison, Gielgud, Richardson and others. All these, he has explained, were unsuspecting subjects of his avid imitation. 'When you are young, this is good, provided you don't mould yourself on one person, and don't *merely* imitate, but allow your own conception to develop. But the great thing about modelling yourself on others is to make yourself think about the part—why did Richardson or Redgrave or Gielgud or Guinness play it that way? When I'm producing young actors, I sometimes mimic the way that some of the older actors, whom they never saw, but whom I *just* saw, played the part. I mimic their accents, their pace and gestures, to give them an idea of how other actors thought about the part, and of what range of variety is possible, to get them to open their minds to the infinite possibilities.'[10]

Every actor, of course, needs to look and learn from life, and for Olivier, so consciously striving for realism, it has been the key to translating technique into action; so important that he once remarked, 'I think if I've got a secret, it's "keep your bloody eyes open, all your senses open. You never know what might be useful." It's like a disease with me. Learning to fly in the Navy during the war, you had to develop a technique, a certain feeling, a poise—it was fatal to be too relaxed, fatal to be too tense. And I thought, "I can use this idea in my acting." It gave me a different sense of acting that I'd been searching for. It had a big effect on me.'[11]

Linked with observation is his masterly use of make-up. Probably no actor except Lon Chaney has used greater quantities of putty and spirit gum. In the early years his love of disguise was prompted by self-consciousness, a reluctance to be seen as himself. But long ago it became much more than that—an aid to determining how a certain character should be played. In *Oh What a Lovely War* he could not get his blimpish field marshal right in his mind's eye until he had hit upon the appropriate hair style for the part. Similarly with the first time he played Astrov: not until the dress rehearsal, when he suddenly saw his face made up in the mirror and jabbed the pince-nez on his nose, did the man become a living person in his mind's eye.

TECHNIQUE. Although he, as much as anyone, is qualified to do so, Olivier has said that he will never write a book on acting technique. The truth is that so much of the mumbo-jumbo about the various schools of acting, about external and internal actors, is tedium to him. And understandably so. He is essentially a *working* actor, not a theorist—a master craftsman who prefers to tackle his construction of a character in a totally professional and business-like fashion without sacrificing practical working time to abstract discussions. He knows what is right for him but would never lay down hard and fast rules for others.

He himself accepts that he is 'a peripheral actor' in that he works mostly from the outside in ('I usually collect a lot of details, a lot of characteristics, and find a creature swimming about somewhere in the middle of them.'[12]). He recognizes, too, that his approach is basically opposite to that of the Actor's Studio ('I am afraid I probably outrage the Method people. They think of me as an external actor because I don't make a study of the way I study. It's primarily a visual thing with me. A man I see on top of a bus might give me an idea; as often as not it's my make-up which determines how a certain character should be played.'[13]). But to classify Olivier simply as an external actor is an over-simplification. He may be suspicious of the intuitive approach, realizing that when you feel yourself inside the part, everything else does *not* necessarily follow. At the same time a deeply thought-out and sympathetic understanding of the character he is preparing to play has been the basis of most of his outstanding performances.

Athene Seyler has observed Olivier's technique over half a century. Far from stressing his external qualities, she says: 'Bernard Shaw made a dictum about acting, to the effect that an actor must get into the character he's playing or get the character into himself.* Larry takes the character into himself. He takes somebody he sees and he cooks it inside the stove of his own emotional understanding. Your ordinary character actor just says, "I'll go and *be* that character." But this is nursery acting. What my great grandchildren do. "Go and be that old lad you see over there," they say. It's not, "Get that old lady and make her into yourself"—and that's what Larry does supremely.'

In exactly the same way it is an over-simplification to stress how an actor like Brando essentially works from the inside out. 'Don't believe Marlon,' said Olivier, talking in 1973 on the N.B.C. television *Today Show* with Barbara Walters. 'Don't tell me he searches inside himself for everything. He looks out, too. He's peripheral, just as any other character is peripheral. You have to be. I want a signal from something to start me off, really. It's a bit of this, that, and the other, something to say . . . he should walk like that, he should stutter, or stoop, or have a way of looking or using his hands, or something, or any little external

---

* In fact, it was Irving who reportedly said, 'There are only two ways of portraying a character on the stage. Either you can try to turn yourself into that person—which is impossible—or, and this is the way to act, you can take that person and turn him into yourself. That is how I do it!'

help. It's better than saying, "Where am I?" It's better to find something outside, for say Richard III, or something like that; or Falstaff, or Toby Belch or "The Entertainer". Well, I ask myself, "Who do I know like that?" It might be me, but it might be a dozen other people as well.'

Kenneth Tynan, champion of the Olivier approach, wrote as long ago as 1951: 'I know of only two actors who can play both the heroes of mind and the (to me) much more important heroes of the body: Olivier and Valk. It is, after all, the physical things which go to make good theatre; noises and body movements are theatrically far more significant than the qualities and essences they cloak. The actor is the tangible foreground of the tragedy; he is primarily a plastic bundle of techniques, not a feeling or a mind. He should build his part from the outside inwards, at whatever cost of private exaltation; his is the business of artificially conjuring up emotion in an audience, not in himself.'[14]

FEELING. This leads us to an alleged flaw in this great actor's art, a 'weakness' based on the belief that Olivier does not really *feel* all that he plays. In this, to a degree, he is the victim of his own technical brilliance—an artist so precise and meticulous in his attention to detail that he is sometimes judged as being the architect of cathedrals of characterization, mathematically faultless in design but somehow lacking in 'soul'.

A leading actress who has worked with him in both classical and modern plays says: 'It's sheer technical ability with Larry, the quality to keep up a performance no matter what. Every move, everything he did, he knew exactly what he was going to do, where he was going to do it and at what time. It's a question of timing more than anything else. I don't think he *feels* anything deeply when he's acting; he's always outside himself, looking on. I don't think he gets involved in his performance. That's the difference between him and Scofield. Where Olivier *does*, Scofield *is*. Larry can simply go on and give a performance, come what may, because he had that wealth of technique behind him.' Then again, an actor who has played with him in many Shakespearean productions says: 'Laurence's technique lies in his ability to put over a wonderful effect which appears to come out of real emotion, although, in fact, he doesn't *feel* anything. Laurence is a trickster; that's what his technique is. He's extremely inventive of tricks to make a performance stand out . . . He is a great showman, a mixture of Douglas Fairbanks and intellectualism.'

This notion that Olivier does not *feel* what he plays is essentially silly. Even Olivier is not so great that he can counterfeit great passion while feeling nothing. Joan Plowright and intimate actor friends know well how disturbed he can be in the hangover of playing a great emotional role. He himself has made his feeling clear on many occasions. Most convincingly, in 1969, he told interviewer Kenneth Harris:

You hear of some of the great men that in the middle of their speeches about passion, power or death they are wondering what won the 3.30, or what they'd like for supper. In my case I feel I am who I am playing. Not *entirely*—how could you, and be sane? (Some actors do go mad, or temporarily mad, of course.) And I think, though I speak only from my own experience, that the actor *must* identify to some extent with his part—the heads of your three children really are there in that basket, and it is your own Juliet who lies there dead and has left you behind for eternity, your own Desdemona you've just strangled. But I do identify easily and naturally. I am interested in what makes people tick. I would be, even if I weren't an actor. Being an actor makes me more so. If you want to interest people, excite them, cater for them, sell something to them—an actor is a salesman, he is selling an illusion all the time—you must know what makes them tick. So if you are playing a part you must ask yourself what kind of man he was. Then, when you know, you must somehow *be* that man—not just the part that shows in the role, but the whole of the man, his whole mind, so what you actually reveal in the role is real and right because in your mind you have got the whole underlying man real and right. It's your sense of the realness of people which gives your rightness about them when you act . . . Oh, God, yes, you have to feel it to do it. If you do it right, you do feel it. The suffering, the passion, the bitterness, you've got to feel them. And it takes something out of you and puts something in, as all emotional experiences do.[15]

The question is not whether Olivier really feels what he is playing, but whether he sufficiently projects that feeling to his audience. It may well be that some untouchable reserve in his own personal nature sets a limit on how far he can plumb the extreme depths of human tragedy and reveal something of himself in playing to emotional extremes. George S. Kaufman saw Olivier's Crassus in *Spartacus* as 'an impeccably patrician performance that fits a certain aloof element in his personality'. That aloofness has often come across most strikingly under the close scrutiny of the camera, especially in *Wuthering Heights* and *Rebecca*. 'On stage,' Ken Tynan says, 'Larry can cry like a child. In *Oedipus* he made this terrible howling noise like a trapped animal. In *Long Day's Journey* he made a ghastly sobbing moan. He has access to all those emotions and he can turn them on like a tap, but he doesn't like to delve very much into emotions.'[16]

It may be argued that Olivier's deep-grained sense of comedy is a limiting factor. He has said that he considers it his life's message to show the minute difference between comedy and tragedy, but he has always preferred comedy to tragedy. 'There is hardly any difference between them. In order to reach the big heights in tragedy you must play very dangerously. Sometimes you have to be almost very funny to be very tragic. I would not mind as Othello rolling about the floor to get laughs. That would be part of the message of tragedy. As long as you make them (the audience) sorry afterwards. Sometimes I want the audience to be on Iago's side. I want them to say, "Get that stupid nigger." But I want them to be sorry afterwards that they felt that. I want the audience to be in a position of the gods—when we are unhappy about a love affair gone wrong or some personal misfortune, the gods are laughing at us and about the absurd things we are sorry about. I want to elevate the audience into that position.'[17]

Dame Sybil Thorndike, most professional and most experienced of all actresses, had the unique advantage of seeing Olivier at work from the dawn of his acting experience. In her ninety-first year, this great lady of extraordinary energy, intelligence, wit and humanity, kindly provided me with this assessment of the actor she had known intimately for more than sixty years:

> I would agree with Agate's remark that Larry is a comedian by instinct and a tragedian by art, because he's worked so very hard at the tragedy. He has pathos, tremendous pathos. But tragedy is bigger still, not pathetic. You are not sorry; you are horrified. This is talking about the spirit of tragedy on the grandest scale. Larry can do tragic parts and pathetic parts, but really big tragedy—well I don't think we've got anybody. John

[Gielgud] is the nearest. Yet I don't think he's such a good actor as Larry. He's not a natural actor like Larry; he had to struggle much harder. Of course, his speech is much better, more beautiful, whereas Larry sacrifices everything to character and you can't always hear what he says. On the other hand, he has got a remarkably flexible voice and can use notes that most actors are denied. High notes. He's got three good octaves—not so rare with a singer but rare with a speaker, particularly English speakers, who only use a few notes and are usually very dull. He uses an enormous scale and that's why he's interesting.

I remember when he made a first entrance in *The Cenci* with Lewis [Casson] and I. He was only a little servant boy saying, 'The master's coming,' but you knew instantly by the way he said it that a horror was coming. He could always do horror wonderfully. He could really *frighten* you. His Button Moulder, for instance. That was the nearest touch he got to tragedy, I think. It was so frightening. But it was the frightfulness of the Devil. The Devil isn't tragic. The Devil is comic. Larry is a comic and sees the world comically. Even tragedy he sees comically. That's what I feel. He can make villainy very attractive.

He is the greatest Shakespearean comedian I have ever seen. And a Shaw comedian. He would always find comedy in any part he played. His Iago was wonderful. There's such a lot of comedy in Iago; he got the fullness of it, the tragedy, too. But he got the tragedy through *character*, not through *feeling*. I don't know whether he felt it deeply or not. Some of his comedy moves you to tears, but that's not being a tragedian. I don't think Larry has the greatness of soul that a great tragedian must have. I don't think he wants to feel as much as the big tragedians feel. He'd laugh first because he always sees the comic side, which is wonderful. There's something awful about great tragedians. They can't laugh.

His double bill of Oedipus and Mr. Puff—that was a thing a tragedian couldn't have done. Of course, he gave the most tremendous performance of Oedipus and it was tragic in that it was horrible. But there was also an hysterical thing about it which I think took charge rather than the big tragedy. He can be very sinister. And when one talks about tragedy he can do the awfulness. It's just the big parts like Lear that he couldn't quite compass. He got a lot of the humour in Lear but I don't think he has the stature you need for great tragedy. Now Johnny Gielgud has the stature, but he couldn't touch half, a quarter, of the things that Larry touches.

Larry is the most lovable person in the theatre. He's got such an enormous sympathy for people. That's what makes him such a frightfully good actor. He's a wonderful family man, and once you're his friend—well, I can't tell you what a friend he has been to me—the best friend I know because he's so deeply, deeply sympathetic and genuinely emotional. His kindness to anybody in any trouble is extraordinary. It's one of his chief characteristics and the reason that he's such a wonderful comedian—because he can get inside anybody and see whether they are troubled.

The Man Behind the Ermine

Sir Laurence Olivier has already chosen his own epitaph: HE'S FUNNY—Phoebe Rice's summing-up in *The Entertainer* of the third-rate music-hall comic she had married. '*He's funny*—tell them that at Westminster Abbey,' he once remarked. 'It's the most wonderful thing in the world to make people laugh.' The 'funny' thing, however, is that Olivier will always be associated with majesty rather than mirth. Dame Sybil Thorndike called him 'the greatest Shakespearean comedian', critics extol the rich vein of humour that runs through his art. The fact remains that he has had few opportunities to make people laugh. It has been his fate to spend the greater part of his career playing soldiers, warriors and kings. His developed powers, as a theatrical demigod able to conjure up the menace of distant thunder and the excitement of electric storms, have over-shadowed his instinctive gifts as a clown.

The general public does not really know the Olivier who so often romped through slapstick sketches in the annual charity spectacular, *Night of a Hundred Stars*, and won louder laughter than the world famous comedians about him. He is firmly cast in the heroic mould, predominantly identified with the giants of classic tragedy on stage and the giants of classic romance on screen. As with the actor, so with the man. Only a privileged few know Larry the hilarious, often bawdy, raconteur; the impulsive joker who, even in his sixties, retained a schoolboyish taste for larks and escapades, and a particular fondness for the *outré*. He is type-cast as the dignified elder statesman of his profession and, having an inbred sense of duty and responsibility, he plays it as a straight part.

Long ago Sir Laurence achieved a status far transcending that of a famous entertainer. He became, whether he liked it or not, an institutional figure of such authority and influence that he needed to guard his every public word and deed. Lady Olivier once explained: 'If you have a husband who is in a very important position, you have to be careful about everything you do or say. Sometimes I forget, but most times I'm careful. I don't see it as a duty because it's enjoyable. It's honouring obligations. Possibly words like honour have gone out of the vocabulary but to me they still exist in the relationship between a man and a woman.' Her husband is the same about honouring obligations as the pre-eminent figure in the theatre. He takes his responsibilities very seriously, moves with Argus-eyed caution.

Yet Olivier would be less than human if he did not allow the instinctive comedian to show himself in public now and then. It does happen, but very rarely indeed. In March 1972, for example, more than 800 people were gathered at the London Coliseum to pay tribute to the late Stephen Arlen, managing director of the Sadler's Wells Opera Company and first administrative director at the National Theatre. The ceremony opened with opera music by Mozart and Wagner and Janacek. Then Sir Laurence mounted the stage holding a sheaf of notes. A serious address was anticipated. Instead, after explaining that it was half a century since he had sat in the Coliseum gallery as a schoolboy watching a music-hall performance, he announced that he was now there to give an audition. He sang, 'Oh come let us bash the door in' to the tune of 'Oh come all ye faithful', and then 'While shepherds washed their socks by night while seated round the tub'. He sustained a vaudeville comic's patter, talked about his father, a clergyman who wore grey flannel trousers and an M.C.C. tie, sang a story about a notice in the lavatory of a South Eastern and Chatham Railway carriage warning passengers against blocking the water system with wrong materials. Finally he paid tribute to Stephen Arlen: 'a wonderful partner, the most satisfactory person in looks, voice and comradeship'. The audience was astonished. Not everyone appreciated that he was giving an audition in the style of Archie Rice and as though he were performing before Mr. Arlen, who, he well knew, preferred broad humour to solemnity. They were geared for Olivier the lord and they had encountered Larry the humorist.

Sir Laurence has always been alive to the danger of being saddled with too stuffy and boring a role. Largely for that reason he was alarmed as well as flattered when Harold Wilson offered him a life peerage. Although he had always discouraged reference to his knighthood on film credits and playbills, he liked being 'Sir Laurence'. It has a romantic and chivalrous ring, and better still was 'Sir Larry', so sporty and popular. But Lord Olivier? That was something else. ('It seemed to suggest a division which I don't like to feel between myself and any other actor and the man in the street.') There was also, characteristically, defensive reasoning behind his reluctance to accept the honour ('I had the thought that, as a target of derision, the actor is a sitting duck in any case, and an actor who is a lord is a duck flying straight towards you; a figure of fun'). Ultimately, after twice declining the honour officially,* he was won over by Wilson's argument that the title would give the acting profession a forum, that by having a seat in the House of Lords he could help all the active arts. It did not make him 'a figure of fun'. It *did* enhance the legend and raise him higher on his Olympian perch.

There was never danger of Lord Olivier's acquiring new high-flown dignity within his own circle of friends. Lady Olivier teased him mercilessly about being 'put out to grass'. His son Richard, aged eight, was far more impressed with England goal-keeper Gordon Banks winning an O.B.E. He was still 'Larry' to Ralphy, Johnny G. and the rest. Elsewhere he resisted undue reverence where he could. His first act as a peer of the realm was to pen a directive to the National Theatre company making it clear that the first person to address him as 'M'Lord' was court-ing instant dismissal. But centuries of tradition were against him. He was not just a lord; he was *the* lord of his profession—unique. Familiar acquaintances might accept him as 'the same old Larry O.'; strangers were more than ever inclined to be overawed in his presence and stand on ceremony for fear of appearing too familiar or disrespectful.

To a degree, Olivier himself added weight to his new image. 'I'm too much of an urchin not to smile slightly at the idea of being a lord,' he said, but he was also too solidly English and conservative, too respectful of tradition, to fall short in playing the part. His maiden speech in the House of Lords was a glorious

* Olivier was following an excellent precedent. In 1883 Irving refused a knighthood because he felt it would impair the unique fellowship existing between actors. Twelve years later he was per-suaded that it would be as much an honour for the profession as for himself.

ten-minute soliloquy, so perfumed with nationalistic feeling that it conjured up echoes of his unforgettable 'Cry "God for Harry, England and St. George!" ' He spoke of 'storybook feudal nostalgia' and reminded his audience that he was the second baron to bear the name Olivier ('The first, incomparably much more deserving, virtuous, illustrious, and in service to his country richer than I can ever hope to be, was my uncle, twice governor of Jamaica, K.C.M.G., friend of Bernard Shaw, the Webbs, and all the eminent Socialists of the day with whom he created the Fabian Society. He entered your Lordships' House the first Labour peer—he seems to have started quite a thing. He served the government in 1925 as Secretary for India, a title once representing one of the richest jewels in the Imperial Crown and which sounds perhaps almost quaint to the retrenched ears whose lobes can only boast the holes to show where once such lush gems hung.')

The new baron entered into a year of negotiations to secure the title of Lord Olivier of Brighton, which required the consent of the four daughters of his uncle Sydney, who had died in 1943 without heir. He also acquired his own coat of arms ('just for fun'), comprising an olive tree and plough, and his family motto was duly recorded in Debrett's Peerage: *Sicut Oliva Virens Laetor In Aede Dei*, loosely translated, 'I rejoice in the House of the Lord even as the olive tree flourishes.'

A peerage allowed him to give new expression to that love of ritual planted in him by his father and fostered by the high church pomp and ceremony of All Saints' to a deep-rooted respect for tradition that no amount of flirting with such anti-Establishment renegades as Osborne and Tynan had significantly weakened. And when the ermined Olivier took his seat in the House of Lords, it was for a magic moment as though nothing had changed since the Forties. No first foreign defeat of English soccer, no dissolution of the Empire, no Suez, no Jimmy Porter, no cynicism of a Permissive Society. Britannia's head was held high, and here again, walking and talking, was the recognizable spirit of that prince who became Henry V and lent majesty to chauvinism and contributed to sustaining millions in their cherished belief that British really is Best.

And in a curious way, seemingly by chance, Olivier's revived image as an Establishment figure was now strengthened by the authoritative parts he was playing in his latest films. Cinemagoers were not seeing Lord Olivier as a seedy Archie Rice but as Lord Dowding, the former Commander-in-Chief of Fighter Command, in *The Battle of Britain*; as Sir John French, Chief of the Imperial General Staff, in *Oh What a Lovely War*; as headmaster Mr. Creakle in *David Copperfield*; as Count Witte in *Nicholas and Alexandra*, and the Duke of Wellington in *Lady Caroline Lamb*. In all these cameo roles, Olivier the clown showed himself only once—with his devastating caricature of the old field marshal cutting a nifty tango at the officers' ball in *O What a Lovely War*. His bemedalled buffoon earned him the displeasure of Sir John French's son, and a British 'Oscar', awarded by the Society of Film and Television Arts, for the Best Supporting Actor of the year.

That four-and-a-half-minute screen appearance as the C.I.G.S. was pure Olivier—gold-braided authority and the most subtle self-parodying manner. It was appropriate, too, that he should have played the Duke of Wellington. In the Thirties he was greatly impressed by his reading of Guedalla's biography of the soldier-statesman, and what impressed him most was the Iron Duke's firm resistance to flattery, a conqueror who refused to become swollen-headed or taken in by praise. The actor has followed the hero's example, neatly cultivating the art of self-effacement and a healthy ability to laugh at himself. He will mock his own performances in an old movie that turns up on television far more cruelly than any critic or satirist would venture to do. Even when *Long Day's Journey* was showing on his home set at Brighton he switched over to Michael Caine's *Alfie*. 'I love watching good acting and I'm bored stiff with my own,' he said.

Charlton Heston first met Olivier when they were dinner guests at William Wyler's house during the filming of *Spartacus*. 'I think there has never been a time when one actor so dominated his time and his profession as Olivier dominates our time and all the rest of us actors. Yet here was the most engaging man, the centre of attraction for everyone, and the outstanding characteristic I noticed about him socially was the way he told stories all evening—and he made himself the butt of all the stories.' Kirk Douglas has a similar memory of him from *Spartacus* and *The Devil's Disciple*. 'I was just dumbfounded by his simplicity and humility. He was the easiest actor to work with that I have ever known. I remember asking him for a piece of advice, and he gave it so modestly and with such humility. I am quick to offer advice, or criticism, but here was Larry, with his tremendous background, being so reticent about making suggestions. He has a quality that I have never encountered in any other member of our profession. He has become a legend that in a sense embraces everyone around him more than it enhances himself. Olivier was always something unique—especially to other actors because actors have a certain kind of self-denigration. Very often they don't have that much respect for themselves as actors. But when you have someone of Olivier's quality, it enhances the entire profession. It gives it a dignity that so many actors, in their insecurity, feel they don't have, and so they grasp at that dignity, clutch at it when they see it in someone else.'

On a public relations level, his self-effacement is liable to appear excessive at times. His performance, for example, on the *Dick Cavett* television talk-show was a masterly marathon of modesty, but the impression of a 'performance' remained, one very carefully studied and rehearsed. The result is that the public *en masse* meets an Olivier who bears little relation to the Larry his closest friends know. They meet instead a kind of compromise between Larry the hearty extrovert with a wicked sense of humour and Larry the remote introvert with a broodingly forceful personality.

Separately, both Joan Plowright and Kenneth Tynan were once asked what image instantly flashes in their mind at the mention of his name. Both gave the same reply: a lion. Lady Olivier said: 'There is something animal-like about him—like the King of the Jungle, I suppose. There is that kind of aloneness, prowling about surveying all he rules and owns—a sort of untouchability, unapproachability.'[1]

Tynan explained: 'Larry has this bottled violence, which is what gives him this great authority on stage—gives his acting a sense of danger. You quite often feel that with enormous effort he is being civil to people that he would not just like to walk away from, but to kick very hard. That is why, when he is prevailed on to make a speech, he puts on a pose of elaborate humility which embarrasses anyone who knows him. He pretends to be such a wilting violet. And you know that he would quite enjoy seeing those people blown up.'[2]

Basically, however, Olivier has got the balance between his public and private style as nearly right as it can be for a man of his temperament. Franchot Tone is an example of an actor who for many years didn't get the balance right and it almost ruined his career. Later, recognizing the errors of his ways, he observed: 'Actors are in a unique position. They are both introspective and exhibitionist. You have to be an introvert before you can find within yourself the symbols of extroversion that are required to put the performance across. It is a paradox . . . Actors suffer from being half narcissistic and half self-critical . . . It is easy to see why actors are insecure in regard to their own personalities. If you're used to building a personality around the work of some-one else, you don't get much time to be yourself. And if you *are* yourself, you may be ruined by the publicity that results. That's why most performers prefer to lead lives more conventional than mine. They know that if their hidden vices were discovered they'd never get another job.'

Sir Laurence has this mixture of the introvert and exhibition-ist. And he certainly suffers from being self-critical. He is so fiercely derogatory about himself that he will talk about Captain Edgar, with his barrack-room vulgarity, quick temper and scheming, bullying nature, as 'one of my autobiographical jobs', and James Tyrone, with his mania for petty economy, as another. He speaks of having a self-detestation, describes himself as frightfully difficult to live with, admits to periods of moodiness and selfishness when he shuts himself in with his work and every-one out, and to having a fearful temper most apt to be ignited by an excess of whisky. It is part of his style to grossly overdramatize his own faults; within the profession, friends and colleagues paint an entirely different picture of the man. Especially he is re-nowned for his immediate and positive response to news of a colleague in distress, and stories illustrating his generosity and thoughtfulness are legion. Simon Williams recalled the day that his father (actor-playwright Hugh Williams) died. They were appearing together in a West End play when it happened. 'Imagine my feelings when I had to go on and play opposite an understudy. I'll never forget Laurence Olivier's kindness at that time. He came and sat in my dressing-room, talking to me and pouring me large drinks until it was time for me to go on.' Athene Seyler remembered the time she was appearing at Chichester and her husband, the late Nicholas Hannen, was seriously ill. Sir Laurence, a lifelong friend, made no reference to her anxiety, offered no emotion-stirring words of comfort. 'He just let me get on with the job. But afterwards, when the play was done, he wrote the most beautiful and kind letter at great length, showing that he had known and had understood and felt deeply all the time. There were some people, who cared much less, who would come up and say, "How is he, darling?" But not Larry. He has great sensitivity. He is the warmest-hearted, the most lovely person.'

'Larry has a tremendous temper, and a sharp tongue, too,' said Dame Sybil Thorndike. 'Anybody who's supposed to be cock of the walk, he can strip down very nicely. He can make you feel a real fool. But, oh, he really is the most lovable person in the theatre, a wonderful family man, and the best friend I know because he's so deeply, deeply sympathetic and frightfully emotional. When Lewis died he was the first person to be here when we came back from hospital; and he is so quick to perceive when you are frightened or nervous on some big emotional occasion. Kindness to anybody in any kind of trouble—that is one of his chief characteristics. He's got such enormous sympathy for people, and that's what makes him such a tremendously good actor. He's always enormous fun with everybody, fooling about with no dignity except an innate dignity. He sees all actors as brothers, friends and countrymen, and as comics.'

'He really is a terribly funny man,' says Michael Jayston. 'Not at all what one expects when meeting him for the first time. Among friends, away from the glare of publicity, he really can be one of the boys. Quite wild. He likes his booze as much as anyone, and when he's relaxed he's the greatest entertainer in the world. During the filming of *Nicholas and Alexandra* in Spain we had a party and he started to reminisce about things, and of course we were trying to pick his brain, asking all those is-it-true kind of questions. Was it true, for example, that Ralph Richardson fell through the ceiling at Notley Abbey? And we found that all those stories were virtually true, and we heard it from the master's mouth. Maybe slightly embroidered, but an absolutely fascinating *tour de force*. Why, he kept going for something like three hours. A riveting performance.'

At times, especially when he is engrossed in his work, Olivier is capable of leaving a different impression. Some actors remember him as an aloof and awesome figure. But his manner can deceive. Laurence Naismith recalls finding him 'rather a frightening man' when he went to work for him in *Richard III* so many years after they had been at school together. No hearty back-slaps, no sentimental reminiscing. Just curt, efficient directives about the business in hand. And yet, many years later, when on tour in a play, Naismith received a long distance telephone call from his wife. Who is Katherine? she wanted to know. A telegram has arrived for you, saying, "Thinking of you especially on this our very special day," signed "Katherine"!' The actor um-ed and ah-ed, stalling and wondering whatever long-forgotten indiscretion could possibly have come to light. And then, finally, the truth dawned. It was from Larry, marking the anniversary of their boyhood appearance together at Stratford in *The Taming of the Shrew*. After so many years of silence he had suddenly had the impulse to make a sentimental gesture

'I think,' Olivier once told Tynan, 'you've got to have a certain edge, that might be traced to being a bit of a bastard, inside. You've got to be a bit of a bastard to understand bastards, and you've got to understand everybody. I think the most difficult equation to solve is the union of the two things that are absolutely necessary to an actor. One is confidence, absolute confidence, and the other an equal amount of humility towards the work. That's a very hard equation.'[3] It is an equation that has troubled him greatly. He finds a need to maintain a personal sense of authority in tackling his work. At the same time he likes to be liked; friendships are vitally important to him. When he accepted control of the National Theatre one of his greatest fears was that he would have to make decisions that might damage his personal relationships. 'I realized I would be very lucky if I had any friends left at the end of five years,' he said. In the end, however, he solved the equation. A current National Theatre player says: 'The love and loyalty that members of the old team feel towards Olivier is really extraordinary. You know, quite honestly, if he had been leaving to form his own company, and he had so desired, he could easily have taken half of the National company with him and left Peter Hall high and dry.'

Olivier commands this tremendous loyalty from those who know and understand him, and he has always had a capacity for enduring friendships—deep, meaningful relationships with a respected few such as Dame Sybil Thorndike and Lewis Casson ('the most wonderful people I have known in my life'), George Relph ('the most honest man I have ever known'), Noel Coward, Tony Bushell, Roger Furse . . . and not least Ralph Richardson.

He and Sir Ralph are bonded together by a half-century of shared experiences and emotions. They were together on the night they heard of King George V's death, the day they heard the Abdication speech, and, most horrific of all, one dreadful night when they discovered a house fire in London's Russell Square and, after sounding the alarm, gleefully climbed aboard the fire engine only to see real-life adventure turn to nightmare as trapped people jumped screaming from upper windows and perished on the ground. They share so many memories that they have made an oath to see the millennium through together.

On the other hand, Sir Laurence is not a man to enter lightly into close personal associations, and the emotional streaking in which so many actors indulge has never been his style. His guarding of the private self is entirely consistent with the man's essential Englishness. He may have inherited a touch of French romanticism and temperament, but basically he is English to the core, in his values, his attitudes, his interests.

'If you passed him in the street, you would never take him for an actor,' says Cathleen Nesbitt. 'He looks like a successful stock-broker.' Nor would this illusion be destroyed if one followed the Englishman home to 'his castle'. He cherishes a family life far removed from the public spotlight. He likes tennis and swimming and motoring, takes more than a passing interest in cricket (as a Lord's Taverner and, like his father, a member of the M.C.C.) and he collects fob watches. Most English of all, he likes garden-ing, and in his years at Notley this extended to a passion for tree-planting, hundreds of them: oaks, willows, poplars, divers flowering trees, whole avenues of limes, an orchard of apples. In *Uncle Vanya* he was speaking as well for himself as for Astrov when he said, 'Maybe I am just a crank but . . . when I plant a birch tree and then watch it put forth its leaves and sway in the wind, my soul is filled with pride.'

Olivier is also an enthusiastic collector of theatrical memora-bilia, with his own mini-museum that includes Kean's sword as Richard III, Irving's dagger as Othello and Garrick's wig as Abel Drugger, and appropriately (since probably no other English actor has equalled Garrick's versatility) he specializes in relics of Garrick—jewellery, engravings, playbills, a Reynolds portrait, a statue. But otherwise the Brighton scene offers little tell-tale evidence of Olivier the actor. Joan Plowright has said: 'You know people would be rather amazed to see Larry at home just with the family. He is so *ordinary*. He just wanders about with his trousers sagging and his braces showing, putting things right, straightening pictures, taking the children off somewhere. He doesn't get recognized at all.'[4] This has been proved many times. 'I remember inviting him into a pub for a beer,' says Frankie Howerd. 'An airman asked for my autograph and I signed, and before I could say anything else the lad had said, "Thank you very much, Mr. Bygraves," and walked away. He never realized that the great Olivier was standing by my side.'

In the end, it is as difficult to define the essence of Olivier's personality as to define the essence of his art. One may analyse the actor but any serious attempt to analyse the make-up of the man is like trying to pick up quicksilver with a fork. And perhaps that is as it should be. He says that he himself does not know what he is like, nor does he wish to know. It is one of his privately expressed theories that you have to be 'a little mad' to touch certain histrionic heights and that he himself might have really gone mad if he had not become an actor and so found an outlet for his emotional energies.

'What is life about?' he asked, speaking from the pulpit of a London church. 'Strife, torment, disappointment, love, sacrifice, golden sunsets and black storms.' And he himself has reflected all the variations in Nature—a mercurial man of infinite sensibility and confusing colours. It partly explains his astonishing versatility and durability as an actor. When he erupts on stage with unrivalled volcanic power he brings to the surface a terrible rage within himself. 'I do not have Larry's fine fury,' Ralph Richardson observed; and Olivier accepts this, seeing temper and temperament as being very much akin, necessary in the actor who seeks to achieve some sudden and startling rise in voltage. Equally, the actor who cavorts on stage with impish delight in the guise of a Puff or a Tattle is revealing something of himself— the spirit of the Larry who masqueraded as an airline steward to welcome the National Theatre company aboard their chartered flight to Moscow; who passed for a vociferous West Indian stagehand and was ordered out of the theatre during a rehearsal of *Othello*; who, disguised beyond recognition in Astrov beard and pince-nez, joined a puzzled group of magistrates on an inspection tour of the newly built Chichester Theatre.

Laurence Olivier is truly a man for all seasons. Athene Seyler who awarded him his first diploma for acting, concludes: 'Now that he has crowned his career I've been trying to think about him in relation to the stage, wondering what it is that keeps him apart from everybody else of his generation. It's a kind of quality of his heart and mind that are on a big scale. He's a universal person. He's got a method of making contact with everything in life.'

★ Theatre Chronology

1917   First public appearance: Brutus in *Julius Caesar*, with
        Ralph Forbes. Production by All Saints Choir School,
        Marylebone.

1918   Maria in *Twelfth Night*, with Fabia Drake. Production by
        All Saints Choir School.

1920   Katherine in *The Taming of the Shrew*, with Geoffrey Heald.
        Production by All Saints Choir School.

1922   Katherine in *The Taming of the Shrew*. Production revived
        at Stratford Memorial Theatre, Stratford-upon-Avon.

1923   Puck in *A Midsummer Night's Dream*. Production by St.
        Edward's School, Oxford.

1924   Pupil at Elsie Fogerty's Central School of Speech Training
        and Dramatic Art, London.
        ASM/general understudy for *Through the Crack* (Algernon
        Blackwood and Violet Pearn) at St. Christopher Theatre,
        Letchworth.
        Lennox in *Macbeth*. Production by Norman V. Norman and
        Beatrice Wilson at St. Christopher Theatre, Letchworth.
        The Suliot Officer in *Byron* (Alice Law), directed by and
        starring Henry Oscar at the Century Theatre, London.

1925   Master Snare and Thomas of Clarence in L. E. Berman's
        production of *King Henry IV, Part II*, with Edmund
        Willard, Alfred Clark and Horace Sequeira, at the Regent
        Theatre.
        Walk-on part as policeman in *The Ghost Train* (Arnold
        Ridley), with Ruby Miller at Brighton Hippodrome; also
        part in curtain-raising sketch. *Unfailing Instinct*.
        Series of parts including Flavius in *Julius Caesar* with the
        Lena Ashwell Players, based at the Century Theatre,
        London.
        Walk-on parts, also ASM, in *King Henry VIII*, with Sybil
        Thorndike and Lewis Casson at Empire Theatre, Lon-
        don.

1926   The Count's servant, also ASM, in *The Cenci* (Shelley), with

Sybil Thorndike, Lewis Casson and Jack Hawkins at the Empire Theatre, London.

The Minstrel in *The Marvellous History of Saint Bernard* (Barry Jackson's version of French mystery play), with Robert Harris. Production by Birmingham Repertory Company at Kingsway Theatre, London.

Minor part in *The Barber and the Cow* (D. T. Davies), with Cedric Hardwicke and Ralph Richardson. B.R.C.'s production at Clacton.

On tour as Richard Coaker in B.R.C.'s production of *The Farmer's Wife* (Eden Phillpotts).

1927   Series of parts with B.R.C. in Birmingham including: an aristocrat in Eden Phillpotts' *Something to Talk About*; Tony Lumpkin in Goldsmith's *She Stoops to Conquer*; title-role in Chekhov's *Uncle Vanya*; Jack Borthwick in Galsworthy's *The Silver Box*; Parolles in *All's Well That Ends Well*; the young American in Elmer Rice's *The Adding Machine*; and Gerald Arnwood in Drinkwater's *Bird in Hand*, with Peggy Ashcroft.

1928   Series of parts with B.R.C. at Royal Court Theatre, London: the young American in *The Adding Machine*; Malcolm in *Macbeth*; Martellus in Shaw's *Back to Methuselah*; title-role in Tennyson's *Harold*; The Lord in *The Taming of the Shrew*.

Gerald Arnwood in *Bird in Hand*, produced by Barry Jackson, with Jill Esmond at Royalty Theatre, London.

Stanhope in *Journey's End* (R. C. Sherriff), directed by James Whale, with Maurice Evans, Melville Cooper and George Zucco at Apollo Theatre, London.

1929   Title-role in *Beau Geste*, directed by Basil Dean, with Madeleine Carroll, Marie Lohr, Edmund Willard and Jack Hawkins at His Majesty's Theatre, London.

Prince Po in *The Circle of Chalk*, directed by Basil Dean, with Anna May Wong at the New Theatre, London.

Richard Parish in *Paris Bound*, with Herbert Marshall and Edna Best at the Lyric Theatre, London.

John Hardy in *The Stranger Within*, with Olga Lindo and Roland Culver at the Garrick Theatre, London.

Hugh Bromilow in *Murder on the Second Floor* (Frank Vosper), with Phyllis Konstam, O. B. Clarence and Viola Lyel at the Eltinge Theatre, New York.

Jerry Warrender in *The Last Enemy* (Frank Harvey), directed by Tom Walls, with Athene Seyler, O. B. Clarence, Nicholas Hannen and Frank Lawton at the Fortune Theatre, London.

1930   Ralph in *After All* (John van Druten), with Elissa Landi
and Cathleen Nesbitt at the Arts Theatre, London.
First film work (see Film Chronology).
Victor Prynne in *Private Lives* (Noel Coward), directed by
Noel Coward, with Noel Coward Gertrude Lawrence and
Adrianne Allen at the Phoenix Theatre, London.

1931   *Private Lives*, with Noel Coward, Gertrude Lawrence and
Jill Esmond, at Times Square Theatre, New York.

1933   Stevan Beringer in *Rats of Norway* (Keith Winter), with
Raymond Massey and Gladys Cooper at the Playhouse
Theatre, London.
Julian Dulcimer in *The Green Bay Tree* (Mordaunt Shairp),
directed by Jed Harris, with James Dale, Leo G. Carroll and
Jill Esmond at the Cort Theatre, New York.

1934   Richard Kurt in *Biography* (S. N. Behrman), directed by
Noel Coward, with Ina Claire, Reginald Tate, Joan Wynd-
ham, Frank Cellier and Sam Livesey at the Globe Theatre,
London.
Bothwell in *Queen of Scots* (Gordon Daviot), directed by
John Gielgud, with George Howe, Glen Byam Shaw,
Campbell Gullan and Gwen Ffrangcon-Davies at the New
Theatre, London.
Tony Cavendish in *Theatre Royal* (Edna Ferber and George
S. Kaufman), directed by Noel Coward, with Marie
Tempest, Madge Titheradge and Mary Merrall at the Lyric
Theatre, London.

1935   Peter Hammond in *The Ringmaster* (Keith Winter), directed
by Raymond Massey, with Dame May Whitty, Colin
Keith-Johnston, Nigel Patrick, Cathleen Nesbitt, Dorothy
Hyson and Jill Esmond at the Shaftesbury Theatre, London.
Richard Harben in *Golden Arrow* (Sylvia Thompson and
Victor Cunard), directed by Laurence Olivier, with Greer
Garson, Helen Haye and Cecil Parker at the Whitehall
Theatre, London.
Romeo in *Romeo and Juliet*, directed by John Gielgud, with
Peggy Ashcroft, Edith Evans and John Gielgud (as Mercu-
tio) at the New Theatre, London.
Mercutio in same production, with Gielgud as Romeo.

1936   Bob Patch in *Bees on the Boatdeck* (J. B. Priestley), with
Ralph Richardson, Raymond Huntley, Kay Hammond and
John Laurie at the Lyric Theatre, London.

1937   Old Vic Season:
Title-role in *Hamlet*, directed by Tyrone Guthrie, with
Michael Redgrave, Cherry Cottrell, Dorothy Dix, Francis L.
Sullivan and George Howe.

Sir Toby Belch in *Twelfth Night*, directed by Tyrone Guthrie, with Alec Guinness, Ivy St. Helier, Jill Esmond and Marius Goring.

Title role in *Henry V*, directed by Tyrone Guthrie, with Ivy St. Helier, Thomas Owen-Jones and Lawrence Baskcomb.

Title role in *Hamlet*, directed by Tyrone Guthrie, with Vivien Leigh as Ophelia, Anthony Quayle, John Abbott and Leo Genn at Kronborg Castle, Elsinore, Denmark.

1937–38 Old Vic Season:

Title role in *Macbeth*, directed by Michel Saint-Denis, with Judith Anderson, Ellis Irving and Andrew Cruickshank.

Iago in *Othello*, directed by Tyrone Guthrie, with Ralph Richardson and Curigwen Lewis.

Frank Vivaldi in *The King of Nowhere* (James Bridie), directed by Tyrone Guthrie, with Marda Vanne.

Title role in *Coriolanus*, directed by Lewis Casson, with Sybil Thorndike.

1939 Gaylord Easterbrook in *No Time for Comedy* (S. N. Behrman), directed by Guthrie McClintic, with Katharine Cornell, Margalo Gillmore, John Williams and Robert Flemyng at the Ethel Barrymore Theatre, New York.

1940 Romeo in *Romeo and Juliet*, directed by Laurence Olivier, with Vivien Leigh as Juliet, Dame May Whitty, Edmund O'Brien, Cornel Wilde, Alexander Knox and Halliwell Hobbs at the 51st Street Theatre, New York.

1944 Appointed Co-director of the Old Vic with Ralph Richardson and John Burrell.

Old Vic Season at the New Theatre, London:

The Button Moulder in *Peer Gynt* (Ibsen), with Ralph Richardson, Sybil Thorndike and Nicholas Hannen.

Sergius Saranoff in *Arms and the Man* (Shaw), with Ralph Richardson, Sybil Thorndike, Nicholas Hannen and Margaret Leighton.

Title role in *Richard III*, directed by John Burrell, with Harcourt Williams, George Relph and Joyce Redman.

1945 Astrov in *Uncle Vanya* (Chekhov), with Ralph Richardson and Harcourt Williams.

Directed *The Skin of Our Teeth* (Thornton Wilder), with Vivien Leigh, Cecil Parker, Joan Young and Terence Morgan:

Old Vic tour of provinces and of Belgium, Holland, Germany and France with *Arms and the Man*, *Peer Gynt* and *Richard III*.

1945–46 Old Vic Season at the New Theatre, London:

Hotspur in *Henry IV, Part I*, directed by John Burrell, with Ralph Richardson and Margaret Leighton.

Mr. Justice Shallow in *Henry IV, Part II*, directed by John Burrell, with Ralph Richardson, Nicholas Hannen and Joyce Redman.

Double Bill: Title role in *Oedipus Rex* (Sophocles, translated by W. B. Yeats), and Mr. Puff in *The Critic* (Sheridan).

1946   *Henry IV, Parts I* and *II, Oedipus Rex, The Critic* and *Uncle Vanya* with Old Vic Company at the Century Theatre, New York.

Title role in *King Lear*, directed by Laurence Olivier. Old Vic production with Pamela Brown, Margaret Leighton, Joyce Redman, Alec Guinness, Nicholas Hannen and George Relph at the New Theatre, London.

1947   Directed *Born Yesterday* (Garson Kanin), with Yolande Donlan and Hartley Power at the Garrick Theatre, London. Received Knighthood 'for services to stage and films'.

1948   Tour of Australia and New Zealand with Old Vic Company:
Sir Peter Teazle in *The School for Scandal* (Sheridan), directed by Laurence Olivier, with Vivien Leigh as Lady Teazle.

Mr. Antrobus in *The Skin of Our Teeth* (Thornton Wilder), directed by Laurence Olivier, with Vivien Leigh as Sabina.
Title role in *Richard III*, directed by John Burrell.

1949   Old Vic Season at the New Theatre, London:
Sir Peter Teazle in *The School for Scandal* (Sheridan), directed by Laurence Olivier, with Vivien Leigh, Mercia Swinburne, George Relph, Terence Morgan and Peter Cushing.

Title role in *Richard III*, directed by John Burrell, with Vivien Leigh as Lady Anne, Peter Cushing, George Relph and Terence Morgan.

Chorus in *Antigone* (Anouilh), directed by Laurence Olivier, with Vivien Leigh and George Relph.

Directed *The Proposal* (Chekhov), with Peter Cushing, Derrick Penley and Peggy Simpson, as curtain-raiser to *Antigone*.

Directed *A Streetcar Named Desire* (Tennessee Williams), with Vivien Leigh, Bonar Colleano, Bernard Braden and Renée Asherson at the Aldwych Theatre, London.

Sir Laurence Olivier (Actor-Manager) took over the lease of the St. James's Theatre, London, for four years.

1950   The Duke of Altair in *Venus Observed* (Christopher Fry), directed by Laurence Olivier, with Heather Stannard, Denholm Elliott, Valerie Taylor, George Relph. Rachel Kempson and Brenda de Banzie at the St. James's.

Directed *Captain Carvallo* (Dennis Cannan), with Peter

Finch, Richard Goolden and James Donald at the St. James's.

1951   Festival of Britain productions at the St. James's Theatre: Caesar in *Caesar and Cleopatra* (Shaw), directed by Michael Benthall, with Vivien Leigh, Robert Helpmann, Wilfred Hyde White, Harry Andrews, Norman Wooland. Maxine Audley and Jill Bennett.

Antony in *Antony and Cleopatra*, directed by Michael Benthall with cast as above.

Caesar and Cleopatra and *Antony and Cleopatra* at the Ziegfeld Theatre, New York.

1952   Directed *Venus Observed* at the New Century Theatre, New York.

1953   Grand Duke of Carpathia in *The Sleeping Prince* (Terence Rattigan), directed by Laurence Olivier, with Vivien Leigh, Martita Hunt, Jeremy Spenser and Richard Wattis at the Phoenix Theatre, London.

1955   Season at the Shakespeare Memorial Theatre, Stratford-upon-Avon:

Malvolio in *Twelfth Night*, directed by John Gielgud, with Vivien Leigh (Viola), Angela Baddeley, Alan Webb, Keith Michell and Michael Denison.

Title role in *Macbeth*, directed by Glen Byam Shaw, with Vivien Leigh (Lady Macbeth) and Keith Michell.

Title role in *Titus Andronicus*, directed by Peter Brook, with Vivien Leigh (Lavinia), Anthony Quayle, Michael Denison, Alan Webb, Maxine Audley and Lee Montague.

1957   Archie Rice in *The Entertainer* (John Osborne), directed by Tony Richardson, with George Relph, Brenda de Banzie, Dorothy Tutin, Richard Pasco, Aubrey Dexter and Stanley Meadows at the Royal Court Theatre, London.

Titus Andronicus: revival of Peter Brook's production on tour to Paris, Venice, Belgrade, Zagreb, Vienna and Warsaw, and closing at the Stoll Theatre, London.

St. James's Theatre lost to property developers.

Archie Rice in *The Entertainer*, reopening at the Palace Theatre, London, with Joan Plowright replacing Miss Tutin, plus Robert Stephens (for Stanley Meadows) and Albert Chevalier (for Aubrey Dexter).

1958   *The Entertainer* at the Royale Theatre, New York.

1959   Title role in *Coriolanus*, directed by Peter Hall, with Edith Evans, Harry Andrews, Robert Hardy, Paul Hardwick, Peter Woodthorpe, Mary Ure and Vanessa Redgrave at the Shakespeare Memorial Theatre, Stratford-upon-Avon.

1960   Directed *The Tumbler* (Benn Levy), with Charlton Heston,

Rosemary Harris and Martha Scott at the Helen Hayes
Theatre, New York.

M. Berenger in *Rhinoceros* (Ionesco), directed by Orson
Welles, with Joan Plowright, Geoffrey Dunn, Peter Sallis,
Alan Webb and Miles Malleson at the Royal Court Theatre,
London.

Rhinoceros transferred to the Strand Theatre, London, with
Maggie Smith replacing Joan Plowright.

Title role in *Becket* (Anouilh), directed by Peter Glenville,
with Anthony Quinn at the St. James's Theatre, New York.

1961   Appointed Director of the new Chichester Festival Theatre.
King Henry II in *Becket*, with Arthur Kennedy as Becket
at the Hudson Theatre, New York.

1962   Chichester Festival Theatre:
Directed *The Chances* (John Fletcher), with Keith Michell,
John Neville and Joan Plowright.

The Prologue and Bassanes in *The Broken Heart* (John
Ford), directed by Laurence Olivier, with Keith Michell,
John Neville, Rosemary Harris and Joan Greenwood.

Astrov in *Uncle Vanya* (Chekhov), directed by Laurence
Olivier, with Michael Redgrave, Joan Plowright, Joan Greenwood and Sybil Thorndike.

Appointed Director of the National Theatre.

Fred Midway in *Semi-Detached* (David Turner), directed
by Tony Richardson, with Mona Washbourne, James
Bolam and Eileen Atkins at the Saville Theatre, London.

1963   Astrov in a revival of his production of *Uncle Vanya* at the
Chichester Festival.

National Theatre opened at the Old Vic:
Directed *Hamlet*, with Peter O'Toole, Michael Redgrave,
Rosemary Harris, Max Adrian and Diana Wynyard.

Astrov in *Uncle Vanya*; the Chichester production directed
by Laurence Olivier.

Captain Brazen in *The Recruiting Officer* (George Farquhar),
directed by William Gaskill, with Robert Stephens, Maggie
Smith, Colin Blakely, Max Adrian and Derek Jacobi.

1964   Title role in *Othello*, directed by John Dexter, with Maggie
Smith, Frank Finlay and Derek Jacobi, at National Theatre
(Old Vic) and at Chichester Festival Theatre.

Halvard Solness in *The Master Builder* (Ibsen), directed by
Peter Wood, with Maggie Smith (followed by Joan Plow-
right) as Hilde Wangel, and Celia Johnson at National
Theatre (Old Vic).

1965   Directed *The Crucible* (Arthur Miller), with Colin Blakely,
John Proctor and Sarah Miles at National Theatre (Old Vic).

National Theatre Company visit to Moscow and Berlin:
Title role in *Othello*, with Billie Whitelaw as Desdemona.
Tattle in *Love for Love* (William Congreve), directed by
Peter Wood, with Colin Blakely, Geraldine McEwan and
Lynn Redgrave.
Tattle in *Love for Love* at the National Theatre (Old Vic).

1966   Directed *Juno and the Paycock* (Sean O'Casey) at the National
Theatre (Old Vic).

1967   Captain Edgar in *The Dance of Death* (Strindberg), directed
by Glen Byam Shaw, with Geraldine McEwan and Robert
Stephens at National Theatre (Old Vic).
Directed *Three Sisters* (Chekhov), with Joan Plowright,
Louise Purnell and Jeanne Watts at National Theatre
(Old Vic).
National Theatre Company tour of Canada (including
Expo '67):
Tattle in *Love for Love*.
Captain Edgar in *The Dance of Death*.
Pulcheux in *A Flea in Her Ear* (Georges Feydeau).

1968   Co-directed (with Donald MacKechnie) *The Advertisement*
(Natalia Ginzburg), with Joan Plowright at the N.T. (Old
Vic).
Directed *Love's Labour Lost*, with Derek Jacobi, Ronald
Pickup, Paul Curran, Jeremy Brett, Joan Plowright and
Louise Purnell at the N.T. (Old Vic).

1969   A. B. Raham in *Home and Beauty* (Somerset Maugham) at
the N.T. (Old Vic).
Captain Edgar in *The Dance of Death* at the N.T. (Old Vic).
Chebutikin in *Three Sisters*, directed by Laurence Olivier,
at the N.T. (Old Vic).

1970   Led N.T. Company to Los Angeles, presenting *Three
Sisters* and *The Beaux Stratagem* (George Farquhar), with
Maggie Smith.
Shylock in *The Merchant of Venice*, directed by Jonathan
Miller, with Joan Plowright, Anthony Nicholls and Jeremy
Brett.
Created Baron Olivier in the Birthday Honours List.

1971   Directed *Amphitryon 38* (Giraudoux), with Christopher
Plummer and Geraldine McEwan. N.T. production at the
New Theatre, London.
James Tyrone in *Long Day's Journey Into Night* (Eugene
O'Neill), directed by Michael Blakemore, with Constance
Cummings, Ronald Pickup and Denis Quilley. N.T.
production at the New Theatre, London.

1972   *Long Day's Journey Into Night* at the N.T. (Old Vic).

1973   Relinquished post as Director of the National Theatre.

Antonio in *Saturday, Sunday, Monday* (Eduardo de Filippo, adapted by Keith Waterhouse and Willis Hall), directed by Franco Zeffirelli, with Joan Plowright, Frank Finlay, Denis Quilley and Anna Carteret at the N.T. (Old Vic).

John Tagg in *The Party* (Trevor Griffiths), directed by John Dexter, with Frank Finlay, Ronald Pickup, Denis Quilley and Anna Carteret at the N.T. (Old Vic).

1974   Directed *Eden End* (J. B. Priestley), with Joan Plowright, Leslie Sands, Michael Jayston and Louie Ramsay at the N.T. (Old Vic).

Presented: *Golden Arrow* (1935); *The Skin of Our Teeth* (1945); *Born Yesterday* (1947); *Daphne Laureola, The Fading Mansion, Romeo et Jeanette* (1949); *The Damascus Blade, Captain Carvallo, Top of the Ladder* (1950); *The Consul*, Orson Welles in *Othello* (1951); *Anastasia* (1953); *Waiting for Gillian, Meet a Body* (1954); *Double Image* (1956); *Summer of the Seventeenth Doll* (1957); *The Shifting Heart, One More River* (1959).

Co-presented: *Bees on the Boatdeck* (1936); *The Happy Time* (1952); *A Lodging for a Bride, Over The Bridge* (1960).

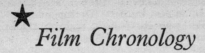

Film Chronology

1930   The Man in *Too Many Crooks* § (20th Century-Fox/UK), directed by George King, with Dorothy Boyd, Bromley Davenport, Mina Burnett, Arthur Stratton and Ellen Pollock.

Peter Billie in *The Temporary Widow* (U.F.A. Anglo-German production), directed by Gustav Ucicky, with Lilian Harvey and Felix Aylmer.

Straker in *Potiphar's Wife* (British International), directed by Maurice Elvey, with Nora Swinburne, Guy Newall and Norman McKinnell.

1931   Lieut. Nichols in *Friends and Lovers* (RKO), directed by Victor Schertzinger, with Adolphe Menjou, Erich von Stroheim and Lily Damita.

Julian Rolph in *The Yellow Passport* (20th Century-Fox), directed by Raoul Walsh, with Elissa Landi and Lionel Barrymore.

1932   Nick Allen in *Westward Passage* (RKO), directed by Robert Milton, with Ann Harding, Zasu Pitts, Juliette Compton and Bonita Granville.

Nicholas Randall in *Perfect Understanding* (United Artists/UK), directed by Cyril Gardner, with Gloria Swanson, John Halliday, Sir Nigel Playfair and Genevieve Tobin.

Clive in *No Funny Business* (United Artists/UK), directed by John Stafford and Victor Hanbury, with Gertrude Lawrence, Jill Esmond, Gib McLaughlin and Edmund Breon (re-issued 1951).

1933   Tested (unsuccessfully) for role of Don Antonio in *Queen Christina* (MGM) directed by Rouben Mamoulian, with Greta Garbo.

1935   Vincent Lunardi in *Conquest of the Air* (Korda), semi-

Dates quoted are the year of production. Unless otherwise stated, the film was released in the same year or the following year.

documentary, with Margaretta Scott, Hay Petrie and Frank-
lyn Dyall (film shelved, later completed and released 1941).
Ignatoff in *Moscow Nights* (Denham), directed by Anthony
Asquith, with Harry Baur, Penelope Dudley Ward and
Athene Seyler.

1936 Orlando in *As You Like It* (Inter-Allied), directed by Paul
Czinner with Elisabeth Bergner, Henry Ainley and Felix
Aylmer.

Michael Ingoldsby in *Fire Over England* (Pendennis),
directed by William K. Howard, with Vivien Leigh, Flora
Robson, Raymond Massey, Morton Selten, Leslie Banks
and Lyn Harding (released 1937, re-issued 1942).

1937 Larry Durrant in *Twenty-One Days* (London Films),
directed by Basil Dean, with Vivien Leigh, Leslie Banks,
Francis L. Sullivan, Hay Petrie and Robert Newton
(released 1940).

Leslie Logan in *The Divorce of Lady X* (London Films),
directed by Tim Whelan, with Merle Oberon, Ralph
Richardson, Binnie Barnes, Gus McNaughton and Morton
Selten.

1938 Tony McVane in *Q Planes* (London Films), directed by
Tim Whelan, with Ralph Richardson, Valerie Hobson,
George Curzon and George Merritt (released 1939, re-
issued 1944).

1939 Heathcliff† in *Wuthering Heights* (New Realm Pictures),
directed by William Wyler, with Merle Oberon, David
Niven, Flora Robson, Geraldine Fitzgerald, Hugh Williams
and Donald Crisp.

Maxim de Winter† in *Rebecca*‡ (Selznick), directed by
Alfred Hitchcock, with Joan Fontaine, Judith Anderson,
Gladys Cooper and George Sanders.

1940 Darcy in *Pride and Prejudice* (MGM), directed by Robert
Z. Leonard, with Greer Garson, Edna May Oliver, Mary
Boland, Edmund Gwen and Maureen O'Sullivan.

Lord Nelson in *Lady Hamilton* (London Films), directed
by Alexander Korda, with Vivien Leigh, Alan Mowbray,
Sara Allgood, Gladys Cooper, Henry Wilcoxon and Juliette
Compton.

1941 Johnnie the Trapper in *49th Parallel* (General Films Dis-
tributors), directed by Michael Powell, with Eric Portman,
Raymond Massey, Leslie Howard, Anton Walbrook and
Glynis Johns.

1943 Ivan Kouznetsoff in *The Demi-Paradise* (Two Cities),
directed by Anthony Asquith, with Penelope Ward, Margaret
Rutherford and Felix Aylmer.

1943–44 Title role† in *Henry V*§ (Two Cities for Rank), produced
and directed by Laurence Olivier‡ (direction with Reginald
Beck), with Renée Asherson, Leslie Banks, Robert Newton,
Ivy St. Helier and Leo Genn (released 1945).

1947 Title role* in *Hamlet*‡ (Two Cities for Rank), directed
and produced by Laurence Olivier, with Jean Simmons,
Basil Sydney, Eileen Herlie, Norman Wooland, Felix
Aylmer and Terence Morgan.

1950 George Hurstwood in *Carrie* (Paramount), directed by
William Wyler, with Jennifer Jones, Miriam Hopkins and
Eddie Albert.

1951 Cameo role as policeman PC 94 in *The Magic Box* (Festival
Films Productions), directed by John Boulting, with Robert
Donat, Maria Schell, Margaret Johnston and all star
cast.

1952 Captain Macheath in *The Beggar's Opera* (British Lion),
directed by Peter Brook, co-produced by Laurence Olivier
and Herbert Wilcox, with Dorothy Tutin, Stanley Holloway,
George Devine, Mary Clare, Hugh Griffith and Daphne
Anderson.

1954 Title role† in *Richard III* (London Films and Laurence
Olivier Productions), directed by Laurence Olivier (with
Anthony Bushell), with Claire Bloom, Ralph Richardson, John
Gielgud, Cedric Hardwicke, Stanley Baxter and Alec Clunes.

1956 The Regent of Carpathia in *The Prince and the Showgirl*
(Laurence Olivier Productions for Warner Bros.), directed
and produced by Laurence Olivier, with Marilyn Monroe,
Sybil Thorndike, Richard Wattis and Jeremy Spenser.

1958 General Burgoyne in *The Devil's Disciple* (United Artists),
directed by Guy Hamilton, with Burt Lancaster, Kirk
Douglas, Janette Scott and Harry Andrews.
Television debut in title role of *John Gabriel Borkman*
(Associated Television), directed by Casper Wrede, with
Irene Worth, Pamela Brown, Maxine Audley, George
Relph, Anthony Valentine and Anne Castaldini.
Charles Strickland¶ in *The Moon and Sixpence* (NBC
Television), directed by David Susskind, with Judith
Anderson, Hume Cronyn, Denholm Elliott, Cyril Cusack,
Geraldine Fitzgerald and Jessica Tandy. (Screened 1960.)

1959 Marcus Crassus in *Spartacus* (Bryna Prod. for Universal
International), directed by Stanley Kubrick, with Kirk
Douglas, Jean Simmons, Charles Laughton, Peter Ustinov
and Tony Curtis.
Archie Rice† in *The Entertainer* (Woodfall Production),
directed by Tony Richardson, with Brenda de Banzie,

Joan Plowright, Roger Livesey, Alan Bates, Albert Finney and Shirley Anne Field.

1961   The Priest in *The Power and the Glory* (Paramount TV production), directed by Marc Daniels, with Julie Harris, George C. Scott, Roddy McDowall and Kennan Wynn.

1962   Graham Weir in *Term of Trial* (Romulus for Warner Bros.), directed by Peter Glenville, with Simone Signoret, Sarah Miles, Hugh Griffith, and Terence Stamp.

1963   Astrov in *Uncle Vanya* (BHE Production), with Michael Redgrave. Film of N.T. production under direction of Stuart Burge.

1965   Inspector Newhouse in *Bunny Lake Is Missing* (Columbia), directed by Otto Preminger, with Keir Dullea, Carol Lynley, Noel Coward and Anna Massey.

Title role† in *Othello* (BHE Production), directed by Stuart Burge. Film of N.T. production, with Frank Finlay and Maggie Smith.

The Mahdi in *Khartoum* (United Artists), directed by Basil Dearden, with Charlton Heston, Richard Johnson and Ralph Richardson.

1968   Premier Kamenev in *The Shoes of the Fisherman* (MGM), directed by Michael Anderson, with Anthony Quinn, Oscar Werner, Leo McKern and David Janssen (released 1972).

Field Marshal Sir John French in *Oh! What a Lovely War* (Cinema International Corporation), directed by Richard Attenborough, with John Gielgud, Ralph Richardson, and John Mills.

Edgar in *The Dance of Death* (BHE), directed by David Giles. Film of N.T. production, with Geraldine McEwan and Robert Lang.

1969   Air Chief Marshal Sir Hugh Dowding in *The Battle of Britain* (United Artists), directed by Guy Hamilton, with Michael Caine, Trevor Howard, Ralph Richardson and Robert Shaw.

Creakle in *David Copperfield* (Omnibus), directed by Delbert Mann, with Robin Phillips, Edith Evans and Ralph Richardson, Michael Redgrave, Susan Hampshire and Sinead Cusack.

Chebutikin in *Three Sisters* (Alan Clore Films/British Lion), directed by Laurence Olivier, with Joan Plowright, Louise Purnell and Sheila Reid. Film of N.T. production.

1971   Count Witte in *Nicholas and Alexandra* (Columbia), directed by Franklin J. Schaffner, with Michael Jayston, Janet Suzman, Tom Baker and Harry Andrews.

The Duke of Wellington in *Lady Caroline Lamb* (EMI),

directed by Robert Bolt, with Sarah Miles, Richard Chamberlain and Ralph Richardson.

1972 Andrew Wyke† in *Sleuth* (Fox–Rank), directed by Joseph L. Mankiewicz, with Michael Caine.

James Tyrone in *Long Day's Journey Into Night* (ATV), directed by Peter Wood. Film of N.T. production, with Constance Cummings, Ronald Pickup and Denis Quilley.

1973 Shylock in *The Merchant of Venice* (ATV), directed by Jonathan Miller. Film of N.T. production, with Joan Plowright, Jeremy Brett and Michael Jayston.

1975 Sir Arthur Granville-Jones ¶ in *Love Among the Ruins* (US/TV), directed by George Cukor, with Katherine Hepburn, Colin Blakely and Joan Sims.

Moriaty in *The Seven Per Cent Solution* (Universal), directed by Herbert Ross, with Nicol Williamson, Robert Duvall and Alan Arkin.

1976 Dr. Christian Szell in *Marathon Man* (Paramount), directed by John Schlesinger, with Dustin Hoffmann, Roy Schneider, William Devane and Marthe Keller.

Nikodemus in *The Life of Jesus Christ* (ITC/RAI), directed by Franco Zeffirelli, with Robert Powell, Rod Steiger and Peter Ustinov.

Cameo role in *A Bridge Too Far* (Joseph E. Levine Presents Inc.), directed by Richard Attenborough, with Robert Redford, Dirk Bogarde, Michael Caine, etc.

Harry Kane in *The Collection* (Granada Television), produced by Laurence Olivier and Derek Granger, directed by Michael Apted, with Alan Bates, Malcolm McDowell and Helen Mirren.

Big Daddy in *Cat on a Hot Tin Roof* (Granada Television), produced by Laurence Olivier and Derek Granger, directed by Robert Moore, with Natalie Wood, Robert Wagner, Maureen Stapleton and Jack Hedley.

First television direction: *Hindle Wakes* (Granada Television), directed and produced by June Howson and Laurence Olivier, with Donald Pleasance, Rosemary Leach, Jack Hedley, Pat Heywood, Rosalind Ayres and Roy Dotrice.

* Best Actor Academy Award.
† Best Actor Academy Award Nomination.
‡ Best Picture Academy Award.
§ Best Picture Academy Award Nomination.
‖ Honorary Academy Award.
¶ 'Emmy' Best Actor Television Award.

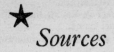

Sources

Chapter 1

1. Sydney Edwards, London *Evening Standard*, January 16, 1970.
2. William Redfield: *Letters From an Actor* (Cassell & Co., Ltd., London, 1966).
3. Olivier on *The Dick Cavett Show*, 1973.
4. Cecil Beaton: *The Happy Years: Diaries 1944–48* (Weidenfeld & Nicolson, London, 1972).
5. Milton Shulman, London *Evening Standard*, July 31, 1950.
6. Robert Muller, London *Daily Mail*, October 5, 1959.

Chapter 2

1. Olivier talking to Kenneth Tynan, B.B.C. television interview, 1967. First published in *Great Acting*, edited by Hal Burton (British Broadcasting Corporation Publications, 1967, and Hill and Wang, New York, 1968).
2. Felix Barker: *The Oliviers* (Hamish Hamilton, London, 1953, and Lippincott, New York, 1953).
3. John Cruesmann, London *Daily Express*, May 25, 1967.
4. Richard Meryman: *Within the Edifice of Olivier*, London *Daily Telegraph* Magazine, No. 432, February 9, 1973.
5. Olivier–Tynan, B.B.C. television interview, 1967.
6. Robert Muller, London *Daily Mail*, October 5, 1959.
7. Felix Barker, 1953.

Chapter 3

1. Olivier talking to Kenneth Harris, *The Observer Review*, London, February 2 and 9, 1969.
2. Olivier–Tynan, B.B.C. television interview, 1967.
3. Marion Cole: *Fogie: The Life of Elsie Fogerty*, *C.B.E.* (Peter Davies, London, 1967).

Chapter 4

1. J. C. Trewin: *The Birmingham Repertory Theatre, 1913–63* (Barrie and Rockliff, London, 1963).

2. Denys Blakelock: *Finding My Way* (Hollis and Carter, London, 1958).

3. Denys Blakelock: *Round the Next Corner* (Victor Gollancz, London, 1967).

4. *Theatre '73*, edited by Sheridan Morley (Hutchinson, London, 1973).

5. Felix Barker: *The Oliviers*, 1953.

6. Denys Blakelock: *Round the Next Corner*, 1967.

7. Olivier–Tynan, B.B.C. television interview, 1967.

8. Ibid.

9. Denys Blakelock: *Advice to a Player: Letters to a Young Actor* (Heinemann, London, 1958).

Chapter 5

1. London *Daily Herald*, May 22, 1930.

2. Jill Esmond talking to Herbert Kretzmer, London *Sunday Dispatch*, April 30, 1961.

3. Noel Coward: *Present Indicative* (Wm. Heinemann, London, 1937, and Doubleday, New York, 1937).

4. *Manchester Evening Chronicle*, September 13, 1930.

5. Noel Coward, 1937.

6. Olivier–Tynan, B.B.C. television interview, 1967.

7. Charles Castle: *Noel* (W. H. Allen, London, 1972, and Doubleday, New York, 1973).

Chapter 6

1. *Memo From David O. Selznick*, selected and edited by Rudy Behlmer (Macmillan, London, 1972, and The Viking Press Inc., New York, 1972). Copyright © 1972 by Selznick Properties, Ltd. Reprinted by permission of The Viking Press, Inc.

2. Thomas Quinn Curtiss: *Von Stroheim* (Angus and Robertson, London, 1971, and Farrar, Straus & Giroux, Inc., New York, 1971).

3. J. B. Priestley: *Midnight on the Desert* (Heinemann, London, 1937).

4. Norman Zierold: *Garbo* (Stein and Day, 1969, and W. H. Allen, London, 1970).

5. *The Dick Cavett Show*, 1973.

Chapter 7

1. Olivier–Tynan, B.B.C. television interview, 1967.

2. Denys Blakelock: *Round the Next Corner*, 1967.

Chapter 8

1. John Gielgud on *The David Frost Show*, December 11, 1970, New York.
2. *Olivier*, edited by Logan Gourlay (Weidenfeld & Nicolson, London, 1973).

Chapter 9

1. Vivien Leigh talking to David Lewin, London *Daily Express*, August 17, 1960.
2. Ibid.
3. Paul Tabori: *Alexander Korda* (Oldbourne, London, 1959, and Heinman, New York, 1959).
4. Janet Dunbar: *Flora Robson* (George G. Harrap, London, 1960).
5. Paul Tabori, 1959.

Chapter 10

1. *Olivier*, edited by Logan Gourlay, 1973.
2. Ibid.
3. Tyrone Guthrie: *A Life in the Theatre* (Hamish Hamilton, London, 1959). Copyright © 1959 by Tyrone Guthrie.
4. George W. Bishop: *My Betters* (Heinemann, London, 1957).
5. C. A. Lejeune: *Thank You for Having Me* (Hutchinson, London, 1964). By permission of the Estate of C. A. Lejeune.
6. Tyrone Guthrie, 1957.
7. Olivier–Tynan, B.B.C. television interview, 1967.

Chapter 11

1. Felix Barker: *The Oliviers*, 1953.
2. David Niven: *The Moon's a Balloon* (Hamish Hamilton, London, 1971, and G. P. Putnam's Sons, New York, 1972). Copyright © 1971 by David Niven.
3. *Memo From David O. Selznick*, 1972.
4. Kenneth Harris, *The Observer Review*, 1969.
5. *Memo From David O. Selznick*, 1972.
6. Ibid.
7. Bob Thomas: *Selznick* (Doubleday and Co., Inc., New York, 1970, and W. H. Allen, London, 1971).
8. Felix Barker, 1953.
9. Elliott Arnold, *New York World Telegram*, June 17, 1939.
10. Kenneth Harris, *The Observer Review*, 1969.
11. *Memo From David O. Selznick*, 1972.

Chapter 12

1. Sir Cedric Hardwicke: *A Victorian in Orbit* (Methuen & Co. Ltd., London, 1961, and Doubleday, New York, 1961).

2. Bob Thomas: *Selznick*, 1970.
3. *Memo From David O. Selznick*, 1972.
4. Ibid.

Chapter 13

1. Brian Aherne: *A Proper Job* (Houghton Mifflin Co., Boston, 1969).
2. Garson Kanin: *Tracy and Hepburn* (The Viking Press Inc., New York, 1971, and Angus and Robertson Ltd., London, 1971). Copyright © 1970, 1971, by T. F. T. Corporation. Reprinted by permission of The Viking Press, Inc.
3. Ibid.
4. Paul Tabori: *Alexander Korda*, 1959.
5. Gwen Robyns: *Light of a Star* (Leslie Frewin, London, 1968).

Chapter 14

1. Kenneth Harris, *The Observer Review*, 1969.
2. Daniel Schwarz: *The Present and Future of Shakespeare* (*The New York Times Magazine*, May 12, 1946).

Chapter 15

1. Olivier–Tynan, B.B.C. television interview, 1967.
2. Ibid.
3. *Olivier*, edited by Logan Gourlay, 1973.
4. Ronald Harwood: *Sir Donald Wolfit, C.B.E.* (Secker and Warburg, London, 1971).
5. John Crusemann, London *Daily Express*, May 25, 1967.
6. Harcourt Williams: *The Old Vic Saga* (Winchester Publications Ltd., London, 1949).
7. *Saturday Review of Literature*, June 8, 1946.
8. Kenneth Tynan: *He That Plays the King* (Longmans, Green and Co., London, 1950). By permission of Curtis Brown Ltd., London, on behalf of the author.
9. Ibid.

Chapter 16

1. *The Film Hamlet: A Record of Its Production*, edited by Brenda Cross (Saturn Press, London, 1948).
2. Alan Wood: *Mr. Rank* (Hodder and Stoughton, London, 1952).
3. *The Film Hamlet*, 1948.

Chapter 17

1. Tyrone Guthrie: *A Life in the Theatre*, 1959.
2. Harcourt Williams: *The Old Vic Saga*, 1949.
3. Kenneth Tynan: *He That Plays the King*, 1950.
4. Gwen Robyns: *Light of a Star*, 1968.

Chapter 18

1. Herbert Wilcox: *Twenty-Five Thousand Sunsets* (The Bodley Head, London, 1967).
2. Ibid.
3. *Olivier*, edited by Logan Gourlay, 1973.
4. Ivor Brown: *Theatre 1954–5* (Max Reinhardt, London, 1955).

Chapter 20

1. Vivien Leigh talking to David Lewin, London *Daily Express*, August 19, 1960.

Chapter 21

1. Spencer Tracy talking to Roderick Mann, London *Sunday Express*, June 5, 1970.
2. Robert Muller, London *Daily Mail*, October 5, 1959.
3. Richard Findlater: *The Player Kings* (Weidenfeld & Nicolson, London, 1971).
4. *Olivier*, edited by Logan Gourlay, 1973.

Chapter 22

1. Laurence Kitchin: *Mid-Century Drama* (Faber and Faber, London, 1960).
2. Olivier talking to Peter Evans, London *Daily Express*, September 25, 1959.

Chapter 23

1. Robert Muller, London *Daily Mail*, October 5, 1959.
2. Olivier talking to Harold Hobson, *The Sunday Times Weekly Review*, London, November 3, 1963.

Chapter 24

1. Virginia Fairweather: *Cry God for Larry* (Calder and Boyars, London, 1969).
2. Leslie Evershed Martin: *The Impossible Theatre* (Phillimore and Co., Ltd., Chichester, Sussex, 1971).
3. Kenneth Tynan: *He That Plays the King*, 1950.
4. *Behind the Scenes: Theatre and Film Interviews* from the *Transatlantic Review*, edited by Joseph F. McCrindle (Sir Isaac Pitman & Sons Ltd., London, 1971).
5. *The Recruiting Officer: The National Theatre Production*, edited by Kenneth Tynan (Rupert Hart-Davis, London, 1965).
6. *Olivier*, edited by Logan Gourlay, 1973.

Chapter 25

1. Tyrone Guthrie: *In Various Directions* (Michael Joseph, London, 1965, and Macmillan Publishing Co., Inc., New York, 1965).
2. *Life* magazine, May 1, 1964.
3. Richard Findlater: *The Player Kings*, 1971.
4. *Olivier*, edited by Logan Gourlay, 1973.
5. *Life* magazine, May 1, 1964.
6. Robert Speaight: *Shakespeare on the Stage* (Wm. Collins, Sons & Co. Ltd., London, 1973).

Chapter 26

1. Sydney Edwards, London *Evening Standard*, May 2, 1967.
2. Sean Day-Lewis, London *Sunday Telegraph*, July 20, 1969.
3. James Thomas, London *Daily Express*, January 27, 1968.

Chapter 27

1. Michael Billington: *The Modern Actor* (Hamish Hamilton, London, 1973). Copyright © 1973 by Michael Billington.
2. Richard Findlater: *The Player Kings*, 1971.
3. Richard Meryman: 'Within the Edifice of Olivier', *The Daily Telegraph* Ltd., 1973.
4. Ibid.

Chapter 28

1. Olivier–Tynan, B.B.C. television interview, 1967.
2. *Olivier*, edited by Logan Gourlay, 1973.
3. Irving Wardle, *The Times Saturday Review*, London, October 27, 1973.
4. Richard Meryman, 1973.

Chapter 29

1. John Crusemann, London *Daily Express*, May 25, 1967.
2. *William Shakespeare's Othello: The National Theatre Production*, edited by Kenneth Tynan (Rupert Hart-Davis, London, 1966).
3. Kenneth Harris, *The Observer Review*, 1969.
4. Ibid.
5. Tyrone Guthrie: *In Various Directions*, 1965.
6. *Olivier*, edited by Logan Gourlay, 1973.
7. Tyrone Guthrie: *Tyrone Guthrie on Acting* (The Viking Press, Inc., New York, 1971 and Studio Vista Ltd., London, 1971). Copyright © 1971 by Tyrone Guthrie. Reprinted by permission of The Viking Press, Inc.
8. Michael Billington: *The Modern Actor*, 1973.
9. Olivier–Tynan, B.B.C. television interview, 1967.
10. Kenneth Harris, 1969.

11. Richard Meryman: 'Within the Edifice of Olivier', 1973.
12. Olivier–Tynan, 1967.
13. Robert Muller, London *Daily Mail*, October 5, 1959.
14. Kenneth Tynan: *He That Plays the King*, 1950.
15. Kenneth Harris, 1969.
16. Richard Meryman, 1973.
17. Sydney Edwards, London *Evening Standard*, May 2, 1967.

Chapter 30

1. Richard Meryman: 'Within the Edifice of Olivier', 1973.
2. Ibid.
3. Olivier–Tynan, B.B.C. television interview, 1967.
4. Richard Meryman, 1973.

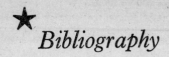

★ Bibliography

General Acknowledgment

Grateful acknowledgment is made to the many critics, reporters and authors—and to their publishers—who have been quoted in the text. Newspapers and magazines consulted by the author include: *The Bioscope, Birmingham Post, Collier's,* London *Daily Express,* London *Daily Herald,* London *Daily Mail,* London *Daily Mirror,* London *Daily Telegraph,* London *Evening News,* London *Evening Standard, Film Weekly, The Hollywood Reporter, Kine Weekly, Life, Manchester Evening Chronicle, Manchester Guardian, Movie Fan, Motion Picture Herald, News Chronicle, New Republic, New Statesman,* New York *Daily News, The New Yorker,* New York *Herald-Tribune, The New York Times,* New York *World-Telegram, The Observer, Photoplay, Picturegoer, Picture Show, Pittsburgh Press, Saturday Review of Literature, The Star,* London *Sunday Dispatch,* London *Sunday Express,* London *Sunday Telegraph,* London *Sunday Times,* London *The Times, This Month, Time, Variety, Weekend Telegraph.* Books consulted include:

Advice to a Player: Letters to a Young Actor by Denys Blakelock (Heinemann, London, 1957).

Agee on Film: Reviews and Comments, by James Agee (McDowell, Obolensky, New York, 1958; Peter Owen Ltd., London, 1967; Grossett and Dunlap, 1969).

Alexander Korda, by Paul Tabori (Oldbourne, London, 1959, and Heinman, New York, 1959).

Anything for a Quiet Life, the autobiography of Jack Hawkins (Elm Tree Books, Hamish Hamilton, London, 1973).

The Barrymores, by Hollis Alpert (Dial Press, New York, 1964, and W. H. Allen, London, 1965).

Billy Rose: Manhattan Primitive, by Earl Conrad (World Publishing Co., Cleveland and New York, 1968).

The Birmingham Repertory Theatre, 1913–1963, by J. C. Trewin (Barrie and Rockliff, London, 1963).

British Film Yearbooks, edited by Peter Noble (Skelton Robinson, London, 1948–50).

British Theatre, by Peter Noble (British Yearbooks, London, 1946).

The Celluloid Mistress, by Rodney Ackland (Allan Wingate, London, 1954).

Charles Laughton and I, by Elsa Lanchester (Faber and Faber, London, 1938).

The Church in Dorking and District, by the Rev. Neville G. T. Stiff (privately published, 1912).

The Contemporary Theatre, 1944 and 1945, by James Agate (George G. Harrap & Co. Ltd., London, 1946).

Cry God for Larry, by Virginia Fairweather (Calder & Boyars, London, 1969).

Curtains, by Kenneth Tynan (Longmans, Green & Co. Ltd., London, 1961 and Atheneum, New York, 1961).

Dorking Parish Magazine.

Drama in the Sixties, by Laurence Kitchin (Faber & Faber, London, 1966).

Early Stages, by John Gielgud (Macmillan & Co. Ltd., London, 1939).

The Film Hamlet: A Record of Its Production, edited by Brenda Cross (Saturn Press, London, 1948).

Finding My Way, by Denys Blakelock (Hollis & Carter, London, 1958).

First Nights and Noises Off, by Beverley Baxter (Hutchinson & Co. Ltd., London, 1966).

Flight 777, by Ian Colvin (Evans Bros. Ltd., London, 1957).

Flora Robson, by Janet Dunbar (George G. Harrap, London, 1960).

Focus on Shakespearean Films, edited by Charles W. Eckert (Prentice-Hall Inc., New Jersey, 1972).

Fogie: The Life of Elsie Fogerty, C.B.E., by Marion Cole (Peter Davies, London, 1967).

The Footlights Flickered, by W. MacQueen-Pope (Herbert Jenkins, London, 1959).

The Fugitive Art: Dramatic Commentaries 1947–51, by T. C. Worsley (John Lehman, London, 1952).

Garbo, by Norman Zierold (Stein and Day, 1969, W. H. Allen, London, 1970).

Garbo, by John Bainbridge (Frederick Muller, London, 1955, and Doubleday, New York, 1955).

The Gay Twenties, A Decade of the Theatre, by J. C. Trewin, with Raymond Mander and Joe Mitchenson (Macdonald, London, 1958).

Great Acting, edited by Hal Burton (The British Broadcasting Corporation, London, 1967, and Hill and Wang, New York, 1968).

Hamlet, the Film and the Play, by Alan Dent (World Film Publishing, London, 1948).

Happy Go Lucky, by Kenneth More (Robert Hale, London, 1959).

The Happy Years: Diaries 1944–48, by Cecil Beaton (Weidenfeld & Nicolson, London, 1972).

He That Plays the King, by Kenneth Tynan (Longmans, Green & Co. Ltd., London, 1950).

A History of St. Edward's School, 1863–1963 (The St. Edward's School Society, 1962).

Hollywood Doesn't Count, by Kyle Crichton (*Collier's* magazine, June 10, 1939).

The Honeycomb, by Adela Rogers St. John (Doubleday & Co., Inc., New York, 1969).

Horror Man, The Life of Boris Karloff, by Peter Underwood (Leslie Frewin, London, 1972).

Horror Movies, by Carlos Clarens (Secker & Warburg, London, 1967).

Immortal Shadows: A Book of Dramatic Criticism, by Stark Young (Charles Scribner's Sons, New York, 1948).

The Impossible Theatre, by Leslie Evershed-Martin (Phillimore & Co. Ltd., Chichester, Sussex, 1971).

In Various Directions, by Tyrone Guthrie (Michael Joseph, London, 1965 and Macmillan Publishing Co., Inc., New York, 1965).

James Agate: An Anthology, edited by Herbert Van Thal (Rupert Hart-Davis, London, 1961).

John Gielgud, The David Frost Show, New York, December 11, 1970.

John Gielgud, by Ronald Hayman (Heinemann, London, 1971).

Kenneth Harris talking to Olivier (*The Observer*, London, February 2 and 9, 1969).

Knight Errant: A Biography of Douglas Fairbanks Jr., by Brian Connell (Hodder & Stoughton, London, 1955, and Doubleday, New York, 1955).

Laurence Olivier, by W. A. Darlington (Morgan Grampian Books Ltd., London, 1968).

Letters From an Actor, by William Redfield (Cassell & Co., Ltd., London, 1966).

Let's Pretend, by Cedric Hardwicke (Grayson & Grayson, London, 1932).

Lewis and Sybil: A Memoir, by John Casson (Collins, London, 1972).

A Life in the Theatre, by Tyrone Guthrie (Hamish Hamilton, London, 1972).

Light of a Star, by Gwen Robyns (Leslie Frewin, London, 1968).

The Making of a National Theatre, by Geoffrey Whitworth, C.B.E. (Faber & Faber, London, 1951).

Margot Fonteyn, by Elizabeth Frank (Chatto and Windus, London, 1958).

Memo From David O. Selznick, selected and edited by Rudy Behlmer (Macmillan, London, 1972, and The Viking Press Inc., New York, 1972).

Michael Redgrave—Actor, by Richard Findlater (Wm. Heinemann Ltd., London, 1956).

Michael Balcon Presents . . . A Lifetime of Films, by Sir Michael Balcon (Hutchinson, London, 1969).

Mid-Century Drama, by Laurence Kitchin (Faber & Faber, London, 1960).

Midnight on the Desert, by J. B. Priestley (Heinemann, London, 1937).

Mind's Eye: An Autobiography, 1927–1972, by Basil Dean (Hutchinson, London, 1973).

The Modern Actor, by Michael Billington (Hamish Hamilton, London, 1973).

The Moon's a Balloon, by David Niven (Hamish Hamilton, London, 1971, and G. P. Putnam's Sons, New York, 1972).

The Movie Moguls, by Philip French (Weidenfeld & Nicolson, London, 1969).

Mr. Rank, by Alan Wood (Hodder & Stoughton, London, 1957).

My Betters, by George W. Bishop (Heinemann, London, 1957).

Noel, by Charles Castle (W. H. Allen, London, 1972 and Doubleday, New York, 1973).

No Leading Lady, by R. C. Sherriff (Victor Gollancz Ltd., London, 1968).

Old Vic Drama, by Audrey Williamson (Rockliff, London, 1948).

Old Vic Saga, by Harcourt Williams (Winchester Publications Ltd., London, 1949).

Old Vic, Gin Palace to National Theatre, by Laurence Olivier (*This Month*, New York, June, 1946).

Olivier, edited by Logan Gourlay (Wiedenfeld & Nicolson, London, 1973).

The Oliviers, by Felix Barker (Hamish Hamilton, London, 1953, and Lippincott, New York, 1953).

Peggy Ashcroft, by Eric Keown (Rockliff, London, 1955).
The Player Kings, by Richard Findlater (Weidenfeld & Nicolson, London, 1971).
Present Indicative, by Noel Coward (Wm. Heinemann, London, 1937).
A Proper Job, by Brian Aherne (Houghton Mifflin Co., Boston, 1969).

The Recruiting Officer: The National Theatre Production, edited by Kenneth Tynan (Rupert Hart-Davis, London, 1965).
Robert Donat: A Biography, by J. C. Trewin (Heinemann, London, 1968).
The Roll of St. Edward's School, 1863–1949, Sixth Edition (St. Edward's School Society, 1951).
Round the Next Corner, by Denys Blakelock (Victor Gollancz, London, 1967).

Selznick, by Bob Thomas (Doubleday & Co., Inc., New York, 1970, and W. H. Allen, London, 1971).
The Set-Up: An Anatomy of the English Theatre Today, by Ronald Hayman (Eyre Methuen, London, 1974).
Shakespeare, by Ivor Brown (Wm. Collins Sons & Co. Ltd., London, 1949).
Shakespeare and the Film, by Roger Manvell (J. M. Dent & Sons, Ltd., London, 1971).
Shakespeare Memorial Theatre 1954–56, by Ivor Brown (Max Reinhardt, London, 1956).
Shakespeare on the Stage, by Robert Speaight (Wm. Collins Sons & Co. Ltd., London, 1973).
Sir Donald Wolfit, C.B.E., by Ronald Harwood (Secker & Warburg, London, 1971).
Spencer Tracy, by Larry Swindell (The World Publishing Co., New York, and Cleveland, 1969, and W. H. Allen, London, 1970).
Sybil Thorndike Casson, by Elizabeth Sprigge (Victor Gollancz, London, 1971).

Thank You for Having Me, by C. A. Lejeune (Hutchinson, London, 1964).
Theatre of Two Decades, by Audrey Williamson (Rockliff, London, 1951).
Theatre 1954–5, by Ivor Brown (Max Reinhardt, London, 1964).
Theatre '73, edited by Sheridan Morley (Hutchinson, London, 1973).
The Theatre Since 1900, by J. C. Trewin (Andrew Dakers Ltd., London, 1951).

Tracy and Hepburn, by Garson Kanin (The Viking Press Inc., New York, 1971, and Angus and Robertson Ltd., London, 1971).

Twenty-Five Thousand Sunsets, by Herbert Wilcox (The Bodley Head, London, 1967).

Two Hundred Years of Dorking Cricket, 1766–1968 (privately published, 1968).

Tyrone Guthrie on Acting, by Tyrone Guthrie (Studio Vista Ltd., London, 1971).

A Victorian In Orbit, by Cedric Hardwicke (Methuen & Co., Ltd., London, 1961, and Doubleday, New York, 1961).

Vivien Leigh: A Bouquet, by Alan Dent (Hamish Hamilton, London, 1969).

Von Stroheim, by Thomas Quinn Curtiss (Angus & Robertson, London, 1971, and Farrar, Straus and Giroux, Inc., New York, 1971).

We'll Hear a Play, by J. C. Trewin (Carroll & Nicholson, London, 1949).

Who's Who in the Theatre (Sir Isaac Pitman & Sons, London).

William Shakespeare's Othello: The National Theatre Production, edited by Kenneth Tynan (Rupert Hart-Davis, London, 1966).

Without Veils: The Intimate Biography of Gladys Cooper, by Sewell Stokes (Peter Davies, London, 1953).

The World Film Encyclopedia, edited by Clarence Winchester (Amalgamated Press Ltd., London, 1933).

A World on Film: Criticism and Comment, by Stanley Kauffman (Harper and Row, New York, 1966).

Years in a Mirror, by Val Gielgud (The Bodley Head, London, 1965).

Index